AF179984

GLOBAL TAXES AND TAXATION

Kruger Brentt
Publishers

GLOBAL TAXES AND TAXATION

Andrew Earle
Dumitru Cristian Tranca
Peter Martelli

Kruger Brentt
Publishers

2025

Kruger Brentt Publishers UK. LTD.
Company Number 9728962

Regd. Office: 68 St Margarets Road, Edgware, Middlesex HA8 9UU

© 2025 AUTHORS

ISBN: 978-1-78715-352-3

Disclaimer:

Every possible effort has been made to ensure that the information contained in this book is accurate at the time of going to press, and the publisher and author cannot accept responsibility for any errors or omissions, however caused. No responsibility for loss or damage occasioned to any person acting, or refraining from action, as a result of the material in this publication can be accepted by the editor, the publisher or the author. The Publisher is not associated with any product or vendor mentioned in the book. The contents of this work are intended to further general scientific research, understanding and discussion only. Readers should consult with a specialist where appropriate.

Every effort has been made to trace the owners of copyright material used in this book, if any. The author and the publisher will be grateful for any omission brought to their notice for acknowledgement in the future editions of the book.

All Rights reserved under International Copyright Conventions. No part of this publication may be reproduced, stored in a retrieval system, or transmitted in any form or by any means, electronic, mechanical, photocopying, recording or otherwise without the prior written consent of the publisher and the copyright owner.

For information on all our publications visit our website at http://krugerbrentt.com/

PREFACE

"Global Taxes and Taxation" embarks on a comprehensive exploration of the multifaceted world of taxation in the global context, offering readers a deep understanding of the principles, practices, and challenges associated with taxation systems across borders. This book serves as an essential resource for students, scholars, policymakers, tax professionals, and anyone interested in navigating the complexities of global taxation.

Taxes are the lifeblood of governments, providing the necessary funding for public services, infrastructure development, social welfare programs, and other essential functions of the state. In an increasingly interconnected world characterized by globalization, digitalization, and cross-border economic activities, the landscape of taxation has become more complex, requiring coordinated efforts and international cooperation to address emerging challenges and ensure fairness and transparency in tax systems.

The primary objective of this book is to provide readers with a comprehensive overview of global taxes and taxation, covering key topics such as international tax law, tax treaties, transfer pricing, taxation of multinational corporations, taxation of digital economy, tax evasion and avoidance, tax havens, and the role of international organizations such as the OECD (Organisation for Economic Co-operation and Development) and the UN (United Nations) in shaping global tax policies.

Each chapter offers insights, theoretical frameworks, empirical studies, and practical examples to help readers understand the principles and practices of global taxation. Contributions from leading experts in the field explore various aspects of taxation from both theoretical and practical perspectives, shedding light on the intricate dynamics of tax systems in different regions and jurisdictions.

Special emphasis is placed on emerging trends and challenges in global taxation, such as base erosion and profit shifting (BEPS), taxation of digital services, carbon taxes and environmental taxation, and efforts to promote tax transparency and combat tax evasion and illicit financial flows. By examining these issues in depth, readers can gain a nuanced understanding of the complexities and controversies surrounding global taxation in the 21st century.

We extend our sincere gratitude to the contributors whose expertise and dedication have enriched this book. It is our hope that "Global Taxes and Taxation" will serve as a valuable resource and reference guide for policymakers, practitioners, academics, and students, facilitating informed dialogue, research, and policy development in the field of international taxation.

Andrew Earle
Dumitru Cristian Tranca
Peter Martelli

CONTENTS

SECTION-1
CORPORATE TAX

1 Chapter

CORPORATE INCOME TAX BASE AND THE CONCEPT IN THE EUROPEAN UNION

1. INTRODUCTION: AN OVERVIEW

The financial and public budget crises that impacted the European Union (EU) nations also brought attention to the issue of tax systems in place in the 27 EU member states. The main objective of EU law is to remove barriers that hinder the operation of the internal market, with a specific focus on enhancing the competitiveness of firms. The notion of a common consolidated corporate tax base (CCCTB) intends to remove barriers to the functioning of the internal market and enhance tax harmonization within the European Union [1].

The chapter examines the fundamental principles of the corporate income tax and provides an overview of the regulations in Polish legislation regarding corporate income tax, along with the draft CCCTB directive. This research focuses on tax revenues and tax costs, specifically excluding revenue that does not qualify as tax revenue and expenses that are not eligible for tax deductions.

2. TAX REVENUES

The corporate income tax is determined by the fundamental concept that the amount of tax owed by the entrepreneur is contingent upon the tax base and tax rates. The tax base is subject to tax harmonization, meaning that it will be set based on consistent regulations applied to all enterprises included in the Common Consolidated Corporate Tax Base (CCCTB) across individual European Union (EU) nations. The tax base is calculated as the taxable income minus the income that is exempt from taxation and the deductible costs. Therefore, in order to ascertain the tax base, it is crucial to specify the concept of tax revenues, income that is not subject to income tax, and expenses that can be deducted. Incorporating these classifications into the framework of a unified corporate tax base should involve the establishment of standardized guidelines for determining the corporate tax base, while respecting the regulations outlined in Council Directives 78/660/EEC and 83/349/EEC, as well as Regulation of the European Parliament and of the Council 1606/2002/EC.

To examine the tax base for corporate income tax in Polish legislation in relation to the CCCTB idea, it is necessary to first establish the definition of the tax base, which refers to the revenue that is subject to taxation. Put simply, this is referred to be the disparity between tax income and the expenses incurred in collecting it.

In accordance with the provisions of Polish law on corporate income tax, income tax represents the excess of the sum of revenues over costs to obtain them achieved in the fiscal year, subject to the special rules for determining the income (revenue) from participation in profits of legal persons and transactions between related parties and entities residing in tax havens.[1] If the deductible costs exceed the amount of revenue, the difference is a loss. In certain situations, the tax base is the income without taking into account tax-deductible expenses. The income indicated in the act is the basis of income taxation regardless of the type of revenue sources from which it accrues.

The Polish law on corporate income tax does not explicitly specify the definition of "income". The rules for the generation of income are defined in Art. 12 of the Act on Corporate Income Tax. Art. 12, par. 1, only contains a catalogue of examples of taxable income subject to corporate income tax. This is indicated by the legislator with the phrase "income particularly includes". This is an open list, and tax revenues particularly include:

1. Received money, cash, including foreign exchange differences
2. Value of goods or rights received free of charge or partially for a fee, as well as the value of other unpaid or partially paid benefits
3. Value (subject to par. 4 item 8 of the Act) of redeemed or expired:
    - Liabilities, including credits and loans and excluding loans amortized from the labour fund
    - Funds in bank accounts (banks)

The literature indicates that, based on the open list contained herein, income can be defined as any enlargement of property resulting in increasing assets or decreasing liabilities [1]. Such definition of tax revenue is also reflected in court decisions. In its judgement of 13 July 2010, the Supreme Administrative Court stated that:

the legislature did not formulate the requirement that income may only cover the benefits mentioned in Art. 12, which are a direct result of achieving the aim of economic activity of a legal person. Therefore any cash deposit may be considered as income of the legal person, provided it meets other requirements set out in section 2 herein. In particular par. 4 of the quoted article contains a list of benefits that cannot be classified as income. It is important to note that the legal norm contained in Art. 12, par. 4 of the act on corporate income tax provides a closed list, the scope of which is not subject to extension or constriction through the use of analogy and extensive interpretation.

Essentially, including a property benefit in the revenues of the legal person is determined by the definitive nature of the benefit in the sense that it definitively actually increases the assets of the legal person. In its judgement dated 27 November 2003, the Supreme Administrative Court in Warsaw stated that "income can include only those values that determine the final increase in the assets of the taxpayer".

At the same time, recognizing a benefit as income is not determined by the fact that it was not included in the list of tax revenues not recognized by legislature. This was pointed out by the Supreme Administrative Court in its judgement in 14 May 1998, in which it stated that:

the essence of the income tax suggests that it is a public and legal burden on the increase in wealth (income) and, therefore, the revenue - as a source of income – is only the value in entering the property of the taxpayer, may increase their assets. Therefore, the money or monetary values received within the meaning of Art. 12, par. 1 item 1 of the Act in question only include such values that increase the assets of the taxpayer, i.e., those they can dispose of as their own.

Taxation should cover all income, unless expressly exempted. Tax-neutral revenues and therefore those that do not constitute bases for determining the taxable income of the taxpayer are listed in Art. 12, par. 4 act on corporate income tax, where an exhaustive list is included. As a result of this regulation, this provision provides a closed list, the scope of which is not subject to extension or narrowing through the use of analogies or broad interpretation.

Income free of income tax includes payments or accrued receivables on the account of the supply of goods and services. Recognizing received or accrued contributions as deferred revenue requires the ability to allocate these payments to future accounting periods. The company must prove (pointing to the provisions of the contract or the content of the invoice) that the supply of goods or services is to take place in the following accounting periods after the accounting period in which the taxpayer receives payment (advance payment). The provision in question applies in particular to services provided on a continuous basis.

According to Art. 12, paragraph 4, item 2, income not constituting tax revenues includes amounts of accrued but not received interest on debt, including outstanding loans (credits). This provision shows that interest is neutral for tax purposes until they paid. The taxpayer receives tax revenue from interest income at the time of actual receipt. In this case, cash accounting will apply, which means that the entity, which is owed interest is required to allocate them to their tax revenues only in the accounting period in which the interest is actually received.

Any decision of contractors regarding, e.g., changes in interest rates on loans, postponement of payments, etc., shall remain tax neutral until actual payment of interest.

Income exempt from taxation also includes revenue generated by redeemed shares in a company in the part constituting the cost of their purchase or acquisition. The matter also applies to the value of assets received by shareholders in connection with the liquidation of the legal entity. On the other hand, the amounts received for the redeemed shares in excess of expenditure on the acquisition of those shares are taxable income.

In accordance with the provisions of the act, tax-exempt revenues are revenues due to redistributable as well as non-redistributable capital, provided for the Code of Commercial Companies. Such subsidies are a variety of cash benefits brought by shareholders for the company to enlarge its assets. Therefore, subsidies do not affect the size of the share capital. Tax income also does not include amounts and values that are in excess of the nominal value of shares, resulting in their release and transferred to the capital.

Neutral tax cash contributions include funds brought to the capital company and noncash contributions. The provisions of the Law on Corporate Income Tax represent that property values brought to cover equity (capital) are not tax income of businesses, which means that the capital raised through the issue of new ordinary shares shall not constitute taxable income. The consequence of this is the fact that expenses related to the acquisition of capital may not be treated as tax-deductible costs. After all, they do not refer to tax income. They are directly related to the performance of a tax-neutral operation on the share capital [2].

In accordance with the provisions of the Polish Law on Corporate Income Tax, the provisions of the act shall not apply to:

- Income from agricultural activities, with the exception of income from special branches of agricultural production
- Income from forestry within the meaning of the forest act
- Revenues resulting from activities, which may not be legally effective contracts
- Revenue (income) of shipowners taxed under the principles arising from the Law of 24 August 2006 on Tonnage Tax.

The presented provisions show that income derived from these activities is not subject to income tax, i.e., it is free from this tax.

In the EU concept of a common consolidated corporate tax base, it has been determined that the tax base is calculated by decreasing income by income exempt from tax, deductible expenses and other deductible items. Next to the definition, a normative interpretation of specific rules for its determination was proposed. It has been stated that income shall be calculated according to the following general principles:

- The accrual basis.
- Gains and losses are recognized only when they are effective (principle of realization).
- Taxable transactions and events are measured individually (the principle of individual valuation).
- Income calculation is performed according to uniform rules, unless exceptional circumstances justify a change (consistency).[2]

The introduction of the said rules would favourably distinguish the CCCTB proposals from those used in Polish law on corporate income tax. The Polish solutions reflect the accrual basis in relation to taxable income and costs. The realization principle can be found in relation to interest income and expenses, but it lacks a general reference to taxable profits and losses. The principles of individual valuation and consistency are also slightly emphasized in Polish law.

The draft directive defines the concepts of revenues, profits and losses. The term "revenues" defines income from sales and all other transactions, without the value-added tax and other taxes and duties collected on behalf of government authorities, in cash or noncash form, including proceeds from the disposal of assets and rights, interest, dividends and other distributions and proceeds from liquidation, royalties, subsidies and grants, gifts received, compensation and voluntary payments. Revenues also include in-kind donations made by the taxpayer. Revenues shall not include equity raised by the taxpayer or debt repaid to the taxpayer. According to the authors of the draft directive, "profit" means a surplus of revenues over deductible expenses and other deductible items in a tax year, and "loss" means the excess of deductible expenses and other deductible items over revenues in a tax year.

It is worth emphasizing that, in accordance with the draft directive, taxation applies not only to noncash donations collected by the recipient but also those transferred by the recipient. In the case of the donor it is in fact a fictitious revenue, resulting from the adoption of a fiction that the donated item has not been donated, but was sold according to its market value. In this way, the tax covers the so-called hidden reserves, i.e., income equal to the difference between the market value and the accounted value of a donation [3]. In the Polish law on corporate income tax, there are no solutions requiring the taxation of the donor; hence, the solutions contained in the draft directive may be considered to be less favourable for Polish enterprises. Such an approach to the valuation of monetary donations received by the recipient is based on Article 22 of the draft directive *Valuation*, which states that:

1. For the purposes of calculating the tax base, transactions are evaluated by:(...)
   a. Their market value, if all or part of the benefit from the transaction, is nonmonetary.
   b. Their market value for monetary donations received by the taxpayer.

The list of exemptions from income tax contained in the draft directive is relatively short. Article 11 *Income exempt from taxation* reads:

The following is exempt from corporate tax:

a. Grants directly related to the acquisition, manufacture or improvement of fixed assets subject to depreciation in accordance with Arts. 32–42
b. Income from the sale of assets referred to in Art. 39, par. 2, including the market value of in-kind donations
c. Distributed revenues received
d. Proceeds from the disposal of shares
e. Income from a facility in a third country

Exemption from tax should also apply to income from dividends, proceeds from the disposal of shares in the company outside the group and the profits of foreign establishments. By granting relief for double taxation, the majority of member states exempts the dividends and proceeds from the disposal of shares, thus avoiding the necessity of calculating the amount to be deducted for tax paid abroad, in particular when while calculating the vested deduction, one must take into account the amount of corporate tax paid by the company paying the dividend. The exemption of income earned abroad meets the same requirement of simplifying the system.

While conducting research on a common consolidated tax base and its importance for the Polish and EU companies, questions were asked regarding the significance of revenues other than tax income. The test results are very interesting also from the point of view of simplifying the Polish tax system. Data showing the answers given by Polish companies is included in Table 1.

The analysis of the data contained in Table 1 shows a high insignificance of amounts of income not constituting tax revenues. This may be due to the fact that many of these exemptions are specific and relate to specific companies, e.g., in the agricultural production and forestry activities in the SEZ. These subjects were relatively few in the total group of companies surveyed.

Table 1. The importance of nontax revenues for polish businesses (0, insignificant; 5, very significant) (in %).

	0	1	2	3	4	5	No answer	Total
Revenues from forestry and agricultural activities	92.86	0.00	0.00	0.00	0.00	3.57	3.57	100.00
Accrued but not received interest on receivables, bank deposits and so on	66.07	16.07	7.14	3.57	1.79	1.79	3.57	100.00
Foreign exchange gains established at the balance sheet date but unrealized	69.64	8.92	5.36	1.79	5.36	5.36	3.57	100.00
Dividends and other revenues from participation in profits of legal persons	80.36	1.79	3.57	8.92	0.00	1.79	3.57	100.00
Returned taxes, charges and expenses not included in KUP	69.64	17.85	5.36	1.79	1.79	0.00	3.57	100.00
Interest received on excess payment of tax	82.15	8.92	5.36	0.00	0.00	0.00	3.57	100.00
Grants, subsidies and payments received to cover the costs or as reimbursement of expenses	87.50	7.14	1.79	0.00	0.00	0.00	3.57	100.00
Income earned from foreign governments derived from non-returnable aid	92.85	1.79	0.00	0.00	1.79	0.00	3.57	100.00
Revenues generated from the economic activity of the SEZ	94.64	1.79	0.00	0.00	0.00	0.00	3.57	100.00
Income from real estate made available free of charge	94.64	1.79	0.00	0.00	0.00	0.00	3.57	100.00
Revenues established by decision of the head of the tax office	94.64	1.79	0.00	0.00	0.00	0.00	3.57	100.00

Source: Author's own calculation based on surveys.

3. COST OF ACQUIRING INCOME

The provisions of the Corporate Income Tax Act do not contain a strict list of expenses that are treated as tax-deductible costs [4]. According to the Act, deductible costs are costs incurred to generate revenue or maintain or secure sources of income, apart from the costs, which are listed numerically in the laws as not deductible.[3] A literal interpretation of this provision leads to the conclusion that all incurred expenses, excluding those restricted by law,[4] are tax-deductible costs as long as they remain in the causal link with revenues, including those aimed at maintaining or securing the functioning of the source of revenue. The provisions of the Act show that it is possible to recognize as deductible costs these expenditures, which—judging rationally—can help to create or increase the company's revenue, provided that the expenditure has not been excluded from such costs. In the jurisprudence of administrative courts and tax authorities, the notion that costs within the meaning of the Corporate Income Tax Act may include those expenses that are in a causal relationship to the economic activity and the revenue obtained in respect thereof has perpetuated.

While defining deductibles for tax purposes, one should not use the definitions contained in other laws, e.g., the Accounting Law. The definitions presented in the theory of economics and finance and accounting law do not apply to the tax law, and for the purposes of interpretation of the texts of acts of tax law, one should only use the definition of tax expense in Art. 15, par. 1 of the Corporate Income Tax Law.[5]

The wording of the provision on tax-deductible costs gives the company the ability to deduct for tax purposes any cost, provided that there is a direct or indirect connection with the activities and that bearing it has or may have an impact on the amount of income earned. Therefore, tax-deductible costs are all rationally and economically reasonable expenses associated with running a business whose goal is to achieve the protection and preservation of sources of income.

The most important prerequisite that must be met for a certain expense to be recognized as tax deductible is that there should be a causal relationship between the expense and the revenue. This involves such relationship that incurring the cost has an impact on the generation or increase of revenue. In its judgement, the court stated:

undoubtedly the costs of revenues must be related to a specific source of revenue, i.e., the amount of income from that source is affected by the costs incurred in order to obtain revenue, i.e., there must be a causal relationship between the expenses incurred and the actual resulting income or the possibility of obtaining that income.

Tax-deductible costs directly related to revenues should be considered these costs which directly affect the revenue acquired from that source. So these are all costs which are essential for the specified source of revenue to bring specific profits. To recognize the expense as tax deductible, it is not always necessary to demonstrate a direct link between it and the revenue. It should be noted that the deductible costs are all expenses incurred in order to obtain revenue, including in those incurred in order to maintain and secure a source of income, so that this source of revenue brings income in the future as well. Therefore, the costs will also include indirect costs associated with the revenue obtained, if it is shown to have been reasonably incurred in order to obtain revenue (including for ensuring the functioning of the source of revenue), even if the revenue is not achieved due to objective reasons.

Deductibles will therefore include such an expense that meets the following conditions:

- It was incurred by the taxpayer; i.e., in the final analysis, it must be covered with resources of the taxpayer.
- It is definitive (actual); i.e., the value of the expenses incurred has not been reimbursed to the taxpayer in any way.
- It remains in connection with the economic activity of the taxpayer.
- It was incurred in order to obtain revenue or maintain or secure the sources of income.
- It was properly documented.
- It cannot belong in the group of expenses that shall not be deemed tax deductibles in accordance with the provisions of the Act.

It should also be noted that the definition formulated by the legislature is very general. Therefore, every expense incurred by the taxpayer should be subject to individual scrutiny in order to carry out its legal qualification. The exception is when the act clearly shows its affiliation to the category of deductible expenses or disables the ability to include it in such costs. In its judgement, the Supreme Administrative Court stated that:

In determining deductible costs, every expense - other than those expressly set out in the Act - requires individual assessments of the direct relationship with income and the rationality of action to achieve this income. Situations, in which this causal relationship is not clear, should therefore be solved according to the principles of rational reasoning, individually for each case.

Expenses not recognized by the legislature as tax-deductible costs can be divided into three groups:

- Expenses that are not included in the cost of revenues beyond the statutorily defined limits or when no distinct conditions are met
- Expenses which, by their nature, are not deductible for tax purposes but in certain circumstances are recognized as such

- Expenses which re absolutely not deductible

Among the presented groups of costs not considered deductible costs, one can distinguish the following groups:

1. Expenditure on the purchase and modernization of fixed assets and intangible assets
2. Losses and penalties, including, e.g.:
    - Loss of prepayments, advances and down payments
    - Interest, contractual penalties and damages
    - Enforcement costs, fines and penalties
3. Liabilities and reserves, including, e.g.:
    - Overdue receivables
    - Reserves created on the basis of the accounting law
4. Taxes
5. Expenditure on the operation of cars not included in fixed assets
6. Other expenses, including, e.g.:
    - Costs associated with tax-free income
    - Representation expenditure

The definition of deductible included in the draft CCCTB directive (on a common consolidated tax base) differs from that recognized in the corporate income tax. According to the provisions in the draft directive:

deductible costs include any costs incurred by the taxpayer for business purposes related to the achievement, maintaining or securing income, including costs of research and development work and the costs of increasing the capital or debt for commercial purposes.[6]

It follows that the deductible cost of doing business should normally include all costs related to sales and costs associated with achieving, maintaining and securing income. The deductibility also covers the costs of research and development and the costs incurred in raising own or foreign equity for the business purposes. The supplement on deductible costs in the draft directive stipulates that:

tax-deductible costs also include donations to charities specified in Art. 16, established in a Member State or in another country covered by the agreement on the exchange of information on request, comparable to the provisions of Directive 2011/16/EU. The maximum amount of deductible costs related to contributions or monetary donations to charities is 0.5% of revenue in the fiscal year.

In the analysis of deductible cost for income tax and the concept of a CCCTB, the category of cause and effect relationship between the income tax and the cost of its acquisition is extremely important. The draft directive stipulates that deductible costs are the "costs incurred by the taxpayer for commercial purposes related to the achievement, maintenance or protection of revenue". This condition, referred to as the "economic purpose test", is ambiguous [5] and imprecise. As indicated earlier, a provision in the Polish law requires an individual approach to every cost incurred by the company, especially when it concerns the so-called indirect costs associated with maintaining sources of income. However, even a thorough analysis does not eliminate tax risks arising from the fact that the assessment made by the tax authority may be different from the subjective assessment of the taxpayer. It is then often the court that decides on the eligibility of cost as a tax cost. In one of its judgements, the Supreme Administrative Court stated:

to include the expense in deductible costs it is not enough to hope that such income would one day be achieved. Each entrepreneur acting professionally must analyse the actions they take, and not just hope that they will prove to be beneficial.

The risk of an erroneous inclusion of a cost into deductibles is also clear from the wording contained in the draft directive. The fact that the wording is imprecise may result in the assessment of the cost incurred by a company also being ultimately carried out by a court, as setting "economic purposefulness" of the expense incurred can be difficult and ambiguous. However, it should be emphasized that the draft directive contains a provision that "deductible cots are considered as such if they are incurred by the taxpayer for business purposes". This wording is still flexible than that contained in the law on corporate income tax.

The draft directive also allows for pro rata write-downs due to depreciation of fixed assets.

Article 14 of the draft directive lists the costs that are not deductible. These include, e.g.:

1. Distributed revenues and repayment of equity or debt
2. 50% of representation cost
3. The transfer of retained profits to other reserves forming part of the company's equity
4. Corporate tax
5. Bribes
6. Fines and penalties paid to a public authority for breach of any legislation
7. Costs incurred by the company in order to generate income exempted from taxation pursuant to Art. 11; the amount of such costs is fixed at a flat rate of 5% of that income, unless the taxpayer is able to demonstrate that he has incurred a lower cost

While analyzing deductible costs for income tax and the CCCTB concept, it is important to note how businesses perceive the burden of costs that are not deductible for tax purposes. Table 2 shows the importance of the costs that are not considered deductibles for Polish companies.

The data contained in Table 2 shows that for Polish company costs that are not considered deductibles in income tax do not have much significance. The least important include fines and penalties, enforcement costs, interest expenses, commissions and foreign exchange differences on loans. In contrast, the cost of interest on loans granted by shareholders has greater importance for tax-payers.

Table 2. The importance of non-deductible costs for polish businesses in income tax (0, insignificant; 5, very significant) (in %).

	0	1	2	3	4	5	No answer	Total
Expenses for the purchase of land or the right of perpetual usufruct of land	66.07	10.71	8.93	1.79	0.00	8.93	3.57	100.00
Costs related to the operation of a car to the extent determined by the value of the car exceeding the equivalent of 20,000 Euro	60.72	12.50	8.93	7.14	3.57	3.57	3.57	100.00
Repayment of loans (credits), excluding capitalized interest on these loans (credits)	46.43	21.42	8.93	8.93	1.79	7.14	5.36	100.00
Interest on liabilities accrued but not paid or written off, including loans	62.50	16.06	1.79	3.57	8.93	1.79	5.36	100.00
Interest, fees and currency exchange differences on loans (credits that increase the cost of investment in development)	73.22	7.14	3.57	1.79	3.57	7.14	3.57	100.00
Enforcement costs related to defaults	75.00	14.29	3.57	0.00	3.57	0.00	3.57	100.00
Fines and penalties	76.78	10.71	5.36	1.79	1.79	0.00	3.57	100.00
Debts written off as overdue	58.93	19.64	3.57	0.00	3.57	1.79	12.50	100.00
Interest on late payment of overdue budget payments and others	55.36	32.14	5.36	3.57	0.00	0.00	3.57	100.00
Reserves formed in accordance with the provisions of the accounting act	62.50	7.14	10.71	3.57	5.36	1.79	8.93	100.00

	0	1	2	3	4	5	No answer	Total
Representation costs	55.36	32.14	5.36	3.57	0.00	0.00	3.57	100.00
Depreciation write-offs calculated for tax purposes more quickly than for accounting purposes	62.50	7.14	10.71	3.57	5.36	1.79	8.93	100.00
Interest on loans granted by shareholders	44.64	25.00	16.07	1.79	3.57	3.57	5.36	100.00
Revaluation of assets in the accounting books	71.42	1.79	12.50	5.36	3.57	1.79	3.57	100.00

Source: Author's own calculation based on surveys.

It is important to note the wording states that revenue, expenses and all other deductible items shall be recognized in the tax year in which they were achieved or incurred. It follows that the tax costs are deducted in the tax year in which they are incurred. Incurring a deductible cost occurs when the following conditions are met: firstly, the obligation to make payments; secondly, the ability to determine the amount of liability with reasonable accuracy; and thirdly, in the case of trading goods, transfer of significant risks and rewards of ownership of goods to the taxpayer, while in the case of services, receiving the services by the taxpayer. It should be stressed that the proposed solution is possible to implement in the Polish law on corporate income tax.

4.COMMONCONSOLIDATEDCORPORATETAXBASE:FUNDAMENTAL ASSUMPTIONS

A document entitled "A Common Consolidated EU Corporate Tax Base[7]" published on 7 July 2004 includes the assumptions of the concept aimed at reducing the costs and barriers to business activity in the European Union. **On 16 March 2011**[8], the European Commission submitted a proposal for the directive on a common consolidated corporate tax base (CCCTB). According to the proposal, the main goal of the concept is to eliminate at least some major tax problems impeding economic growth on the EU single market. Due to the lack of uniform corporate tax regulations, interdependence of domestic tax systems often results in double taxation. Hence, enterprises have to deal with heavy administrative burdens and high costs associated with conforming to tax regulations. Such a state of affairs discourages companies from making investments in the EU and consequently hinders the achievement of priorities included in *Europe 2020*—a strategy for smart, sustainable and inclusive growth.[9]

Common consolidated corporate tax base is a major initiative designed to eliminate obstacles to the creation of a single market.[10] It is considered[11] an initiative stimulating growth that should be undertaken in the first place in order to facilitate economic development and create new jobs. CCCTB concept would guarantee the coherence of domestic tax systems but no harmonization of tax rates.

According to the proposal for the directive, tax rates ought to be subject to fair competition. Different rates enable particular countries to maintain a certain level of tax competition on internal market. Furthermore, fair competition based on tax rates provides a greater transparency and allows the member states to take into account the competitiveness of their markets and budgetary requirements while determining tax rates [6].

Supporting research and development is one of the fundamental objectives included in the directive under discussion. As part of common consolidated corporate tax base, all costs associated with R&D are tax-deductible expenses. For enterprises that would decide to adopt the system, such an approach will be an incentive to further investment in research and development. In case of economic losses which are subject to cross-border compensation, consolidation within the framework of CCCTB will contribute significantly to reducing the tax base. Nevertheless, the implementation of CCCTB will expand the average EU tax base mainly due to the option taken as far as the depreciation of assets is concerned.

The introduction of CCCTB would reduce or even eliminate barriers to conducting cross-border activity in the European Union. This is of profound importance for enterprises regardless of their size. In the case of small- and medium-sized companies, costs involved in adjusting the activity to regulations imposed in particular countries are a major barrier. Compared to the turnover of such firms, these costs are an important item. As for large enterprises, the possibility of cross-border settlement of tax losses is the main advantage of the new solution.

A system will be chosen voluntarily. Since not all enterprises conduct their activity abroad, CCCTB will not require companies which do not intend to expand their business outside their homelands to cover costs associated with adopting a new tax system. Only methods for determining tax base will be subject to harmonization. It will not be the case with financial statements. Therefore, the member states will still apply domestic principles of financial accounting, and CCCTB will impose autonomous regulations on calculating corporate tax base. These regulations will not exert any effect on producing annual and consolidated financial reports. As for CCCTB, certain enterprises would have to follow uniform tax rules (applicable in the entire European Union) and would deal with single tax administration (one-stop shop). Having decided to apply common consolidated corporate tax base, the company is no longer subject to domestic corporate tax system as far as all the issues regulated by joint regulations are concerned. Enterprises conducting activity in more than one state will benefit from the possibility of cross-border loss relief and lower the costs involved in conforming to corporate tax regulations. The possibility of direct consolidation of profits and losses for the purpose of calculating the EU tax base is a major step towards reducing overtaxation in a cross-border context. At the same time, it is a step towards improving the existing conditions, namely, in the scope of tax neutrality of domestic and cross-border activity. This will lead to a more effective fulfilment of internal market potential.[12]

The main advantage of implementing CCCTB for enterprises is the reduction of costs associated with observing tax regulations. Data published by the European Commission indicates that the introduction of the aforementioned concept may lower such costs by circa 7%. Actual reduction of the costs under discussion may have a major impact on enterprises' potential and willingness to expand their business and enter foreign markets (especially the companies that have operated only on regional markets so far).[13]

The directive under consideration provides a complete set of corporate tax regulations. It specifies which entities may select tax system, method of determining tax base, relief scope and methods. Furthermore, it introduces regulations on combating fraud, proposes a method for the apportionment of consolidated base and specifies how CCCTB system is to be administered by the member states in line with "one-stop shop" principle.

Optional implementation of CCCTB entails that it will be the 28th tax system adopted by the 27 member states. In other words, certain enterprises or individual taxpayers will choose fiscal regime referred to in the directive or follow their domestic tax systems. Therefore, the proposal is a major step towards the harmonization of corporate income tax which, by improving the internal competitiveness of the EU, is to restrict harmful internal competition.

In the context of following the principles of income tax, and particularly the principle of tax system coherence and transparency, it should be emphasized that the directive under discussion provides a complete regulation on CCCTB. Directive on CCCTB and related issues should be implemented only when all the aspects to determining the tax base and its apportionment are known and so are the mechanisms that underlie the functioning of administration in such the new system. Needless to say, the system has to be comprehensive and coherent.

5.COMPARISONOFCORPORATEFINANCEANDCAPITALSTRUCTURE WITH THE CCCTB IDEA

Issues relating to the effect that income tax has on capital structure are very complex. Attention should be paid to fundamental questions regarding tax solutions suggested in CCCTB concept in the context of corporate finance theory. As far as research on capital structure and its impact on goodwill are concerned, major breakthrough was achieved by Franco Modigliani and Merton H. Miller. In 1958 they published an article entitled *The Cost of Capital, Corporation Finance and the Theory of Investment* [7]. Publications has been started discussion that is held up to the present day. The discussion centres on the consequences of the capital structure imposed by the company for its finance and goodwill [8]. According to the theory developed by Modigliani and Miller, in the world without taxes, both the goodwill and weighted average costs of capital (WACC) do not depend on capital structure.

In 1963 Modigliani and Miller published an article which was a correction to the capital structure irrelevance proposition. It was then that they addressed the problem hitherto explored by corporate finance. **Major difficulty lays in defining the role of tax in shaping the financial policy to be pursued by the company** [9]. The authors under discussion presented a different view on the effect that the capital structure had on the goodwill. Having in mind corporate income tax, they were inclined to believe that under such circumstances the level of foreign funding to the enterprise was optimum and therefore the capital structure was optimum. Taking into account the tax differentiation (**tax asymmetry**) was a key to the analysis. The asymmetry is between income generated by shareholders and creditors at the company level [10]. Costs associated with interest on foreign capital reduce income tax base, unlike retained dividends and profits [11]. Hence, the utilization of outside capital involves interest tax shield. If interest is subtracted from corporate tax base, the goodwill of business entity which utilizes debt financing exceeds the goodwill of the company which does not utilize foreign capital (by the compound value of tax shield).

Introducing the tax system allowing to reduce the tax base by expenses such as interest on debt, Modigliani and Miller proved that less expensive foreign capital (due to interest tax shield) increased the goodwill. At the same time, they were the first to stress the importance of tax for financial policy pursued by the company and aimed at increasing its goodwill.

The theory formulated by Modigliani and Miller in 1963 highlighted **the role of tax in corporate finance**. They proved that it was possible to shape the capital structure and goodwill through tax policy. It is worth emphasizing that this aspect to tax has not yet been noticed by employees responsible for tax management in enterprises. Nowadays, tax is often treated as a fiscal burden and not a flow that may be managed in order to exert an influence on the goodwill. **With reference to the concept of CCCTB, the aforementioned theory states reasons for introducing one corporate tax system in the entire European Union so that all entities**

have equal opportunities for developing their goodwill through tax policy.

As for factors determining the capital structure in a given company, attention was also paid to the role of the other, namely, non-debt tax shields, resulting from depreciation and investment allowances, that may lessen the effect of interest of tax shield. Non-debt tax shields enabled to modify the research conducted by Miller by adding the concepts framed by DeAngelo and Masulis. They highlighted the role of investment tax shield in determining optimum tax structure. Furthermore, they proved that the goodwill of company with high non-debt tax shield may be the same as the goodwill of entity with high debt and thereby high interest tax shield. The higher the depreciation tax shield, the lower the interest shield. Such a conclusion was drawn by Masulis. In other words, the variety of tax shields enables one to create capital structure optimum for every company and the economy. Capital structure is optimum at a certain debt level, when the total value of tax shields (interest and depreciation) is a maximum allowance under certain fiscal conditions [12].

Based on the theory developed by Modigliani and Miller as well as the research conducted by DeAngelo and Masulis, it can be stated that **taking into account income tax and depreciation costs enables the companies to increase their goodwill through tax benefits.** Therefore, the optimum capital structure of the company does not stem only from the share of equity and outside capital in the aforementioned structure but is also a consequence of financial system solutions adopted as far as income tax is concerned.

The analysis of the theories referred to in the present paper suggests that debt and interest tax shield are particularly relevant to shaping the optimum structure of capital. So are system solutions for recognizing tax effects of debt financing. Solutions aimed at determining the level and structure of capital have been included in the proposal for the directive on CCCTB. It would be a simplification to put into practice an assumption that interest lessens the debt cost by recognizing it as a deductible expense.

According to Corporate Income Tax Act, tax-deductible expenses do not include loan (credit) repayment, except for capitalized interest on the loan (credit). In other words, interest is recognized as a deductible expense once it has been capitalized. In legal terms, in the case of contract relationship, payment is one form of discharging the liabilities by a debtor due to which the debt is amortized.

General principles formulated in the Act enable one to account for interest expenses by recognizing them as deductible costs. Obviously, there are exceptions to the rule (e.g. interest, calculated to date of handing over a fixed asset for use, is capitalized to its original value and effectively recognized as deductible cost through capital allowance). Therefore, according to the Act under discussion, the term "tax-deductible expenses" does not refer to "accrued but not paid or amortized interest, including interest on loan (credit)".

Other types of expenses associated with incurring a debt by the company are commissions and charges. As to the principle, commission is an expense not directly incurred to accomplish the goal for the sake of which the loan has been taken out but is a source of funding. As for the moment of recognizing commission as a deductible expense, one should pay attention to the regulation included in the Act according to which tax-deductible costs, other than costs directly associated with revenues, are deductible once they have been incurred (on such a date). In line with the Act under discussion, Polish companies can recognize paid and capitalized interest and costs associated with incurring the debt as tax-deductible costs. Therefore, it should be verified if solutions proposed by the legislator are significant to Polish enterprises. Table 3 shows the survey results.

Table 3. Significance of tax-deductible expenses associated with debt utilization in the opinion of Polish enterprises (0, insignificant, 5, significant) (in %).

	0	1	2	3	4	5	Absence of answer	Total
Costs associated with repayment of loan (credit) except for capitalized interest on the loan (credit)	46.4	21.4	8.9	8.9	1.8	7.2	5.4	100
Accrued but unpaid or amortized interest on debt, including loan (credit)	62.5	16.1	1.8	3.5	8.9	1.8	5.4	100
Interest, commission and exchange differences between loans (credits) increasing the cost of investment during its realization	73.2	7.1	3.6	1.8	3.6	7.1	3.6	100
Interest on loans granted by shareholders	80.4	1.8	5.3	1.8	1.8	5.3	3.6	100

Source: Based on the questionnaire survey.

Polish enterprises do not prioritize tax strategies for recognizing the deductibility of costs related to loan utilization. More than 45% of the surveyed firms fail to acknowledge that the expenses related to loan repayment are not eligible for deduction. Less than 7% of entities believe this to be a significant limitation. Moreover, Polish enterprises do not have any issues with regards to the inability to decrease the tax base on accrued interest that has not been paid or capitalized. Only a small number of organizations consider the significance of interest and commissions paid during the actual execution of investments, which constitute their initial worth. This is particularly true for the interest on loans provided by shareholders. Polish entrepreneurs fail to recognize the significance of deductible expenses in minimizing the actual cost of obtaining foreign financing through loans and credits. Furthermore, the study respondents do not perceive any issue with the fact that interest on debt may only be acknowledged as a tax-deductible expense if it is either paid or capitalized. In this connection, it can be said that Polish firms have the ability to adopt the ideas proposed by the European Commission within the discussed scope.

When developing the tax system as part of the CCCTB concept, we focused on achieving a balance between flexibility and standardization of legislation. We also considered the specific and general aspects of the suggested solutions in the idea, as well as their attractiveness compared to domestic solutions. Granting firms the freedom to select the taxation system empowers them to influence the composition and magnitude of the tax foundation.

The topic being discussed does not specifically pertain to interest charges as deductible costs for tax purposes. By a broad definition, all the expenses that the corporation incurs and pays to service its debt are considered deductible costs. The repayment of the obligation, such as the credit principle, will not qualify as a tax-deductible expense. This method is exactly the same as the one suggested in the Corporate Income Tax Act.

When examining deductible expenses according to the CCCTB approach, the accrual basis is especially important. Under the current Corporate Income Tax Act in Poland, interest is considered a tax-deductible item in accordance with the cash basis accounting method. The accrual basis is also employed in the context of MSR/MSSF. Consequently, it can be inferred that interest expenses will decrease the taxable amount after the tax has been computed, but before it is actually paid. This approach is advantageous for businesses and aligns tax concepts with accounting solutions.

6. CONCISE SUMMARY

The income tax system in both Poland and the European Union need significant reform. The necessity to enhance the Polish system arises from the significant deterioration of the tax law and the substandard quality of legislation. Uniformity is necessary within the Union to enhance its competitiveness against China, Russia, and the United States. At present, the European Union (EU) countries do not form a unified entity when it comes to business income tax. Instead, there are 27 distinct participants that compete with each other both within the EU and internationally. The objective should be to standardize the corporate income tax system for all enterprises in the EU, ensuring comparable working conditions in terms of income tax and presenting a cohesive entity externally from the Union. The CCCTB concept proposes the unification of the tax base, which refers to the principles governing the calculation of revenues and tax costs.

AT A GLANCE

The chapter examines the foundation of the corporate income tax and provides an overview of the regulations in Polish legislation regarding corporate income tax, along with the proposed common consolidated corporate tax base (CCCTB) directive. An examination of tax income and tax expenses, with a specific focus on non-tax income and non-deductible spending, is not taken into account. The chapter focused on carrying out a survey. Questionnaires were distributed to 1000 Polish enterprises that are liable to pay corporate income tax. The companies were chosen randomly from the entire pool of businesses in Poland. Surveys were distributed to 500 companies located in the European Union (EU), with a focus on Germany, the UK, France, the Netherlands, Italy, and the Czech Republic. A total of 112 Polish enterprises and 50 foreign companies responded to the study. The survey revealed that both Polish and international operators were predominantly comprised of limited liability firms and joint stock entities. The initial phase of the study was conducted between 2010 and 2011. In 2012, the study was replicated, and an additional 200 surveys were distributed to Polish companies, with 15 of them providing responses.

REFERENCES

1. Iwin-Garzyńska J. Common consolidated corporate tax base (CCCTB) in the theory of corporate finance. International Journal of Accounting and Taxation. June 2016;4(1):17-51. ISSN: 2372-4978 (Print), 2372-4986 (Online), Published by American Research Institute for Policy Development. DOI: 10.15640/ijat.v4n1a2
2. Iwin-Garzyńska J. Introduction to the Study on Harmonization of Corporate Tax in the European Union in Light of the Theory of Corporate Finance. Szczecin: Uniwersytet Szczeciński; 2015
3. Marciniuk J. Podatek dochodowy od osób prawnych. In: Komentarz. Warsaw: C.H. Beck; 2010. pp. 246-247
4. Litwińczuk H, editors. Wspólna korporacyjna podstawa opodatkowania w UE a opodatkowanie dochodu spółek w Polsce, ed. Warsaw: Oficyna Prawa Polskiego, Wydawnictwo Wiedza i Praktyka; 2011
5. Kubacki R. Koszty Uzyskania przychodów W Podatkach Dochodowych. Wrocław: Unimex; 2012. p. 39

6. Iwin-Garzyńska J. In: Iwin-Garzyńska J, editor. Opodatkowanie przedsiębiorstw W Unii Europejskiej – założenia Koncepcji wspólnej Skonsolidowanej Korporacyjnej Podstawy Opodatkowania, Opodatkowanie przedsiębiorstw. Wybrane Zagadnienia. Warsaw: Difin; 2013. p. 208

7. Modigliani F, Miller MH. The cost of capital, corporation finance and the theory of investment. American Economic Review. 1958;48:261-297

8. Modigliani F, Miller MH. Corporate income, taxes and the cost of capital. A correction. American Economic Review. 1963;53:433-443

9. Ashton DJ. Corporate financial policy: American analytics and U.K. taxation. Journal of Business Finance and Accounting. 1991;4:465-482

10. Matin JD, Cox SH, McMinn RD. The Theory of Finance. Evidence and Applications: The Dryden Press, Chicago; 1988. p. 656

11. Schall LD, Haley CW. Introduction to Financial Management. New York: McGraw-Hill International Editions; 1991. p. 429

12. Martin JD, Cox SH, McMinn RD. The Theory of Finance. Chicago: Evidence and Applications. The Dryden Press; 1988. p. 347

2 Chapter

GLOBAL IMPLICATIONS OF CORPORATE INCOME TAXES AND RELATED DISRUPTIONS

1. INTRODUCTION: AN OVERVIEW

Corporate income taxes (CIT) are paid by multinational corporations operating in many countries. Hence, the design, administration, and compliance of the system have a significant global dimension. The scientific and professional literature addresses this subject through the examination of tax competitiveness, tax coordination, and tax harmonization. The scientific inquiry into international tax rivalry and related subjects has a long-standing history. The interest has been fueled by a growing movement of money over the past four decades, as well as mounting worries about capital flight and the reduction of public revenue caused by base erosion and profit shifting. The issue arises from the governments' conflicting objectives. Governments aim to encourage investment by offering advantages, such as favorable tax treatment, to potential investors in the country, region, or location. By engaging in tax competition, governments participate in detrimental or inefficient practices. However, it is essential for governments to gather an adequate amount of tax money to ensure the provision of satisfactory public services and meet other demands from the public. This requires a complex process of finding a balance between those aims. Reduced income might result in inadequate delivery of public services or necessitate challenging policy choices at the higher government or supranational level, such as tax coordination and harmonization.

Studies in public economics theory outline the circumstances in which tax competition can have either detrimental or beneficial economic consequences [1, 2, 3]. These conditions exhibit a wide range of variations and are frequently challenging to harmonize in theoretical models. Empirical study often yields inconclusive results. The negative economic consequences of tax competition involve the reduction of taxes on mobile factors of production, which results in a decrease in the supply of public services and hampers governments' attempts to redistribute money. The beneficial impacts of tax competition are mostly endorsed by proponents and adherents of public choice theory, who observe efficiency-enhancing effects in tax competition. It restricts the inclination of local governments to excessively expand and curbs the development of an excessively powerful state [4, 5]. The empirical research on tax competitiveness presents a similarly varied depiction [1, 3].

This chapter aims to consolidate the increasing body of research on the economic consequences of tax competition. It encompasses an examination of the most recent developments in corporate income tax (CIT), foreign direct investment (FDI), and profit shifting. The subject is highly significant as tax avoidance and evasion, specifically through base erosion and profit shifting, have been ongoing and may be rising due to the increasingly advanced tax-reducing methods employed by multinational corporations and people who are more mobile [6, 7, 8, 9, 10].

The subsequent sections will (1) examine the theory of tax competition, including the "basic tax competition model" and its expansions, (2) present current patterns in corporate income tax rates and revenue in the European Union and Organisation for Economic Co-operation and Development (OECD) countries, (3) provide an overview of empirical research on tax competition, including evidence of the connection between tax rates and foreign direct investment (FDI), and (4) outline the existing knowledge regarding the extent of tax avoidance through base erosion and profit shifting. Ultimately, the final portion comes to a close.

2. TAX COMPETITION THEORY

There is an extensive literature on the theory of tax competition. The modern literature on tax competition began with Oates's discussion on the potential efficiency problems associated with competition for capital by local governments [2, 11]. Under certain assumptions, small jurisdictions competing for mobile capital reduce tax rates to such level that leads "to less than efficient levels of output of local services" ([1] p. 654). In a small jurisdiction, competition leads to the abandonment of taxes on capital income altogether which produces "race to the bottom" ([1] p. 651). Oates' concludes that this behavior is inefficient that rests on the idea that this a zero-sum game. When all governments behave this way, none gain and consequently communities are all worse off than they would have been if local managers had made decisions based on marginal costs [2]. More recent interest in the topic was prompted in part by fears that tax competition among the increasingly economically integrated EU nations will over time significantly reduce the level of capital income taxation to the extent of announcing the death of CIT [12]. Thus, governments must solely rely on financing their expenditures from the taxes on immobile factors of production (labor/land) and on consumption taxes, which have their own constraints and disadvantages.

"Basic tax competition model" has been built by Zodrow and Mieszkowski [13] and Wilson who formalized the notions on tax competition developed by Oates

[2]. Alternatively, the model is known as a ZMW model or a simpler version, according to Wilson [2], is known as ZM model [14]. Similar to Tiebout's model [15], the ZM model is built on those assumptions "(1) A large number of homogenous jurisdictions; (2) Perfectly competitive markets; (3) A Nash equilibrium in which each jurisdiction takes as fixed the after-tax return to capital and the tax rates set by other jurisdictions; (4) Fixed population and land in each jurisdiction; (5) Identical tastes and incomes for all residents of all jurisdictions; (6) A fixed national capital stock that is perfectly mobile across local jurisdictions; (7) A single good that is produced by capital and the fixed factor (labor/land) in each jurisdiction; (8) Government services that are "publicly provided private goods," benefit only residents, have no spillover effects to other jurisdictions, and can be modeled as purchases of the single private good;(9) Two local tax instruments—a "property tax" that applies to capital income and a head tax; (10) Local governments that act to maximize the welfare of their (identical) residents" ([1, 15] p. 654).

In the ZM model, interjurisdictional competition results in "race to the bottom," as all taxes on capital income are eliminated. Governments are only able to impose taxes on immobile factors of production only. The insight of this result serves as a model for a "small open economy" [16].

An important assumption of the basic tax competition model is that local public services are essentially another consumption good that enters individual utility functions. However, as Sinn correctly observes, one of the most important roles of government is to redistribute income which has nothing to do with consumption goods [17]. Income redistribution at least partially represents social protection against income uncertainty attributable to different macroeconomic shocks and, more broadly, differences in natural endowments and access to education. Private markets fail to insure against income uncertainty and other risks; therefore, public programs designed to smooth such shocks improve both equity and efficiency of resource allocation. Tax competition results in lower tax rates on mobile factors of production and thus limits the power of governments to engage in redistributive activities. It imposes important social costs. In case of perfect mobility of both capital and highly skilled labor, tax competition implies that only benefit taxes can be levied and the policy of income redistribution is given up. Though Sinn's observation relaxes one of the assumptions of the basic model, it fundamentally reinforces the central message of the basic model.

Since the development of the basic tax competition model, many extensions have been added by changing one or several assumptions of the basic model; for complete list and details, see Zodrow [1]. Some of those modifications support the results of the basic model and find inefficiencies due to tax competition, while others find efficiency enhancing effects of tax competition. The extensions that assume heterogeneous rather than homogeneous jurisdictions and include trade among members of the union or trade with the rest of the world find harmful effects to tax competition. The modification of the model which assumes variable labor supply (instead of fixed) also does not change the results of the basic model.

Another departure from the ZM model is the existence of "interregional externalities." In this case, the actions that one region's government takes to increase the welfare of its own residents lead to reductions in the welfare of residents in other regions. In the tax competition literature, this externality is often described as a "fiscal externality," which occurs through the effects of one region's public policies on the government budgets in another region [18]. For example, when a region lowers its tax rate on mobile capital, it gains capital at the expense of other regions, causing their tax bases to fall and, hence, their tax revenues to decline. Because governments are assumed not to possess unlimited taxing powers, the presence of such externalities reinforces the message of the ZM model (Wilson [2]).

However, other extensions of the basic model, such as the existence of international trade with the presence of agglomeration economies [19] and international public good spillovers do not support the conclusion of the ZM model. Adding the combination of labor mobility and population scale economies to the model yields interesting results. With scale economies, underprovision of local public services tends to decline and disappears entirely in the limiting case of a pure public good [1]. Therefore, this extension contradicts the proposition of the basic tax competition model.

A special niche in this discussion is reserved for public choice literature, which traditionally argues that jurisdictional governments in the union do not act to maximize the welfare of their residents but to achieve their own objectives that are typically positively related to the size of the budget. Under this view, government bureaucrats strive to maximize the budgets of their agencies and increase their own power and prestige. In the public choice literature, tax competition is not a source of inefficiency. On the contrary, tax competition serves a valuable social purpose in constraining government officials who are naturally predisposed to raise revenue to serve their own rather than public interests. To Brennan and Buchanan for instance, "... tax competition among separate units ... is an objective to be sought in its own right" ([4] p. 186). In this context, tax competition plays an important role in limiting budget-maximizing behavior of government officials. It restricts the growth of public finance and curbs the expansion of a Leviathan state.

The results of the tax competition literature are mixed to such a degree that it is difficult to draw unambiguous conclusions. It is obvious that the key point of the basic tax competition model (as well as those extensions that reinforce its conclusions) is that tax competition is harmful and leads to inefficient underprovision of public services. On the other hand, some of the extensions to the basic model suggest that tax competition may be desirable as it limits the undue expansion of public budgets.

3. EMPIRICAL EVIDENCE OF TAX COMPETITION

3.1. Trends in corporate income taxes

As a consequence of the difficulty to develop one and conclusive theory, the empirical literature on tax competition burgeoned in recent years. However, meta-analysis reveals that results are as diverse as those in theoretical analyses [3]. First, the empirical evidence of tax competition and "race to the bottom" depend on the choice of parameters. Second, the findings are not conclusive. For example, there is mixed evidence if rate reductions in the face of increased international capital mobility are actually occurring. At first glance, the reduction of CIT rates is undisputable. CIT statutory rates[1] have decreased substantially in the EU over the past 22 years, with the average rate falling from 35% in 1995 to 22% in 2017, which constitutes a fall of 37.4% from 1995 to 2017 in EU 28 countries [20]. As indicated in Figure 1, the decrease of CIT rates in new EU member states (those who joined EU in 2004 and later) is even more substantial. The average statutory rates have decreased from the average rate of 31% in 1995 to 18% in 2017. This constitutes a fall of 43.6% or an average annual rate of minus 3% during the same period. In old EU member states (EU-15), statutory rates fell at an average annual rate of -2% as shown in Figure 2.

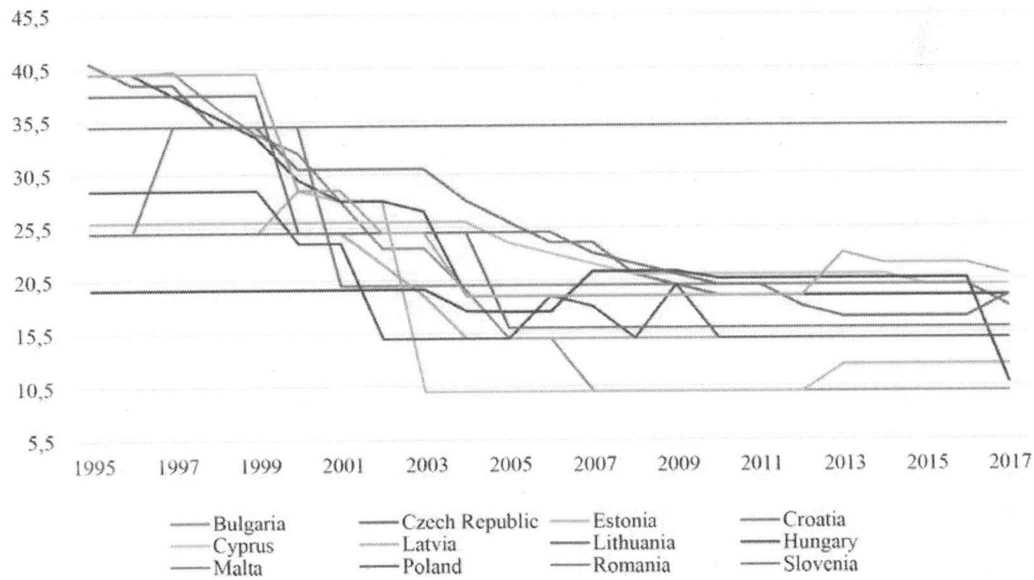

Figure 1. Statutory corporate income tax rates for new EU member states. Source: European Commission. Data on Taxation (2017).

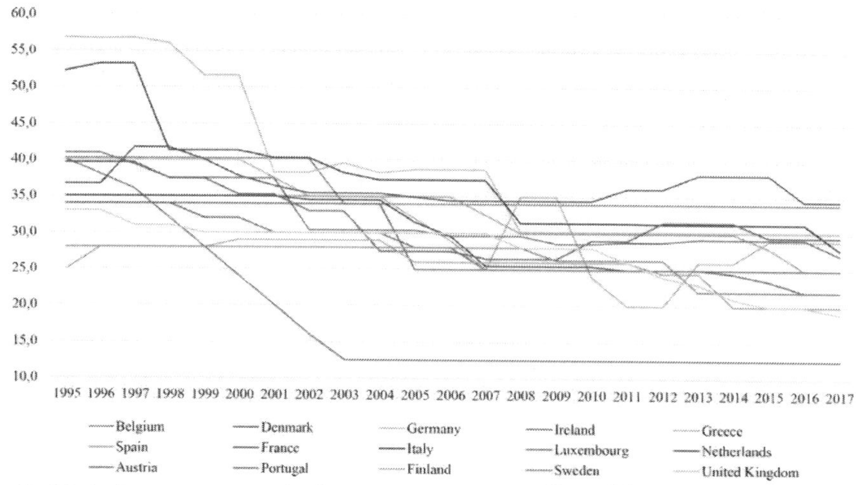

Figure 2. Statutory corporate income tax rates for old EU member states (EU-15). Source: European Commission. Data on Taxation (2017).

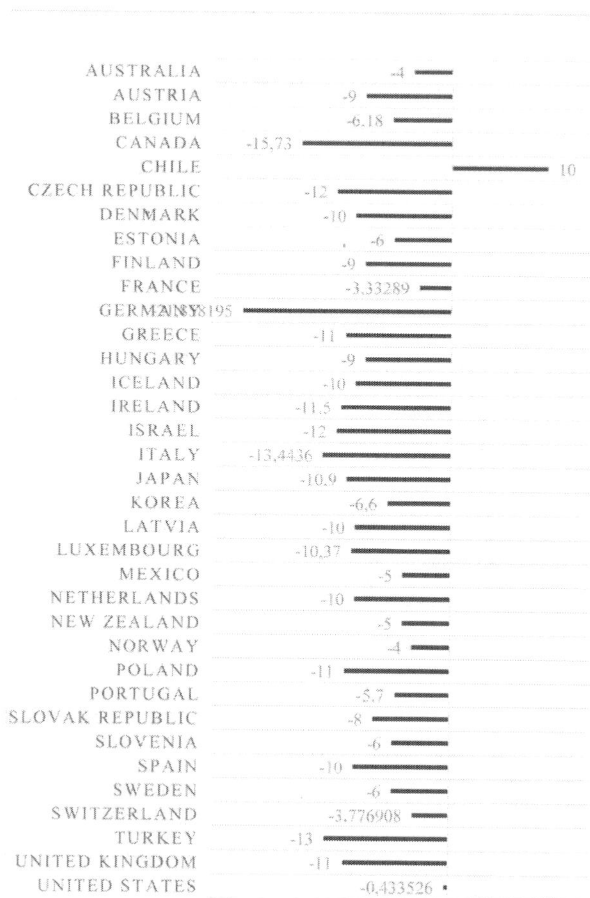

Figure 3.Statutory corporate income tax rates in OECD countries. Difference from 2000 to 2017. Source: OECD (2017).

As indicated in Figure 3, in OECD countries combined central and local government, average statutory rates have fallen by 25.6% from an average CIT rate of 32.5% in 2000 to an average CIT rate of 24.2% in 2017 [21]. The statutory rates have fallen in virtually each OECD member state with an exception of Chile where CIT rate has increased by 10% points. The largest fall in the CIT statutory rate has occurred in Germany, albeit from a very high level of 52% in 2000 to 30.2% in 2017, while the change of CIT rate in the United States was incremental (-0.43% points).

However, this evidence becomes less remarkable when base-broadening measures[2] are taken into account leading to much less conspicuous fall in average effective tax rates. As shown in Figure 4, average effective tax rates measured as CIT revenue as a % of GDP has stayed overall even. They have decreased by 15% from 2000 to 2014 or at an average annual rate of -1.12%, with the effects of the economic boom and recession standing out.

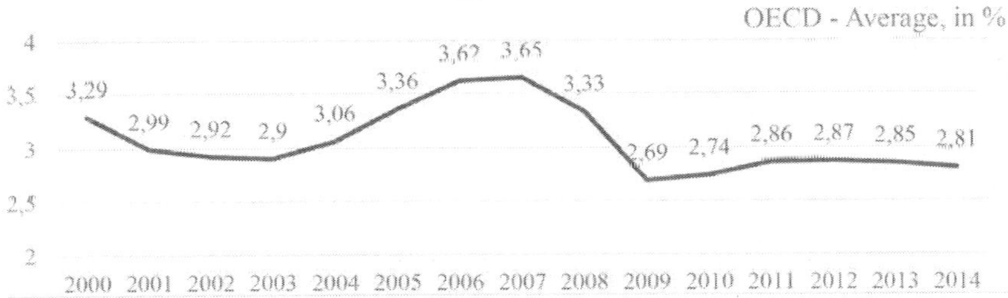

Figure 4. Corporate Income Tax Revenue as percentage of GDP, OECD countries. Source: OECD (2017).

These trends support previous findings by Grubert that the greatest declines in tax rates were in small, open and relatively poor countries—the countries that are arguably most vulnerable to the effects of tax competition, like new EU member states [22]. These results suggest that the rate reductions predicted by the theory of tax competition are actually occurring. Indeed, governments engage in two-dimensional tax competition. They concurrently compete over effective marginal tax rates for capital and over statutory rates for profits [23]. Evidence from Belgium suggests of regional tax competition taking place between different regions, with a lower effective tax rate (ETR) in the peripheral region of Wallonia than in Flanders [24].

However, it should be noted that reasons other than the tax competition for mobile capital might explain the fall in statutory CIT rates. In particular, this result can be explained by the reforms undertaken by policy makers to adopt base-broadening, rate-reducing measures consistent with persisting reform recommendations to improve the efficiency, equity, and simplicity of the tax system [25]. Besides, reductions in statutory rates can also be explained as an attempt to minimize a country's vulnerability to the use of transfer pricing by multinational enterprises to move deductions to high-tax countries and receipts to low-tax countries [26]. This is consistent with tax avoidance problem caused by capital mobility and tax rate differentials discussed in the following sections.

3.2. Tax rates and foreign direct investment

Since the 1980s, the relation between FDI and corporate taxation policy has been widely studied, and the pioneers in research have focused primarily on the FDI flows sensitivity to capital tax rate [3]. Despite abundant literature, the consensus on the effect of the corporate taxation on FDI in todays' globalized economies has not been reached. Some of the studies find no impact of tax reduction on FDI, but the other studies argue about the negative relationship between taxation policies and FDI gravity.

Hunady and Orviska examine EU countries (except Estonia due to the unavailability of certain data) in the period between 2004 and 2011 and find no statistically significant effect of statutory corporate tax rate on the flow of FDI [27]. Similarly, Kersan-Skabic using data on EU transition economies fails to find evidence that tax rates significantly affect the long-run elasticity of FDI [28]. Studies of Daniels and Egger based on data from the US and other OECD countries basically do not confirm a precise impact of tax rates on the long-run elasticity of foreign investment [29, 30].

There exist even fewer studies which find any positive effect of corporate taxes on FDI. Herger finds that tax elasticity varies depending on the FDI strategy (with vertical FDI being in general more responsive) [31]. Salihu and Faria focus on emerging economies and they show that there is a positive relationship between FDI and the avoidance of corporate tax [32, 33]. Their research is based on Malaysian companies. The findings indicate that investors seek to avoid taxes in both host and parent countries.

The heterogeneity of empirical findings led to a need for concise and comprehensive review of the existing empirical evidence. In the meta-analysis undertaken by Feld and Heckemeyer, a pooled effect based on the median result taken from each primary study was found. It amounts to semi-elasticity for company taxes on FDI (percentage reaction of FDI to one percentage point change in the tax burden) of 1.68 in absolute terms [3].

4. DISTORTIONARY EFFECTS OF DIFFERENTIAL TAX REGIMES

4.1. Distortionary effects of corporate income tax

As stressed by Cnossen and many others, even confined to the tax system of one country, the defects of the corporate income tax are numerous as it causes distortions of asset mix, capital allocation, financing and payout decisions, and the choice of organizational form [1, 34]. The main problem with capital taxation is that effective corporate tax and personal tax rates on investment returns vary depending on the choice of financing [35]. Investment can be made either through equity or debt. As a rule, debt finance is favored against equity finance because interest payments are deductible under most tax systems. The tax-favored status of debt discriminates against corporations that face difficulties in attracting debt [35]. Therefore, newly founded corporations have to sustain higher capital costs because of taxation than older, established corporations with either easier access to debt financing or sufficient retained profits to finance new investments.

The corporation's dividend policy produces yet another example of discrimination. Profits can be either distributed to shareholders as dividends or retained. When earnings are retained, the shareholders, instead of receiving dividends, benefit from an increase in the market value of the company. As a result of this bias in favor of retentions, equity funds may be locked in within certain companies rather than allocated between companies in the most efficient manner by financial markets [36]. Broadly, debt finance is favored against equity finance, and individual investors are discriminated relative to corporate investors. Therefore, differential tax rates and other tax structure features inherent to CIT distort investment decisions that should be based solely on economic costs and gains. Those features produce worldwide implications through the operations of multinationals.

4.2. Tax avoidance

As shown in Figure 5, OECD member states have widely diverging statutory CIT rates that may have externality effects on other member states. Statutory rates vary from 8.5% in Switzerland to 35% in the United States.

Varying tax systems directly influence the extent of tax evasion. The primary distinction between tax evasion and tax avoidance typically lies in the legality of the former. Avoidance typically involves exploiting and manipulating tax laws to minimize the amount of taxes paid. It encompasses a wide spectrum of behaviors. An example is to hire a tax professional to notify you about the deductibility of income obtained from actions that have already been completed. Another illustration is altering the legal structure of a particular operation, such as restructuring a business from one type of corporation to another, reclassifying regular revenue as capital income, or adjusting the timing of a transaction to change the tax year it falls under [37].

International investors frequently have a wide range of options for organizing and funding their investments, facilitating transactions between affiliated parties in various countries, and distributing profits to investors. Advanced strategies for international tax avoidance sometimes involve shifting taxable income from high-tax jurisdictions to low-tax jurisdictions, and may also involve manipulating the timing of income recognition for tax purposes. Given that interest payments are typically eligible for tax deductions, but profits are subject to taxation, it is advantageous for corporations to utilize debt for financing foreign subsidiaries in countries with high tax rates, and to employ equity for financing subsidiaries in countries with low tax rates [8].

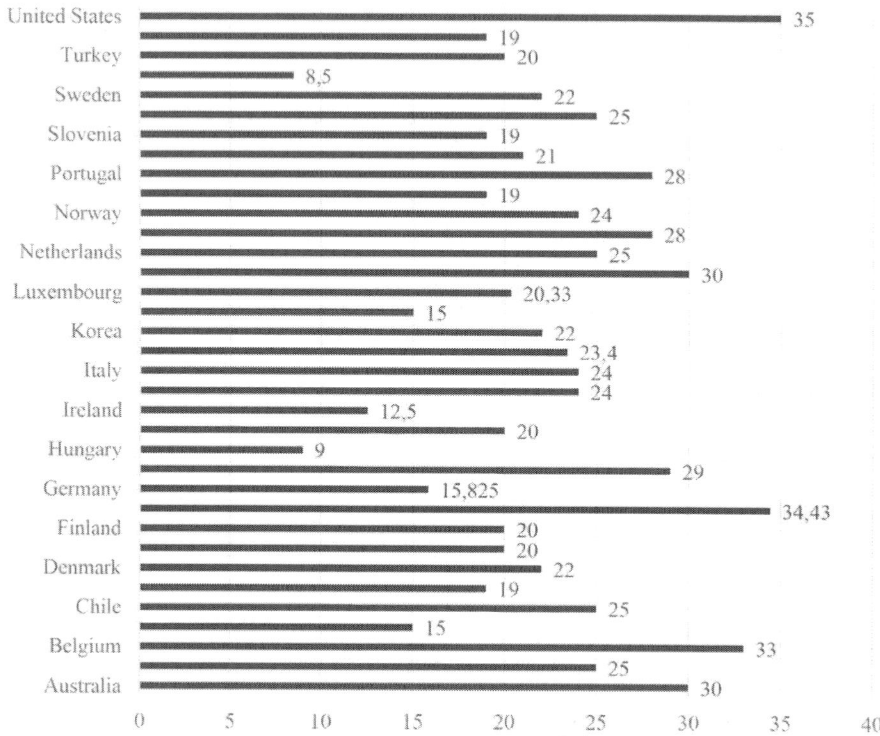

Figure 5. Statutory corporate income tax rates of the OECD countries in 2017 (in %). Source: OECD, 2017.

One further method to decrease the amount of taxes on passive income is by utilizing hybrid corporations or hybrid instruments, which are subject to varying treatment in different jurisdictions. In the late 1990s, the USA implemented a new legislation aimed at streamlining the determination of whether a company was classified as a corporation or a partnership. The application of the concept to foreign conditions has resulted in a scenario where an entity can be acknowledged as a corporation in one jurisdiction but not in another. As an illustration, a subsidiary of a US parent company located in a nation with low tax rates can provide a loan to its subsidiary in a country with high tax rates. The interest on this loan is considered deductible because the high-tax jurisdiction acknowledges the subsidiary as an independent corporation. Furthermore, there are hybrid securities that can circumvent taxation by being classified as debt in one jurisdiction and as equity in another [8].

The empirical evidence strongly supports these motivations. The profitability of multinational corporations, as reported, is negatively correlated with local tax rates. This link is, to some extent, due to tax-driven debt financing (thin capitalization), the pricing of intrafirm transfers, royalty payments, and similar strategies. Grubert conducts a study where he calculates distinct equations for dividend, interest, and royalty payments made by foreign subsidiaries to American parent companies. He discovers that there is a correlation between high corporate tax rates in the countries where American subsidiaries are situated and increased interest payments, as well as decreased dividend payout rates [22]. The reported profitability patterns align with other signs of deliberate tax evasion practices. It is generally acknowledged that companies modify prices for transactions within the company in order to minimize their overall tax liabilities. There is significant evidence indicating that transfer pricing in US trade prices is driven by tax considerations. Typically, multinational corporations gain advantages by lowering the prices paid by their subsidiaries in countries with high tax rates for goods and services delivered to subsidiaries in countries with low tax rates [7, 38]. Previous studies have discovered substantial impacts of tax rates in both affiliate and parent countries on the profit shifting behavior of multinational firms. However, the extent of these effects differs. The measured results in semi-elasticities vary from nearly zero to significantly above one [39].

The research findings about profit shifting behavior by US businesses are corroborated by evidence from Europe. Weichenrieder, using data on German inbound and outbound foreign direct investment (FDI), discovers an empirical relationship between the tax rate in the parent company's home country and the after-tax profitability of its German subsidiary. This correlation supports the notion of profit shifting behavior. According to the findings, a 10% increase in the tax rate of the parent's home country results in an approximate 0.5% improvement in the profitability of the German subsidiary [40]. Huizinga and Laeven utilize a distinctive dataset that includes comprehensive information about the parent firms and subsidiaries of European multinationals. They construct a model and conduct an empirical analysis to investigate the degree of profit shifting within Europe by European multinationals. The average semi-elasticity of reported profits in relation to the top statutory tax rate is found to be 1.3, while the projected shifting costs amount to 0.6% of the tax base. The researchers have determined that foreign profit shifting results in a significant redistribution of company tax income at the national level [41]. The research provides evidence that income shifting occurs in response to variations in corporation tax rates and that a unilateral increase in the corporate tax rate leads to significant revenue loss. This conclusion is reinforced by analyzing data from a wide range of OECD nations [42].

An exception to the findings that corroborate the main message of the basic tax competition model is presented in the research by Han and Leach. In their study, they propose a model where governments compete by offering financial incentives to attract particular enterprises to their jurisdictions [43]. Equilibrium is defined by three stipulations of the additional taxes. Under two of these criteria, there is no misallocation of capital, whereas under the third specification, there may or may not be capital misallocation. This outcome starkly contradicts the fundamental tax competition paradigm, which asserts that competition among governments typically results in an inefficient distribution of resources.

International tax avoidance is clearly a lucrative endeavor. A minimal amount of tax is levied on the income generated from overseas sources by companies based in the United States [8]. This has serious consequences for national tax policy. The increased global movement of economic activity significantly limits the ability to impose excessive taxes on domestic income-generating activities. The significance of this concern prompts the question of whether there is still such a thing as a purely domestic tax policy. Essentially, increased tax coordination across countries could potentially be a solution to this global issue.

4.3. The revenue loss estimates of base erosion and profit shifting (BEPS)

Following the global financial crisis and subsequent budgetary challenges in various nations, there was increased focus from the public and policymakers on the tax evasion practices of multinational corporations. In a similar vein, researchers made more significant endeavors to determine the magnitude and characteristics of the related tax losses.

Corporate tax is a significant contributor to government revenue in all global regions. According to Figure 6, the OECD governments, on average, generate roughly 10% of their overall tax revenue from CIT, which is equivalent to nearly 3% of GDP. Although there is an annual variation, this is the general trend. In lower-income nations, the proportion of overall tax revenues contributed by CIT is higher on average compared to high-income countries [6].

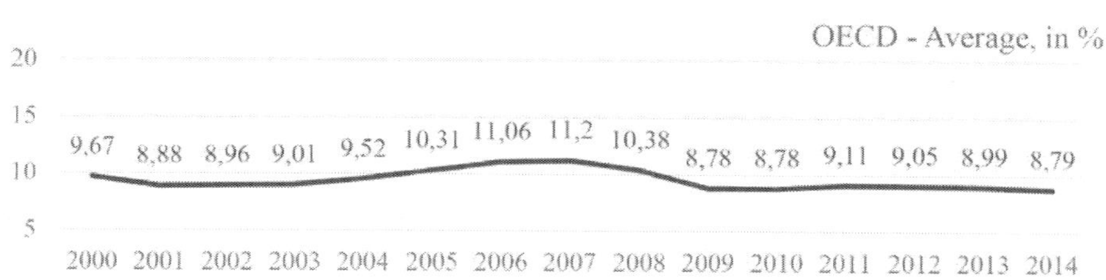

Figure 6. Taxes on corporate income as percentage of total taxation, OECD average. Source: OECD, 2017.

Estimating the worldwide losses caused by base erosion and profit shifting necessitates intricate and meticulous research. The most extensive research on this topic is currently provided by the researchers Crivelli et al. from the International Monetary Fund (IMF) and Cobham and Janský, whose study was recently published by the United Nations University World Institute for Development Economics Research (UNU-WIDER) in Helsinki [6, 9, 45].

Crivelli et al. analyze the size and characteristics of international fiscal externalities by utilizing panel data from 173 countries spanning a period of 33 years. Specifically, their attention is directed towards the repercussions of tax policy choices made in one jurisdiction on others. The researchers have created and employed a novel approach that enables them to differentiate between spillover effects resulting from actual investment choices and those resulting from avoidance strategies. They also measure the financial losses caused by the latter. Overall, experts calculate that the global revenue losses amount to approximately US$650 billion each year, with approximately one-third of these losses affecting developing countries. In emerging countries, the concentration as a proportion of gross domestic product (GDP) is slightly larger than in OECD economies [45].

Cobham and Gibson demonstrate that the anticipated losses amount to approximately 2-3% of overall tax revenue in OECD countries, but in poorer countries, the losses are significantly higher, ranging from 6-13% [46].

Utilizing a methodology used by academics at the International Monetary Fund, Cobhan and Jansky have calculated that there are around US$500 billion in annual revenue losses worldwide [6], based on an enhanced dataset. While wealthy economies like the United States experience the greatest losses, lower-income countries face more significant relative losses. Although the exact figures for this deliberately concealed occurrence are inherently unknown, the scale of its impact implies that multinational corporations have the potential to significantly harm the economic progress of nations.

In a study focused on individual countries, Clausing utilized survey data from the Bureau of Economic Analysis to analyze US multinational corporations from 1983 to 2012. The findings indicate that profit shifting is estimated to have resulted in a loss of corporate tax revenue for the US government, ranging from $77 billion to $111 billion by 2012. Furthermore, these losses have significantly grown in recent years [7]. Other researchers support these findings and suggest that the United States may lose over $100 billion annually due to profit shifting by international corporations [8].

Nevertheless, the accumulated losses are immense. According to recent calculations, Fortune 500 companies are evading up to $767 billion in US federal income taxes by keeping over $2.6 trillion of profits abroad under the label of "permanently reinvested" funds. According to the most recent annual financial reports, 29 of these firms have disclosed that they paid an income tax rate of 10% or lower in the countries where their revenues are nominally located. This suggests that a majority of these profits are probably being retained in offshore tax havens [47].

This can be interpreted as proof that reducing corporation tax rates is an efficient measure to combat tax avoidance. More focused research, such as the studies conducted by Cobham and Janský (2017) and Clausing [7], present compelling evidence that profit shifting has significantly increased despite a decrease in effective tax rates. In their study, Cobham and Janský (2017) provide evidence of effective tax rates ranging from 0% to 5% for US-based multinational companies in jurisdictions where profit shifting is prevalent. This is in contrast to the typical tax rates of 15% to 20% in the USA and other economies [6].

5. CONCISE SUMMARY

The literature survey in this chapter indicates that tax competition and its associated issues continue to be a top priority for both policymakers and researchers. Given that governments are tasked with the dual objective of attracting investment to their territory and generating sufficient public income to fund public services, tensions inevitably develop. To promote foreign direct investment (FDI) and other types of investment, governments provide tax advantages to prospective investors. However, this frequently entails participating in detrimental rivalry with other jurisdictions. This behavior is wasteful due to its zero-sum nature. When governments universally adopt this behavior, no one benefits, and as a result, communities suffer more than they would have if public managers had made judgments based on marginal costs. Tax competition can result in a decrease in tax revenues and cause inefficient underprovision of public services.

The new empirical evidence confirms the fundamental premise of the basic tax competition theory that there is indeed a competition for capital taking place. It is demonstrated by the overall decrease in official and actual corporate income tax rates, as well as the responsiveness of foreign direct investment to the tax burden. Moreover, aside from the inefficiencies in capital allocation that result from legitimate economic activity, the differing tax systems also give rise to additional distortions, such as tax arbitrage and tax avoidance by multinational corporations. Base erosion and profit shifting result in substantial income losses for governments worldwide. According to recent estimates, several countries have incurred significant losses, amounting to a whopping $767 billion in US federal income taxes [47].

The magnitude of revenue losses due to tax avoidance by multinational companies and other distortions arising from differential tax regimes call for the re-examination of CIT policies and tax coordination, and/or harmonization at the international level.

AT A GLANCE

The objective of this chapter is to examine the most recent advancements in corporate income tax (CIT), with a specific emphasis on its international dimensions and related discrepancies. This chapter relies on evidence presented by prominent tax professionals and serious academic research. This chapter analyzes and combines information on tax competitiveness, the correlation between tax rates and foreign direct investment (FDI), and tax avoidance due to varying tax systems. Statistical data provided by the OECD and European Commission is used to identify trends in the growth of CIT. Multiple studies conducted using global, regional, and country-specific datasets provide evidence that tax competition for capital does exist, albeit the extent of its impact varies. There is ample evidence indicating that tax avoidance and evasion, namely through base erosion and profit shifting, have been ongoing and may be increasing.

REFERENCES

1. Zodrow GR. Tax competition and tax coordination in the European Union. International Tax and Public Finance. 2003;10(6):651-671
2. Wilson JD. Theories of tax competition. National Tax Journal. 1999;52(2):269-304
3. Feld LP, Heckemeyer JH. FDI and Taxation: A Meta-Study. In: Discussion Paper No. 08-128, C.f.E.E. Research, Editor; 2008
4. Brennan G, Buchanan JM. The Power to Tax: Analytic Foundations of a Fiscal Constitution. Cambridge: Cambridge UP; 1980
5. Niskanen WAJ. Bureaucracy and Representative Government. New Brunswick (USA): Aldine Transaction; 1977
6. Cobham A, Janský P. Global Distribution of Revenue Loss from Tax Avoidance: Re-estimation and Country Results, in WIDER Working Paper 2017/55. 2017, UNU-WIDER Helsinki
7. Clausing KA. The Effect of profit shifting on the corporate tax base in the United States and beyond. National Tax Journal. 2016;69(4)
8. Gravelle J. Tax Havens: International Tax Avoidance and Evasion. Federal Publications; 2015

9. Tax Justice Network. New Estimates Reveal the Extent of Tax Avoidance by Multinationals. 2017 August 17, 2017; Available from: https://www.taxjustice.net/2017/03/22/new-estimates-tax-avoidance-multinationals/
10. Altshuler R, Grubert H. Repatriation taxes, repatriation strategies and multinational financial policy. Journal of Public Economics. 2003;87(1):73-107
11. Oates WE. Fiscal Federalism. New York: Harcourt Brace Jovanovich; 1972
12. De Mooij RA. Will Corporate Income Taxation Survive? De Economist. 2005;153(3):277-301
13. Zodrow GR, Mieszkowski P. Pigou, Tiebout, property taxation, and the underprovision of local public goods. Journal of Urban Economics. 1986;19(3):356-370
14. Keen M, Konrad KA. The Theory of International Tax Competition and Coordination. Working Paper 2012 – 06; 2014. DOI: http://dx.doi.org/10.2139/ssrn.2111895
15. Tiebout CM. A pure theory of local expenditures. The Journal of Political Economy. 1956;64(5):416-424
16. Razin A, Sadka E. International tax competition and gains from tax harmonization. Economics Letters. 1991;37(1):69-76
17. Sinn H-W. Tax harmonization and tax competition in Europe. European Economic Review. 1990;34:489-504
18. Wildasin DE. Interjurisdictional capital mobility: Fiscal externality and a corrective subsidy. Journal of Urban Economics. 1989;25:193-212
19. Baldwin R, Krugman P. Agglomeration, Integration and Tax Harmonization. Centre for Economic Policy Research; 2000
20. European Commission, Data on taxation. Taxation and Customs Union 2017
21. OECD, Statutory Income Tax Rate. 2017
22. Grubert H. Tax planning by companies and tax competition by governments: Is there evidence of changes in behavior? In: Hines JJR, editor. International Taxation and Multinational Activity. Chicago: University of Chicago Press; 2001. pp. 113-139
23. Devereux MP, Lockwood B, Redoano M. Do countries compete over corporate tax rates? Journal of Public Economics. 2008;92(5):1210-1235
24. Vandenbussche H, Crabbé K, Janssen B. Is there regional tax competition? Firm level evidence for Belgium. De Economist. 2005;153(3):257-276

25. McLure CE, Zodrow GR. Treasury I and the tax reform act of 1986: The economics and politics of tax reform. Journal of Economic Perspectives. 1987;1(1):37-58

26. Slemrod J. The taxation of foreign direct investment: Operational policy perspectives. In: Poterba JM, editor. Borderline Case: International Tax Policy, Corporate Research and Development, and Investment. Washington, DC: National Academy Press; 1997. pp. 11-38

27. Hunady J, Orviska M. Determinants of foreign direct investment in EU countries – Do corporate taxes really matter? Procedia Economics and Finance. 2014;12:243-250

28. Kersan-Skabic I. The importance of corporate taxation for FDI attractiveness of southeast European countries. Panoeconomicus. 2015;62(1):105-122

29. Daniels JP, O'Brien P, von der Ruhr MB. Bilateral tax treaties and US foreign direct investment financing modes. International Tax and Public Finance. 2014;22(6):999-1027

30. Egger P, Raff H. Tax rate and tax base competition for foreign direct investment. International Tax and Public Finance. 2014;22(5):777-810

31. Herger N, Kotsogiannis C, McCorriston S. Multiple taxes and alternative forms of FDI: evidence from cross-border acquisitions. International Tax and Public Finance. 2015;23(1):82-113

32. IA, Annuar HA, Sheikh Obid SN. Foreign investors' interests and corporate tax avoidance: Evidence from an emerging economy. Journal of Contemporary Accounting & Economics. 2015;11(2):138-147

33. Faria JR. Location clusters, FDI and local entrepreneurs: Consistent public policy. Journal of the Knowledge Economy. 2015;7(4):858-868

34. Cnossen S. Company taxes in the European Union: Criteria and options for reform. Fiscal Studies. 1996;17:67-97

35. S. How much tax coordination in the European Union? International Tax and Public Finance. 2003;10(6):625-649

36. Parthasarathi S. Tax Policy Handbook. Washington D.C: International Monetary Fund: International Monetary Fund; 1999

37. Slemrod J, Yitzhaki S. Tax Avoidance, Evasion, and Administration. NBER Working Paper No. 74732000. DOI: 10.3386/w7473

38. Hines JRJ. Lessons from behavioral responses to international taxation. National Tax Journal. 1999;52(2):305-322

39. Dowd T, Landefeld P, Moore A. Profit shifting of U.S. multinationals. Journal of Public Economics. 2017;148:1-13
40. Weichenrieder AJ. Profit shifting in the EU: evidence from Germany. International Tax and Public Finance. 2009;16(3):281-297
41. H, Laeven L. International profit shifting within multinationals: A multi-country perspective. Journal of Public Economics. 2008;92(5):1164-1182
42. EJ, Beetsma RMWJ. Why pay more? Corporate tax avoidance through transfer pricing in OECD countries. Journal of Public Economics. 2003;87(9):2225-2252
43. Han S, Leach J. A bargaining model of tax competition. Journal of Public Economics. 2008;92(5):1122-1141
44. OECD, Tax on Corporate Profits (indicator). 2017
45. E, De Mooij R, Keen M. Base erosion, profit shifting and developing countries. FinanzArchiv: Public Finance Analysis. 2016;72(3)
46. Cnossen S. Corporation taxes in the European Union: Slowly moving toward comprehensive business income taxation? International Tax and Public Finance. 2017
47. on Taxation and Tax Policy, Fortune 500 Companies Hold a Record $2.6 Trillion Offshore. 2017, Institute on Taxation and Tax Policy Washington, D.C

3
Chapter

THE EFFECTS OF TAXES ON THE BUSINESS SECTOR IN SLOVAKIA

1. INTRODUCTION: AN OVERVIEW

Taxes are a crucial component of a nation's economic policy. They constitute a fundamental source of income for the state budget or municipal budgets. Each tax under the tax system has a specific rationale and serves a distinct purpose. Tax issues are complex and challenging. The goal of tax optimization is to provide a tax system that is both efficient and straightforward for each corporate entity [16].

The primary issue concerning taxes in the European Union is the conflict between tax harmonization and tax competition [15]. The fundamental components of the tax process are crucial instruments that influence the taxation of business entities and have a substantial effect on the calculation of the taxable amount and the resulting tax obligation [1]. An essential requirement for enhancing the business environment is the regulation of laws to provide assistance for entrepreneurs, aiming to achieve an ideal equilibrium between tax revenues, specifically the tax burden on businesses, and the appeal of the country for labor and capital. In light of the challenging economic circumstances, the tax administration is adapting its anti-tax approach and shifting its focus towards other domains. The company sector is currently facing difficulties in fulfilling its tax responsibilities while also striving to generate additional value in the business [14].

It is crucial to have a comprehensive understanding of all legal regulations in the corporate environment and to employ legal strategies to maximize the tax base. The primary objective of businesses is to maximize their tax efficiency by strategically managing their tax base and implementing value-added activities that result in tax reduction across all tax categories. Multimodal transport in EU states offers a chance to adopt a more environmentally friendly approach and completely waive vehicle taxes [13]. These prospects also open up possibilities for innovative business ventures (Table 1).

Table 1. Taxes in Slovakia.

Taxes in Slovakia			
Direct taxes	**Asset taxes**	**Local taxes**	**Indirect taxes**
Income tax	Property tax	Tax of dog	Value added tax
	Vehicle tax	Tax of non-winning game machines	Consumer tax of alcohol
		Local income tax	Consumer tax of tobacco
		Tax of vending machines	Consumer tax of mineral oil
		Tax of nuclear facility	Costumer tax of electricity, coal, gas
		Tax of using historical part of town	
		Tax of using public area	

Source: Refs. [2, 3, 4, 8, 9, 12].

2. MACROECONOMIC INDICATORS OF TAXES

The tax-deductible burden refers to the extent of taxation or the proportion of GDP comprised of taxes and levies. What is the total amount of resources that the country has available for redistribution through public finances? The Paying Taxes research 2017 reveals that companies in Slovakia face a tax burden that is 10% higher than the average tax burden worldwide and in the EU/EFTA. Key macroeconomic variables used to measure fiscal burden include tax quota 1, tax quota 2, tax multiplier, expenditure multiplier, and multiplier of balanced budget. The tax quota is a macroeconomic indicator that focuses on maximizing tax revenues, which are a key component of the state budget. It does not take into account the specific impact of taxes and levies on economic entities and individuals. This indicator serves as a primary tool for implementing fiscal policy.

Table 2. Taxes quota in Slovakia.

Years	DK I (%)	DK II (%)
1995	24.8	39.6
1996	23.0	38.7
1997	21.9	36.6
1998	21.5	36.2
1999	21.2	35.1
2000	19.8	33.8
2001	18.7	32.9
2002	18.4	32.9

Years	DK I (%)	DK II (%)
2003	19.0	32.7
2004	18.6	31.6
2005	18.8	31.4
2006	17.5	29.2
2007	17.4	29.0
2008	17.1	28.8
2009	16.3	28.8
2010	15.8	28.1
2011	16.3	28.6
2012	15.7	28.2
2013	16.7	30.2
2014	17.5	31.1
2015	18.1	32.1

Source: Eurostat.

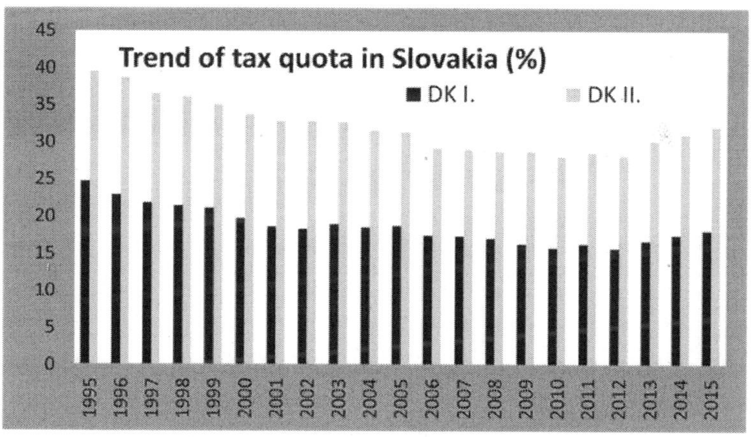

Figure 1. Trend of tax quota in Slovakia. Source: Eurostat.

The World Bank Group and the consulting firm PwC have released a study aimed at simplifying and reducing tax liabilities in business around the world. The study involved 190 countries of the world. The study highlighted the global most common element of tax reforms over the period under review for the introduction of an electronic system for filling in and paying taxes.

3. TAX RATES OF DIRECT TAXES IN SLOVAKIA

Tax rates are a fundamental competitive tool and a means of tax harmonization. Setting tax rates is the responsibility of individual EU states, hindering tax harmonization in the EU. Tax rates are an indicator of differences in tax systems across EU countries. We determine the tax rate in terms of income of a natural person and a legal entity. The natural person uses the tax rate based on the tax base reduced by non-taxable parts and the tax loss and the special rate of income tax on the dependent activity of selected constitutional agents, whose income is also taxed at this special rate (the President of SR, Member of the Slovak Republic, and the Vice-Chairman of the Supreme Audit Office of the Slovak Republic) [7]. The tax rate is based on 176.8 times the current living wage (Table 3).

Table 3. Tax rate in Slovakia.

Years	Tax rate for tradesman (%)	Tax rate for tradesman (%)	Tax rate for tradesman (%)
2007	19	—	—
2008	19	—	—
2009	19	—	—
2010	19	—	—
2011	19	—	—
2012	19	—	—
2013	19	—	—
2014	19	25	5
2015	19	25	5
2016	19	25	5
2017	19	25	5

Source: Ref. [9].

The tax liability of a legal person is determined from the tax base reduced by the tax loss according to the applicable tax rate. The legal entity was required to pay the tax license for the first time in 2015 for the taxable period of 2014 as the minimum corporate income tax. The new tax law, which will enter into force on January 1, 2018, will be cancelled, the last taxable period for which taxpayers-legal entities will be required to pay tax licenses will be 2017 if the tax year is a calendar year. If the taxpayer is not a taxable person on the last day of the taxable period and has an annual turnover not exceeding EUR 500,000, a tax license of EUR 480 shall apply. If the taxpayer is a value added taxer at the last taxable date and has an annual turnover not exceeding EUR 500,000, he pays a tax license of EUR 960. If the taxpayer attains an annual turnover of more than EUR 500,000 at the last taxable date, regardless of whether or not he is a taxable person, he has a tax license of EUR 2880 (Table 4).

Table 4. Tax rate for company in Slovakia.

Years	TAX rate for company (%)
2007	19
2008	19
2009	19
2010	19
2011	19
2012	19
2013	23
2014	22
2015	22
2016	22
2017	21

Source: Ref. [9].

The natural reaction of each business entity to taxing is the search for tax optimization within legal procedures. In order to minimize the indirect tax liability, entrepreneurs may consider the decision on voluntary registration as a value added tax payer. In order to minimize the tax burden on local taxes, entrepreneurs consider regional differentiated tax burdens. In the case of income tax, entrepreneurs consider decisions of long-term nature, including choosing a suitable form of business, choosing the way to apply tax expenses, choosing the way to procure long-term tangible and intangible assets, choosing the depreciation method and using the possibility of aborting the depreciation, non-taxable and deductible items from the tax base, the possibility of applying the tax deducted as a tax advance. Income tax in the Slovak legal system is a common denomination for two types of taxes: the income tax of a natural person and the corporate income tax. Many EU countries complain that some Member States have an unfair advantage from low corporate tax rates. Their aim is to determine the minimum rate of tax within the European Union. In Switzerland, Spain, Italy, England and Austria, income tax has always been relatively high. Taxes have set these countries virtually exclusively on the basis of their national needs. The tax rates in Bulgaria, Cyprus, Romania, Hungary and the Czech Republic had to be set to motivate Western European companies to shift production (Figure 2).

Taxation of the economic activity of business entities can be judged at a double level. One is the effort of the state and the self-government to maximize revenue into public budgets that needs to be taken into account in the context of the impact of individual taxes on the behavior of taxpayers and the entire society. The second is the interests of taxpayers and their attitudes toward taxation. Tax harmonization exists where taxpayers face similar or equal tax rates regardless of whether they are working, buying, buying or investing.

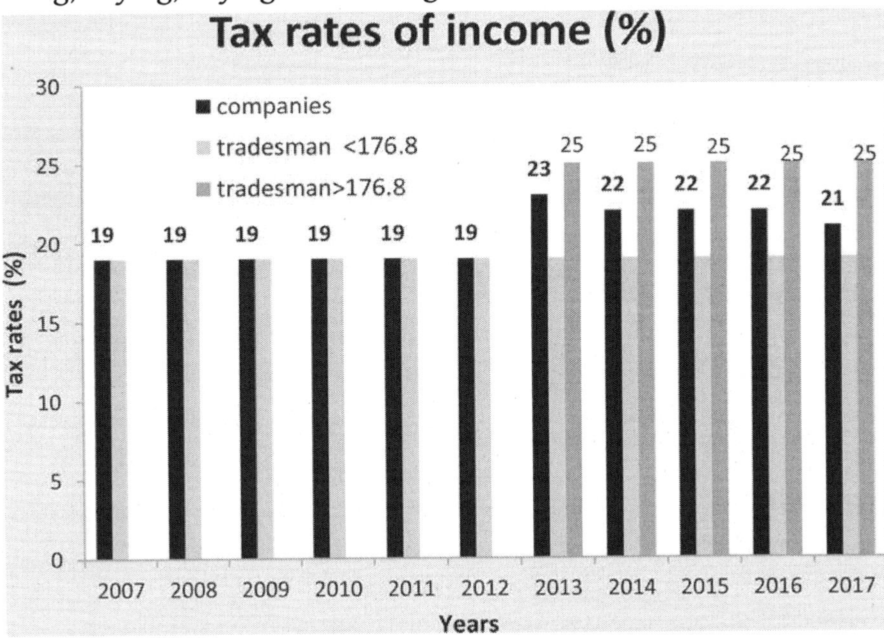

Figure 2. Tax rates of income. Source: Ref. [9].

Harmonized tax rates eliminate budget competition. Tax harmonization can be achieved in two different ways: explicit and implicit tax harmonization. Explicit tax harmonization occurs when countries agree to set minimum or equal tax rates. The EU requires its Member States to apply a minimum standard rate of 15% VAT. The EU has harmonized taxes on fuels, spirits and tobacco, and efforts to harmonize corporate and personal income taxes. In such a direct form of tax harmonization, taxpayers are not able to benefit from better tax policy in other countries, and governments are not under the pressure of competitive discipline. Tax competition is desirable for many reasons. The most important thing is that it underpins economic growth by encouraging policy-makers to make a meaningful tax policy.

4. LIMIT ON TAX RETURN

Tax return is the document FO, PO. Its purpose is to grant income that is subject to tax. The result is a quantification of the tax, which can be compared with the tax advances paid. The resulting tax arrears FO, PO will transfer the state through the tax office. Tax return always refers to a certain period, calendar year, marketing year and specific tax, income tax, value added tax (Table 5) [9].

Table 5. Tax return limit in Slovakia.

Years	Limit
2007	1586.93 €
2008	1634.73 €
2009	2012.85 €
2010	1773.00 €
2011	1779.65 €
2012	1822.37 €
2013	1867.97 €
2014	1901.67 €
2015	1901.67 €
2016	1901.67 €
2017	1901.67 €

Source: Ref. [9].

Table 6. Non-taxable portion in Slovakia.

Years	Month part	Year part
30.6.2017	316.94 €	3803.33 €
2016	316.94 €	3803.33 €
2015	316.94 €	3803.33 €
2014	316.94 €	3803.33 €
2013	311.32 €	3735.94 €
2012	303.72 €	3644.74 €
2011	296.60 €	3559.30 €
2010	355.48 €	4025.70 €
2009	355.48 €	4025.70 €
2008	272.46 €	3269.47 €
2007	264.49 €	3173.87 €

Source: Ref. [9].

For tax purposes, two types of tax returns are available: type A and type B. Type A is intended for taxpayers who have income only from dependent activity under Section 5 of the Income Tax Act. Type B is intended for taxpayers who have income, which are subject to tax according to §5 to §8 of the Income Tax Act. Tax returns are required to be paid by natural persons whose income for the taxable period exceeds 50% of the amount of the taxable amount of tax to the taxpayer if the income derived from the non-taxpayer receives income from abroad, the revenue for which tax cannot be deducted and also if the taxpayer did not ask the employer to perform the annual settlement of deductions for tax on dependent activity. The tax return is required to be paid by an employee who has income from dependent activity from several employers or other types of taxable income. Tax returns are required to be filed by natural persons whose earnings for a taxable period do not exceed 50% of the taxable amount of tax on the taxpayer but show a tax loss. The tax return is also filed by a lawyer, a PO person (Figure 3).

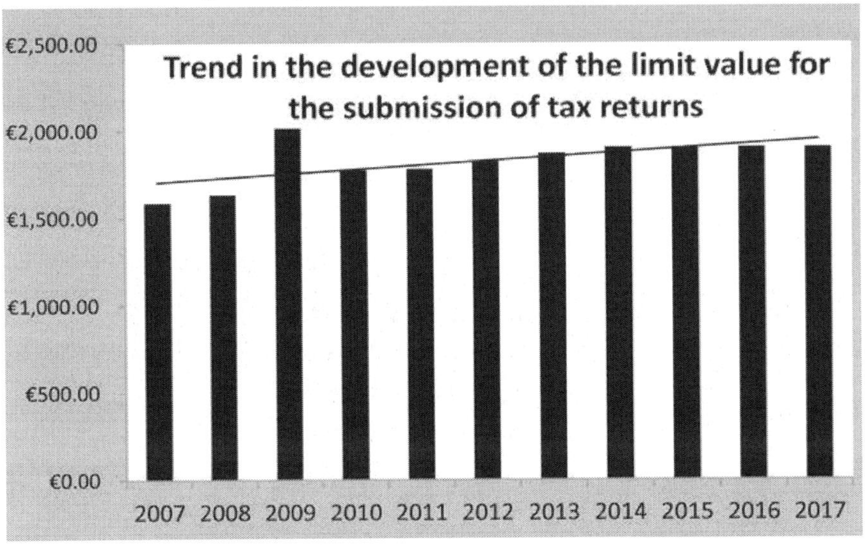

Figure 3. Trend of limit value of tax returns. Source: Ref. [9].

5. TAX INDICATORS IN SLOVAKIA

The term non-taxable portion of the taxable amount is the statutory value for tax purposes of the taxpayer's tax base, which is based on the subsistence level. The amount of the tax base is related to the amount of the non-taxable portion. The Income Tax sets a limit of 100 times the amount of the applicable living wage. If the tax base is lower or equal to 100 times the living wage, the non-taxable portion of the tax base per year is calculated at 19.2 multiple of living wage. If the taxable amount of the taxpayer's tax exceeds the amount of 100 times of living wage, the non-taxable portion of the taxable amount is calculated as the difference of 44.2 times of living wage and ¼ of the tax base. If the result is equal to or less than zero, the non-taxable portion is zero. The non-taxable amount of the taxable amount of the taxable person cannot be claimed by the taxpayer who, from the beginning of the tax period (from 1 January), receives a retirement pension, early retirement pension, social security reimbursement premium, old-age pension, retirement pension or foreign compulsory insurance pension, to whom a retirement pension has been redeemed at the beginning of the current or previous tax period (calendar year), and at the same time, if his or her pension is higher than the non-taxable portion of the taxable person's tax base. Where the amount of the retirement pension is lower than the amount of the taxable amount of the taxable amount of the taxable amount, the taxpayer is entitled to claim only the difference between the non-taxable portion of the taxable amount of the taxpayer and the retirement pension (Table 6).

Non-taxable portion of the tax base

- Non-taxable portion of the tax base of the taxpayer
- Non-taxable portion of the taxable income of the spouse (spouse)
- Non-taxable portion of the tax base for contributions to supplementary retirement savings (third pillar)

5.1. Non-taxable portion of the tax base on wife, husband

In this type of non-taxable part, the income of his wife, husband is assessed in addition to the taxable person's tax base, which fulfills at least one of the following conditions during the period: she takes care of a child living in common household, she was unemployed, she is a person with a disability, she tooks a care allowance. Include every income, including income tax, maternity and sickness benefits, all kinds of pensions and prizes, between the wife's (our husband's) incomes. This revenue is reduced by compulsory premiums paid and contributions to health and social insurance. We do not include an employee's bonus, tax bonus, retirement pension, state social benefits in our wife's (our husband's) income. State social benefits include childbirth allowance and surcharge for birth grant, contribution to parents who are simultaneously born with three or more children or who have been repeatedly born twins or more children over the course of 2 years at the same time, a funeral grant, parental allowance, child allowance and surcharge for baby allowance, Christmas contribution to pensioners, retirement allowance by political prisoners.

5.2. Non-taxable portion of the tax base for contributions to supplementary retirement savings (third pillar)

It is a part of the taxpayer's contribution to supplementary retirement savings (up to the third pillar). The non-deductible part of the tax base also includes contributions to supplementary pension savings abroad of the same or similar type. The maximum amount of this non-taxable portion is €180 for a taxable period. This amount is fixed by the Income Tax Act. The limit applies to all taxpayers (domestic and foreign employees, tradesmen, etc.) as well.

In order to claim this taxable amount, the taxpayer has to meet the following conditions: the participant under which he paid contributions for supplementary pension savings was concluded after December 31, 2013 or was amended and the change in the plan was canceled, the taxpayer has not entered into a contract with another participant who does not meet the conditions laid down by the law on supplementary retirement savings (Figure 4).

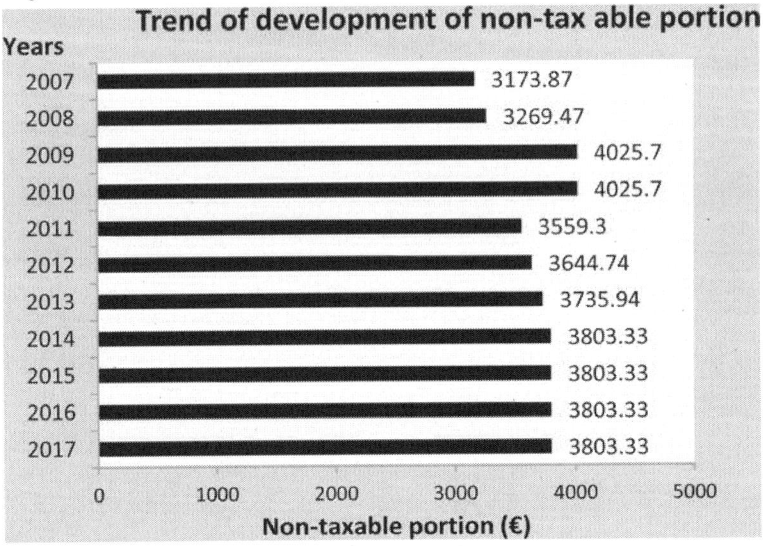

Figure 4. Trend of non-taxable portion in Slovakia. Source: Ref. [9].

The development of a non-taxable portion of the tax base is based on the development of the subsistence level. The minimum age has not changed for the last 4 years, and therefore there has been no change in the taxable portion of the tax base. The non-taxable portion of the tax base affects the amount of tax liability of business entities and individuals. This is a legal form of tax deduction, which the taxpayer optimizes the tax base.

The taxpayer is entitled to claim a non-taxable portion of the tax base only from the sub-base of the tax on income from dependent activity, business income, other self-employment, rental, use of the work and artistic performance.

5.3. Living wage

The subsistence minimum is defined as the socially recognized minimum income threshold for a natural person under whom a state of material need arises. The subsistence sums are adjusted each year to July 1 of the current calendar year. If the legislation does not change, to 30.6. it is repeat date every year by the Ministry of Labour, Social Affairs and the family of the Slovak Republic [5, 9, 10]. The sum of the subsistence minimum is a relatively important reference (Figure 5).

The subsistence sums help in a universal way to find out in what financial situation the persons under review are located. The subsistence amount for one adult physical person, or the coefficient increasing this amount affects a number of other indicators in the tax and social spheres.

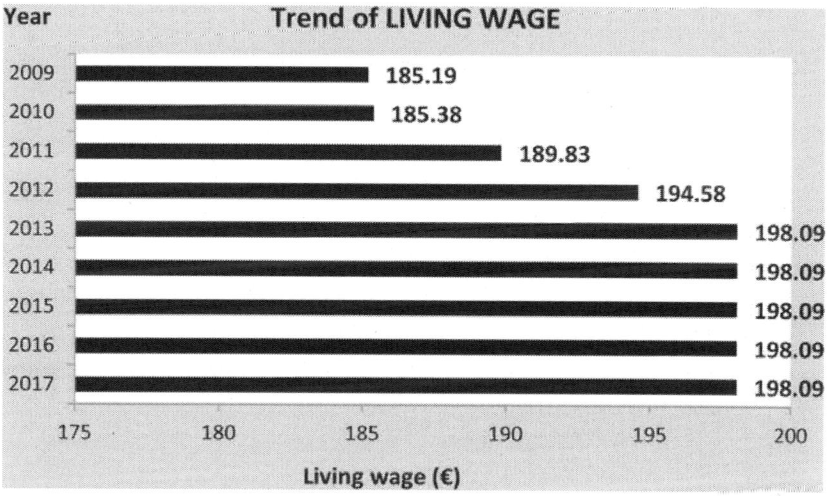

Figure 5. Trend of living wage in Slovakia. Source: Ref. [10].

These include, for example, the amount of the tax bonus, the amount of non-taxable portions of the tax base, the amount of the tax base, after which the individual has to apply a higher rate of income tax (25%), the amount of the allowance and the surcharge for the child allowance, the amount of the unreachable amount for the execution charges [6, 9, 10]. The above minimum subsistence also affects the entitlement to early retirement or the minimum retirement age (Table 7).

Table 7. Living wage in Slovakia.

Years	Living wage		
	Adult	Adult Jointly assessed person	Child Dependent
2017	198.09 €	138.19 €	90.42 €
2016	198.09 €	138.19 €	90.42 €
2015	198.09 €	138.19 €	90.42 €
2014	198.09 €	138.19 €	90.42 €
2013	198.09 €	138.19 €	90.42 €
2012	194.58 €	135.74 €	88.82 €
2011	189.83 €	132.42 €	86.65 €
2010	185.38 €	129.31 €	84.61 €
2009	185.19 €	124.81 €	81.66 €

Source: Ref. [10].

5.4. Minimum wage

The minimum wage is determined on the basis of key factors that affect it. Basic factors influence determination of minimum wage are economic and social situation in the country, consumer price developments, employment developments, average monthly wage developments in the national economy, and the development of the subsistence minimum. The concept of the minimum wage is the lowest possible wage that must be paid to the employee for a work-related or similar employment relationship to ensure the minimum level of employee's income for the work done but also for the natural persons performing for the employer under one of the agreements on work performed outside the employment (work agreement, agreement on students' brigade work) [11]. The amount of the minimum wage is set by the Government of the Slovak Republic each year by two amounts: in euros per month (monthly minimum wage) and in euro per hour worked (hourly minimum wage). The amount of the monthly minimum wage applies only to employees who are remunerated in the form of a monthly wage. Employees who are remunerated by another form of wage, such as monthly wages (hourly wages), are based on the hourly minimum wage when assessing their legal entitlements to wage levels. If the employee has a shorter than the prescribed weekly working time or does not work all the working days or hours in the month, the monthly minimum wage is reduced in proportion between the actual times worked and the monthly working time fund. The amount of the minimum wage in euro per month is rounded to the nearest 10 eurocent (Table 8) [11].

Table 8. Minimum wage in Slovakia.

Years	Minimum wage/Monthly wage (€)
2017	435
2016	405
2015	380
2014	352
2013	337.70
2012	327.20
2011	317
2010	307.70
2009	295.50
2008	269
2007	269
2006	252
2005	229
2004	216

Source: Ref. [11].

The minimum wage is not established in Finland, Austria, Denmark, Italy, Malta and Cyprus. Among the most advanced countries where the minimum wage is the highest are Luxembourg, Ireland, the Netherlands, Belgium, Germany and France (Table 9).

Table 9. Minimum wage in Europa.

Country	Minimum wage
Luxembourg	1999 €
Ireland	1563 €
The Netherlands	1552 €
Belgium	1533 €
Germany	1486 €
France	1482 €
England	1400 €
Spain	825 €
Slovenia	804 €
Malta	735 €
Greece	684 €
Portugal	650 €
Estonia	470 €
Poland	454 €
Slovakia	435 €
Hungary	410 €
Croatia	410 €
The Czech Republic	408 €
Latvia	382 €
Lithuania	381 €
Romania	274 €
Bulgaria	220 €

Source: Eurostat.

The purpose of setting a minimum wage is to protect employees and employers. The minimum wage fulfills two basic functions—social protection—the minimum wage must ensure to employee socially acceptable of wage - minimum in height of living wage. And ensures wage competition - adequate labor assessment economically critical - the minimum wage motivate people to work, not to take social benefits, to protect employees againts unfair competition on the labor market. The minimum wage in Slovakia has been growing steadily since 2003 (Figure 6).

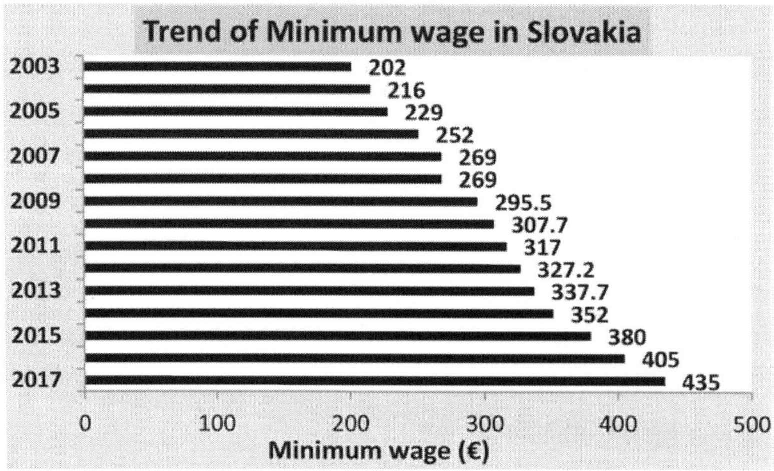

Figure 6. Trend of minimum wage in Slovakia.

The national minimum wage has 22 states from the 28 EU Member States, with the exception of Denmark, Italy, Cyprus, Austria, Finland and Sweden. When comparing EU countries and outside the Eurozone, the minimum wage is influenced mainly by the level of the exchange rate between the national currency and the Euro. The differences between the minimum wage levels in the EU countries are striking. The maximum difference in the minimum wage recorded in the EU countries is € 1729. Within EU countries, it is not always clear that the minimum wage is valid on a monthly basis; some countries may have it on an hourly or weekly basis.

5.5. Tax bonus

We understand the tax bonus as a tax concession or tax benefit, which is provided to a taxpayer who is living with a child, in the form of a reduction in income tax or tax advances that the taxpayer would otherwise have to pay. For the purposes of the tax bonus, a child may not have the same permanent residence as a taxpayer. The temporary stay of a child outside the household (e.g., a child studying in another city and staying on board) does not affect the application of the tax bonus. The law does not require the same taxpayer's and child's residence, but that the taxpayer and the child live in one household. In accordance with Section 115 of the Civil Code, households are natural persons who live together and share the costs of their needs together (Table 10).

Table 10. Tax bonus in Slovakia.

Years	Tax bonus (€)
2017	21.41
2016	21.41
2015	21.41

Years	Tax bonus (€)
2014	21.41
2013	21.41
2012	21.03
2011	20.51
2010	20.02
2009	20.00
2008	19.32
2007	18.42
2006	17.92

Source: Ref. [9].

The amount that a taxpayer reduces the tax can be seen as a tax credit or tax benefit to the person who receives it after the specified conditions have been met, the amount of the tax bonus is reduced by the tax (not the tax base). It can be claimed by a taxpayer who has had taxable income in the taxable period: from dependent activity, at least six times the minimum wage or from business, other self-employment and from renting six times the minimum wage and reported the tax base (the tax base from of revenue); only one taxpayer may apply if the conditions for applying the tax bonus are met by more taxpayers and, unless otherwise agreed, the tax bonus for all dependent children is applied or awarded in the following order: mother, father, other eligible person; the taxpayer can apply the tax bonus even if the child has a temporary residence outside the household, for example, if the child is studying at secondary school outside of his/her permanent residence, and he/she is staying at the boarding school (Figure 7).

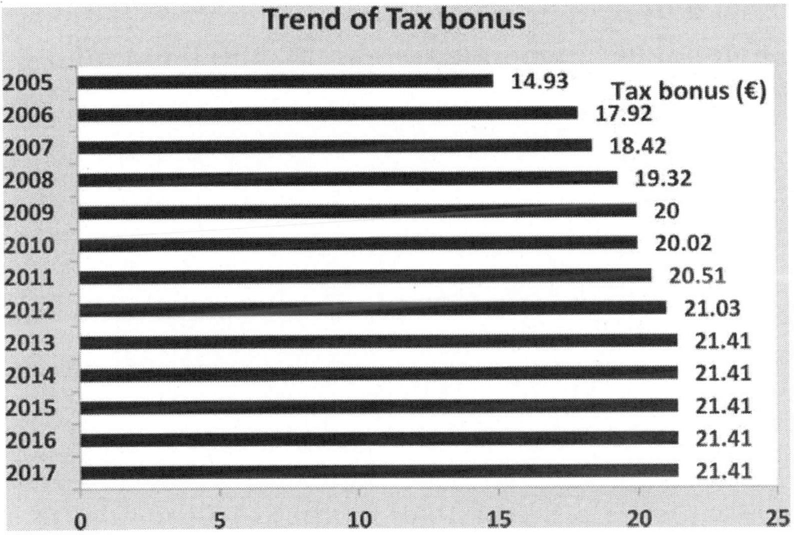

Figure 7. Trend of tax bonus in Slovakia. Source: Ref. [9].

6. IMPACT OF TAXES TO BUSINESS SECTOR

The business environment is characterized by constant changes in the law, resulting in legislative uncertainty. Businessmen in Slovakia must constantly observe what changes they are about and how they will affect their business. Their attention is not entirely entrepreneurial because they have to deal with different bureaucratic requirements, but also with accounting and legal problems. Business costs are increasing, which negatively affects their competitiveness and leads to the demotivation of business expansion, innovation or improvement of their services. In order to maintain economic growth in Slovakia, it is necessary to improve the business environment, thereby increasing employment, but also booming small- and medium-sized enterprises, especially in the case of economically weaker regions. The need to remove administrative and regulatory barriers in the business sector is a priority for economic growth (Figure 8).

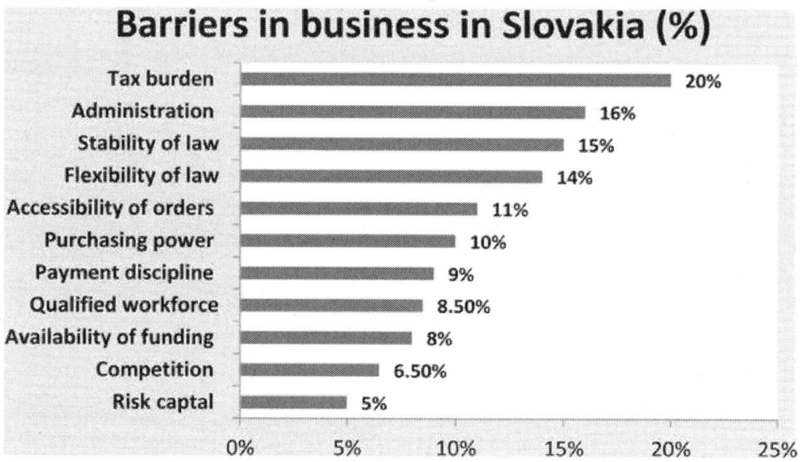

Figure 8. Barriers in business in Slovakia. Source: Research in Slovakia.

7. CONCISE SUMMARY

The tax policy of Slovakia should be oriented on fostering the business climate. Within fiscal policy, the primary macroeconomic objectives are to secure funds for state spending, influence the economic and social policy of the state, maintain the stability of the currency through taxes, credit and monetary policy, and address unemployment and tax-related issues in the state economy. Aside from the macroeconomic perspective on the significance of taxes, the microeconomic standpoint also plays a role. This involves monitoring changes in tax laws and how they affect businesses. It influences the tax base through legal tools of tax policy, such as depreciation policy, as well as factors that impact the tax base of economic entities, like non-taxable items. The establishment of fundamental tax institutions in Slovakia indicates the government's commitment to fostering a favorable business climate. Examination of the primary institutions involved in the tax process reveals minor variations across the 10-year period being studied, despite minimal modifications in fundamental institutions. Foundational institutions are mechanisms for maximizing the tax revenue, which has an impact on the operations of both individuals and businesses in Slovakia. The country's tax policy is adaptable to address changes in all aspects of social life. Its primary objective is to resolve issues concerning the tax burden on entrepreneurs, such as double taxation. This is being gradually addressed through the implementation of double taxation treaties.

AT A GLANCE

The tax policy of Slovakia should be oriented on fostering the business climate. Within fiscal policy, the primary focus is to secure funds for state spending in order to influence economic and social policies. This includes managing taxes, currency stability, credit and monetary policy, unemployment, and addressing tax-related issues in the state economy. Aside from the overall economic understanding of the significance of taxes, the specific examination of tax laws and their effects on businesses, known as the microeconomic perspective, also shapes the tax base through legal tools of tax policy (such as depreciation policy) and factors that impact the taxable income of economic entities (such as non-taxable items). This chapter focuses on the examination of direct and indirect taxes in Slovakia and their influence on the business industry. The objective of this chapter is to emphasize the trajectory of tax rate evolution between 2007 and 2017, as well as the key elements that exert a substantial influence on the magnitude of taxes in Slovakia. Reducing taxes has a beneficial impact on economic growth, but the steady increase in tax rates is a significant obstacle to the corporate sector.

REFERENCES

1. Burak E, Nemec J. Main factors determining the Slovak tax system performance. Journal of Public Administration and Policy. 2016;9(2):185-197
2. Law 609/2007 consumer tax of electricity, coal, gas
3. Law 106/2004 consumer tax of tobacco
4. Law 222/2004 value added tax
5. Law 354/2011 financial institute
6. Law 431/2002 Z. financial accounting
7. Law 563/2009 administration of taxes
8. Law 582/2004 local income taxes
9. Law 595/2003 income tax

10. Law 601/2003 living wage
11. Law 663/2007 minimum wage
12. Law 98/2004 consumer tax of mineral oil
13. Ližbetinová L, Fábera P, Jambal T, Caha Z. Road tax as an economic tool of the support for the development of multimodal transport in selected EU states. In: International Scientific Conference LOGI 2017. Vol. 134. Nov 8, 2017
14. Maličká L, Šulíková V, Šoltés M. Relationship between fiscal decentralization and economic growth in European Union countries and Slovakia. Ekonomický časopis. 2017;65(9):856-875
15. Stoličná Z, Černička D. Tax systems changes in V4 countries during financial crisis. International Business Information Management Association Conference. May 3–4, 2017. pp. 2546-2551
16. Teplická K, Daubner M. Study of the relation between tax competition and tax burden in European Union member states. Ekonomický časopis, 2013;61(2):172-186

SECTION-2

TAXATION, ECONOMIC GROWTH AND WELFARE STATE

4 Chapter

THE RELATIONSHIP BETWEEN TAXATION AND ECONOMIC GROWTH IN NIGERIA, A COUNTRY ABUNDANT IN NATURAL RESOURCES

1. INTRODUCTION: AN OVERVIEW

1.1. Taxation

Taxation is a crucial tool that governments use to generate money and stimulate economic growth and development.Governments utilize tax money to fulfill their conventional roles, which include providing public goods and services, maintaining law and order, defending against external invasion, and regulating commerce and business to preserve social and economic stability [1]. Efficient tax revenue mobilization decreases an economy's reliance on unpredictable external inflows.Two Taxation provides governments with increased flexibility in shaping and managing their development plans. It also incentivizes states to enhance their domestic economic policies, thereby creating a favorable atmosphere for essential foreign direct investments. Additionally, taxation reinforces the sense of responsibility and transparency between governments and their citizens [2]. The global financial and economic crisis of 2008/2009 taught countries valuable lessons about the importance of focusing on efforts to mobilize internal resources, such as boosting tax revenues, and reducing reliance on foreign financial flows and export income.Three

While tax structures may differ significantly between countries, the main goal of any tax structure is to achieve optimal revenue and economic growth while minimizing distortions. Various nations possess distinct ideologies on taxation and employ diverse approaches to tax acquisition. Similarly, countries allocate their money in various ways that have distinct impacts on economic growth [3]. Agell et al. [4] have contended that the various applications of total government expenditure have varying effects on growth, and the same principle applies to the methods used to generate tax income. Romer [5] highlights the significance of elements like as the 'spill-over effect and learning by doing' in which enterprises' unique choices to invest in capital, research and development, or human capital can generate positive external impacts that benefit the entire economy. Solow [6] was the pioneer in analyzing the impact of taxation on economic growth. He contended that tax policy does not influence steady state growth. In other words, tax policy, independent of any distortion, does not alter long-term economic growth rates, even if it decreases the level of economic output in the long run. He stated that the various uses of total government expenditure have distinct effects on growth, and the same rationale applies to the methods of raising tax income. The economic expansion of Singapore, for example, can be ascribed to the low levels of corporate and personal income taxes. Furthermore [8], it is believed that there is a distinct disparity in taxation between developing countries and developed countries. Developing countries acquire approximately two-thirds of their tax revenue from indirect taxes, whereas industrialized countries obtain two-thirds of their tax revenue from direct taxes. However, they proposed that the tax system can be altered over time in order to optimize economic growth.

1.2. Taxation–theoretical underpinnings

Despite the varying perspectives on the impact of taxation on economic growth, there are significant conceptual questions regarding the ideal level of taxation for a specific objective, whether it be promoting growth or generating revenue. These questions include how the tax burden should be distributed among taxpayers, the extent of government involvement in taxation, and how tax revenues should be allocated to different public goods and services.

Lindahl [9] sought to tackle these inquiries by employing a model that enables the assessment of the degree to which the state provides goods and services, as well as the proportionate tax burdens of two individuals who have the freedom to express their preferences for state services in relation to their corresponding tax obligations. The core premise of the Lindahl model is the voluntary transaction between the taxes contributed by two individuals and the services provided by the government. The Lindahl model aimed to address three key issues: determining the level of state involvement, distributing total expenditure across different products and services, and allocating the tax burden among taxpayers.

Based on Figure 1, assuming a linear and homogeneous production of goods and services, SS' represents the supply curve of state services. DDa and DDb are the demand curves of two individuals, A and B, respectively. The vertical summation of these demand curves gives the community's total demand curve for state services, which is represented by DDl. When the amount of state services generated is ON, A contributes NE, B contributes NF, and NG indicates the cost of provision. As the state does not generate profits, it raises its supply to the level of OM. At this level, A contributes MJ while B contributes MR, which together equals the cost of supply, MP. P represents the specific point at which equilibrium is achieved by the voluntary exchange of commodities and services, resulting in a balance between supply and demand (SS = DD).

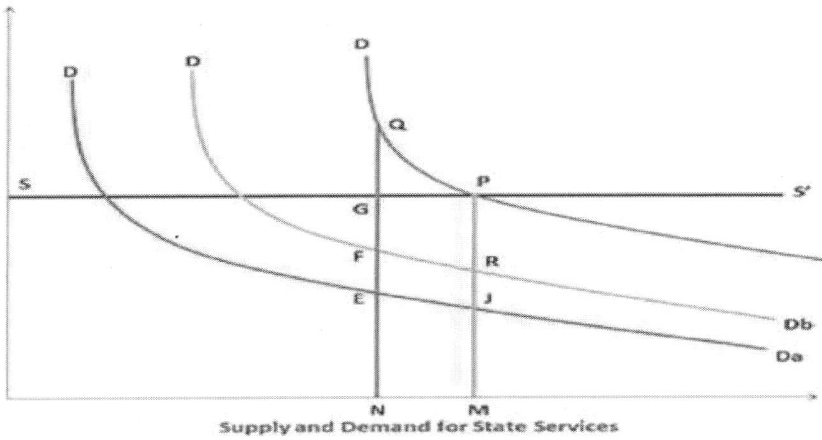

Figure 1. Lindahl model

Many economists however, tend to favour the Bowen approach [10] since it can be easily adapted to depict what happens when social goods are produced under conditions of increasing costs, as opposed to Lindahl model which assumes linear and homogenous production (Figure 2).

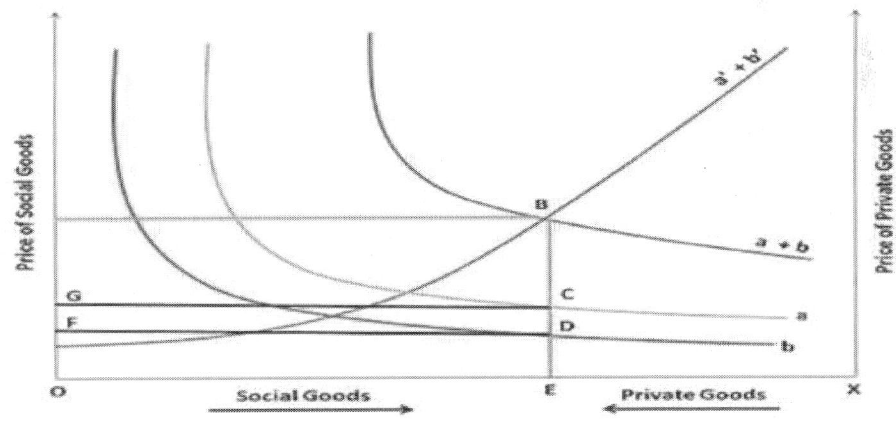

Figure 2. The Bowen model.

The model assumes the existence of one social good and two tax-payers - A and B whose demand curves are represented, respectively, by a and b; with a + b being the total demand. The supply curve 'a + b' implies that the social goods are produced under conditions of increasing cost. But economic theory posits that the cost of producing social goods is the value of private goods foregone; that is 'a + b' is also the demand curve of private goods. The intersection of the cost and demand curves at B therefore, gives a determination of how a given national income should, according to tax-payers' desire, be shared between social and private goods - OE social goods and EX private goods. At the same time, it is possible to determine the tax shares of A and B, which are represented, respectively, by GCEO and FDEO out of the total tax requirement represented by area ABEO.

1.3. What ails the Nigerian tax system?

Irrespective of how a country chooses to share the tax burden among tax payers or allocates tax revenues among various goods and services, the tax revenue to gross domestic product (GDP) ratio is generally accepted as a crude measure of the tax effort of a given country and can be used as a basis for cross country comparisons. Compared to similar economies in Africa, Nigeria has a very low tax revenue to GDP ratio, with the bulk of government revenue being derived from oil and gas sector.[4] Between 1981 and 2015, revenues from the oil and gas sector accounted, on average, for 75% of total government revenues, with the non-oil sector, of which taxation is part, contributing, on average, the remainder 25%, albeit with wide annual fluctuations [11]. Nigeria discovered oil in 1956 at Oloibiri in the Niger Delta after half a century of oil exploration, but commercial exploitation only started in 1968. By 1972, the oil sector share in total revenue was 54.4% against 45.6% share from non-oil sector. But by 1974 oil share of total revenue had increased to 82.1% with only 17.9% revenue accruing non-oil sector. Following the glut in the world oil prices in the later part of the 1970s however, the oil share in total revenue fell to 61.8% in 1978 while non-oil sector's share rose to 38.2%. More recently, the oil sector share in total revenue has been on an upward trajectory peaking at 88.6% in 2006. As at 2012, oil sector share in total revenue stood at 75.3% while non-oil sector accounted for 24.7% of the total revenue [11]. Overall, tax revenue, as a proportion of GDP, has been on a downward trend in the recent past. From a high of 5.459% in 2009, the tax to GDP ratio stood at 1.557% in 2012 which compares unfavourably with, for instance, the situation in South Africa, with a tax to GDP ratio of 26.81 and 25.52%, respectively, in 2009 and 2012.[5]

Despite the many policy, legislative and administrative reforms effected in the recent past,[6] the Nigerian tax system is still riddled with several challenges which limit its optimal performance. These challenges have been highlighted, variously, by [12, 13, 14, 15, 16, 17]; and include, but are not limited to the following: non-availability of tax statistics, inability to prioritise tax efforts, poor tax administration, multiplicity of taxes, regulatory challenges, tax evasion, tax avoidance, structural problems in the economy and a thriving underground economy. The role of taxation in promoting economic growth in Nigeria has therefore, not been optimally felt, owing to defective tax policy framework and administrative mechanisms. Tax administration process and the institutions saddled with the responsibility of tax collection often suffer from limitations in skilled manpower and financial resources; and appropriate tools and technology required to meet the ever-increasing challenges and difficulties associated with tax administration. Over the years, Nigeria has relied heavily on crude oil exports as a major source of government revenue, and consequently, neglecting other critical sectors of the economy that would have broadened the country's tax base. However, the high volatility associated with crude oil prices has made it imperative for the country to explore other sources of revenue to help fund public expenditure.

In this chapter, we examine the relationship between the availability of higher resource revenue—oil revenue in this case, and lower taxation effort of other (non-oil) revenue categories and the effects of these on growth. Specifically, we seek to examine the role of Petroleum Profit Tax in stimulating economic growth in Nigeria; determine the contribution of Companies' Income Tax to economic growth in Nigeria; ascertain the impact of Customs and Excise Duties on economic growth in Nigeria; determine factors responsible persistent low tax efforts in Nigeria; and recommend plausible policy proposals for enhancing optimal and effective tax administration in Nigeria. Whereas previous studies (See for instance [1, 18, 19]) have aggregated the various components of taxation and analysed their impact on economic growth, we disaggregate the various components of taxation in Nigeria with a view to ascertaining their respective influences on economic growth in Nigeria. We also expand the scope of the study to capture the effects of the most recent reforms and policy instruments relating to taxation in the Nigerian economy such as the Company's Income Tax (Amendment) Act. 2007; the Federal Inland Revenue Services (Establishment) Act, 2007 and the Personal Income Tax (Amendment) Act, 2011. More broadly, we examine taxation as an instrument for stimulating economic growth in Nigeria, by tracing trends and performance of various categories of taxes. We also present a cross-country analysis of tax effort in Nigeria and a select group of African countries.

2. A REVIEW OF THE NIGERIAN TAX SYSTEM

2.1. Policy, legal, and institutional reforms: a historical overview

Policy, legislative and administrative reforms of the Nigeria tax system predate independence and can be traced back to early twentieth century when the then High Commissioner of the [then] Northern Protectorate issued the Stamp Duties Proclamation in 1903, followed immediately thereafter in 1906 by the Native Revenue Proclamation. This latter Proclamation systematised all the pre-colonial taxes by defining taxable rates; and procedures for assessment and collection, as well as penalties for default thus eliminating arbitrariness that had hitherto characterised the Nigerian tax system. It introduced the four certainties essential in tax practice: what to pay, when to pay, where to pay and who to pay to. The same Proclamation was re-issued as the Native Revenue Ordinance in 1917 to cover the

Southern territories and by 1927, was applicable in the whole country. The year 1943 was a watershed period in the history of the Nigerian tax system as it witnessed the creation of the Inland Revenue Department (renamed the Federal Board of Inland Revenue in 1958), the precursor to the present day Federal Inland Revenue Service (FIRS). Following independence in 1960, other legal and institutional reforms were effected in 1961 through the establishment of the Federal Board of Inland Revenue (FBIR) and the Body of Appeal Commissioners as the first point of call for tax dispute resolution. In the same year, the Joint Tax Board (JTB) was created with the primary responsibility of ensuring uniformity of standards and application of Personal Income Tax.

Other major reforms to the tax system were effected in 1982 with the establishment of the Chartered Institute of Taxation of Nigeria [24] and 1993 with a review of the composition of the FBIR and establishment of the present day Federal Inland Revenue Service (FIRS) as the operational arm of the FBIR; as well as a review of the functions of the JTB. Further changes were effected in 2007 with the granting of financial and administrative autonomy to the FIRS following the recommendations of the 'Study and Working Group on Nigerian Tax System' which had been set up in half a decade earlier. These, and other reforms[7] represented the first major attempt at shifting focus away from oil to a more sustainable source of revenue, that is, the non-oil sector. Since then, a raft of changes that cut across organisational restructuring of the Federal and State authorities, the enactment of a National Tax Policy, funding, legislation, taxpayer education, dispute resolution mechanism, taxpayer registration, human capacity building, automation of key processes, refund mechanism and several other areas have been effected.

The foregoing would lead to one logical question: why so many reforms? Given the low tax to GDP ratio, it is plausible to assume that the need to address the problem of low tax returns motivated the Nigerian Government to embark on these reforms. The scope of, and frequency with which tax reforms have been implemented should however, be viewed within the broader context of the structure of Nigeria's economy and the centrality of taxes to the attainment of national development objectives. In specific terms, four main considerations seem to have informed these frequent tax reforms: the need to diversify the revenue portfolio to safeguard against the oil price volatility in the global market; the need for an accurate and reliable determination of the optimal tax rate, since Nigeria operates on a cash budget system, where expenditure proposals and overall fiscal management are anchored on revenue projections; historical overreliance on petroleum and trade taxes while overlooking direct and broad-based indirect taxes such as value added tax (VAT); and the ever-widening fiscal deficit, an ever-present threat to macroeconomic stability. According to [20], the objectives of tax reforms in Nigeria include the need to bridge the gap between the national development needs and the funding of the needs; achieve improved service delivery to the public; improve on the level of tax derivable from non-oil activities, vis-à-vis revenue from oil activities; constantly review the tax laws to reduce/manage tax evasion and avoidance; and improve the tax administration to make it more responsive, reliable, skilful and taxpayers friendly, as well as achieve other fiscal objectives such as managing inflation and improving balance-of-payment conditions. But the fiscal objectives were only a means to an end. The end objectives of the tax policy reforms were to generate revenue; promote growth and development; ensure effective protection for local industries and encourage greater use of local raw materials; promote value addition and greater geographical dispersion of domestic manufacturing capacities; and create jobs. And although specific policy, legal and institutional measures have varied over time, these objectives have remained relatively unchanged.

2.2. Taxation laws and regulations: who taxes what?

Tax regulations and laws refer to the embodiment of rules and regulations relating to tax revenue and the various kinds of taxes. A tax administration that encourages voluntary compliance, resolutely and legally enforces compliance, treats the tax payer as partner, rewards pro-tax behaviour and operates in an environment of accountability is a preferred tax system [21].

The federal system of government in Nigeria implies that fiscal power is based on a three-tiered tax structure: Federal, State and Local Governments, each of which has, in principle, different and distinct tax jurisdictions. Specifically, the Federal government taxes corporate bodies while State and Local Governments tax individuals. The Taxes and Levies (approved list for Collection) (Decree, 1998) gives the Federal, State and Local Governments the responsibilities for collecting the taxes and levies listed in, respectively, Parts I, II and III of the schedule to the Decree.

Part 1 of the schedule contains taxes to be collected by the Federal Government. These include: Companies Income Taxes; Withholding tax on companies, residents of the Federal Capital Territory, Abuja and non-resident individuals; Petroleum profits tax; Value added tax; Education tax; Capital gains tax on residents of the Federal Capital Territory, Abuja, bodies corporate and non-resident individuals; Stamp duties on bodies corporate and residents of the Federal Capital Territory, Abuja; and personal income tax of members of the Armed Forces of the Federation, members of the Nigeria Police Force, residents of the Federal Capital Territory, and staff of the Ministry of Foreign Affairs and non- resident individuals.

Similarly, Part II of the Schedule presents taxes and levies to be collected by the State Governments and they include: Personal Income Tax in respect of –Pay-As-You-Earn (PAYE) and direct taxation (Self-Assessment); Withholding tax (individuals only); Capital gains tax (individuals only); Stamp duties on instruments executed by individuals; Pools betting and lotteries, Gaming and casino taxes; Road taxes; Business premises registration fee; Development levy (individuals only); Right of Occupancy fees on lands owned by the State Government in urban areas of the State; and Market taxes and levies where State finance is involved.

Part III of the Schedule contains taxes and levies to be collected by the Local Governments and these include: Shops and kiosks rates; Tenement rates; On and Off Liquor Licence fees; Slaughter slab fees; Marriage, birth and death registration fees; Naming of street registration fee, excluding any street in the State Capital; Right of Occupancy fees on lands in rural areas, excluding those collectable by the Federal and State Governments; Market taxes and levies excluding any market where State finance is involved; Motor park levies; Domestic animal licence fees; Bicycle, truck. Canoe, wheelbarrow and cart fees, other than a mechanically propelled truck; Cattle tax payable by cattle farmers only; Merriment and road closure levy; Radio and television licence fees (other than radio and television transmitter); Vehicle radio licence fees (to be imposed by the Local Government of the State in which the car is registered); Wrong parking charges; Public convenience, sewage and refuse disposal fees; Customary burial ground permit fees; Religious places establishment permit fees; and Signboard and Advertisement permit fees.

And to address the hitherto inherent conflict of fiscal responsibilities and powers among the three tiers of government, the 1999 Constitution classifies governmental taxation responsibilities and powers into *exclusive*, *concurrent* and *residual* lists. The National Assembly, is empowered to issue legislation on the taxation of incomes, profits and capital gains, and on matters classified in the concurrent list—particularly those related to the division of public revenue. The State Houses of Assembly may prescribe the collection of any tax, fee or rate, or the administration of a law to provide for such collection by a local government council or any tax, fee or rate not expressly stipulated as being within the authority of the Federal government. The State government is empowered to impose tax on all items in the concurrent list as well as residual matters but to the extent that such laws are consistent with those of the National Assembly.

In sum, the Federal Government is limited to eight specific taxes while the State and Local Governments were restricted to 11 and 20, respectively. However, the Federal government controls most of the buoyant tax handles, accounting for 99% of the tax revenue. The most important tax laws in Nigeria include Company Income Tax Act (CITA), Capital Gains Tax Act and Stamp Duties Act, all enacted in 1990; value added tax (VAT) Act and Education Ac, both enacted in 1993; Personal Income Tax Act (PITA) of 2004; and the Petroleum Profit Tax Act and Information Technology Development Act, both enacted in 2007. In reality however, Nigeria's tax administration environment is fraught with the problem of multiple taxation, which in the extreme compels companies to pay income tax to Federal Government, and other wide ranging taxes, levies and rates, to State and Local governments. This may be due, in part, to declining and fluctuating earnings from oil and the need by various tiers of Government to raise own revenue.

2.3. A review of national tax policies

Tax policy provides a set of rules, *modus operandi* and guidance for all stakeholders in the tax system. Tax policy formulation in Nigeria is the responsibility of the FIRS, Customs Services, Nigerian National Petroleum Corporation (NNPC), and other agencies of government but under the guidance of the National Assembly. A good tax policy needs to satisfy both *efficiency* and *equity* criteria. Any tax policy is, however, continually subjected to pressure and changes. According to [22], the best approach to reforming taxes is one that considers taxation theory, empirical evidence and political and administrative realities and blending these with a good dose of local knowledge and sound appraisal of the prevailing macroeconomic and international situation to produce a feasible set of proposals sufficiently attractive to be implemented and robust enough to withstand changing times.

Whereas during the pre- Structural Adjustment Programmes (SAP) era tax policies were aimed at boosting government revenue; ensuring effective protection for local industries and equity in the geographic dispersion of manufacturing activities, the introduction of the SAPs in 1986 witnessed a shift in policy focus to using taxes to boost productivity and competitiveness of business enterprises; promoting exports of manufactures; and reducing the tax burden of individuals and companies. The specific measures introduced included a review of custom and excise duties; reduction of company and income taxes; granting of a wide array of tax exemptions and rebates; introduction of capital allowance; expansion of duty drawback and manufacturing-in-bond schemes; elimination of excise duty; introduction of VAT; and monetizing of fringe benefits and increase in tax relief to low-income earners [23].

More recently, a National Tax Policy (NTP) adopted in 2010 sought to provide a set of guidelines, rules and *modus operandi* that would regulate Nigeria's tax system and provide a basis for tax legislation and tax administration. The 2010 NTP seeks to resolve some inherent problems of the existing tax system such as multiple taxation; uncertainty and leakages in the tax system; lack of accountability of tax revenue and expenditure; inadequate clarity on taxation powers of each level of government and encroachment on the powers of one level or state by another; uncertainty in the tax system and increasing cost of tax compliance due to lack of skilled manpower, inadequate funding, improper delegation of tax powers to third parties; the non-refund of excess taxes to taxpayers, due to the lack of an efficient system and funds; obsolete laws which do not reflect Nigeria's current realities; and the lack of a specific policy direction for tax matters in Nigeria, as well the absence of laid down procedures for the operation of the various tax authorities. The 2010 policy in effect has shifted focus from direct taxation to indirect taxation. Its strategy is to reduce companies' income tax rate from 30 to 20%, top rate personal income tax rate from 25 to 17.5% and a gradual increase in the rate of VAT from the current level of 5%. These strategies are aimed at encouraging investments, creating employment, increasing tax compliance and limiting opportunities for tax avoidance.

3. METHODOLOGICAL APPROACH

3.1. Review of the literature

The relationship between taxation and economic growth has been widely studied. Some of these studies suggest that tax policies have positive and significant impact on the rate of growth of output, while others have observed that there is an inverse relationship between the two variables, that is, tax policies have a negative and significant impact on growth. Haq-Padda and Akram [25] examined the impact of tax policies on economic growth using data from Asian economies. They established that there is no empirical evidence that tax policies adopted by developing countries in Asia have a permanent effect on the rate of economic growth, a finding that is inconsistent with the endogenous class of growth models. The results of their study suggest that the relationship between aggregate output and the tax rate is best described by the neo-classical growth models because a higher tax rate permanently reduces the level of output but has no permanent effect on the output growth rate. Consequently, they recommended an optimal tax rate to finance the budgets, with debt instrument used in financing transitory expenditure while permanent expenditures are to be financed through taxes.

In a cross-country analysis, Ramot and Ichihashi [26] used panel data from 65 countries covering the period 1970–2006 to examine the effects of tax structure on economic growth and income inequality and established that company income tax (CIT) rates have a negative impact both on economic growth and income inequality. They also established that personal income tax rate does not significantly affect economic growth and income inequality. The authors therefore, recommended that there is a need to develop a modest design into the tax system since countries which are able to mobilise tax resources through broad-based tax structures, coupled with efficient administration and enforcement of the tax system' are likely to enjoy faster growth rates than countries with narrow tax base and lower efficiency in tax administration. Also, governments should reduce tax evasion, which, they averred, occurs among the highest income group and has potential to distort horizontal and vertical equity in income redistribution. Finally, they recommended that very high earners or the highest income group should be subjected to high and rising marginal tax rates.

Ariyo [14] evaluated the productivity of the Nigerian tax system given the negative impact of persistent unsustainable fiscal deficits on the Nigerian economy for the period 1970–1990 to devise a reasonably accurate estimation of Nigeria's sustainable revenue profile. The results of the study showed a satisfactory level of productivity of the Nigerian tax system. The author therefore, recommended for an improvement of the tax information system to enhance the evaluation of the performance of the Nigerian tax system and facilitate adequate macroeconomic planning and implementation. Kneller et al. [27], taking account of the financing assumption associated with government budget constraints, studied the effect of the structure of taxation and public expenditure to the steady-state growth and established that non-distortionary taxation and productive expenditure enhance economic growth, a finding consistent with the Barro model [28].

Widmalm [29] in a study established that there exists a negative relationship between personal income tax, measured by average income tax, and economic growth, while corporate income tax does not correlate with growth at all. In their estimation, Lee and Gordon [30] found out that the concrete tax rates that greatly affect economic growth are the top statutory company income tax (CIT) rates. From their estimation, they established that only the CIT rate had a significant negative impact on economic growth in all their regressions by controlling the endogeneity of tax measures while the personal income tax (PIT) rate and its progressivity did not significantly affect economic growth. The results of Lee and Gordon [30] are supported by the findings of Arnold [31] who established that the CIT and PIT rates reduce the economic performance of a country. Analogously, Padovano and Galli [32] argued that average tax rates lead to several biases and concluded that taxation has no impact on growth because of the possibility of high correlation with average fiscal spending.

Poulson and Kaplan [33] explored the impact of tax policy on economic growth within the framework of an endogenous growth model using data from 1964 to 2004. In this model, differences in tax policy can lead to different paths of long-run equilibrium growth. They used regression analysis to estimate the impact of taxes on economic growth. Their analysis revealed that higher marginal tax rates had a negative impact on economic growth. Jibrin et al. [34] used ordinary least squares (OLS) method to examine the impact of Petroleum Profit Tax on Economic Development in Nigeria for the period 2000–2010. Their findings revealed that Petroleum Profit Tax has a positive and significant impact on Gross Domestic Product. The authors therefore, recommended that government should improve on the effectiveness and efficiency of the administration and collection of taxes with a view to increasing government revenue.

Enokela [35] explored the relationship between VAT and economic growth of Nigeria using secondary data and multiple regressions. The results revealed that gross domestic product (GDP) is positive and statistically significant to value added tax; Government capital expenditure (GCE) is positive but insignificant to value added tax; and gross domestic product per capita (GDPPC) is negative and statistically significant to value added tax. The researcher recommended a zero tolerance for corruption to enable the revenue generated from VAT to be channelled to appropriate developmental projects. In a related strand of literature, Emmanuel [36] examined the effects of VAT on economic growth and total tax revenue in Nigeria using data covering the period 1994–2010. He formulated two hypotheses: that VAT does not have significant effects on GDP; and VAT does not have significant effects on total tax revenue. The results of the regression analysis show that VAT has significant effect on GDP; and also on total tax revenue. He therefore, encouraged government to sensitise the people to enable it increase the tax rate in order to increase its annual revenue for economic development. Relatedly, in a study by Wambai and Hanga, [37] titled '*Taxation and Social Development in Nigeria: Tackling Kano's Hidden Economy*', they found that the attitude of the government towards taxation need to change and recommended a tax system that concentrates on establishing simplicity, predictability and neutrality while Olusanya et al. [38] in investigating taxation as a fiscal policy instrument for income redistribution among Lagos state civil servants using Spearman's Rank Correlation coefficient found a positive relationship between tax as a fiscal policy instrument and income redistribution.

Tosin and Abizadeh [39] studied economic growth and tax charges in OECD countries from 1980 to 1999; their study reveals that economic growth measured by GDP per capita has significant effect on tax mix of GDP per capita. The study recorded a decline in shares of payroll, goods and services and positive growth from personal and property taxes. At the regional level, Chiumia and Simwaka, [40] analysed the effects of taxation in sub-Saharan Africa. They found that taxes levied on personal and corporate income reduces economic growth. From their study, one could be tempted to conclude that the tax structure is largely irrelevant in less developed economies, although we know from theory that embedded in an effective tax system are benefits for both the taxpayers and the government.

3.2. Model specification and estimation technique

The model specified for this study is adopted from Appah [41], Okafor, [42], Ogbonna and Ebimobowei [43] and Nwakanma and Nnamdi, [19]. We used a multiple linear regression model to capture the relationship between taxation and economic growth in Nigeria for the period 1986–2015. Included in the model are; real gross domestic product growth rate (RGDPgr), as the dependent variable; and companies income tax (CIT) revenue, petroleum profit tax (PPT) revenue, as well as customs and excise duties (CED) revenue as the explanatory variables.[8]

1. Petroleum profit tax (PPT) is the tax imposed on companies which are engaged in the extraction and transportation of petroleum products. It is related to rents, royalties, margins and profit-sharing elements associated with oil mining, prospecting and exploration leases [44]. Apart from providing revenue for the government, PPT also serves as an instrument through which the government regulates the number of participants in the petroleum industry and gain control over public assets [45]. In the context of Nigeria, like in other developing countries, the PPT is, in a sense, an instrument for wealth re-distribution between the wealthy and industrialised economies who own the technology; and expertise and technical know-how, as well as the capital needed to develop the oil and gas sector [34].
2. Companies income tax (CIT) is charged on the profit or gain of any company accruing in, derived from, brought into, earned in or received in Nigeria. The tax rate has been 30% and it is applied on the total profit or chargeable profit of the company but was reduced to 20% under the new (2010) tax policy. It should be noted that oil marketing companies, oil services companies are liable to tax under CITA at the rate 20% and Education Tax at the rate of 2% on the assessable profit.
3. Custom Duties constitute one of the oldest kinds of modern taxation in Nigeria having been introduced in 1860 as import duties. Excise duties are *ad-valorem* taxes on the output of manufactured goods and are administered by the country's Custom Service. They are taxes on the country's imports charged either as a percentage of the value of the imports or as a fixed amount contingent on quality.

The model was thus explicitly specified as:

$$RGDPgr = a_0 + a_1 CIT + a_2 PPT + a_3 CED + U \quad (1)$$

where: RGDPgr = Real Gross Domestic Product growth rate; CIT = Companies Income Tax; PPT = Petroleum Profit Tax; CED = Customs and Excise Duties; and U = Stochastic error term while a_{0-} a_3, are parameters of the model.

The coefficients of all the explanatory variables are expected to be either positive or negative, depending on the peculiarity of the country's tax structures. The intercept term is expected, *a priori*, to be positive as tax variables are not the only contributors to the country's economic growth rates.

We employed the ordinary least square (OLS) method of estimation based on the desirable properties it possesses and the relative simplicity of its application. We carried out unit root test at 5% level of significance to assess the stationarity of the time series data. Descriptive analysis was also carried out regarding tax trends and tax efforts in Nigeria, to determine the effectiveness of existing tax structures towards enhancing optimal and effective tax administration. Finally, we used descriptive analysis to evaluate relevant national and cross-country tax data, with a view to evaluating their inherent patterns and trends, and determining the implications of these patterns and trends for tax policies and administration in Nigeria.

3.3. Evaluation criteria and data sources

The results were evaluated based on the following criteria: economic *a-priori* criterion, statistical criterion and econometric criterion. We carried out tests to check if the signs and magnitudes of the estimated parameters conform to what economic theory postulates. The coefficient of determination (R^2), was estimated to capture the proportion of the total variation in the dependent variable, Real GDP growth rate, that can be explained by the explanatory variables explicitly captured in the model. We also used the F-test to test whether the explanatory variables included in the model are, jointly, significant or not in determining the level of economic growth while the T-Test was used to test the statistical significance of individual parameters of the regression model. To test autocorrelation, we adopted the Durbin Watson (D-W) statistic because of the absence of lagged dependent variables in the specified regression model while for Heteroscedasticity, we adopted the White's General Heteroscedasticity Test to ensure that the variance of the stochastic error term is constant. Our regression analysis relied heavily on secondary data published by the Central Bank of Nigeria (CBN), the National Bureau of Statistics (NBS), and Federal Inland Revenue Service (FIRS) covering the fiscal period 1986–2015 while data for descriptive analysis of tax trends in Nigeria, as well as cross country tax trends and performance among selected African countries, were sourced from FIRS and the International Monetary Fund (IMF).

4. REGRESSION RESULTS AND ANALYSIS OF TAXATION TRENDS

4.1. Results and discussions

To address the phenomenon of spurious regression usually associated with nonstationary time series data, we carried out the Augmented Dickey Fuller (ADF) unit root test at 5% level to ascertain the stationarity status of each individual time series data; the results of which are shown in Table 1 below.

Table 1. ADF unit root test results.

Variables	ADF statistic	Order of integration
RGDPgr	-4.103592	I(0)
CIT	-3.262681	I(1)
CED	-4.473805	I(1)
PPT	-3.102251	I(1)

Source: Authors' computation.

From Table 1, the time series data for RGDPgr is stationary at level, implying that the time series data on Real Gross Domestic Product growth rate is integrated of order zero (0) while the annual time series data on CIT, CED and PPT are all stationary at first difference, implying that they are integrated of order one (1). The finding with respect to Companies Income Tax, Customs and Excise Duties and Petroleum Profit Tax substantiates the theoretical assertion that most economic time series are usually not stationary at level, but they attain stationarity after first differencing.

Based on the results shown in Table 2 below, the estimated regression equation (Eq. (1)) becomes:

$$RGDPgr = 2.771101 + 0.0000326CED - 0.00000926CIT - 0.000850PPT \qquad (2)$$

Table 2. Summary of regression results.

Variable	Coefficient	Standard error	T-statistic	P-values
C	2.771101	0.888043	3.120460	0.0044
CED	3.26E-05	1.08E-05	3.013292	0.0057
CIT	-9.26E-06	7.45E-06	-1.242312	0.2252
PPT	-0.000850	0.001434	-0.592753	0.5585
Adjusted R^2	0.195645			
D.W statistic	1.707596			
F-statistic	3.351249			0.034229

Source: Authors' computation.

From the estimated regression results, the intercept term is positive (2.771101), implying that the growth rate of the Nigerian economy retains a positive value when all the explanatory variables explicitly captured in the regression model are held constant; that is, economic growth rate is dependent on other variables other the explanatory variables captured in the model. The signs of the coefficients of explanatory variables explicitly captured in the regression model conform to the *a-priori* expectations as the impact of tax variables on growth can either be positive or negative, depending on the internal dynamics of the economy as well as the incidence of the various categories of taxes. The coefficient of customs and excise duties is positive while the coefficients of Companies Income Tax (CIT) and Petroleum Profit Tax (PPT) are negative. The estimated regression results show that, a unit change in Customs and Excise Duties will result in an average change in Real Gross Domestic Product growth rate of 0.0000326 units, holding all other explanatory variables in the regression model constant while the coefficient of Companies Income Tax implies that a unit change in Companies Income Tax will result in an average change in Real Gross Domestic Product growth rate of -0.00000926 units, holding all other explanatory variables in the regression model constant. Similarly, the coefficient of Petroleum Profit Tax implies that a unit change in Petroleum Profit Tax will result in an average change in Real Gross Domestic Product growth rate of -0.000850 units, holding all other explanatory variables in the regression model constant.

The Adjusted R^2 from the estimated regression model shows that only about 20% (0.195645) of the changes in Real Gross Domestic Product growth rate (RGDPgr) can be explained by the explanatory variables explicitly captured in the regression model, implying that the regression model has a poor fit. The low R^2 is an indication that the tax variables explicitly captured in the regression model have not significantly influenced the total change in Real GDP growth rate in Nigeria. This poor tax performance as a driver of economic growth can be attributed to the economy's heavy reliance on commodity export (crude oil) as a major driver of economic growth and the perpetually low tax to GDP ratio as a result of the plethora of challenges facing the Nigerian tax administration system discussed Section 2.

Based on the students' T-test for each of the parameters in the model, the coefficient Customs and Excise Duties is statistically significant at 5% level of significance, while the coefficients of Companies Income Tax and Petroleum Profit Tax are not statistically significant at 5% level of significance. This implies that Customs and Excise Duties do have significant impact on the growth rate of Real Gross Domestic Product (RGDPgr), while Companies Income Tax (CIT) and Petroleum Profit Tax (PPT) have not contributed significantly towards stimulating economic growth in Nigeria during the period under review.

We also employed the F-Statistic (ANOVA) to establish the overall significance of the regression at the 5% significance level. The results show that the equation or model employed is statistically significant with P- value of 0.034229 and F = 3.351249, implying that the relationship between the growth rate of Real Gross Domestic Product and all the explanatory variables explicitly captured in the regression model is statistically significant at 5% level of significance. Thus, even though some of the individual coefficients of some of explanatory variables are not statistically significant, they are, jointly, statistically significant. That is, during the period under review, all the tax variables explicitly captured in the regression equation jointly exerted significant effect on economic growth in Nigeria.

Lastly, we evaluated the results based on econometric criteria. The estimated Durbin Watson statistic (D-W = 1.707596) shows that the regression model is devoid of first order serial correlation. Also, the White's test of heteroscedasticity was carried out to ensure that the variance of the error term is constant. Since the calculated value of the test statistic is 5.147783, which is lower than the 5% critical value of 7.81 (P-value = 0.525004), the null hypothesis that the model is devoid of first order serial correlation is accepted; the disturbances of the regression model are homoscedastic.

4.2. An examination of tax patterns in Nigeria and a few chosen African nations.

The dynamics of taxation and economic growth in Nigeria should be understood not just from the perspective of the tax revenues discussed in the preceding section, but also from an analysis and discussion of other aspects of Nigeria's tax revenue and the broader tax system, some of which may not easily lend themselves to econometric analysis.

Figures 3 and 4 below present recent trends in oil and non-oil tax revenues, as well as the share of oil and non-oil tax revenue as a percentage of total government revenues.

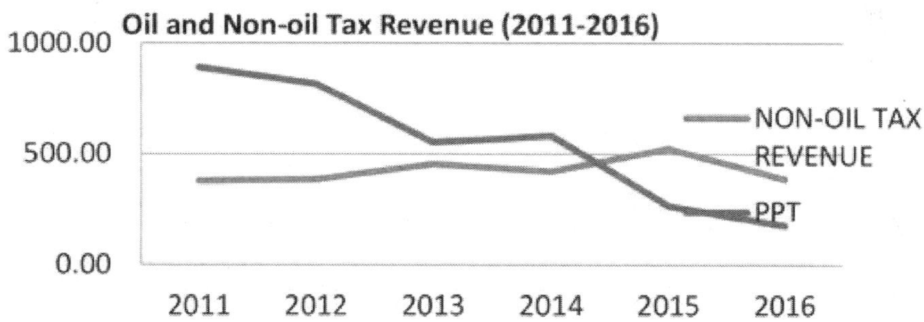

Figure 3. Oil and non-oil revenue—recent trends. Authors' computation from Federal Inland Revenue Service (FIRS) figures.

As shown in the Figure 3, there has been a steady decline in oil tax revenue in Nigeria from 2011 to 2016. It is noteworthy to mention that oil tax revenue remained higher than the non-oil tax revenue from 2011 to 2014 which marked the beginning of the huge slump in oil prices in the global market. From 2014 however, non-oil tax revenues, though generally declining, albeit at a slower pace, began to outperform oil revenues. It follows therefore, that oil revenue as a percentage of total revenues has been on the decline in the recent past. The converse holds true for non-oil revenues as shown in Figure 4 below.

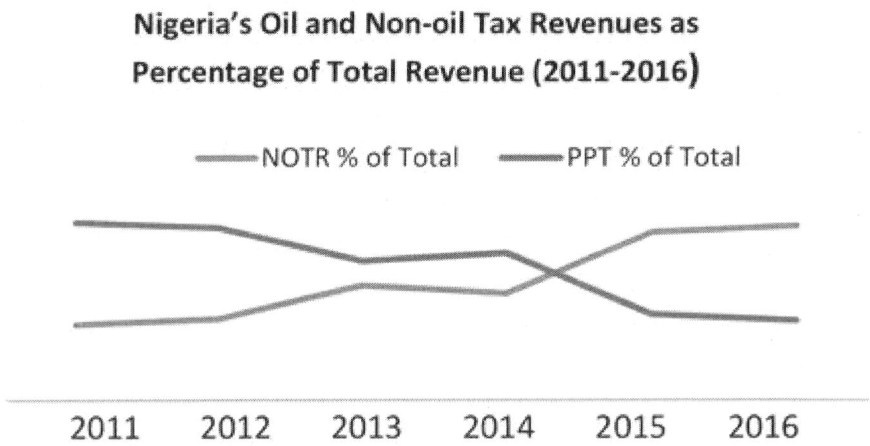

Figure 4. Oil and non-oil revenue as percentage of Total revenue (2011–2016).

From Figures 3 and 4, it is apparent that there is a need to pay more attention to other critical sectors of the economy, beyond oil, from which revenue can be generated in order attain fiscal stability and engender macroeconomic stability. An important question thus arises: since taxation is an important fiscal policy instrument for domestic resource mobilisation and economic growth, is Nigeria' tax effort optimal for the desired impact on economic growth? In an attempt to address this policy question, we reviewed comparative tax efforts in Nigeria and selected African countries, focussing on the tax to GDP ratios, over the period 2003–2011.

From Figure 5, it is apparent that, historically, Nigeria lags other African countries in terms of the tax to GDP ratio, that is, tax effort. Over the 2003–2011 period, the average tax revenue as a percentage of GDP for Nigeria was 2.93%, with the corresponding figures for Egypt, Ghana, Kenya, South Africa and Algeria being 14.62, 15.89, 16.10, 25.48 and 35.04%, respectively. Algeria's tax effort, that is, tax to GDP ratio, is 12 times Nigeria's tax effort, while South Africa's tax effort is approximately 10 times that of Nigeria. Nigeria tax efforts is less than one fifth that of neighbouring Ghana. The low tax to GDP ratio can be attributed to structural defects associated with overreliance on oil revenue as the main source of government revenue and the consequent neglect of other critical sectors of the economy. This low performance of the non-oil tax revenue has great potential of creating substantial macroeconomic instability and consequently, negatively impacting growth and development owing to the volatility associated with oil prices and the critical role of public expenditures in stimulating economic activities. Nigeria's low performance in terms of tax revenue as a percentage of GDP also points to the existence of unexploited 'fiscal space' or untapped potential for tax revenue mobilisation.

Figure 5. Tax revenue (% of GDP) for selected African countries (2003–2011). Source: IMF.

5. CONCISE SUMMARY

This chapter explores the correlation between taxation and economic growth in Nigeria from 1986 to 2015. It specifically analyzes the impact of Companies Income Tax, Customs and Excise Duties, and Petroleum Profit Tax. The empirical findings indicate that taxation had a substantial influence on the growth rates of Real GDP in Nigeria over the examined period. Nevertheless, the tax contribution to the growth rate of the Nigerian economy is below the ideal level considering the number of economic activities, total value of production, and the country's potential for revenue generation. This discovery has significant implications for both policy formulation and decision-making regarding the improvement of Nigeria's tax systems and the mobilization of domestic resources. In addition, when comparing Nigeria's tax performance to that of other African countries, it becomes evident that Nigeria falls behind in terms of tax effort, which refers to the percentage of tax income relative to the GDP. Therefore, it is necessary to implement policy measures that enhance tax revenues and taxation capacity in order to create more income that can effectively boost economic growth. It is expected that continuous tax policy and institutional reforms, along with strategies to diversify and transition the economy away from excessive dependence on the oil and gas sector, will not only increase the importance of non-oil tax revenues, but also enhance the overall tax effort. This will enable taxation to become a significant tool of fiscal policy, ensuring both macroeconomic stability and consistent economic growth.

The Government of Nigeria should establish a suitable tax system that focuses on expanding the revenue base and, in certain instances, increasing tax rates to improve the role of taxation in promoting economic growth and development. The tax administrative system in Nigeria should be enhanced to overcome the current obstacles that are hindering growth in tax administration. Moreover, it is important to promote voluntary adherence by means of ongoing taxpayers' education and the establishment of an efficient tax administration system. Furthermore, it is advisable for tax enforcement authorities to establish strong connections with professional bodies that deal with tax issues. This will help to garner their assistance in combating tax malpractices and other types of fiscal corruption. Furthermore, the regulatory bodies tasked with the duty of tax collection should be better empowered to ensure that taxpayers adhere to the regulations. Government should increase accountability and openness in managing tax income to ensure the supply of public goods and services. This would promote tax compliance among taxpayers. Finally, as a component of the wider economic diversification initiative, the utilization of tax revenue mobilization should be employed as a policy tool to transition from the past excessive dependence on oil earnings to non-oil earnings, which are more stable and hence crucial for the country's overall macroeconomic stability.

AT A GLANCE

This chapter investigates the correlation between taxation and economic growth in a country abundant in resources, with Nigeria serving as a specific example. We investigate the relationship between the availability of higher resource revenue and the reduced taxation effort of other revenue categories, as well as the impact of these factors on economic growth. The stated model is estimated using the Ordinary Least Squares (OLS) estimation approach. Furthermore, a comprehensive study is conducted to evaluate the efficacy of the current tax structures in Nigeria by examining tax trends and tax efforts. This research also includes an examination of pertinent national and cross-country statistics. Empirical findings demonstrate that taxes exerts a substantial influence on the rates of growth of Real GDP. Nevertheless, the ratio of tax contribution to the growth rate is insufficient when considering the magnitude of economic activity and the value of total output. Nigeria's tax effort is comparatively lower than that of other African countries, indicating a significant untapped potential for increasing revenue mobilization. We suggest that the Government should establish a suitable tax system that focuses on expanding the tax base and, in certain instances, raising tax rates to enhance the tax effort and ensure that taxation contributes optimally to economic growth and development.

REFERENCES

1. Adereti S, Sanni M, Adesina J. Value added tax and economic growth of Nigeria. European Journal of Humanities and Social Science. 2011;10(1):456-471

2. UN (United Nations). Taxation and technology Transfer: Key Issues. New York and Geneva: UNCTAD; 2005
3. Masood M, Sohaib Y, Syed A. Tax revenue and economic growth; an empirical analysis for Pakistan. Journal of World Applied Sciences. 2010;10(11)
4. Agell J, Olindh T, Ohlesson H. Growth and the public sector; a critical review essay. European Journal of Political Economic. 1997;13(1):33-52
5. Romer P. Increasing returns and long-run growth. The Journal of Political Economy. 1986;94(5):1002-1037
6. Solow R. A contribution to the theory of economic growth. Quarterly Journal of Economics. 1956;70:65-94
7. Atkinson A. The welfare and economic performance. National Tax Journal. 1995;48:171-198
8. Burges R, Stern N. Taxation and development. Journal of Economic Literature. 1993;31:762-830
9. Lindahl E. Classics in the Theory of Public Finance. 1st ed. London: Macmillan; 1958
10. Bowen H. The interpretation of voting in the allocation of economic resources. Quarterly Journal of Economics. 1943;58
11. CBN (Central Bank of Nigeria). Annual Report and Statistical Bulletin. Abuja: CBN; 2015
12. FRN (Federal Republic of Nigeria). Report of Vision 2010 Committee. Abuja: FRN; 1997 p. 60-75
13. . Personal Income Tax Act 1993. Abuja: Federal Ministry of Finance; 2002
14. A. Productivity of the Nigerian Tax System: 1970-1990. Kenya: African Economic Research Consortium; 1997. pp. 1-50
15. C. Income Tax Law and Practice in Nigeria. Ibadan: Heinemann Educational Books Nigeria Limited; 2001
16. A. Internally generated revenue at the local government: issues and challenges. Presentation presented at the Workshop on Revenue Generation at the State Government Level; 2003; University of Ibadan
17. L, Chukwuma E, Umobong A. Tax system in Nigeria: Challenges and the way forward. Research Journal of Finance and Accounting. 2012;3(5):1-14
18. N. Stimulating economic growth through an efficient tax system. A Paper Presented at the Second Annual Conference of The Chartered Institute of Taxation of Nigeria; 2000

19. P, Nnamdi K. Taxation and national development. Research Journal of Finance and Accounting. 2013;4(19):176-180
20. B. Managing the tax reform process in Nigeria. Niger Account. 2009;42(1):45-51
21. J. Towards a people-focused tax system in Nigeria. Guage–A Quarterly Publication of Federal Inland Revenue Service (FIRS) Oct-Dec 2009
22. S, Nobes C. The Economics of Taxation. 8th ed. Birmingham: Fiscal Publications; 2008
23. Odusola A. Tax policy reforms in Nigeria. United Nations University-World Institute for Development Economics research. 2006 (UN-WIDER-2006). Working paper No. 2006/03. ISSN: 1810-2611
24. CITN (Chartered Institute of Taxation of Nigeria). CITN Nigerian Tax Guide Statutes; 2002
25. Haq-Padda I, Akram N. The impact of tax policies on economic growth: Evidence from. Asian Economies. 2011
26. Ramot Ichihashi M. The effects of tax structure on economic growth and income inequality. Presentation presented at; 2012; Hiroshima University, Japan. 2
27. Kneller R, Bleaney M, Gemmell N. Fiscal policy and growth: Evidence from OECD countries. Journal of Public Economics. 1998;74:171-190
28. R. Government spending in a simple model of endogenous growth. Journal of Political Economics. 1990;98:103-125
29. Widmalm F. Tax structures and growth: Are some taxes better than others? Public Choice. 2001;107(3/4):199-219
30. Lee Y, Gordon R. Tax structure and economic growth. Journal of Public Economics. 2005;89(5-6):1027-1043
31. Arnold J. Tax policy for economic recovery and growth. Economic Journal. 2008;12(1):59-80
32. Padovano F, Galli E. Tax rate and economic growth in the OECD countries (1950-1990). Economic Inquiry. 2001;1(39):44-57
33. Poulson B, Kaplan J. State income taxes and economic growth. Cato Journal. 2008;28(1)
34. Jibrin S, Blessing S, Ifurueze M. Impact of petroleum profit tax on economic development of Nigeria. British Journal of Economics, Finance and Management Sciences. 2012;5(2):60-72

35. Enokela S. The impact of value added tax on economic development of Nigeria. Journal of Social and Management Sciences. 2010;3(2):19-40
36. Emmanuel C. The effects of value added tax on the economic growth in Nigeria. Journal of Economics and Sustainable Development. 2003;4(6):190-202
37. Wambai U, Hanga B. Taxation and societal development in Nigeria: Tackling Kano's hidden economy. International Journal of Academic Research in Business and Social Science. 2013;3(3):113-125
38. Olusanya S, Peter M, Oyebo A. Taxation as a fiscal policy instrument for income redistribution among Lagos state civil servants. IOSR. Journal of Humanities and Social Sciences. 2012;5(10):60-70
39. Tosin M, Abizadeh S. Economic growth and tax components: An analysis of tax changes in OECD. Journal of Applied Economics. 2005;37:2251-2263
40. Chiumia A, Simwaka K. Tax policy development, donor inflows and economic growth in Malawi. Journal of Economics and International Finance. 2012;4(7):159-172
41. Appah E. The problems of tax planning and Administration in Nigeria: The federal and state governments experience. International Journal of Labour Organisation Psychology. 2010;4(1-2):1-14
42. Okafor R. An analysis of the preference of organizational forms for small scale Investors in Nigeria: Issue of income tax consideration. Journal of Association of National Accountants of Nigeria. 2012;16(1):6-17
43. Ogbonna G, Ebimobowei A. Impact of tax reforms and economic growth of Nigeria: A time series analysis. Current Research Journal of Social Sciences. 2012;4(1):62-68
44. Ekeocha P, Ekeocha C, Malaolu V, Oduh M. Revenue implications of Nigeria's tax system. Journal of Economics and Sustainable Development. 2012;3(8):206-215
45. Abdul-Rahamoh O, Taiwo F, Adejare A. The analysis of the effect of petroleum profit tax on Nigerian economy. Asian Journal of Humanities and Social Sciences (AJHSS). 2013;1(1)

5 Chapter

AN ANALYSIS OF THE STRUCTURE AND PATTERNS OF TAXES AND TAX REVENUES IN THE UNITED KINGDOM

1. INTRODUCTION: AN OVERVIEW

The tax system in the UK encompasses a diverse array of taxes. For a comprehensive overview of the intricate system, readers are encouraged to see Pope and Waters [1]. The primary taxes comprise:

- Personal income tax. Almost all forms of income are subject to tax but the rate of tax applied is determined by a series of income bands and subject to allowances against tax. Every taxpayer is given a personal allowance (£11,000 in 2016–2017) which is deducted from their pre-tax income before income tax is levied. The allowance is reduced for incomes over £100,000. The rate of tax varies according to bands. In 2016–2017 the basic tax rate of 20% was applied up to an income of £32,000, a higher rate of 40% for incomes between £31,785 and £150,000 and an additional rate band of 45% for income over £150,000. The UK Government estimates there to be about 30.1 million income tax payers in 2016–2017, including some 609,000 basic rate (only) payers and about 4.4 million in the highest band.
- National Insurance Contributions (NICs). The origins of NICs were as compulsory contribution to a National Insurance fund, which was linked to benefits that could be paid to the contributor. Over the years the link between contributions and payments has gradually disappeared and there is now considerable overlap between NICs and the general budget. Employers and employees are subject to NIC's (at different rates) and the self-employed at a different rate again. The NIC rate for income from employment between £155 and £827 per week was 12% in 2016–2017.
- Corporation tax. This tax is levied on the profits of UK resident corporations and on the UK profits of non-resident corporations. Losses may be offset against future profits for tax purposes. The rate of corporation for the 2017–2018 tax year is scheduled at 19%.

- Value added Tax (VAT). Value added is a tax on the value added at each stage of production. By the stage of final consumption it is, in effect, levied on the value of the good or service. The standard rate of VAT is currently 20%. A small number of goods are taxed at a reduced rate and a range of products are exempt from VAT in the UK.
- Excise taxes. Excise duties are levied on alcoholic drinks, fuels and tobacco products. These duties are typically levied at a specific rate (for example, per litre) but there is also an ad valorem component.
- Capital gains tax. This tax is applied to the gains accruing from the buying and selling of financial and other assets. Like income tax there is a tax free threshold (£11,100 for individuals in 2016–2017). The rate of capital gains tax varies according to the individual's income tax band.
- Council tax. The revenues from council tax go to local rather than national government. Council tax is levied on an assessed value of domestic residences, with the rate of tax depending on within which band the assessed value of the property falls.
- Business rates. These are another tax which generates local rather than national government revenues. They are levied on the assessed rentable value of business and commercial properties.
- Inheritance tax. Inheritance tax applies to transfers of assets in excess of £325,000 after or immediately before death. The standard rate is 40% of the value exceeding £325,000. Some reduced rates and exemptions apply.
- Other taxes. These include stamp duty levied on transactions involving assets such as land, property and financial securities. Taxation of North Sea oil and gas is, essentially, a variant of corporation tax. A bank levy is applied to the liabilities and equity of banks. A number of indirect taxes also exist. These include an excise tax on motor vehicles, air passenger duty, a climate change levy, an insurance premium tax, a landfill tax and duties on gambling

In order to comprehend the impacts and fundamental patterns of the UK tax system, it is necessary to simplify its complexity. It is particularly logical to analyze the makeup of tax revenues in the UK in order to determine which taxes have the greatest impact on government income and how they have changed over time.

2. THE COMPOSITION OF UK TAX REVENUES

2.1. UK tax revenues by type of tax

Figure 1A displays the breakdown of tax receipts in the United Kingdom for the tax year 2008–2009, whereas Figure 1B illustrates the breakdown for the year 2015–2016.

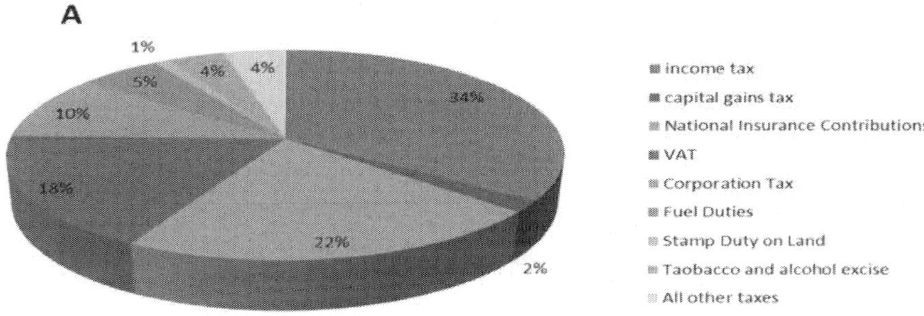

Source: HMRC Statistics

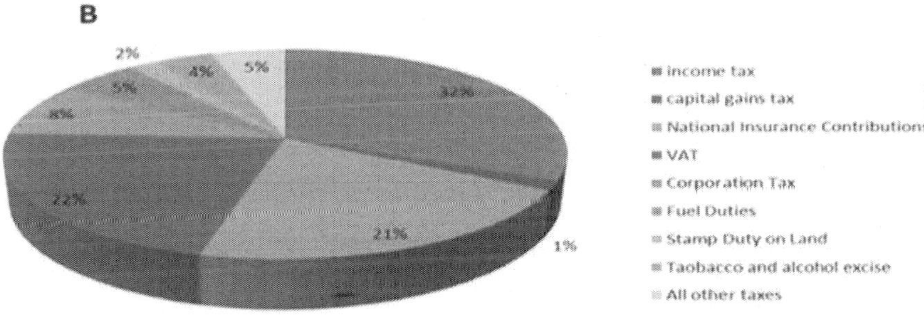

Source: HMRC Statistics

Figure 1. (A) Composition of UK tax receipts for tax year 2008–2009. (B) Composition of UK tax receipts 2015–2016.

In terms of trends the composition of UK tax revenues by type of tax has been stable between 2008 and 2009 and 2015–2016. In 2008–2009 income tax accounted for 34% of total tax revenues and in 2015–2016, in both periods representing the largest revenues for any of the taxes. The next largest contributor to overall tax revenues in 2015–2016 was VAT, comprising 22% of revenues (against 18% in 2008–2009). The contribution of NICs declined slightly in relative importance from 22% of revenues in 2008–2009 to 21% in 2015–2016. Very roughly about three quarters of UK tax revenues in both 2008–2009 and 2015–2016 was made up from three taxes—income tax, NICs and VAT. Corporation tax, the next biggest contributor, declined slightly in relative importance from 2008–2009 to 2015–2016.

Table 1 provides details of the revenues of individual taxes and their evolution over time. As has already been seen three taxes jointly provide about 75% of total UK tax revenues—income tax, NICs and VAT. Fuel duties have consistently yielded significant revenues (£27.6 billion in 2015–2016). A range of excise duties on tobacco and alcoholic drinks yielded a combined total of about £20 billion in the 2015–2016 tax year. Of the smaller taxes Stamp Duty Land Tax has shown a substantial increase in revenues between 1999 and 2016, as has capital gains tax and air passenger duty. Revenues from some taxes such as that on petroleum revenue have tended to exhibit volatility between 1 year and another but revenues from most taxes show a pattern of steady evolution over time.

Table 1. Decomposition of UK tax revenues (£ million).

	1999-00	20005-06	2009-10	2015-16
Total HMRC receipts	294,177	402,874	414,920	533,686
Income Tax	93,910	134,916	144,881	168,451
Capital Gains Tax	2,122	3,042	2,491	7,060
NICs	56,354	85,522	95,517	113,701
VAT	56,779	72,856	70,160	115,415
Corporation Tax (Onshore)	33,054	35,048	31,630	43,872
Corporation Tax (Offshore)	1,268	7,307	4,998	538
Bank Levy	-	-	-	3,392
Petroleum Revenue Tax	853	2,016	923	-562
Fuel duties	2,121	9,323	5,921	-24
IHT	22,515	23,438	26,197	27,623
Shares	2,047	3,259	2,384	4,650
Stamp Duty Land Tax	3,711	3,465	3,017	3,320
Tobacco duties	3,184	7,454	4,886	10,682
Spirits duties	5,683	7,959	8,813	9,485
Beer duties	1,804	2,309	2,570	3,147
Wines duties	2,813	3,076	3,182	3,271
Cider duties	1,657	2,308	2,949	3,973
Betting & Gaming	155	168	311	296
Air Passenger Duty	1,514	1,421	1,439	2,666
Insurance Premium Tax	882	905	1,856	3,077
Land fill Tax	1,423	2,343	2,259	3,293
Climate Change Levy	430	733	842	919
Aggregates Levy	-	744	695	1,763
Customs Duties	-	326	275	356
Source: HMRC Statistics	2,043	2,258	2,646	3,089

The composition of tax receipts in the UK remains surprisingly consistent in terms of the numerous types of taxes imposed. The key sources of UK tax revenues have remained consistent over the years, with few changes in their proportionate contribution to the overall revenue. The only significant difference between 2008 and 2009 and 2015–2016 is a rise in the relative significance of VAT receipts, which comes at the cost (mostly) of income tax and NICs.

2.2. Tax revenues by country within the UK

Figure 2 presents the composition of UK tax revenues by component country for three different time periods—2000–2001, 2007–2008 and 2015–2016.

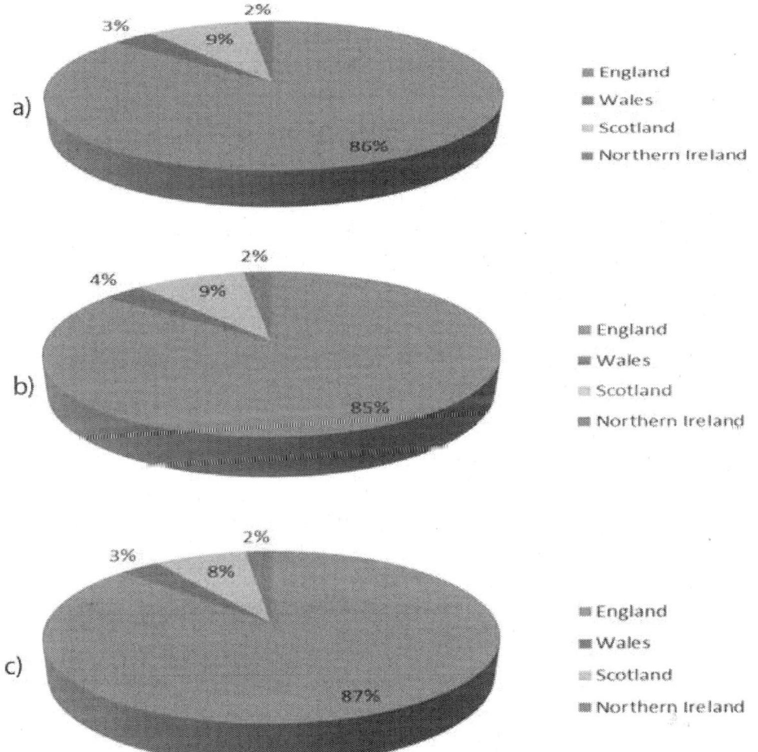

Figure 2. UK tax receipts by country (a) 2000–2001, (b) 2007–2008, and (c) 2015–2016.

The results show a stable pattern of UK tax receipts by country. In all three time periods Northern Ireland accounts for about 2% of total tax revenues, Wales for 3–4% and Scotland for 8–9%. In each time revenues from England dominate the UK total. Receipts from England accounted for 86% of the total in 2000–2001 and 87% of the total in 2015–2016.

3. INTERNATIONAL COMPARISONS

Figure 3 compares tax revenues as a percentage of GDP for a sample of countries for both 1995 and 2014. The UK is slightly below the average for all OECD countries (33% in 1995 and 34% in 2014). As a share of GDP the UK's tax revenues increased slightly from about 30% in 1995 to approximately 32% in 2014. For the majority of other countries in the sample such changes that occurred in the share of tax in GDP tended to be modest. In consequence, countries such as Chile, the United States and Switzerland were low tax in both 1995 and 2014. High tax countries in both 1995 and 2014 included Denmark, France and Italy.

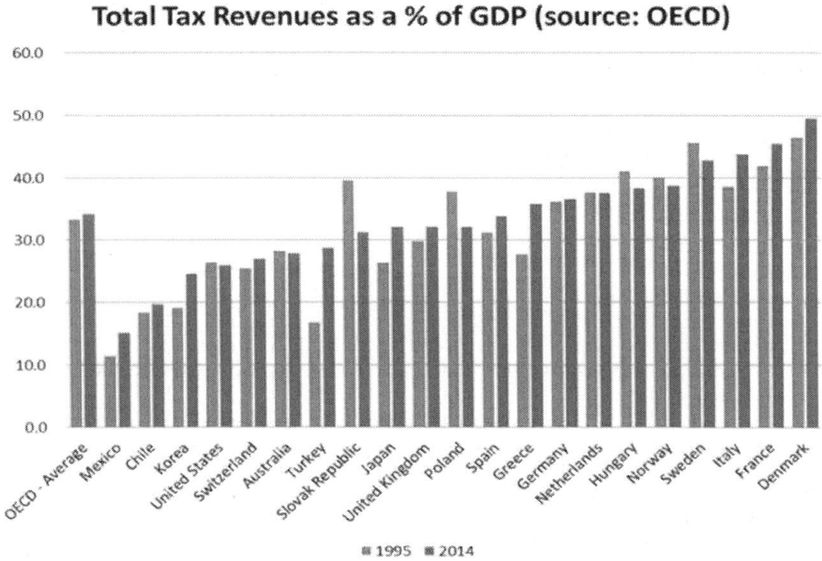

Figure 3. International comparisons of the tax burden.

Countries which showed significant increases in the share of tax in GDP between 1995 and 2014 included Turkey and Greece. Countries with a significant reduction in the share of tax in GDP included Slovakia and Poland.

3.1. International comparisons in tax composition

Table 2 presents comparisons between the UK and several other countries in the composition of their tax revenues at several points in the period between 1990 and 2014.

Table 2. International comparisons in the composition of tax revenues.

UK	1990	2000	2005	2010	2014
Taxes on income, profits and capital gains of individuals	29.4%	29.3%	29.1%	28.7%	27.4%
Taxes on income, profits and capital gains of corporates	9.9%	9.7%	9.3%	8.7%	7.5%
Social security contributions (SSC)	17.0%	17.0%	18.9%	19.0%	18.7%
Taxes on payroll and workforce	0.0%	0.0%	0.0%	0.0%	0.0%
Taxes on property	8.2%	11.6%	12.0%	12.0%	12.7%
Taxes on goods and services	31.0%	31.9%	30.3%	30.9%	33.2%
United States					
Taxes on income, profits and capital gains of individuals	37.7%	42.2%	35.4%	34.8%	39.3%
Taxes on income, profits and capital gains of corporates	7.5%	7.9%	11.0%	7.6%	8.4%

UK	1990	2000	2005	2010	2014
Social security contributions (SSC)	25.6%	23.6%	24.5%	26.1%	24.1%
Taxes on payroll and workforce	0.0%	0.0%	0.0%	0.0%	0.0%
Taxes on property	11.6%	10.2%	11.4%	13.1%	10.8%
Taxes on goods and services	17.6%	16.1%	17.7%	18.3%	17.4%
France					
Taxes on income, profits and capital gains of individuals	10.7%	18.0%	18.0%	17.1%	18.7%
Taxes on income, profits and capital gains of corporates	5.3%	6.9%	5.5%	5.6%	5.1%
Social security contributions (SSC)	44.1%	36.0%	37.0%	38.4%	37.4%
Taxes on payroll and workforce	1.9%	2.3%	2.7%	3.2%	3.5%
Taxes on property	6.3%	6.9%	7.7%	8.4%	8.5%
Taxes on goods and services	28.4%	25.9%	25.5%	24.9%	24.1%
Malaysia					
Taxes on income, profits and capital gains of individuals	11.0%	13.5%	9.9%	15.1%	13.9%
Taxes on income, profits and capital gains of corporates	31.4%	38.4%	46.8%	46.6%	52.6%
Social security contributions (SSC)	0.0%	1.9%	1.6%	1.7%	1.5%
Taxes on payroll and workforce	0.0%	0.0%	0.0%	0.0%	0.0%
Taxes on property	3.1%	3.4%	3.9%	4.0%	3.4%
Taxes on goods and services	51.3%	38.4%	33.4%	27.3%	22.8%
Argentina					
Taxes on income, profits and capital gains of individuals	0.1%	6.4%	5.7%	5.0%	8.8%
Taxes on income, profits and capital gains of corporates	0.0%	10.8%	13.7%	10.5%	9.3%
Social security contributions (SSC)	25.3%	15.8%	12.2%	21.2%	21.6%
Taxes on payroll and workforce	0.0%	0.0%	0.0%	0.0%	0.0%
Taxes on property	12.7%	6.4%	11.2%	9.0%	9.1%
Taxes on goods and services	55.7%	56.5%	54.6%	52.4%	49.5%
Source: OECD Tax Statistics					

For the US income tax is the single largest contributor to overall tax revenues, accounting for about 39% of total revenues in 2014. For the UK, in contrast, income tax was the second largest source of revenues at about 27% of the total in 2014. For the UK, VAT was the largest contributor at around 33%. In both the UK and the US the contribution of taxes on corporate income and on property are of broadly comparable significance. The US also differs from the UK with a greater contribution of social security payments but a substantially lower relative contribution from taxes on goods and services.

In France the relative contribution of social security to overall tax revenues (37% in 2014) is close to double that of the UK (19% in 2014). The UK earns proportionately more from personal income tax, corporate income tax and from taxes on goods and services than does France.

The composition of Malaysian tax revenues is almost wholly different to that of the UK. In Malaysia in 2014 receipts from taxes on corporate income accounted for about 53% of total tax revenues. The comparable figure for the UK was just 7.5%. Social security contributions and property taxes account only for a minimal share of Malaysian tax revenues but represent a more significant share of overall UK revenues. Personal income tax in the UK is approximately double the share of tax revenues of that in Malaysia (14% compared to 27% in 2014).

Argentina too has a fundamentally different composition of tax revenues than the UK. In the UK revenues from personal income tax represent the second largest share of overall receipts. In Argentina they accounted for less than 9% of the total, even less in earlier years. Taxes on goods and services are the dominant source of tax revenues for Argentina, accounting for almost 50% of total revenues. In the UK they are the single largest contributor but still account for approximately one third of the total.

4. TRENDS IN UK TAX REVENUES

Figure 4 plots monthly revenues from personal income tax between January 2002 and September 2016. These are measured in constant price terms, using the UK retail price index to adjust. To the extent that these tax revenues are dominated by income from employment it might be expected that monthly revenues would be fairly stable over time. In contrast, Figure 4 shows that revenues from personal income exhibit a high degree of volatility over time To provide a clearer a trend was fitted by using a simple linear regression in Eviews7. The results of this estimated trend are also reported in Figure 4. This shows a slight and steady increase in the real value of revenues from personal income tax over the period.

Figure 5 presents a similar analysis for National Insurance Contribution (NIC) revenues over the same period (January 2002–September 2016) in constant price terms. As with personal income tax monthly revenues exhibit considerable volatility. Again a trend was fitted using an OLS regression in Eviews7. The trend, as with personal income tax, shows a steady rise in the real value of NICs over the period.

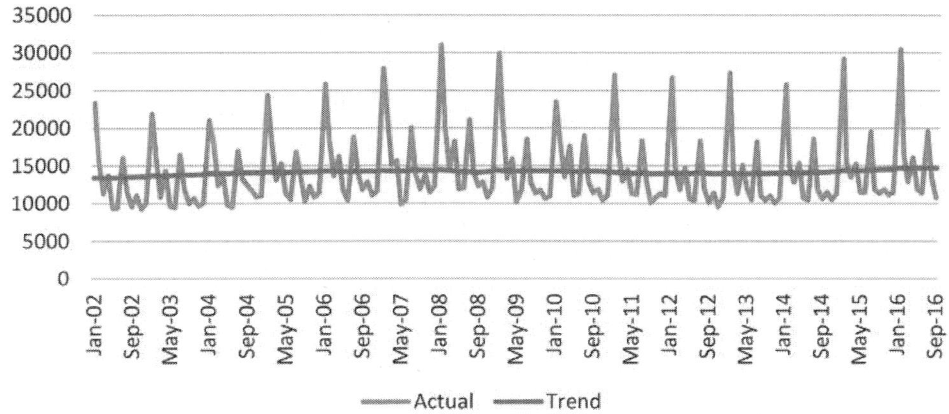

Figure 4. Personal income tax revenues in constant prices (May 2014 = 100).

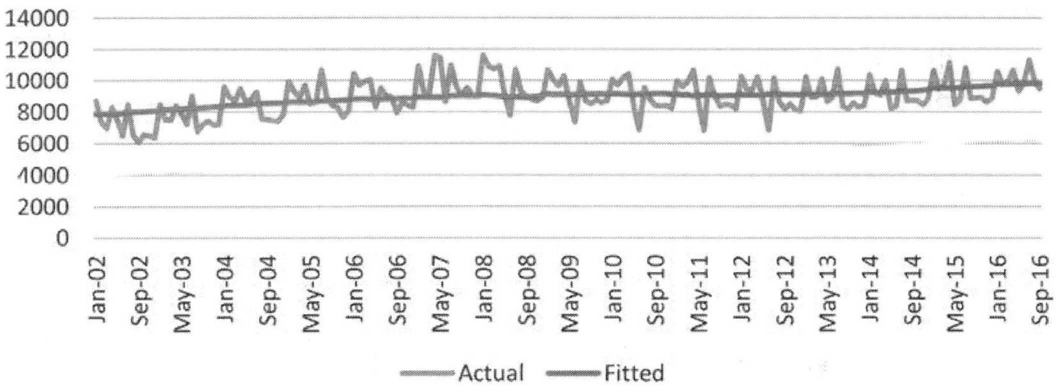

Figure 5. Monthly NIC revenues (constant prices).

Figure 6 presents monthly data on VAT revenues from April 2008 until August 2016 (earlier data were not available). Yet again receipts show considerable volatility over time. As with both personal income tax and NICs OLS regression was used to construct a trend line. The trend, as with the other two taxes, has been for a steady but gradual increase in revenues from VAT.

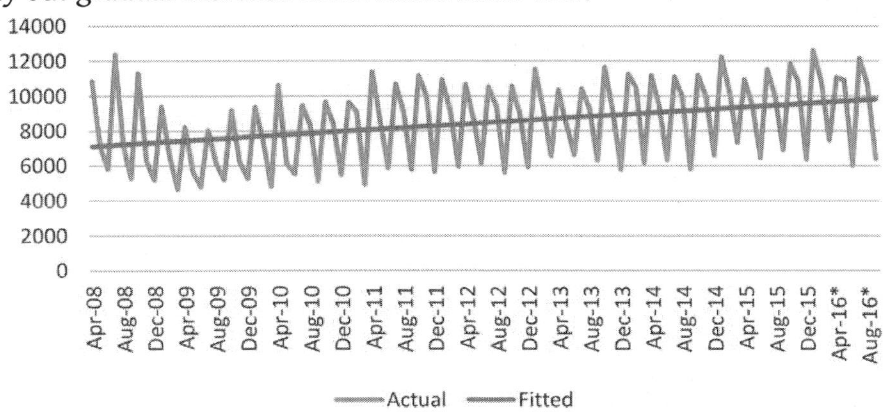

Figure 6. Monthly VAT revenues (constant prices).

Finally, Figure 7 presents a similar graphical analysis for monthly UK tax revenues (measured in constant price terms) from the period April 2008–September 2016. As with the earlier charts a trend was estimated using OLS regression in Eviews7. Total tax revenues (as shown by the trend line) remain volatile from 1 month to another but the trend is almost constant in real terms, exhibiting a very slight and gradual increase over the period.

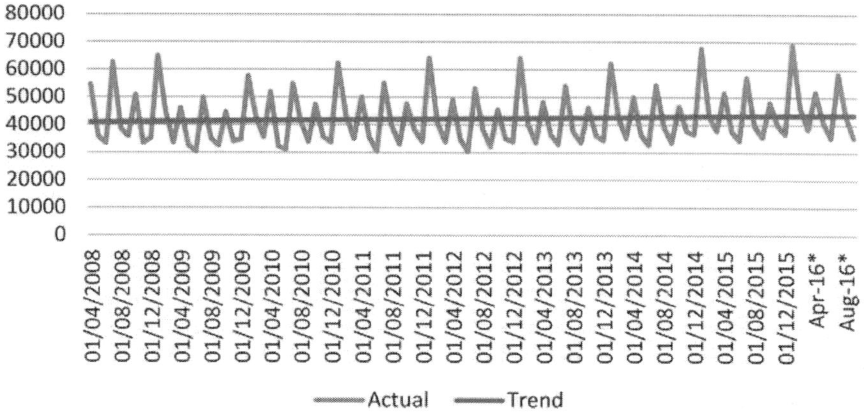

Figure 7. Total monthly tax revenues (in constant prices).

Taken overall, the figures for individual taxes and for overall tax revenues all share more or less common trends. That is, tax revenues in constant prices terms have tended to be stable over longer periods of time (the trend) but volatile between 1 month and another. The trend is for the real value of tax revenues to grow slowly and slightly i.

5. PREDICTING FUTURE TAX COLLECTIONS IN THE UNITED KINGDOM

An extensive literature exists concerning political bias in budgetary and tax revenue forecasting. Bischoff and Gohout [2] found some evidence of upward bias in tax projections in West German states. Buettner and Kauder [3], also working with data from Germany, found that Federal tax revenue forecasts were typically unbiased but still influenced by government. Jochimsen and Lehmann [4] examined national tax revenue forecasts for a sample of 18 OECD countries. They find strong support for a politically partisan effect on national forecasts of tax revenues. Brogan [5] in a study of US states found evidence of systematic under forecasting of tax revenues. Brück and Stephan [6] studied budget deficit forecasts for a sample of Eurozone countries. They found evidence of an association between politics and systematic over or under forecasting with, of course, some countries performing worse than others in this respect. Perhaps one of the most extensive and systematic studies of political influence on budget (and tax revenue) forecasting was provided by Frankel [7]. This found evidence of systematic bias in official forecasts.

Another closely related strand of the literature addresses how political influence on tax revenue forecasting might be reduced. Concern with politically influenced government revenue forecasting has led some authors such as Auerbach [8] to advocate budget rules, combined with better forecasting techniques. Frankel [7] finds budget rules not to be particularly effective but instead found the use of independent expert panels to reduce forecast bias. Frankel and Schreger [9] studied government revenue and budget forecasts in Eurozone countries, finding lower bias in those countries that have adopted budget rules. Leal et al. [10] argue in favour of transparent methods in revenue forecasting combined with clear procedures. Jonung and Larch [11] analysed the link between policy and forecasts and considered how the policy framework might be reformed to reduce influence on revenue forecasts. They argue strongly that revenue forecasts should be conducted by an independent authority to reduce potential political bias.

In the UK precisely such an independent authority exists. The *Office for Budget Responsibility* (OBR) was established by government in 2010. Its function is to provide independent analysis of public finance. Specifically it has five main roles:

- To produce detailed 5 year forecasts twice per year
- Evaluation of government performance in relation to its fiscal targets
- of the sustainability of public finances
- Fiscal risk evaluation
- of the costing of government tax and welfare measures

The OBR produces forecasts for overall revenues and also on a tax by tax basis. They use a variety of different modelling and forecasting techniques. A crude generalization would be that those taxes most closely related to economic behaviour such as personal income tax, NICs and VAT tend to be forecasted using a detailed structural of the economy. Other, smaller taxes, less obviously related to the business cycle are sometimes forecast by time series methods.

OBR reports do not just provide forecasts but also an evaluation of errors in past forecasts. A specimen of such an evaluation from the OBR's October 2016 report [12] is reproduced below (Table 3).

Table 3. Specimen OBR revenue forecast evaluation.

2015-16 VAT forecast errors						
		£ billion				
	Forecast	Outturn	Error	*of which:*		
				Economic factors	Fiscal forecasting errors	Policy changes

2015-16 VAT forecast errors						
March 2014 forecast	115	116.4	1.4	-1.9	3.8	-0.4
March 2015 forecast	114.3	116.4	2.1	-0.7	2.8	0

Source: Office for Budget Responsibility, October 2016 report

6. LOCAL TAXES

Table 4 reports collections of the two main local taxes—council tax and non-domestic rates. The information is for England rather than the UK as a whole. Collections of both taxes are reported both in terms of value and in relation to national tax receipts. Collections of local taxes are not included in the national tax receipts figure so the percentages are not shares, just a guide to the relative significance of local taxes.

Table 4. Local tax collections for England.

Tax Year	Council tax		Non-domestic rates	
	Collected £ million	Relative to national tax receipts	Collected £ million	Relative to national tax receipts
2011-12	22,083	5.4%	20,824	5.1%
2012-13	22,378	5.5%	21,873	5.3%
2013-14	23,386	5.5%	22,661	5.3%
2014-15	24,052	5.4%	23,066	5.2%
2015-16	24,782	5.3%	23,621	5.1%

Source: office at National Statistics

The results show that receipts from local taxes have broadly kept pace with national tax receipts from 2011 to 2012 until the most recent tax year. The two local taxes combined have consistently raised revenues roughly equivalent to 10% of national tax receipts.

7. CONCISE SUMMARY

This analysis of the structure and trajectory of tax revenues in the United Kingdom has offered a glimpse into an intricate system of diverse taxation. In the United Kingdom, there is a wide array of diverse taxes imposed at the national level. Examining the revenues generated by each of the many taxes is crucial for priority, both in terms of budget planning and for analyzing the potential macroeconomic effects.

When considering the overall tax burden as a percentage of GDP, the UK does not fall into the category of either a severely taxed or lightly taxed economy. In Figure 3, the UK was positioned in the middle range among the selected nations in terms of tax receipts as a proportion of GDP, both in 1995 and 2014. The tax-to-GDP ratio in the UK has exhibited a consistent level of around 30%.

The primary sources of tax revenue in the UK for the fiscal year 2015-2016 were personal income tax, which accounted for 32% of total receipts, value-added tax (VAT), which accounted for 22% of the total, and national insurance contributions (NICs), which accounted for 21%. Collectively, these three taxes constituted 75% of the total tax collections in that particular year. The structure of tax revenues in the UK has mostly remained consistent over time. For instance, in 2008-2009, the combined contribution of the three most significant taxes accounted for little more than 75% of the total.

When comparing tax revenues among different countries, the UK shows similarities to the US and France. In these countries, the main sources of revenue are personal income tax, social security contributions, and taxes on goods and services. In Malaysia, the primary source of income is derived from taxes on corporate profits, which contrasts significantly with the revenue sources in the UK. In Argentina, the majority of the total revenue comes from taxes on products and services, while personal income tax contributes only a minor portion.

In order to analyze developments in the tax revenues of the United Kingdom more thoroughly This study analyzed the monthly tax revenues for the three most significant taxes. We observed substantial variations in monthly receipts over time, therefore we applied an econometric trend to the data after adjusting them to constant price terms. The real value of tax receipts for all three primary taxes has consistently increased at a gradual pace in constant price terms. In other words, the rise in the actual worth of tax receipts has roughly matched the increase in the actual worth of GDP.

The research on budgetary forecasting, which include tax revenues, presents empirical evidence of possible political bias in the estimates of numerous nations. The independent Office for Budget Responsibility (OBR) provides tax revenue predictions in the UK. The OBR not only publishes revenue predictions for specific taxes but also provides retroactive information on the sources of mistake in previous forecasts. Ultimately, the study analyzed the income obtained by local government in England from the primary local taxes, namely council tax and non-domestic rates. The revenues generated from each of these levies have maintained a consistent level in comparison to the overall national tax receipts. Each tax has generated receipts about equal to 5% of the total national tax revenues during a sustained period of time.

AT A GLANCE

This study examines the structure and patterns of tax revenues in the United Kingdom. It offers a concise summary of the intricate structure of various taxes in the UK. Approximately 75% of all tax receipts are attributed to three primary taxes: personal income tax, national insurance contributions (NICs), and value added tax (VAT). This distribution has been consistent over a significant length of time. The tax composition of the UK is comparable to that of the US and France, as these countries rely on the same three categories of tax to generate their revenues. It has little resemblance to either Malaysia or Argentina. The paper analyzes the monthly tax revenues in the UK for these three taxes, utilizing econometrically calculated patterns. The analysis reveals that, when adjusted for inflation, revenues have exhibited a gradual and consistent increase over time, closely aligning with the expansion of real GDP. In the UK, tax revenue forecasting is mostly conducted by an autonomous organization that releases projections for specific taxes at the level of receipts. This significantly decreases the likelihood of political bias in these revenue projections.

REFERENCES

1. Pope T, Waters T. A survey of the UK tax system. In: IFS Briefing Note BN09. 2016
2. Bischoff I, Gohout W. The political economy of tax projections. International Tax and Public Finance. 2010;17(2):133-150
3. Buettner T, Kauder B. Political biases despite external expert participation? An empirical analysis of tax revenue forecasts in Germany. Public Choice. 2015;164(3-4):287-307
4. Jochimsen B, Lehmann R. On the political economy of national tax revenue forecasts: Evidence from OECD countries. Public Choice. 2016:1-20
5. Brogan M. The politics of budgeting: Evaluating the effects of the political election cycle on state-level budget forecast errors. Public Administration Quarterly. 2012:84-115
6. Brück T, Stephan A. Do Eurozone countries cheat with their budget deficit forecasts? Kyklos. 2006;59(1):3-15
7. Frankel J. Over-optimism in forecasts by official budget agencies and its implications. Oxford Review of Economic Policy. 2011;27(4):536-562
8. Auerbach AJ. On the performance and use of government revenue forecasts. National Tax Journal. 1999:767-782
9. Frankel J, Schreger J. Over-optimistic official forecasts and fiscal rules in the Eurozone. Review of World Economics. 2013;149(2):247-272

10. Leal T, Pérez JJ, Tujula M, Vidal JP. Fiscal forecasting: Lessons from the literature and challenges. Fiscal Studies. 2008;29(3):347-386
11. Jonung L, Larch M. Improving fiscal policy in the EU: The case for independent forecasts. Economic Policy. 2006;21(47):492-534
12. Office of Budget Responsibility, Forecast Evaluation Report, October 2016

6 Chapter

HOW DOES A WELFARE STATE ATTAIN FISCAL SUSTAINABILITY? AN ANALYSIS OF THE EFFECTS OF TAX FAIRNESS

1. INTRODUCTION: AN OVERVIEW

The chapter commences by addressing the assertion that all welfare states encounter fiscal challenges. Put simply, it arises from the inquiry: "Are there any methods to guarantee the financial viability of the welfare state while upholding the necessary level of welfare expenditure?" Neo-Marxist theorists in the early stages of their development anticipated that the fiscal crisis of the welfare state was inevitable as a result of inherent contradictions within the capitalist system of production. These contradictions give rise to a conflict between the increase of wealth and the need to justify its distribution [1, 2]. According to Streeck [3], the 2008 global financial crisis was an unavoidable result of the precarious marriage of capitalism and democracy in capitalist nations. His thesis posits that the financial crisis occurred due to the dismantling of democratic capitalism, as a result of capital that operates outside of democratic oversight during the shift towards neoliberalism in the postcapitalist transition. This argument also involves the reevaluation and application of new Marxist theories in the current context.

Nevertheless, it is challenging to acknowledge these assertions when we consider that the recent economic downturn has not occurred in all developed western welfare nations. It is difficult to definitively claim that the fiscal crisis of the welfare state is unavoidable. This is because Nordic countries, which offer extensive welfare benefits, do not experience this crisis. However, it is observed in Southern Europe, where welfare spending is low and the social security system is not as well-established as in other western welfare states. Hence, it is imperative to ascertain the type of welfare state that can maintain fiscal sustainability, as well as discern the distinction between fiscally sustainable nations and those that are not sustainable.

If the government has enough fiscal space and can handle increasing debt without harming fiscal sustainability for welfare spending, the issue of fiscal sustainability will not become a major concern. Ways to secure financial resources include increasing taxes or non-tax revenue, cutting public spending, adjusting expenditure priorities, improving expenditure efficiency, issuing currency, and receiving foreign aid. An effective approach for advanced welfare states to alleviate budgetary pressures is to either enhance tax collections or decrease welfare spending on significant public outlays. Frequently, in affluent nations, reductions in expenditure are regarded as more advantageous than increases in revenue [6]. There is a contention that making changes by reducing public spending is less likely to cause a recession compared to increasing taxes, and it may also have a beneficial effect on economic growth. According to this claim, the most effective approach to guarantee the long-term financial viability of a welfare state is to decrease welfare spending.

While reducing welfare spending may not be the sole solution to the financial problem confronting the welfare state, it is important to note that cutting public spending is not always viable or practical. Alesiana and Giavazzi [6] emphasize that implementing public spending reduction initiatives alongside suitable monetary policy is crucial for achieving sound financing, but it may not always be feasible. It is worth mentioning that European Union (EU) countries have restricted their monetary policies to operate only at the national level [7]. Moreover, the abrupt decrease in welfare benefits frequently triggers resistance from the public in the form of limitations on the government's ability to address welfare needs arising from new social dangers, as well as political opposition from individuals who previously benefited from welfare programs [8, 9]. Undoubtedly, reallocating and streamlining expenses can be an effective method of obtaining financial resources within a specified budget in the near future. Over time, the diminishing benefits of budget rebalancing and rationalization always decrease, making them no longer a core option [5].

Hence, our attention should be directed towards the mobilization of resources to ensure reliable and long-lasting funding [5]. This study specifically examines the tax system, which serves as the primary means of generating revenue for advanced welfare countries compared to other ways of resource mobilization. Taxation is crucial in maintaining the capability of national policies [10]. Additionally, it has the potential to either stimulate or hinder the growth of capital accumulation, which serves as the foundation for the tax revenue of welfare states, by influencing the investment, savings, and labor habits of individuals and corporations [11]. Furthermore, taxation plays a crucial role in regulating the individuals within a political community and establishing a reciprocal obligation between them. The formation of taxation is intricately linked to the sustainability of both political and social aspects [12].

The subsequent section, Section 2, analyzes previous studies on the factors that influence the long-term financial viability of the welfare state. The purpose is to identify the shortcomings of these studies and introduce the strategy of this current study, which aims to overcome these limitations. Section 3 outlines the research methodology utilized in this study. Section 4 presents the findings of the investigation, while Section 5 explores the consequences and significance of this study.

2. THEORETICAL BACKGROUND

2.1. Existing research on determinants of fiscal sustainability

Studying the financial challenges of the welfare state is a fundamental and recurring topic in welfare state research. The subject matter is categorized into two types of studies: those that examine economic issues and those that examine institutional factors.

2.1.1. Economic factors

Macroeconomic determinants affecting the fiscal sustainability of the welfare state encompass economic growth rates, interest rates, the disparity between economic growth rates and interest rates, economic openness, financial market accessibility, and inflation.

The fiscal viability of the welfare state is directly linked to economic growth [13, 14, 15, 16]. If the economy has consistent growth, the tax can be effortlessly collected. Specifically, a progressive tax system can be implemented with increasing tax rates corresponding to increases in income, resulting in a tax rate growth that surpasses the rate of economic growth. Furthermore, the inflation that occurs alongside economic expansion can result in a significant reduction in the value of debt. This is because debt is considered a nominal asset, with a fixed value that is carried forward into the future. During the low growth phase, tax revenue was constrained, leading to a probable rise in real debt burdens. Furthermore, as a result of the decline in income, it was inevitable that the debt burden would escalate.

The effects of interest rates on national debt have also been important [13, 16]. In the context of the emphasis on interest rates, some studies have focused on the initial level of debt [17, 18]. This is because countries with high initial debt have high interest rates on national debt, and their fiscal capacity is sensitive to changes in interest rates [19]. Therefore, there is a greater risk that fiscal sustainability will be weaker than that found in countries with low debt level.

Meanwhile, some studies have demonstrated that primary balance is important [14, 20]. Sakuragawa and Karou [14] examined the phenomenon that the real interest rate on government bonds is low, while the national debt surge is comparable to the gross domestic product in developed countries as well as Japan by incorporating the concept of intermediation cost is explained. Specifically, government bonds are not very sensitive to interest rate changes because intermediation costs lower deposit interest rates and bond return replaces deposits. Therefore, they argued the interest rate was not the primary factor, but, rather, the level of the primary balance.

Some have paid attention to access to markets where the government can borrow money [21, 22, 23, 24]. Drelichman and Voth [23] attempted to account for the fact that eighteenth-century England, whose financial position was worse than Spain's in the sixteenth century, did not face insolvency. Specifically, England was able to borrow at a lower rate of interest than the market interest rate through financial repression, so the cost of interest was low. Thus, the interest burden on repayment of government bonds could be significantly reduced. Moreover, with financial globalization, the government took notice not only of the domestic market, but also the foreign market. In particular, low-income countries with low financial capacity can reduce the burden of foreign debt by improving access to financial markets due to globalization [13, 22, 24], while developed countries do not have a statistically significant impact of the global capital market on fiscal sustainability [24].

In the past, inflation was the main variable of fiscal soundness [25]. Because the national debt is a nominal asset, a slight rise in prices alone can significantly lower the real value of government bonds. However, recently developed countries have guaranteed the independence of the Central Bank in order to prevent inflation risks arising from the arbitrary use of monetary policy. Thus, the importance of monetary policy and inflationary taxation on fiscal soundness has weakened [26]. Especially in the case of European Union countries, it is argued that monetary policy cannot be utilized in accordance with the reality of each country, and thus, it is further argued that there is a limit to the guarantee of financial stability [13, 26].

As faith in monetary policy diminished, the significance of fiscal policy started to be highlighted [26]. The primary factor of utmost significance is the demographic phenomenon of population aging. The aging of the population results in a decline in the workforce available to contribute to public finance, an escalation in the responsibility of providing care, and a rise in welfare expenditure for the elderly. Consequently, this could escalate the fiscal strain on the government and compromise financial stability. Government spending can have a favorable impact on the sustainability of national debt, although this depends on the specific industry or kind of expenditures. Kaplanoglou and Rapanos [27] show that enhancing the progressive tax burden can help achieve fiscal sustainability in terms of financial revenues.

2.1.2. Institutional factors

Institutional factors identified in the empirical study are divided into two areas: political systems and financial systems. The former is a form of political decision-making [28], such as the electoral system or the political decision-making, and the latter implies a condition that restricts the adoption of fiscal policy [28].

The influence of elections has been considered important in relation to political institutions [29, 30, 31, 32, 33, 34, 35]. Theoretically, as politicians have incentive to increase the likelihood their reelection by using more public spending and debt accumulation. In addition, this may cause financial instability when financial status is arbitrarily adjusted in a strategic act to hinder the ability of the next elected candidate to enact policy. The empirical research also examines the relationship between political change and national debt accumulation, but the results are not constant [36, 37]. Some authors point out that these inconstant results are related to the lack of control over the nature of political systems in each country [38], because the structure of decision-making changes the incentives of politicians [39].

At first, decentralization has become a major concern in terms of the decision-making structure of fiscal policy. When there are a large number of participants in the decision-making process, each participant may represent only a narrow range of interest groups. Therefore, it may not be easy to reach consensus due to conflicting interests among participants. Indeed, if there is a structured coalition government or a strong bipartisan system, fiscal soundness is likely to be undermined [40]. In addition, there are slight differences in operational definitions, but generally, it is argued that the higher the number of expenditure departments or the larger the size of the Cabinet, the lower the financial performance [41, 42, 43, 44]. In addition, there is a tendency for expansion of deficit and debt when there are a large number of effective political parties in the coalition or there is a small share of the ruling party in Parliament [43, 45].

The ideological composition of the Cabinet was also affected. The greater the proportion of politicians supporting a left-wing ideology in the Cabinet, the greater the likelihood that the state's fiscal soundness will deteriorate [43]. Traditionally, politicians who support a leftist ideology are relatively supportive of public spending, particularly welfare spending, and have a tolerance for fiscal deficit [46, 47]. However, it is difficult to say with certainty that finances are unstable in the tradition of a representative system. This is consistent with Schmidt [48], who contended that the political composition or ideological differences of a government should not only lead to differences in financial performance, but that the political and economic conditions of each country should also be taken into account. In countries where a social democratic ideology is dominant within the Cabinet, social security spending is generally high, but the level of welfare spending and debt accumulation in these countries has not been high since mid-1970s [48]. While the left wing is generally favorable to a high tax burden and increased public spending, it is also true that differences in the composition of financial and tax systems have played a more important role than ideology in actual history [10].

As mentioned above, the influence of political formulations is limited, and studies focusing on financial systems have recently expanded. Since 1970s, OECD countries have pursued a series of reforms to effectively manage government spending growth and overcome fiscal deficits [49, 50]. In addition, it is necessary to establish a budget system for total budget allocations. In recent empirical studies, the introduction of a top-down budgeting system has had a positive effect on fiscal soundness [27]. In addition, the introduction of explicit fiscal rules has proved effective [51].

The introduction of a fiscal system that controls public expenditures and revenue levels is effective in promoting fiscal soundness, but caution is needed in interpreting it. First, the effectiveness of the fiscal system affects final fiscal performance in combination with the attributes of the political system in each country [52]. Indeed, Hallerberg et al. [32, 33] formulate a centralization index and a rule index for the political system and fiscal policy decision structures to determine their impact on the rate of change in national debt. According to their results, strong fiscal rules in a representative council system and a concentration of decision-making power over fiscal policy decisions in a majoritarian system or among mixed-government countries have a statistically significant effect on reducing the national debt ratio.

2.2. Limitations of existing studies and approaches of this study

There are two limitations in the existing research in identifying the determinants of fiscal sustainability of the welfare state. These are further divided into two dimensions: the measurement of dependent variables and the composition of independent variables.

2.2.1. Measuring the fiscal sustainability of the welfare state

In the previous study, the fiscal sustainability of the welfare state has been replaced by the level of the primary balance or the national debt level. However, the financial condition of the state cannot be exclusively evaluated using either values, because it means that even if deficit occurs, state can recover fiscal balance without default [53, 54, 55]. Moreover, the financial problems of the welfare state are not problems that can be solved through the technicalities that control the level of public expenditures or tax revenues. This is, in the end, a matter of politics [8]. Therefore, in order to gain a comprehensive understanding of fiscal sustainability, it should be conceptualized and measured in accordance with the economic structure and institutional capacity of the state.

Related to this, the research of Ostry et al. [56] and Ghosh et al. [57] is useful. Their research reflects the context in which public finance is embedded [58]. Changes in financial conditions do not always cause financial crises in the welfare state. We must consider the political, economic, and social contexts that might lead to a financial crisis.[2] They define the fiscal space as the gap between the debt limit and current debt level implied by the country's historical fiscal adjustment for understanding fiscal sustainability like Figure 1 [56, 57].

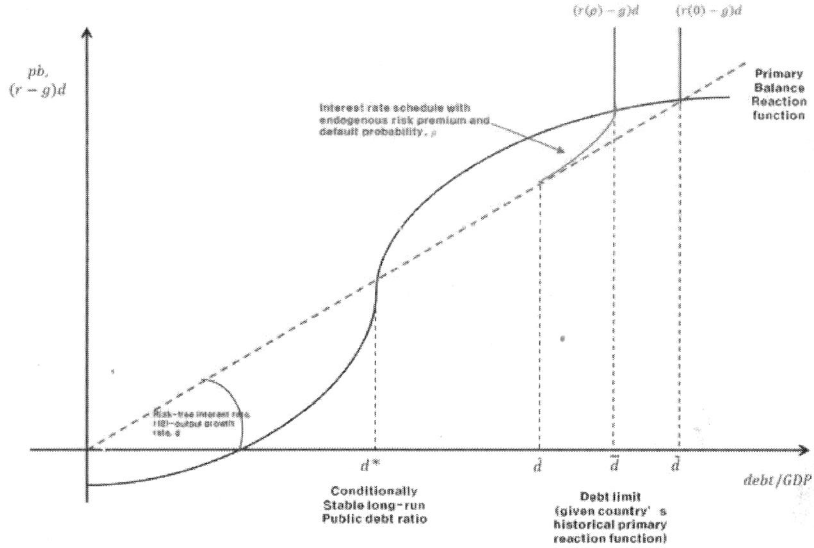

Figure 1. Determination of debt limit from Ostry et al. [56]: 8; Ghosh et al. [57]: F11.

First, the solid line represents the behavior of the primary balance as a function of debt. It reflects the nonlinear relationship between the primary balance and the public debt. Specifically, the primary balance shows little response to rising debt at very low levels of debt. Fiscal policy makers do react to changes in the level of public debt unless the public debt is fairly high [59], so the increase in the primary balance appears negligible. However, excessively high levels of debt may make it difficult to offset debt accumulation, because the marginal response of the primary balance to public debt is lower [60] and adjustment effort peters out as tax increases or spending cuts become politically infeasible [61].

Next, the dashed line shows the effective interest rate schedule, given the interest rate-GDP growth rate differential multiplied by the debt ratio. At low levels of debt, the interest rate is the risk-free rate, by assuming that output growth is independent of the public debt or the interest rate, so this schedule is simply a straight line with a slope determined by the risk-free interest rate-growth rate differential. When there is an unexpected economic shock, there is a stronger likelihood that public debt will accumulate, which means the debt reaches the debt limit, the interest rate is rapidly increased because of risk premiums. In this case, creditors may be reluctant to buy public bonds because of concerns about the potential for the country to declare bankruptcy. To secure public finances, countries should be willing to raise the interest rate through the application of risk premiums because of the increased default risk. This is represented by the solid rising curve between $\hat{d}$ and d^{-}.

Between these two lines, there are several intersections. The lower intersection ($d*$) defines the conditional stable point. There is positive relationship between the primary balance and the public debt, so if a shock raises the debt level above this point, then the primary balance in subsequent periods will offset the higher interest payments and the debt ratio returns to its long-run average. However, the upper intersection (d^{-}) cannot guarantee fiscal sustainability. If the debt exceeds this point, then it will rise forever, because the primary surplus will never be enough to offset the growing debt. This point represents the public debt limit, which is the critical point of debt led by the historical fiscal response without special action of the government [56]. If there is no fiscal space and a debt limit, current fiscal stance does not take the ability to afford the debt burden. That is, country is not always facing a fiscal crisis, but it is difficult to ensure the fiscal sustainability unless significant change of current fiscal stance [56].

In this study, I analyze the fiscal sustainability of the welfare state by determining the fiscal space of the welfare state using the methods employed by Ostry et al. [56] and Ghosh et al. [57]. Nevertheless, I have incorporated further factors to assess the fiscal sustainability inside the welfare state. Initially, I choose variables to calculate the fiscal reaction function, relying on theoretical principles and prior research. I removed several variables (openness, inflation, oil prices, and nonoil commodity prices) that were identical and substituted them with more suitable variables in order to prevent issues with multicollinearity. Furthermore, while assessing the budgetary sustainability of the welfare state, I specifically consider public welfare spending rather than the whole public expenditure. Furthermore, the interest rate is determined using the vector autoregressive (VAR 1) model, as proposed by Polito and Wickens [62, 63]. This approach is employed to circumvent the issues arising from arbitrary rules and to accurately capture the endogenous connection between debt and interest rate.

2.2.2. Determinants of fiscal sustainability of welfare states

Although the composition of the national finance has recently been pointed out as a determinant of fiscal sustainability [6, 27], empirical research has lacked reflection them. In the previous study, total public spending and total tax burden level were mostly considered, focusing on identifying whether spending cutoff strategies and tax expansion strategies are more effective to ensure fiscal sustainability [56, 64]. It is true that those were difficult to suggest specific policy measures to enhance the fiscal sustainability of the welfare state. Related to this, this study focuses on tax structure as a determinant of fiscal sustainability of welfare state.

Basically, tax is a representative resource mobilization tool of the advanced welfare state. Therefore, the level of tax burden in terms of public revenue should be discussed in relation to the fiscal sustainability of the welfare state. In order to cover welfare expenditures, a certain level of tax burden must be guaranteed, but if the tax burden is too high, it is not easy to increase the burden level [19, 65]. There are many reasons for the increase in incentives for tax avoidance and tax evasion. On the other hand, too low level of tax burden can also negatively impact fiscal sustainability. This is because there is a high possibility that sufficient financial resources are not available for public expenditure.

In addition, the structural characteristics of tax, especially tax equity, should be considered as the main factors. Because taxation inevitably violates the private ownership of a member, a lack of reasonable grounds for who owes taxes can lead to tax resistance and promote social conflict and division. Therefore, taxes must be imposed on the basis of justifiable grounds to secure political support for welfare states [12]. Indeed, the views on the taxation of the public are determined not by the level of burden but by the fairness of burden [27, 66]. The fairness of taxation can be defined as the principle of the ability to pay and the benefit principle. The former is the view that members of society are obliged to pay taxes regardless of the benefits they receive from the state as a member of the state. Accordingly, it is fair and desirable to pay taxes according to the ability to pay or to charge. On the other hand, the principle of benefit attaches importance to the exchange of benefits from tax and public goods, with the view that the taxpayer will pay the benefits of the provision of national services. In other words, it is fair to pay fair compensation for benefits.

Tax on the basis of each principle can have a different impact on the fiscal sustainability of a welfare state. First, in relation to the principle of ability to pay, direct taxation with a high tax rate can have a negative impact on economic growth by lowering incentives for labor and high tax evasion in the high-income class. On the basis of this, the enhancement of tax progressivity may hinder the fiscal sustainability of the welfare state. However, it is also true that people are not always opposed to high-level taxation [67]. In addition, the Progressive Tax System can be designed to lower income inequality by designing the higher income group to pay a higher tax burden than the low-income group, thus contributing to social sustainability by preventing conflicts between taxpayers and beneficiaries due to worsening income distribution.

Meanwhile, the horizontal equity, one part of ability to pay, is also considered. Related to this, the possibility of taxation of capital and property is lowered due to the intensification of tax competition caused by globalization [68], and advanced welfare countries have shown a tendency to rely on a consumption tax rather than an income tax. Unlike in the past, the gap between the labor and the capital is significantly increasing, while the gap between the labor and the consumption is significantly decreasing. Recalling that vertical equity and horizontal equity are inseparable, and that inequity on one side is not offset by the achievement of equity through other principles [69], the inhibition of confidence that the tax burden is fairly distributed can make it difficult and may not only lead to a lack of financial resources to support the welfare state, but also to difficulties in obtaining political support. Thus, the widening gap between tax sources have a negative effect on the fiscal sustainability of the welfare state as the level of equity is raised to the level of horizontal equity.

On the other hand, social security contributions and the contributions of the private sector are closely related to the principle of benefit. This is mainly used for specific social security purposes so that it can maintain actuarial soundness and positively affect the fiscal sustainability of the welfare state. In addition, political support will likely be high because it pays for the benefits that will come in the future [70]. Particularly in the case of contributions by the private sector, the loyalty of the contributors may be higher because it is more exclusive than the social security tax. However, this may lead to the undesirable exclusion of low-income people, which may hinder social and political sustainability. In this sense, it is possible that the social security system is limited to a small number of full-time workers and the corporation, so it leads to unfairness in the tax burden and severe tax resistance [71, 72, 73].

As mentioned above, each aspect of equity in the tax structure may have different impacts on the fiscal sustainability of the welfare state. In addition, the tax structure may change the impact of welfare expenditures on the fiscal sustainability of a welfare state. First, increasing welfare expenditures worsens the nation's financial condition. However, if the level of welfare spending is combined with a sufficient level of tax burden and a fair tax burden, then the negative impact of welfare expenditures may decrease [61, 74]. Thus, we must examine the moderating effects of tax structure on the impact of welfare expenditures and fiscal sustainability, as well as the direct effects of tax structure on fiscal sustainability.

3. RESEARCH METHOD

3.1. Analysis target and timing

The analysis of national finances should incorporate careful selection of the analysis target because analysis results may be different depending on which country is analyzed. Because, there is a huge gap between the high- and low-income countries' socioeconomic development levels, especially in terms of the level of public expenditures, the taxation capacity, and the tax structure, so it is necessary to analyze the two groups separately. This chapter analyses the 17 OECD countries, and considering the possibility of data access and the analysis of OECD major countries is reasonable in order to draw implications in the establishment of a welfare state with a financial balance. Specifically, the analysis includes Austria, Belgium, Canada, Denmark, Finland, France, Germany, Greece, Italy, the Netherlands, Norway, Portugal, Spain, Sweden, Switzerland, the United Kingdom, and the United States.

Next, this chapter analyzes the fiscal sustainability of welfare states over the course of 28 years, from 1986 to 2013, while the independent variables, including tax structure and welfare expenditures, are based on the period from 1985 to 2012, lagged term (t - 1), considering temporal precedence as a requirement for causality.[3] Those OECD countries have undergone a series of welfare and tax reforms to alleviate the burden of national financing, having experienced severe economic downturns during the mid to late 1970s. Since the effects of reform are not immediately apparent, but, rather, come after a certain period of time, this study has limited its analysis to late 1980s, specifically since 1986 (independent variables since 1985). In addition, until early 1990s, most advanced welfare states demonstrated a relatively moderate increase in national debt. However, since mid-1990s, sovereign debt has soared, and concerns about the national debt have become more widespread since the 2008 global financial crisis. Therefore, it is possible to derive timely policy implications for ensuring the fiscal sustainability of the welfare state by analyzing the period when the national debt had soared and a widespread financial crisis occurred.

3.2. Method of analysis

This study constructs simultaneous equations to control the inverse causal relationship between welfare expenditures and fiscal sustainability by examining the effects of tax structure on the fiscal sustainability of the welfare state. Existing studies have focused on the impact of fiscal spending on fiscal soundness [55, 64]. It is not only welfare expenditures that affect national finances, but also the government's fiscal capacity for welfare expenditures, which will be limited if finances are not sufficient in the long term. In other words, the financial condition of the state also affects welfare expenditures. If the effect of financial power on welfare expenditures is not reflected in the analytical model, there is a possibility that the estimation will be biased due to the endogeneity problem. In this study, the simultaneous equations model is set and analyzed. Thus, this study constructs a simultaneous equations model with two dependent variables. The first dependent variable is the fiscal sustainability of the welfare state and is measured by the fiscal space of each year on each welfare state. The second dependent variable is the level of public social welfare expenditures, which reflects public welfare efforts or the level of benefits enjoyed by the public.

Model estimations are adopted as a three-step least-squares method devised by Zellner and Theil [75]. This is a combination of the two-step least-squares method and the seemingly unrelated regression model, and all of the equations comprising the simultaneous equations are simultaneously estimated so that the correlation between the error terms of each equation is reflected in the analysis [75]. Using this method, we can derive the coincidental estimator from the simultaneous equations model and find a more efficient estimator than the one using the two-step least-squares method. Additional consideration utilizing national panel data is also considered for treating the endogeneity problem caused by non-modeled factors in the use of national panel data, which may lead to bias in statistical estimation. Specifically, a fixed-effects model with national dummy variables is constructed and analyzed in each equation of simultaneous equations. Additionally, the financial capacity of advanced welfare states has undergone structural changes since late 2000s [76], so the equations analyzed reflect the effect of timing changes, including year dummy (before 2008 and after then) variables.

3.3. Operational definition of variables

3.3.1. Dependent variables

The fiscal sustainability of the welfare state, the first dependent variable, is measured as fiscal space, which can be specified by the gap between current debt levels and debt limits according to Ostry et al.'s [56] and Ghosh et al.'s [57] method of calculating. Fiscal space is not merely a source of funds to meet the current welfare needs of the public. Rather, it plays an important role in resource mobilization to cover future spending, as well as cushioning against unexpected risks [77, 78]. In other words, the issue of fiscal space is a question of whether countries can finance their obligations, including social security, without sacrificing economic growth and stability based on fiscal sustainability [5, 50]. Therefore, fiscal space can be a useful tool in examining the fiscal sustainability of the welfare state.

In order to derive the abovementioned fiscal space as shown in Figure 1, it is necessary to estimate the fiscal reaction function and select the appropriate gap between the interest rate and the growth rate [57]. This is because it is necessary to determine the debt limit of each country on the basis of the intersection of the estimated base on the fiscal reaction function and the interest repayment schedule. This study estimates the fiscal reaction function through pooled time series analysis and uses a vector autoregressive model for estimation to establish the gap between the appropriate interest rate and the growth rate. The description of variables used for estimating the fiscal reaction function is shown in Table 1.[4]

Table 1. Variables for estimating the fiscal reaction function.

Categories			Definition	Sources
Dependent variable		Primary balance	Government net borrowing or net lending excluding interest payments on consolidated government liabilities /nominal GDP	OECD Economic Outlook OECD Social Expenditures database
Independent variables	Finance	Lagged debt	General government debt/nominal GDP	
		Output gap	Difference between actual and potential (calculated using the Hodrick-Prescott filter) real GDP	
		Welfare expenditures	Public social expenditures	
		Inflation	$\Delta CPI_t/CPI_{t-1}$	
	Economic structure	Unemployment	(unemployed/labor force population) × 100	OECD Employment and Labor Market Statistics database
		Service industry	(Workers in service industry/total employment) × 100	
		Part-time worker	(Non-voluntary part-time workers/labor force population) × 100	
		Self-employed	(Self-employed/labor force population) × 100	
		Capital openness	Chinn-Ito index	Chinn-Ito index (KAOPEN) http://web.pdx.edu/~ito/Chinn-Ito_website.htm

Categories			Definition	Sources
Independent variables	Political and fiscal systems	Age dependency	(People over age 65/total population) × 100	OECD Employment and Labor Market Statistics database
		Future dependency	(People over age 65/population of ages 15–64) × 100, years ahead	
		Election	Dummy variable of election (election: 1 no election: 0)	
		Political stability	Ideological differences between current and former Cabinet	
		Majority system	Majority system:1; others: 0	Comparative political dataset/IMF fiscal rules database
		Centralization	Index of federalism, the strength of the bicameral legislature, effective number of parties, and the independence of the financial management organization	
		Fiscal rule	Index of introduction of fiscal rules, legislative base of rules, existence of the multiyear spending limit, exception and financial monitoring system	

Next, one of the most important points to be considered in determining the national debt limit, along with the estimation of the fiscal reaction function, is how to define the long-term interest rate [56].[5] This study estimates the interest rate through vector autoregulation (VAR), similar to the works of Polito and Wickens [62, 63]. This is because it not only avoids arbitrary problems, but also reflects the endogenous relationship between the interest rate and the national debt level (Table 2). In this study, the autoregressive model is used to model the endogenous relationship between the interest rate and the national debt, adding government revenue, government spending, debt, the economic growth rate, the inflation rate, and short- and long-term interest rates [62, 63]. The gap between these estimates and the average real growth rates of the countries from 1985 to 2013 are used to calculate the debt limit and determine fiscal space based on this. The contents and data sources of the variables used for estimating the fiscal reaction function are shown in Table 3.

Table 2. Descriptive statistics of variables for estimating fiscal reaction function.

Categories			Mean	Standard deviation	Minimum	maximum
Dependent variable	Primary balance		0.249	3.693	-10.505	15.786
Independent variables	Finance	Lagged debt	71.681	28.763	16.079	166.190
		Output gap	-0.049	2.622	-13.851	9.579
		Welfare expenditures	22.763	4.857	10.565	35.517
		Inflation	2.935	2.755	-0.900	23.015
	Economic structure	Unemployment	7.636	3.940	0.457	24.885
		Service industry	2.679	0.793	1.232	5.384
		Part-time worker	3.071	1.649	0.295	9.714
		Self-employed	15.987	9.116	6.596	50.708
		Capital openness	1.929	0.908	-1.188	2.390
		Age dependency	15.466	2.015	10.255	21.080
		Future dependency	31.238	5.987	18.478	51.991
	Political and fiscal systems	Election	0.292	0.455	0.000	1.000
		Political stability	0.353	0.772	0.000	3.000
		Majority system	0.177	0.382	0.000	1.000
		Centralization	0.672	0.115	0.370	1.000
		Fiscal rule	0.419	0.172	0.242	0.908

Table 3. Variables for estimating long-term interest rate.

Variables	Definition	Sources
Public debt	General government public debt as a percentage of GDP	OECD Economic Outlook No. 97 (Edition 2015/1)
Government revenue	Total government revenue as a percentage of GDP	
Government expenditure	Total government expenditure as a percentage of GDP	
Output gap	Difference between actual GDP and potential GDP	
Inflation	The annual percentage change in the cost to the average consumer of acquiring a basket of goods and services	
Long-term interest rate	Interest rate of government bonds maturing in 10 years	
Short-term interest rate	Interest rate which is money market rate	
Note: Each variable in the estimated variables is included from t-1 to t-n. t = 1, ..., 27.		

The second variable that is influenced by or dependent on other factors is the amount of money spent on public welfare. This refers to the extent of social welfare spending by the government, specifically in terms of the benefits provided to the general populace. The ratio of total public welfare expenditures to the gross domestic product is utilized to regulate variations in the level of welfare spending based on the economic size of each country.

3.3.2. Independent variables

Tax structure, a major independent variable, is divided between the ability to pay principle and the benefit principle. The former is divided into horizontal equity and vertical equity. In the following section, the operation of each principle is described in detail.

3.3.2.1. Measurement of horizontal equity

Horizontal equity identifies the tax rate gaps between labor and assets and labor and consumption, which are major tax sources because guaranteeing horizontal equity means that equity is ensured among the tax bases [69]. In particular, despite the weakening of the tax base, labor taxation is the most basic tax in all countries, so horizontal equity is defined based on the labor tax. Specifically, each tax rate on the labor, capital, and consumption of households is derived, and the tax rate differences between labor and capital taxation and labor and consumption tax are calculated based on the method proposed by Macdaniel [79].[6] According to the study, the government's tax revenue is divided into labor tax, capital tax, private consumption tax, and private investment tax. Moreover, the average tax rate of each tax base is calculated by dividing each tax revenue from each source into the corresponding tax sources [79].

3.3.2.2. Measurement of vertical equity

Vertical equity, one aspect of the ability to pay principle, is measured by the relative ratio of the marginal tax rate among income groups. In the comparison of tax progressivity among countries, a structural approach has been utilized to compare statutory tax rates, as well as comparisons within specific income groups. In this study, the structural approach is used for cross-country comparisons, although it is recognized as a valid criticism that it is difficult to reflect differences in taxable income using this [84, 85]. This study reflects the differences between progressivity in the low-income class (67% of the average wage and the average wage) and progressivity in the high-income class (comparison between the average wage and the average wage of 167%) considering data accessibility. In addition, this study measures the actual burden level, excluding benefits by subtracting the transfer of cash so as to more accurately measure the progressivity. For the values which are calculated as mentioned above, the higher the value, the stronger the progressivity, and the lower the value, the more regressive it is. This approach has the advantage of reflecting the degree of progressivity. The marginal tax rate data among the income groups for estimates of progressivity were used by Nickell [86] and the OECD Taxing Wages Database. That database provides marginal tax rates for OECD countries between 1960 and 2004. On the basis of this, the OECD has calculated the marginal tax rates of each country since 2000, and this study combines both datasets.

3.3.2.3. Measurement of the benefit principle

The benefit principle is specified by the share of social security contributions in GDP. [73]. The social security contribution is a welfare state resource that is provided through contributions made by both employers and employees. This is a fixed use, and it is based on a burden corresponding to the benefits, so it is related to the benefit principle [73]. In addition, the proportion of private contributions to welfare resources supplements the benefit principle. Private contributions are generally designed to benefit contributors and are not reflected in government finances, but they can have a positive impact on the maintenance of public welfare programs. Thus, this study uses the share of social security contributions and the share of private contributions as proxies of the benefit principle.

3.3.2.4. Measurement of the generosity of the welfare system

To identify the simultaneous equations model, the second equation, which has welfare expenditures as a dependent variable, requires additional exogenous variables, excluding the fiscal sustainability variable with endogeneity.[7] In this study, it is possible to identify the model by introducing the generosity of the public pension, unemployment insurance, and disease insurance of the Comparative Welfare Entitlement Dataset 2 (CWED2). These variables are calculated by taking into account the replacement rate, qualifications, scope or coverage, and waiting period [87, 88] (Table 4).

Table 4. Variables for estimating determinants of fiscal sustainability of welfare state.

Categories		Variables		Definition	Sources
Equation. 1	Dependent variable	Fiscal sustainability		Fiscal space	OECD National account
	Independent variables	Welfare expenditures		Total public welfare expenditures/nominal GDP	OECD Social Expenditure Statistics
		Tax burden		Total tax revenue/nominal GDP	OECD Tax Dataset
		Ability to pay principle	Horizontal equity	Gap between effective tax rate on labor and capital	OECD National account
				Gap between effective tax rate on labor and consumption	
			Vertical equity	((1 - marginal tax rate of average wage 67%)/(1 - marginal tax rate of average wage 100%)) - 1	Nickell [86] OECD Tax Dataset
				((1 - marginal tax rate of average wage 100%)/(1 - marginal tax rate of average wage 167%)) - 1	
		Benefit principle		Social security contribution/nominal GDP	OECD Revenue Statistics: financing of social security benefits
		Mandatory private contribution/ total social security revenue			
Equation 2	Dependent variable	Welfare expenditures		Total public welfare expenditures/nominal GDP	OECD Social Expenditure Dataset
	Independent variables	Fiscal sustainability		Fiscal space	OECD National account
		Generosity of public pension		Index of public pension considering the replacement rate, qualifications, scope or coverage, and waiting period	Scruggs et al. [88] CWED2
		Generosity of public unemployment insurance		Index of unemployment insurance considering the replacement rate, qualifications, scope or coverage, and waiting period	
		Generosity of sickness insurance		Index of sickness insurance considering the replacement rate, qualifications, scope or coverage, and waiting period	

4.DETERMINANTSOFFISCALSUSTAINABILITYINWELFARESTATE

In the first equation, where fiscal space as the proxy of fiscal sustainability is a dependent variable, welfare expenditures have a negative impact on the fiscal sustainability of the welfare state at a statistically significant level. Moreover, although the magnitude of the negative impact of welfare spending in the lagged term is somewhat smaller, the increase in welfare spending in the medium term tends to lower fiscal space even further. On the other hand, the results of the second equation with welfare expenditures as a dependent variable demonstrate that welfare expenditures increase as the fiscal space increases at a statistically significant level in the medium-to-long term. This supports the argument that it is essential to secure fiscal space for the continuation of the welfare state in the long term [5].

If we look only at the results of the first equation, it may be argued that public welfare spending must be reduced, because welfare spending lowers the nation's fiscal space. However, considering the political resistance that may be caused by the reduction of welfare expenditures, it is necessary to examine how financial resources can positively influence fiscal sustainability. At first, increase of tax revenue may offset the negative impact of welfare expenditures on the fiscal sustainability of the welfare state as well as positively affect the fiscal sustainability of the welfare state (Table 5).

It is noted that the perception of tax burden is not absolutely influenced by the level of the burden, but, rather, it is influenced by equity [27, 66]. This study examines the level of tax burden and the taxation specified by the fairness principle and analyzes the effects of taxation on the fiscal sustainability of the welfare state. In addition, the impact of welfare expenditures on fiscal sustainability may change according to tax structure characteristics. Even if increases in welfare expenditures negatively affect national finances, the public may be willing to accept the financial burden in the long run by recognizing the tax burden differently, considering the benefits of the fiscal expenditure and the fairness of the tax burden [61, 74]. For example, a fair tax burden may offset the negative effects of welfare spending and may also have a positive impact on fiscal sustainability. For this reason, this study focuses on the moderating effect of the tax structure on the relationship between welfare expenditures and fiscal sustainability, as well as the direct effect of the tax structure on fiscal sustainability.

Table 5. Determinants of fiscal sustainability on welfare state.

Dependent variables	Independent variables	Model 1		Model 1	
		Coefficient	Standard error	Coefficient	Standard error
Fiscal sustainability Equation 1	Welfare expenditure (t - 1)	-4.32	0.35***	-3.74	0.34***
	Welfare expenditure (t - 5)			-1.79	0.39***
	Tax burden	1.01	0.50*	1.84	0.52***
	Gap between effective tax rate on labor and capital	1.64	2.23	-2.66	4.07
	Gap between effective tax rate on labor and consumption	-83.60	22.70***	-131.0	22.53***
	Progressivity (low income group)	-23.78	8.80**	-31.50	9.79**
	Progressivity (high income group)	4.37	7.72	-0.18	7.51
	Social security contribution	3.80	1.21**	4.75	1.17***
	Mandatory private contribution	0.97	0.22***	0.99	0.21***
	Welfare expenditures * tax burden			0.24	0.05***
	Welfare expenditures * gap between effective tax rate on labor and capital			-4.32	3.50
	Welfare expenditures * gap between effective tax rate on labor and consumption			-11.85	3.97**
	Welfare expenditures * progressivity (low income group)			3.36	2.04
	Welfare expenditures * progressivity (high income group)			-0.77	1.56
	Welfare expenditures * social security contribution			0.29	0.12*
	Welfare expenditures * mandatory private contribution			0.08	0.04*
	Constant term	139.13	24.05***	141.22	23.26***

Dependent variables	Independent variables	Model 1 Coefficient	Standard error	Model 1 Coefficient	Standard error
Welfare expenditures Equation 2	Fiscal sustainability (*t* – 1)	-0.07	0.01***	-0.07	0.01***
	Fiscal sustainability (*t* – 5)	0.05	0.01***	0.05	0.01***
	Generosity of public pension	0.44	0.16**	0.40	0.16*
	Generosity of public unemployment insurance	0.42	0.16*	0.42	0.17*
	Generosity of sickness insurance	0.65	0.24**	0.65	0.24**
	Constant term	11.67	2.51***	11.66	2.52***
Number of obs	Equation 1	304		303	
	Equation 2	304		303	
F value	Equation 1	792.60***		779.06***	
	Equation 2	122.71***		123.37***	

*p < 0.05.
**p < 0.01.
***p < 0.001.
†p < 0.1.

Specifically, the gap in the tax base, especially the gap between labor taxation and consumption taxation, hinders the fiscal sustainability of the welfare state in terms of horizontal equity. In addition, the negative effect of welfare expenditures on fiscal sustainability tends to become larger as the gap between labor and consumption increases. On the other hand, the direct effect of the gap between labor and capital taxation does not have a statistically significant effect. Although the impact of the gap between labor and capital taxation on fiscal sustainability is not statistically significant, the negative effects of welfare expenditures on fiscal sustainability intensify when tax equity is not guaranteed. In other words, if the tax burden is not distributed fairly among the tax base (labor, capital, and consumption), it is difficult to guarantee the fiscal sustainability of the welfare state.

Second, the effect of the level of vertical equity on the fiscal capacity of the welfare state is mixed. The increase of the progression in low-income groups has a statistically significant negative impact on fiscal capacity, while the increase of progressivity in the high-income group is not statistically significant, although it demonstrates a positive impact. In addition, the latter also alleviates the negative impact of welfare expenditures at a statistically significant level. Related to this, it is worth noting that severe income tax burdens on low-income households may have a negative impact on improvements to the fiscal sustainability of the welfare state.

It is crucial to highlight the connections between the ability to pay principle and the budgetary viability of the welfare state. This is also linked to the combination of analysis outcomes in terms of vertical equity. The welfare state's golden age, spanning from 1930 to 1960, was sustained on the principle of fiscal capacity. As the concept of social justice rooted on fairness became more widely accepted, there was an increased call for redistribution of wealth, leading to a strengthening of the progressive nature of income tax. This is because in the context of social problems generated by the dominance of the capitalist economic system, the government makes sincere efforts to control the working class and address the inequality resulting from this imbalance. It is challenging to assert that higher levels of progressive taxation invariably result in more tax avoidance by the high-income class [67].

Nevertheless, if it is acknowledged that progressive tax burdens are unjust, their consequences may differ, as the high load can promote tax evasion [67]. In the 1970s, taxes were increased at a higher rate than income, leading to intense political unrest. To prevent corporations from moving capital overseas and skilled labor from emigrating, most high-income countries ceased rising income taxes. The issue is in the potential trade-off between reducing the tax burden on capital and maintaining fairness in the distribution of taxes across different income levels. This trade-off could result in a negative impact on horizontal equality with labor taxation and the decrease of tax progressivity [68]. If the principle of ensuring the ability to pay is not assured, it can lead to a reduction in tax progressiveness and an increase in the likelihood of tax avoidance.

Vertical equity and horizontal equity are inherently interconnected. Both principles have distinct objectives that they aim to accomplish, and it is not possible for one principle to substitute the other. Put simply, the inequities resulting from each equity principle cannot be balanced out by achieving equity through other equity enhancements. Therefore, each principle must be addressed directly to rectify the injustice on either side [69]. When the principle of vertical equality fails to provide tax benefits to enterprises and individuals with high incomes, it may lead to a violation of the fair burden condition. This can increase people's aversion to paying taxes and encourage tax cheating, even if horizontal fairness is improved. Thus, achieving fairness in distributing the burden based on one's ability to pay can be accomplished when both horizontal equity and vertical equity successfully achieve their respective objectives. Taxation will subsequently serve to make a good contribution to budgetary sustainability.

Conversely, the rise in social security payments has a favorable impact on the long-term financial stability of the welfare state, aligning with the benefit principle. Additionally, it helps counterbalance the adverse effects of welfare spending on fiscal sustainability. Furthermore, the rise in compulsory private payments has a beneficial impact on fiscal sustainability, although not being accounted for in the government's financial records. These public financing sources that are linked to the benefit principle are very politically acceptable due to the ease of obtaining political support for the burden based on the direct benefit to the individual [89]. Furthermore, private compulsory contributions can help reduce the financial strain on a nation that lacks public welfare initiatives. Thus, to ensure the long-term financial stability of the welfare state, it is imperative to broaden the funding sources by effectively utilizing both social security contributions and private contributions.

5. CONCISE SUMMARY

This study aims to identify the factors that determine the long-term financial viability of the welfare state, with a specific focus on the tax system. According to the study's findings, it is crucial to get financial resources in order to sustain the welfare state. While fiscal space may not immediately contribute to the growth of welfare expenditures, it does have a significant impact in the medium-to-long term. The issue lies in the fact that an escalation in welfare spending might potentially deteriorate fiscal sustainability. It is not always suitable to address this by reducing welfare expenditures in order to expand fiscal space, as this aligns with the viewpoints of those who oppose the welfare state. Thoughtlessly reducing welfare spending is not feasible due to the need for collaborative social efforts to address various social problems. Similarly, continuously increasing welfare spending without considering the fiscal space can gradually undermine the financial foundation of the welfare state. Hence, it is crucial to explore methods of upholding welfare expenditure while guaranteeing budgetary viability.

The analytical results clearly demonstrate that the tax burden level plays a crucial role in maintaining fiscal sustainability in the welfare state. Tax income serves as the financial foundation for sustaining the welfare state. Therefore, enhancing tax compliance to counterbalance the adverse effects of rising welfare expenditures will foster social unity. Nevertheless, the national endeavor to sustain the welfare encompasses more than simply gathering extra revenue. The onerous burden does not invariably yield a favorable effect on fiscal sustainability, and it is not always feasible for a nation to amass additional tax resources to augment welfare. Hence, the crucial factor to examine about total tax revenue is the method by which it is generated, since the choice of approach significantly affects the influence of taxation on the sustainability of economic, political, and social dimensions. According to this study, ensuring tax fairness helps maintain the financial stability of the welfare state. The tax structure's various components may enhance the fiscal sustainability of the welfare state in a beneficial manner.

The principle of ability to pay, when applied to the tax base and progressivity, can contribute positively to the long-term financial stability of the welfare state, promoting equity. The correlation between narrowing the disparity in labor taxation and consumer taxation is evidently crucial in guaranteeing fiscal sustainability. The implementation of a consumption tax may have a more favorable impact on social and political sustainability, as well as economic sustainability, compared to labor taxes. Advanced welfare countries have shown interest in indirect taxation, specifically consumption tax, as a means to generate public revenues and address financial crises. This approach is favored over direct taxes like income tax and corporation tax, which are more susceptible to economic fluctuations [90, 91, 92, 93]. Furthermore, it can aid in achieving intergenerational parity by alleviating the financial strain on elderly households, which tend to bear a greater burden [94]. Furthermore, if the labor taxation basis is compromised as a result of labor market dualization and decreasing employment rates, implementing a consumption tax grounded in universal solidarity can be an effective method to ensure a broad tax base.

However, if we just depend on the growth of the consumption tax, it can impose an excessive burden on the low-income class because of the regressive nature of the tax. Thus, it is imperative to guarantee enough welfare benefits for individuals with low incomes, in conjunction with a progressive taxation system, to alleviate the regressive burden and reduce the disparity between consumption tax and labor tax. Enhancing vertical equality can have a dual benefit: it can improve the long-term financial stability of the welfare state and ensure the tax system's political legitimacy. Additionally, it can help alleviate the regressive impact that may arise from implementing a consumption tax. It is important to highlight that implementing a progressive tax on those with high incomes does not necessarily result in tax avoidance. For instance, when the tax burden aligns with the corresponding benefits supplied by the state, a progressive tax leads to an increase in tax compliance. Therefore, in order to preserve the long-term financial stability of the welfare state, it is necessary to implement a consumption tax that distributes the tax burden fairly among all individuals based on their ability to pay.

Incorporating both the ability to pay principle and the benefit principle into the financial foundation of the welfare state is beneficial for ensuring the long-term financial stability of the welfare state. Increasing social security contributions or private contributions also yields a favorable impact on fiscal sustainability in accordance with these principles. Nevertheless, the provision of public services through these channels is restricted to a limited group of permanent staff, which can potentially lead to labor tax resistance and the marginalization of individuals with low incomes, irregular employment, or unemployment. Therefore, in order to sustain solidarity, it is necessary to diversify the funding sources of the welfare state by combining the ability to pay principle with the benefit principle.

AT A GLANCE

This study aims to discover the institutional characteristics of financially sustainable welfare governments that prioritize tax structure. This study examines the fiscal sustainability characteristics of each welfare state by analyzing data obtained from 17 OECD nations between 1986 and 2013. The three-step least-squares method is employed to analyze the relationship between budgetary sustainability and welfare expenditures in a model of simultaneous equations. Consequently, raising the tax burden level typically has a beneficial impact on the long-term financial viability of the welfare state. Nevertheless, the crucial aspect to be taken into account is the method of generating tax income, which has an impact on the long-term viability of the economic, political, and social aspects in ensuring fiscal sustainability. It is crucial to increase the fairness in the distribution of taxes based on the premise of ability to pay. Enhancing vertical equity can also have a beneficial impact on fiscal sustainability by ensuring the political acceptance of the tax and reducing the regressive burden that may arise from the implementation of a consumption tax. Ultimately, it is advantageous for the long-term financial stability of the welfare state to broaden its sources of funding by integrating both the ability to pay principle and the benefit principle.

REFERENCES

1. O'Connor J. The Fiscal Crisis of the State. New York: St. Martin's Press; 1973
2. Gough I. The Political Economy of the Welfare State. London: MacMillan Publishing Company; 1979
3. Streeck W. Buying Time: The Delayed Crisis of Democratic Capitalism. Verso: Brooklyn, NY; 2014
4. Heller PS. Understanding Fiscal Space. IMF Policy Discussion Paper, no, 05/04 Ed. Washington, DC: International Monetary Fund; 2005
5. Harris E. Financing social protection floors: Considerations of fiscal space. International Social Security Review. 2013;66:111-143
6. Alesina A, Giavazzi F. The austerity question: 'How?' is as important as 'how much? In: Corsetti G, editor. Austerity: Too Much of a Good Thing? Centre for Economic Policy Research. 2012. pp. 11-15

7. Delong JB. The austerity question: 'How?' is as important as 'how much? In: Corsetti G, editor. Austerity: Too Much of a Good Thing? Centre for Economic Policy Research. 2012. pp. 17-21
8. Guy P. Fiscal Strains on the Welfare State: Causes and Consequeces. In: Levine CH, Rubin I, editors. Fiscal Stress and Public Policy. Everly Hills, Calif: Sage Publications; 1980. pp. 23-47
9. Pierson P. Irresistible forces. Immovable objects: Post industrial welfare states confront permanent austerity. Journal of European Public Policy. 1998;4:539-560
10. Kettl DF. Deficit Politics: The Search for Balance in American Politics. New York: Longman; 2003 ch3
11. Swedberg R. The Economics and Sociology of Capitalism. Princeton, NJ: Princeton University Press; 1991
12. Martin W, Mehrotra AK, Prasad M. The Thunder of History: The Origins and Development of the New Fiscal Sociology. In: Martin W, Mehrotra AK, Prasad M, editors. The New Fiscal Sociology: Taxation in Comparative and Historical Perspective. Cambridge: Cambridge University Press; 2009
13. Agnello L, Castro V, Sousa RM. What determines the duration of a fiscal consolidation program? Journal of International Money and Finance. 2014;37:113-134
14. M, Karou H. Fiscal Sustainability in Japan. Japanese Economic Review. 2010;61(4):517-537
15. J. Determinants and consequences of fiscal procyclicality and sustainability [dissertation]. Ann Arbor: The University of York (United Kingdom); 2012
16. Aspromourgos T, Daniel R, White G. Public debt sustainability and alternative theories of interest. Cambridge Journal of Economics. 2010;34:433-447
17. Chalk NA. The sustainability of bond-financed deficits: An overlapping generations approach. Journal of Monetary Economics. 2000;45:293-328
18. A, Ardagna S, Perotti R, Schiantarelli F. Fiscal policy, profits, and investment. American Economic Review. 2002;92:571-589
19. European Union, editor. Progress and Key Challenges in the Delivery of Adequate and Sustainable Pensions in Europe. European Commission Economic and Financial Affairs; 2010
20. A. An endogenous growth model with public capital and sustainable government debt. Japanese Economic Review. 2007;58:345-361

21. CA. The precarious fiscal foundations of EMU. DNB Staff Reports 1999, No. 34. ed. DNB; 1999

22. D, Kumar M. Financial Globalization and Fiscal Performance in Emerging Markets. IMF Working Paper, No.05/212; 2005

23. M, Voth H-J. Debt sustainability in historical perspective: The role of fiscal repression. Journal of the European Economic Association. 2008;6:657-667

24. JP, Fiess N, MacDonald R. The global dimension to fiscal sustainability. Journal of Macroeconomics. 2011;33:137-150

25. R, van Winibegen S. Inflacton and the Financing of Government Expenditure in Turkey. World Bank; 1987

26. Sehovic D. The impact of the great recession on monetary and fiscal policy in developed market economics. Business. Systems Research. 2015;6(1):56-71

27. G, Rapanos VT. Tax and trust: The fiscal crisis in Greece. South European Society and Politics. 2013;18(3):283-304

28. Rose S. Institutions and fiscal sustainability. National Tax Journal. 2010;63:807-837

29. Besley T, Case A. Incumbent behavior: Vote-seeking, tax-setting, and yardstick competition. American Economic Review. 1995;85:25-45

30. Carey JM, Niemi RG, Powell LW. The effects of term limits on state legislatures. Legislative Studies Quarterly. 1998;23(2):271-300

31. Carey JM, Niemi RG, Powell LW. The effects of term limits on state legislatures: A new survey of the 50 states. Legislative Studies Quarterly. 2000;31(1):105-134

32. Hallerberg, M. Strauch, R., von Hagen J. The design of Fiscal Rules and Forms of Governance in European Union Countries. European Central Bank Working Papers No. 419; 2004

33. M, Strauch R, von Hagen J. The design of fiscal rules and forms of governance in European Union countries. European Journal of Political Economy. 2007;23(2):338-359

34. Illera RM, Mulas-Granados C. What makes fiscal consolidations last? A survival analysis of budget cuts in Europe (1960-2004). Public Choice. 2008;134:147-161

35. Miriam AG, Lucio P. Pork-barrel politics in Postwar Italy, 1953-94. American Journal of Political Science. 2008;52(2):268-289

36. Crain M, Tollison R. Time inconsistency and fiscal policy: Empirical analysis of U.S. STATES. 1969-89. Journal of Public Economics. 1993;51:153-159

37. Franzese, Robert J. The positive political economy of public debt: An empirical examination of the OECD postwar experience. 2002. Available at SSRN: https://ssrn.com/abstract=1084130 or http://dx.doi.org/10.2139/ssrn.1084130

38. Persson T, Tabellin G. Macroeconomic Policy, Credibility and Politics. Chur, Switzerland: Harwood Academic Publishers; 2000

39. Bulow J, Rogoff K. Sovereign debt: Is to forgive to forget? American Economic Review. 1989;79(1):43-50

40. Ko H. Empirical analysis of fiscal soundness and public social expenditure: A lesson for the future direction of the Korean welfare state. Asian Social Work and Policy Review. 2014;8(1):16-33

41. Kontopoulos Y, Perotti R. Fragmented Fiscal Policy. New York: Columbia University; 1997

42. Kontopoulos Y, Perotti R. Government fragmentation and fiscal policy outcomes: Evidence from the OECD countries. In: Poterba J, von Hagan J, editors. Fiscal Rules and Fiscal Performance. Chicago: University of Chicago Press; 1999

43. Volkerink B, Hann J. Fragmented government effects on fiscal policy, new evidence. Public Choice. 2001;109:221-242

44. Perotti R, Kontopolos Y. Fragmented fiscal policy. Journal of Public Economics. 2002;86:191-222

45. Ricciuti R. Political fragmentation and fiscal outcomes. Public Choice. 2004;118(3-4):365-388

46. Iverson T, Soskice D. Electoral institutions and the politics of coalition: Why some democracies redistribute more than other. American Political Science Review. 2006;100(2):165-180

47. Iverson T, Soskice D. Distribution and redistribution: The shadow of the nineteen Century. World Politics. 2009;61(3):438-486

48. Schmidt. The welfare state and the economy in periods of economic crisis: A comparative study of twenty-three OECD nations. European Journal of Political Research. 1983;11:1-26

49. A. Budgeting for fiscal space. OECD Journal on Budgeting. 2009;9(2):1-18

50. Marcel M. Budgeting for fiscal space and government performance beyond the great recession. OECD Journal on Budgeting. 2014;13(2):1-37

51. Bohn H, Inman RP. Balanced Budget Rules and Public Deficits: Evidence from the U.S. States. National Bureau of Economic Research Working Paper No. 5533; 1996

52. Hallerberg M, von Hagen J. Electoral institutions, cabinets negotiations, and budget deficits within the European Union. In: Poterba J, von Hagen J, editors. Fiscal Rules and Fiscal Performance. Chicago: University of Chicago Press; 1999

53. Croce E, Hugo Juan-Ramon V. Assessing Fiscal Sustainability: A Cross Country Comparison. Washington, DC: International Monetary Fund; 2003

54. Richter C, Paparas D. How Reliable Are Budget Sustainability Tests A Case Study for Greece? International Network for Economic Research Working Paper; 2012

55. Afonso A, Jalles JTA. Longer-run perspective on fiscal sustainability. Empirica. 2014;41:821-847

56. Ostry JD, Ghosh A, Kim JI, Qureshi MS. Fiscal Space. Washington, DC: IMF Staff Position Note 10/11 September; 2010

57. Ghosh AR, Kim JI, Mendoza EG, Ostry JD, Qureshi MS. Fiscal Fatigue, Fiscal Space and Debt Sustainability in Advanced Economies. National Bureau of Economic Research Working Paper No.16782.; 2013

58. Campbell JL. The state and fiscal sociology. Annual Review of Sociology. 1993;19:163-185

59. Bajo-Rubio O, Carmen D, Vicente E. Is the budget deficit sustainable when fiscal policy is nonlinear? Journal of Macroeconomics. 2006;28:596-608

60. Mendoza EG, Ostry JD. International evidence on fiscal solvency: Is fiscal policy "responsible"? Journal of Monetary Economics. 2008;55(6):1081-1093

61. S. Tax mixes and the size of the welfare state: Causal mechanisms and policy implications. Journal of European Social Policy. 2006;16:360-373

62. V, Wickens M. Assessing the fiscal stance in the European Union and the United States, 1970-2011. Economic Policy. 2011;68:601-629

63. Polito V, Wickens MA. Model-based indicator of the fiscal stance. European Economic Review. 2012;56(3):526-551

64. A, Abeysinghe T. The experience of some OECD economies on tax smoothing. Applied Economics. 2013;45:2305-2313

65. H. Understanding the Finance of Welfare. The Policy Press: University of Bristor, UK; 2009

66. JL. What American think of taxes. In: Martin IW, Mehrotra AK, Prasad M, editors. The New Fiscal Sociology: Taxation in Comparative and Historical Perspective. Cambridge: Cambridge University Press; 2009

67. Doerrenberg P, Peichl A. Progressive taxation and tax morale. Public Choice. 2013;155(3-4):293-316. DOI: 10.1007/s11127-011-9848-1

68. Genschel P. Globalization amd the trasformation of the tax state. European Review. 2005;13:53-71

69. S. Welfare State Changes and its Relationship with Tax Structures (in Korean) [Dissertation]. Seoul, Korea: Chung-Ang University; 2010

70. E, Steinmo S. The end of the strong state? On the evolution of Japanese tax policy. In: Martin W, Mehrotra AK, Prasad M, editors. The New Fiscal Sociology. Cambridge: Cambridge University Press; 2009

71. Ferrera M. The southern model of welfare in social Europe. Journal of European Social Policy. 1996;6(1):17-37

72. M. Welfare states and social nets in Southern Europe: An introduction. In: Maurizio, editor. Welfare State Reform in Southern Europe: Fighting Poverty and Social Exclusion in Italy, Spain, Portugal and Greece. London and New York: Routledge; 2005. pp. 1-32

73. Obinger H, Wagsshal U. Social expenditure and revenues. In: Castles FG, Leibfried S, Obinger H, Pierson C, editors. The Oxford Handbook of the Welfare State. London, UK, Oxford; 2010. pp. 333-352

74. S. Taxation and Democracy: Swedish, British and American Approaches to Financing the Modern State. New Haven: Yale University Press; 1993

75. Zellner A, Theil H. Three-stage least squares, simultaneous estimation of simultaneous equations. Econometrica: Journal of the Econometric Society. 1962;30(1):54-78

76. P, Mendoza EG, Zhang J. What is a Sustainable Public Debt? NBER Working Paper, No. 21574; 2015

77. I, Chaim J, Cummins M. Identifying Fiscal Space—Options for Social and Economic Development for Children and Poor Households in 184 Countries. UNICEF Social and Economics Policy Working Paper; 2011

78. I, Cummins M, Karunabethy K. Fiscal Space for Social Protection Options to Expand Social Investments 187 Countries. Geneva: International Labour Office; 2015

79. Macdaniel C. Average Tax Rates on Consumption, Investment, Labor and Capital in the OECD 1950-2003. Arizona University; 2007

80. J. Indicators of Fiscal Sustainability. Washington DC: IMF Working Paper; 1991

81. E, Razin A, Tesar L. Effective tax rates in macroeconomics. Journal of Monetary Economics. 1994;34(3):197-323

82. Carey D, Rabesona J. Tax ratios on labour and capital income and on consumption. OECD Economic Studies No. 35, 2002/2; 2002

83. Carey, D., Rabesona, J. Tax rations on labour and capital income and on consumption. In: P. Sorensen, edior. Measuring the Tax Burden on Capital and Labour. Cambridge, MA: MIT Press; 2004

84. Attinas M-G, Checherita-Westphal C, Rieth M. Personal Income Tax Progressivity and Output Volatility Evidence from OECD Countries. European Working Paper. No. 1380; 2011

85. Paturot D, Mellbye K, Brys B. Average Personal Income Tax Rate and Tax Wedge Progression in OECD Countries. OECD Taxation Working Papers, No. 15, OECD Publishing; 2013

86. W. The CEP-OECD Institutions Data Set (1960-2004). London, UK: London School of Economics and Political Science; 2006

87. Scruggs L. Social Welfare Generosity Scores in CWED 2: A Methodological Genealogy. CWED Working Paper Series. WP 01; 2014

88. Scruggs L, Detlef J, Kati K. Comparative Welfare Entitlements Dataset 2 Codebook. Version 2014-03. University of Connecticut and University of Greifswald; 2014

89. Lieberman ES. Taxation data as indicators of state-society relations: Possibilities and pitfalls in cross-national research. Studies in Comparative International Development. 2002;36(4):89-115

90. Kato J. Regressive Taxation and the Welfare State. Path Dependence and Policy Diffusion. Cambridge: Cambridge University Press; 2003

91. Beramendi R, Rueda D. Social democracy constrained: Indirect taxation in industrialized democracies. British Journal of Political Science. 2007;37:619-641

92. Kneller R, Bleaney MF, Gemmel N. Fiscal policy and growth: Evidence from OECD Countrie. Journal of Public Economics. 1999;74:171-190

93. Kneller R, Bleaney MF, Gemmel N. Testing the endogenous growth model: Public expenditure, taxation, and growth over the long run. Canadian Journal of Economics. 2001;34(1):36-57

94. Jones R, Fukawa SK. Achieving Fiscal Consolidation while Promoting Social Cohesion in Japan. OECD Publishing. Paris: OECD Economics Department Working Papers. NO. 1262; 2015

7 Chapter

EFFICIENT TAXATION OF CONSUMPTION IN THE CONTEXT OF DYNAMIC CHANGES

1. INTRODUCTION: AN OVERVIEW

Taxation serves as the primary revenue stream, derived from the exercise of governmental sovereignty. Within this framework, taxation serves as a fundamental political instrument employed by states to achieve economic, social, and political objectives. Taxation, when used as a fiscal policy tool, enables states to implement successful strategies to achieve their macroeconomic objectives. Tax policies play a crucial part in achieving the macroeconomic goals listed above, as taxation is a powerful weapon for the government to influence the economy. According to the social state model, taxation functions as a means of transferring resources. Promoting equality and justice for every individual is widely recognized as a primary responsibility of states towards its inhabitants.

In order to ensure equality and justice, it is necessary for the state to redistribute resources collected through taxation from higher income groups to lower income groups, allowing citizens from all income brackets to access public services. Within this context, taxation serves as the primary means of transferring resources between different socioeconomic levels.

The optimal taxation literature extensively discusses the comprehensive design of taxes, which are crucial policy tools for the state to achieve efficacy and equality. Optimal taxation is a tax system that takes into account the competing goals of equality and economic efficiency in society, with the aim of maximizing social wealth as the primary objective.

Given the current circumstances, where the government possesses imbalanced knowledge regarding an individual's social and economic attributes, the objective of redistributing income can be achieved by implementing taxes that cause distortions. To achieve income justice, the state can utilize distortionary taxes, although this approach requires sacrificing economic efficiency. Optimal taxation focuses on the tax subject, tax rate, and tax base in order to reduce inefficiencies in generating a specific amount of tax income.

Within this perspective, there are two primary studies in the field of optimum taxation that pertain to the taxation of a certain issue. Ramsey [1] examined the optimal taxation issue from the perspective of consumption, while Mirless [2] focused on revenue as the subject of taxation in his seminal research. Both research aimed to identify the optimal tax rates within the specific tax framework.

In the Ramsey approach to optimal taxation, the assumption is made that governments cannot use lump sum taxes to generate the necessary budget revenue. As a result, they must rely on distortionary taxes, which leads to a loss of wealth in terms of economic efficiency and deviates from the optimal solution. Ramsey focuses on the tax subject and rate that will minimize efficiency loss within this framework. According to the Ramsey approach, there is a consensus that the government has the authority to implement a linear income tax in addition to a commodities tax [3].

The concept of optimal commodity taxation, first introduced by Ramsey in 1927 and further developed by modern approaches, is founded on the principle of the inverse elasticity rule. This rule suggests that goods with low demand elasticity should be subject to higher tax rates in order to minimize efficiency loss. Additionally, the Corlett-Hauge Rule states that goods that complement leisure and influence consumer preferences between work and leisure should also be taxed at a higher rate.

Ramsey's inverted elasticity rule proposes that taxes should be levied at a higher rate on items with low demand elasticity and at a lower rate on goods with high demand elasticity, in order to achieve equal impact on all goods.

The primary criticism of this rule stems from the observation that essential products, which are necessary for meeting basic necessities, have a low price elasticity of demand. Conversely, luxury goods have a high price elasticity. It is argued that taxing luxury products at a lower rate than essential goods, based on the idea that consumers are similar, has a detrimental impact on the fairness of taxation.

The belief that luxury items exhibit high demand elasticity while necessary products exhibit low demand elasticity may be subject to revision when considering both short and long time periods and taking into account the competitive dynamics that drive market economies. For enterprises operating in the market economy, the fundamental objective is to maximize profits. In order to achieve this, two crucial factors to consider are the total revenues and demand elasticity of their products. Companies have the potential to boost their overall revenue by reducing the demand elasticity for their products. Within this particular framework, companies strive to diminish the susceptibility of their produced goods to fluctuations in price.

With the opening of markets to foreign countries and the liberalization of trade, the size of the market and the level of innovation grow. This can lead to an increase in the price elasticity of demand, particularly for essential commodities, since there is a greater chance for substitution. [5, 6, 7] However, in order to mitigate this risk, companies attempt to reduce the responsiveness of demand for their products by establishing strong brand identities and fostering customer loyalty to these brands [8]. Brand loyalty, particularly in product categories that include luxury goods like technology gadgets and automobiles, diminishes buyers' responsiveness to changes in the product's price.

Changing market conditions alter the demand elasticity of luxury and necessity products within this framework. Consequently, it becomes necessary to reevaluate the fundamental assumptions of optimal taxation and the criticisms directed towards it.

2. OPTIMAL TAXATION

The most fundamental goal of economic and fiscal policies is to maximize wealth. This goal includes quite large sub-goals, such as providing stability, growth, efficient allocation of resources, and fair income distribution. Tax is the primary fiscal tool to be used in reaching the goals in question. Among the tax applications that are under the changing and developing state understanding, what type of taxation is the taxation that serves the goal of wealth maximization is considered in the literature especially in the framework of "Optimal Taxation" theory.

While within classical welfare economics understanding, optimal taxation theory considers taxes as effective tools in assuring resource allocation; new welfare economics' view of utility measurement and impossibility of inter-personal comparisons caused economic area of interest to rotate to Pareto efficiency. This situation focused on substitution effect of taxes, creating efficiency loss and lasted until the study of Mirrlees [2], which targets resolution of equality and efficiency conflict.

In this context, optimal taxation is the taxation that reflects the preferences of the society between equality and efficiency with rivaling goals, and that has social wealth maximization as the starting point. Within this scope, balance between the goals of justice (equality) in taxation and economic efficiency is tried to be redressed. On the other hand, trade-off between these goals created different approaches to the topic.

Existence of the relevant trade-off depends on the existence and influence of distortionary taxes. In today's conditions, in which the state has asymmetrical information about the individual's social and economic characteristics, the goal of income redistribution can be possible through the use of distortionary taxes.

The state can assure income justice by using distortionary taxes only by conceding economic efficiency. Because of this reason, optimal taxation lays emphasis on tax subject, tax rate, and tax base, which will minimize efficiency loss in securing a certain amount of tax revenue.

3. DISTORTIONARY TAXES AND EFFICIENCY LOSS

In general terms, distortionary taxes can be defined as taxes that will influence or change economic decisions of taxpayers. The main reason for distortionary taxation on the other hand is to assure redistribution of revenue, which is one of the fundamental functions of the state and thus to achieve a society structure more egalitarian than the one that could have been achieved via a uniform lump-sum tax [9].

The state, which has a social aim of distributing the tax burden in a fair and balanced way within the scope of fiscal policy, needs distortionary taxes in order to realize this aim. State's complete and absolute knowledge about the characteristics of each individual in the society underlies this need. In this context, use of distortionary taxes is a consequence of the aim to redistribute revenue in a world, where the state knows characteristics of individuals only incompetently [9]. Within this scope, in the assurance of justice (equality), individuals having the same ability to pay will be assumed to be in equal conditions, and same amount of taxes will be taken from them [10].

When different abilities to pay are at stake, the state redistributes revenue in a way to load a greater amount of public expenditures to higher income groups. Different societies may have different preferences on equality and efficiency. These differences bring along different tax systems in practice. Discussions on how progressive tax structure should be in order to enable equality are a result of value judgments about equality. In this context, inequality reduced through progressive tax structure can only be possible by the acceptance of a certain amount of efficiency loss.

According to Diamond and Mirrless [11], administratively, it is not possible for the state to realize its revenue distributer goal on the grounds of social justice and revenue creator goal on the grounds of public finance, through lump-sum taxes. Since lump-sum tax is not appropriate, optimal taxation will only be a taxation that will not impair the efficiency of production. This on the other hand is only possible if the taxation on the final production can be diversified between products at no cost [12].

In the light of these explanations, optimal tax structure is defined as the tax structure, which reflects the preferences of the society between the balance of efficiency loss and equality and maximizes social wealth. Optimal taxation theory seeks answers basically to the following questions:

1. On what will the tax be taken from (income-consumption-wealth)?
2. If the tax will be taken on consumption, is it going to be at a fixed rate?
3. If the tax will be taken on wealth, how will the tax base be? [13]
4. In the following parts of this study, optimal taxation will be taken on consumption.

4. OPTIMAL COMMODITY TAXES: RAMSEY RULE

The main topic of discussion in the literature regarding optimal commodity taxes, which are approached under the heading of optimal taxation, is about the proportional structure of the taxes in question. In this context, literature searches which tax rates, single rate or varying, will create optimal results in the construction of optimal commodity taxes. Within this scope, while on one side, there is the view arguing that a single rate tax will not damage market forces and will be synonymous with a fixed rate tax on income [14]; on the other side, optimal commodity taxes within the context of Ramsey and varying rates take place.

Ramsey rule involves taxing commodity and zero capital taxes in the long run [15] for minimizing the deadweight loss. For public choice theory, equilibrium taxes and feasible tax structure apart from Ramsey analysis are important subjects because tax system can cause rent seeking when it is used as an income distribution tool [16, 17].

Optimal commodity taxation, which was proposed in 1927 by Ramsey and whose theoretical structure has developed through today's modern approaches, is based on the inverse elasticity rule, which claims goods with low demand elasticity to be taxed at a higher rate will reduce efficiency loss, and Corlett-Hauge Rule, which claims leisure complement goods that will change the preferences of consumers between working and leisure on behalf of working need to be taxed at a higher rate.

As seen in Figure 1 , tax application may cause a decrease in social wealth by changing price before and after tax. The reason behind this is the decline of production under the amount before tax because of the change in price. Minimization of this efficiency loss, which is also called excess tax burden or deadweight loss (DWL), is the purpose of the tax systems.

Under the assumption that characteristics of individuals can only be known deficiently and thus lump-sum taxes are not applicable, Ramsey searched the tax structure that will minimize efficiency loss (deadweight loss) associated to the collection of a specific amount of tax revenue. Excess tax burden is caused by the reduction in equilibrium quantity because individuals change their behaviors and consume taxed product less. Decrease in the quantity of the product depends on demand elasticity. According to Ramsey rule, tax rate imposed on the good with high elasticity should be lower than the tax rate imposed on the good with low elasticity [18]. In this way, as seen in Figure 1 , decrease in the equilibrium quantity of goods would be minimized.

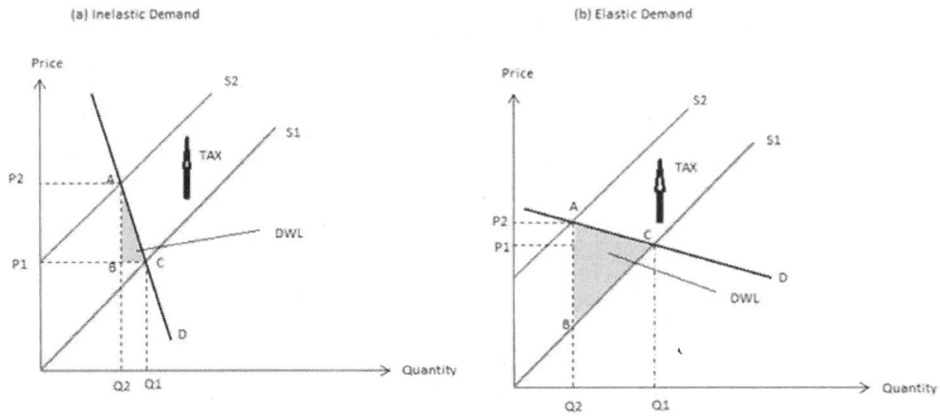

Figure 1. Deadweight loss of taxation. Source: Ref. [44].

Under the assumption that people resemble each other, Ramsey taxes are expressed as the sum of the inverses of supply and demand elasticity.

$$\frac{t}{p} = \mathrm{k}\left(1/n_u^d + 1/n^s\right) \tag{1}$$

In this equation, *t* represents tax rate per unit, *p* represents price after tax, n u d represents compensated elasticity of demand, and n s represents supply elasticity [9].

In the inverse elasticity rule suggested by Ramsey, under the assumption that supply curve is finite or, in other words, a horizontal supply curve exists, tax is stated to be inversely proportional to compensated demand elasticity. Accordingly, all goods to be affected equally from taxes are aimed by collecting lower rates of taxes from goods with high price elasticity of demand and higher rates of taxes from goods with low price elasticity of demand.

Within the framework of this purpose, Sandmo [19] expresses that Ramsey rule can be based on the following three hypotheses:

1. Being able to minimize efficiency loss, which occurs as a result of distortionary taxation, is possible through tax applications with a low substitution effect. Because of this reason, goods with prices that do not create substitution effect are the ideal subject of the tax. In other words, in cases where lump-sum taxes cannot be imposed, commodity taxes with similar effects should be imposed.
2. Goods, which will be taxed at high rates, should have a high leisure complementary level.

Elasticity of substitution between goods and leisure lies behind the fact that single rate tax, which does not change the relative prices of goods and will not be different from the lump-sum tax that will be imposed on labor income, is not optimal [14].

However, according to Corlett-Hague Rule, varying tax rates, in which leisure complementary goods that will change the preferences of consumers between working and leisure in favor of working will be taxed at higher rates, serve for the assurance of optimality in commodity taxes. In this context, Diamond [11] proposed leisure complementary goods to be taxed at relatively higher rates intended to the efficiency purpose.

3. Tax rates are expected to be inversely proportional with uncompensated own-price elasticity of demand.

The most important criticism toward the Ramsey rule composed of above-mentioned hypotheses is caused by the fact that necessity goods devoted to meet basic needs to have low price elasticity of demand and luxury goods to have high price elasticity. Under the assumption that consumers resemble each other, taxation of luxury goods at a lower rate compared to necessity goods is claimed to influence justice of taxation negatively.

5. REDISTRIBUTION AND RAMSEY TAXES

Ramsey taxes, which were pointed out in the above section in detail, are criticized because of its current assumptions and negativity they might create in income distribution.

At this point, first main criticism to Ramsey analysis is the assumption that all individuals resemble each other. The fundamental reason for the state to use distortionary taxes instead of lump-sum taxes is to have redistribution goals, which are not possible to attain in another way. In case this assumption is valid, there are no causes of the state for not imposing lump-sum taxes.

Nevertheless, when taxes are imposed within the context of inverse elasticity rule, an equal amount of decrease in demand in all goods will be caused by collecting lower rates of taxes from goods with a high possibility of change in demand amount and at higher rates from goods with a low possibility of change in demand amount; and thus, efficiency loss will be minimized. According to this approach, taxation of necessity goods, which have low compensated demand elasticity and have a large share in the consumer's budget, at a higher rate than luxury goods comes to the fore [9].

Generally, price elasticity of demand for good, which are consumed with the purpose of meeting basic needs, is low, while price elasticity of demand for luxury goods is high. Based on this rule, tax rate to be imposed on basic necessity goods will be high, and tax rate to be imposed on luxury goods will be low. What needs attention here is the assumption that consumers are alike. However, since income distribution and demand for different products will vary, such a rule will create negative results in terms of tax equity especially in developing countries. Ramsey defended this rule by placing economic efficiency to forefront. Therefore, although theoretically consistent, this analysis becomes contradictive in practice with the influence of socio-political reasons [20].

In short, when Ramsey's suggestion is applied, low-incomers, who relatively allocate majority of their income to necessity goods, have to face a high tax burden. Therefore, a conflict between the goals of decreasing the efficiency cost of tax and equitable tax emerges. Ramsey rule puts forward what needs to be done when efficiency purpose is desired to be pursued. Goal of justice is not within this rule's field of interest [18].

As a result in optimal commodity taxation, Ramsey's analysis requires a careful analysis of: the constraints on taxation; the elasticities of demand and supply; and the structure of the economy [21].

6. CHANGING DEMAND ELASTICITIES

Criticisms done within the context of the basic assumptions of Ramsey taxes' inverse elasticity rule become more serious especially on the topic of income redistribution. Inverse elasticity rule creates a conclusion in line with efficiency but to the detriment of equality by suggesting taxation of necessity goods, which occupy a heavy place in the consumption basket of lower income groups, at a high rate and goods appealing to higher income groups at lower rate depending on demand elasticity.

Besides the assumptions in inverse elasticity rule mentioned above that are subject to criticisms, another topic to be emphasized is whether demand elasticity varies within the framework of macroeconomic and microeconomic variables. A change that may occur in demand elasticity of luxury and necessity goods may build a fairer structure for the inverse elasticity rule in terms of income distribution, and the abovementioned taxes criticized in practice within the context of enabling justice in income distribution, which is among the main functions of the state, may be reassessed as part of changing demand elasticity. Under this assumption, in this part, changes in elasticity of luxury and necessity goods that could be created by macrovariables and microvariables within the changing economic conjuncture will be addressed.

6.1 Short- and long-term changing demand elasticity

Existence of substitution possibility is the primary element affecting demand elasticity. Existence of close substitutes for some goods increases price elasticity of the demand in question. As seen in Figure 2 , since development of substitution opportunities take time, while in short term, price elasticity of demand for many products is low, elasticity may increase in the long term [22]. Durable consumer goods have a different structure compared to other goods in short and long term elasticity. Despite the fact that elasticity differences are observed between terms in these goods as well, price elasticity of demand is more elastic for these goods in the short term, while it weakens in the long term [23].

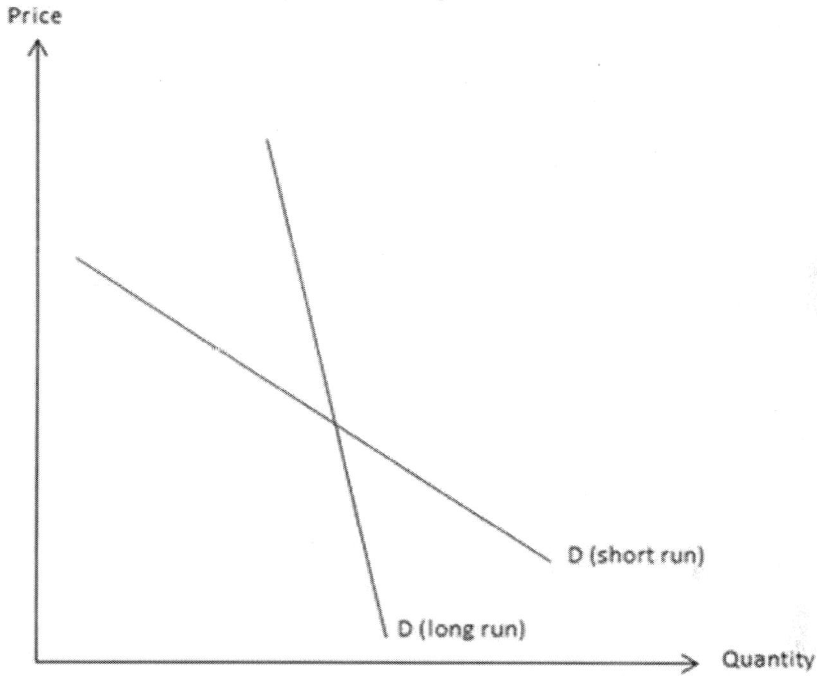

Figure 2. Changing demand elasticity.

At this point, the most basic example is the price elasticity of demand for oil changing in short and long terms against OPEC cartel shock in 1970s. Sudden price increase experienced in the so-called period was received with highly inelastic price elasticity of demand at a level that did not cause a change in the amount demanded in the short term; however, fuel efficient solutions with the technology developed in the long term allowed price elasticity of demand to increase.

In this way, short and long term price elasticity of demand for products with substitutes that need time to be developed may differ. Because of this reason, although goods with low price elasticity of demand are advised to be taxed at higher rates in Ramsey taxes within the tax structure that will not damage efficiency, in the long term, price elasticity of demand for many goods including necessity goods increases. In such a case, since tax rates will decline as part of increased elasticity, it will be difficult to achieve the budget revenue planned in the beginning without negatively affecting efficiency.

6.2 Commercial liberalization and changing demand elasticity

Criticism of Ramsey taxes, which will be applied within the scope of the inverse elasticity rule because luxury goods have high demand elasticity and necessity goods have low demand elasticity, because of its elasticity assumptions may change as part of competition, which is the main abettor of market economy today. Total revenue and demand elasticity for products are important variables in providing profit maximization, which is the principal purpose of firms competing in market economy.

Firms can increase their total revenues by decreasing the demand elasticity for their products. In this context, firms aim to decrease the vulnerability of the products they produce against price changes. Thus, they can increase their total revenues by raising product prices [24]. Yet, together with the increased competition, efficiencies [25, 26] increase, and together with liberalization, market size [27] increases.

Especially, liberalization in commerce influences export and import performances of industries, declines in tariffs cause scale increases [28], and thus, competition escalates [29]. As supported by quite a few studies, high protectionism in commerce leads firms to produce under optimal scale, and output increases to be negatively affected [30].

Commercial liberalization on the other hand allows the tariff structure to soften, large-scale firms to rise together with the increase in competition, and output levels of small-scale firms to rise [29]. Diversity increased in the market structure that grew by this means enhances the substitution opportunity between goods and thereby increases price elasticity of demand. By this way, the scale that increased through liberalization and competition raises diversity of goods and services and therefore their substitutability and serves for the increase of price elasticity of demand of all necessity and luxury goods.

6.3 Market size, innovation, and changing demand elasticity

In one of the first studies investigating the relationship between market size and innovation, Griliches [31] put forward in 1957 the existence of a significant relationship between technological change and technological adaptation and profitability and market size. In other studies analyzing different sectors following this study, a significant relationship between market size and innovation and innovation elasticity was exhibited [32, 33, 34]. In this context, the innovation process, which improves as market size grows, increases price elasticity of demand by supporting the increase of product range [35].

In the light of these analyses, macroeconomic variables, such as short and long term structures, commerce liberalization and competition, market size, and innovation, affect and change the price elasticity of demand for luxury and necessity goods. This change generally reveals itself as the increase of price elasticity of demand for goods. This macrochange of demand elasticity in both luxury and necessity goods composes a risk for firms in microterms. On the other hand against this risk, firms try to decrease the demand elasticity for their products by creating brands and increasing loyalty to these brands [8].

Brand loyalty decreases the sensitivity of consumers to the prices of products especially in product groups such as technological products and automobiles. At this point, it is useful to mention about brand loyalty as a microvariable effective on price elasticity of demand.

6.4 Brand loyalty and changing demand elasticity

While price elasticity of demand increases as part of macrovariables, this increase in elasticity requires different precautions to be taken, since it would negatively influence profit maximization goal. One of the fundamental elements for the firms to obtain their profit maximization goal is to be able to increase total revenue with price increases they gathered by decreasing substitutability opportunities and price elasticity of demand for their products [24]. Within this scope, primary methods for dropping price elasticity of demand for the firms' products at microlevel are creating or strengthening brand loyalty.

According to Palumbo and Herbig [36], brand loyalty, which has different definitions in literature, is in the most general sense a situation, in which consumers continuously tend to seek and purchase only a certain brand even when competitor businesses offer lower prices and sales promotions.

Brand loyalty to be also high in high-priced products [37] leads the consumer, whose brand loyalty increased, to be less sensitive to price changes. Firms, with a purpose of increasing market share and profitability, try to reduce the vulnerability of their products against substitution opportunities and price changes by raising loyalty to their brands. Within this framework, a close relationship between market share and purchase possibilities of brand loyal consumers, who do not respond to price changes, is in question [38].

Brand loyalty provides some advantages to firms against competition. These advantages can be listed as follows:

- Creating brand loyalty decreases an important amount of advertising and promotion costs [39]. Together with the fall in costs, consumers loyal to brand will be loyal to the brand and not be sensitive to price changes as long as they resolve problems they experience about the product.

- Brand loyalty ensures competitive advantage to businesses. It builds a large entrance barrier to new entrant businesses. These barriers lower price elasticity of demand by complicating substitution of products firms produce.
- Brand loyal consumers do not oppose to pay a higher price for the products and services the business offers, and this increases the profitability of the business in short and long term.
- They do not abandon the brand immediately after they experience a negative situation about the brand.

All these advantages enabled by brand loyalty on the other hand serve price elasticity of demand for the product to fall.

Brand loyalty with regard to Ramsey taxation has importance especially in terms of decreasing price elasticity of demand for luxury goods. Brand loyalty to be high especially in luxury goods [40] drops price elasticity of demand to the so-called goods by weakening substitution possibilities and thus weakens the sensitivity of consumers of luxury goods the price changes of these goods.

All these macrovariables and microvariables change price elasticity of demand for luxury and necessity goods as part of differential tax rates in optimal commodity taxes. Additionally, they give way to Ramsey's inverse elasticity rule to be re-evaluated as part of criticisms it receives about income distribution. At this point, price elasticity of demand for luxury and necessity goods rises depending on short and long term effect, commercial liberalization, and increased competition and innovation, which are all macroeconomic variables.

Thus, demand elasticity of necessity goods, which have a large share in the consumption spending of lower level income groups, increases as part inverse elasticity rule; and therefore, tax rates decrease in line with the increase in elasticity. A decline in the tax rate, which the lower income level group will be exposed to as part of inverse elasticity rule, may create a more agreeable result in income distribution.

The influence microvariables have on price elasticity of demand on the other hand is important especially for luxury goods. Firms, aiming to increase their total revenues by reducing demand elasticity for their products, have the purpose of decreasing the vulnerability of their products against price changes. Since brand loyalty, which is one of the primary microvariables firms use within this framework, is high especially in luxury goods as mentioned above, it affects price elasticity of demand for the goods.

Created brand loyalty prevents change in consumer preferences by reducing substitution possibilities of luxury goods and decreasing price elasticity of demand.

By this way, in a tax that will be applied as part of inverse elasticity rule, luxury goods will be subject to high-rate taxes because of low demand elasticity. And therefore since aforementioned goods share in the consumption basket is very low for lower level income groups and high for higher level income groups, effect of this taxation, which is applied by considering elasticity, might be positive on income distribution.

Within this scope, while justice in income distribution is served on one hand, a certain budget revenue of optimal taxation goal is achieved through taxing goods with low demand elasticity at a high rate, and this goal is achieved without damaging any economic decisions or in other words without spoiling economic efficiency. Both inverse elasticity rule and leisure complementary goods, which will change preferences of consumers between working and leisure in favor of working, to be taxed at higher rates play a role. The fact that luxury goods are mostly substitutes of leisure lead to this conclusion.

Beginning from this century, labor market and accordingly preferences between leisure and working started to change. In this context, leisure industry has boomed. In many societies, leisure was equalized with luxury goods such as motor sports and traveling and became a symbol of postmodernity [41].

Thus, luxury goods have been effective in the change of the decision for working as a complementary of leisure. While luxury goods with a declined price elasticity of demand as part of brand loyalty are taxed at a higher rate with regard to inverse elasticity rule; at the same time, preferences of individuals in favor of working were strengthened by imposing taxes on leisure complementary goods and thus raising the cost of leisure.

Keeping in mind that criticisms Atkinson and Stiglitz [42, 43] made with regard to differential consumption taxes in terms of economic efficiency, the assumption that the single rate consumption tax will result efficiently in terms of optimal taxation, and under the agreement that other assumptions of Ramsey rule remain the same, demand elasticity of necessity and luxury goods, which changed with the influence of macrovariables and microvariables, will be able to serve in enabling the aimed public revenue without contradicting justice in income distribution under inverse elasticity rule.

7. CONCISE SUMMARY

The optimal taxation literature argues that redistributive policies aimed at achieving equality might have negative consequences due to the tradeoff between equality and efficiency. This creates a quandary where policies that promote equality may hinder economic efficiency. The primary issue in this matter arises from the inability to achieve a certain budget revenue target using lump-sum taxes due to the presence of asymmetrical knowledge between the state and individuals, as well as the necessity for distortionary taxes. Within this particular scenario, a proposed solution found in the literature is the implementation of an optimal commodities tax.

The topic in optimal tax application revolves around the choice between implementing a single tax rate or a differential tax rate in order to achieve efficiency.

Ramsey's study on optimal commodity taxes, which propose that items should be taxed in inverse proportion to their price elasticity of demand, is considered one of the key studies in the field. The Ramsey rule suggests that goods with a low price elasticity of demand should be taxed at higher rates. Its objective is to maintain individuals' consumption decisions for goods with increasing prices unchanged, particularly for goods with low elasticity. This is done to prevent the formation of deadweight loss or wealth loss in the economy. The dominant concern for economic efficiency in this rule is heavily criticized due to the emergence of unequal distribution resulting from the premise that all individuals are alike.

Ramsey proposes using the inverted elasticity rule to determine tax rates. According to this rule, commodities that are considered essential items and make up a significant portion of the consumption basket for lower income groups should be taxed at higher rates. On the other hand, things that are more appealing to higher income groups should be taxed at lower rates, taking into account their demand elasticity. The crucial aspect in this context is if the price elasticity of demand for goods undergoes any changes as a result of macrovariables and microvariables.

The price elasticity of demand for luxury and necessary items increases based on the short and long-term effects, commercial liberalization, and heightened competition and innovation. These factors are all macroeconomic variables. However, the high level of brand loyalty, which is the primary microeconomic factor, particularly for luxury items, has an impact on the price elasticity of demand for these goods.

Furthermore, the imposition of greater taxes on luxury products, based on the idea that they are complementary to leisure activities, can potentially influence the choices made by persons who are employed. Considering the criticisms of Ramsey's rule on economic efficiency in relation to differential taxation, it is worth reevaluating the application of the rule of inverse elasticity to promote equality.

AT A GLANCE

Optimal taxation refers to a tax system that takes into account society's preferences for both equality and economic efficiency. The main objective is to maximize overall social welfare. Ramsey's optimal taxation of commodities is determined by the principle of inverse elasticity, which states that taxing things with low demand elasticities at higher rates will minimize efficiency losses. The criticism of this rule stems from the observation that essential products, which are necessary for meeting basic needs, have a low degree of responsiveness to changes in price, known as price elasticity of demand. In contrast, luxury items exhibit a high degree of responsiveness to price changes. Assuming that customers are alike, it is contended that levying luxury products with a lower tax rate compared to essential goods will adversely impact tax fairness. Fluctuations in market conditions alter the responsiveness of demand for luxury items and necessity products, necessitating a reassessment of the fundamental assumptions underlying optimal taxation and the complaints leveled against it. The present study aims to examine the varying degrees of responsiveness of demand in relation to changing market conditions within the framework of trade liberalization. Given these discoveries, a reevaluation of the most effective taxes on goods will take place.

REFERENCES

1. Ramsey F. A Contribution to the theory of taxation. The Economic Journal. 1927;37:47-61
2. Mirrlees JA. An exploration in the theory of optimum income taxation. The Review of Economic Studies. 1971;38:175-208
3. Golosov M, Tsyvinski A. Designing optimal disability insurance: A case for asset testing. Journal of Political Economy. 2006;117:257-279
4. Corlett WJ, Hague DC. Complementarity and the excess burden of taxation. Review of Economic Studies. 1953;21:21-30
5. Barron JM, Umbeck JR, Waddell GR. Consumer and competitor reactions: Evidence from a field experiment. International Journal of Industrial Organization. 2008;26:517-531
6. Hummels D, Lugovskyy V. International Pricing in a Generalized Model of Ideal Variety. Mimeo: Purdue University; 2008
7. Tybout J. Plant- and firm-level evidence on the 'new' trade theories. In: Choi EK, Harrigan J, editors. Handbook of International Trade. Oxford: Basil-Blackwell; 2003. pp. 388-415
8. Bucklin RE, Gupta S, Siddarth S. Determining segmentation in sales response across consumer purchase behaviours. Journal of Marketing Research. 1998;35:189-198
9. Stiglitz JE. Economics of Public Sector. 3rd ed. New York: WW Norton & Co; 2000. 848 p

10. Musgrave R. ET, OT and SBT. Journal of Public Economics. 1976;6:3-16
11. Diamond PA, Mirrlees JA. Optimal taxation and public production I-II. American Economic Review. 1971;61:261-278
12. Munk KJ. Welfare Effects of Tax and Price Changes Revisited. School of Economics and Management Economics Working Paper. University of Aarhus. 2008;2008:3
13. Şen H, Şağbaş İ. Vergi Teorisi ve Politikası. 2nd ed. Ankara: Kalkan Ofset; 2016. 512p
14. Sorensen PB. The theory of optimal taxation: What is the policy relevance? International Tax and Public Finance. 2007;14:383-406
15. Chamley C. Optimal taxation of capital income in general equilibrium and infinite lives. Econometrica. 1986;54:607-622
16. Buchanan JM. Public Finance in Democratic Process. Chapel Hill: University of North Carolina Press; 1967
17. Buchanan JM. Taxation in fiscal exchange. Journal of Public Economics. 1976;6(1-2):17-29
18. Savaşan F. Piyasa Başarısızlığından Devlet Başarısızlığına Kamu Ekonomisi. 6th ed. Bursa: Dora Yayıncılık; 2016. 399p
19. Sandmo A. A Reinterpretation of elasticity formulae in optimum tax theory. Economica. 1986;54:89-96
20. Pınar A. Maliye Politikası. 2nd ed. Ankara: Naturel Kitap; 2006. 369 p
21. Stiglitz J. In praise of frank Ramsey's contribution to the theory of taxation. The Economic Journal. 2015;125:235-268
22. Lipsey RG, Courant PN, Ragan CT. Economics. 12th ed. New York: Addison-Wesley; 1999. 840 p
23. Pindyck R, Rubinfeld D. Microeconomics. 8th ed. New York: Pearson; 2013. 768p
24. Perreault WD, Cannon JP, McCarthy EJ. Essentials of Marketing. 13th ed. New York: The McGraw-Hill; 2012. 654 p
25. Galdon-Sanchez JE, Schmitz JA. Competitive pressure and labor productivity: World iron-ore markets in the 1980s. American Economic Review. 2002;92:1222-1235
26. Nickell SJ. Competition and corporate performance. Journal of Political Economy. 1996;104:724-746

27. Syverson C. Market structure and productivity: A concrete example. Journal of Political Economy. 2004;112:1181-1222
28. Head K, Ries J. Rationalization effects of tariff reductions. Journal of International Economics. 1999;47:295-320
29. Tybout J, Melo J, Corbo V. The effects of trade reforms on scale and technical efficiency: New evidence from Chile. Journal of International Economics. 1991;31:231-225
30. Caves R. Scale openness and productivity in manufacturing. In: Caves R, Krouse L, editors. The Australian Economy: A View from the North. Sydney: The Brookings Institution; 1984
31. Griliches Z. Hybrid corn: An exploration in the economics of technological change. Econometrica, 1957;XXV:501-522
32. Acemoglu D, Linn J. Market size in innovation: Theory and evidence from the pharmaceutical industry. The Quarterly Journal of Economics. 2004;119:1049-1090
33. Lakdawalla D, Sood N. Incentives to innovate. In: Oxford Handbook of the Economics of the BioPharmaceutical Industry. New York, NY: Oxford University Press; 2012
34. Hansen RW, Grabowski HG, Lasagna L. Cost of innovation in the pharmaceutical industry. Journal of Health Economics. 1991;10:107-142
35. Desmet K, Parente SL. Bigger is better: MARKET size, demand elasticity and innovation. International Economic Review. 2010;52:319-333
36. Palumbo F, Herbig P. The multicultural context of brand loyalty. European Journal of Innovation. 2000;3:116-124
37. Tranberg H, Hansen F. Patterns of brand loyalty: Their determinants and their role for leading brands. European Journal of Marketing. 1986;20:81-109
38. Dyson P, Farr A, Hollis NS. Understanding, measuring, and using brand equity. Journal of Advertising Research. 1996;36:9-21
39. Blackston M. The qualitative dimension of brand equity. Journal of Advertising Research. 1995;35:2-7
40. Denoue M, Saykiewicz JN. Brand loyalty as a tool of competitive advantage. Journal of Management and Business Administration Central Europe. 2009;17:36-45
41. Campo S, Hamada T, Barbiroli G, Sassen S, Masini EB, Nkwi PN, Sichone O, Momoh A. Social and Economic Development. United Kingdom: Encyclopaedia of Life Support Systems. EOLSS Publishers/UNESCO; 2010

42. Atkinson A, Stiglitz JE. The design of tax structure: Direct versus indirect taxation. Journal of Public Economics. 1976;6:55-75
43. Atkinson A, Stiglitz JE. Lectures in Public Economics. New York and London: McGraw-Hill Book Company; 1980
44. Available from: http://ppt-online.org/28345/10/03/2017

8

Chapter

THE RIGHT TO WATER AND HYDRIC INJUSTICE: AN ANALYSIS OF THE CONSTITUTIONALITY OF TAX INCENTIVES FOR THE HYDRO-INTENSIVE INDUSTRIAL AND PORT COMPLEX OF PECÉM-CEARÁ

1. INTRODUCTION: AN OVERVIEW

The present circumstances of climate change present significant difficulties to the world order, as well as to the required contemplation in the realm of critical thought. Morin and Kern analyze the current state of the Earth as a "polycrisis," or a collective crisis, which encompasses the interconnected crises of development, modernity, and societies. They also refer to the Earth as the "Earth-Homeland" and humanity as the "humankind-community of destiny." These terms are used to describe the complex and multifaceted nature of the civilizational crisis we are facing [1]. The water crisis is a prominent aspect of the global climate situation, which highlights the key issues with Brazil's current growth policies. Within this particular environment, the State of Ceará is currently facing the negative consequences of the water crisis.1 The uneven distribution of water and its concentrated allocation to large-scale development businesses are clear indicators of the problem.

The Industrial and Port Complex of Pecém2 is a notable example of a water-intensive and polluting industry, which depends on government subsidies and public infrastructure to ensure its viability. These subsidies undermine the effectiveness of the Right to Water and the requirements of the National Policy for Water Resources. This research aims to examine how the mechanisms of the unjust allocation of water jeopardize the fundamental Right to Water and perpetuate the exclusivity of access to this essential resource. The case of the Industrial and Port Complex of Pecém serves as our point of reference.

Our analysis focuses on the examination of taxing and charging instruments and their consistency with the legal system. This analysis examines the economic legal tools that provide subsidies to such an enterprise from two perspectives: the first perspective focuses on the equilibrium between constitutionally safeguarded assets, while the second perspective explores the systematic interpretation of laws within the hierarchy below the constitution.

Conceptual rigor is essential for accurately differentiating and understanding the legal instruments being analyzed. The Industrial Complex of the Port of Pecém benefits from a comprehensive package of state incentives.

1. The State Act n. 14.920/2011 authorizes the Companhia de Gestão de Recursos Hídricos (Company for Management of Hydric Resources, COGERH, in Portuguese acronym) to grant to the companies Porto do Pecém Geração de Energia S/A (08.976.495/0001-09) and MPX Pecém II Geração de Enerbia S/A (CNPJ 10.471.487/0001-44,) 50% discount on the cost of water tax.
2. The State Act n. 14.456/2009 ratifies the deal in which the "State commits to make feasible the negotiations with CSP to adjust the cost of average tax charged per m^3 **of raw water offered in the moment of initialization of the industrial installations."**
3. The State Act n. 15.593/2014, the State of Ceará authorized the concession of ownership to MPX Energia S/A of buildings in the plots of land 720 and 722, destined to the implementation of the Energetic Substation of Pecém II, in the Municipality of São Gonçalo do Amarante, through extra-judicial agreement of disappropriation.
4. The State Act n. 14.863/2011 authorizes the state to exchange the immobile good denominated Sítio Bom Jesus with the immobile present in the Anexo II, correspondent to a smaller part of the immobile with number registration 4509, of the 2nd Office of Immobile Registration of São Gonçalo do Amarante, of propriety of Rex Empreendimentos Imobilirários Ltda.
5. The State Act n. 16.024 granted tax benefits to the other unity of the Complex, to be build, reducing in 58.8% the basis for calculation of the Tax of Goods Circulation and Provision of Service of Interstate and Intercity Transportation (ICMS, in Portuguese Acronym,) incident on the internal operations and on the importation of natural gas destined to the thermal-electric power plant, resulting in a tax burden equivalent to 7%. It is important to underline that the reduction is destined to internal operations of natural gas being destined to the thermal-electric power plant that is intended to build and operate in the Complex.

The research will analyze these institutes collectively, while also making distinctions based on their specific legal categorization. Some of these reductions in tariffs are considered public prices, which are fees charged by private individuals providing public services for profit, without any tax or legal obligation. Below are the reductions in the cost of water tariffs.

The tax exemptions are classified under a different legal category. The tributes provide a tangible display of the authority of the government, encompassing taxes, fees, and donations. The regulation is constitutionally enforced in accordance with the principles of the economic order. Compulsory benefits are mandated by law and must be precise and divisible when charged for services.

The other subsidies are non-monetary in nature, but rather consist of tangible benefits, such as the granting of land and infrastructure for the firm. This research focuses on analyzing the economic institutions that decrease fees and taxes, interpreting them within the constitutional and legal framework that governs the subject.

The initial premise of the study posits that the vertical and horizontal efficacy of fundamental rights supports the notion that the safeguarding of the human right to water should be ensured through both tariff and tax mechanisms. The right to water is governed by a complicated normative framework, wherein the tariff mechanisms prioritize the economic model over the norms that guide water use priorities, so disregarding the protective logic of the environment.

Therefore, we stress that the granting of tariff and tax subsidies is not solely at the discretion of public managers but must primarily be fully compliant with the legislative framework. However, it is crucial to secure legal safeguards for water in order to examine the legal and economic tools.

2. THE HYDRIC CRISIS IN THE BACKGROUND OF THE ANTHROPOCENE AND OF THE CLIMATE CHANGES: THE BRAZILIAN NORTHEASTERN SEMI-ARID

In the context of how the case under study is inserted, it should be pointed out that the planet is immersed in a social-environmental and civilizational crisis yet not experienced by the human society. Its graver and more evident face, but not the only one, is the super warming of Earth and the climate changes. Even with the presentation of the 5th Assessment Report on Climate Change of the Intergovernmental Panel on Climate Change (IPCC), the publicizing of the previous report in February 2007 caused an unvulgar impact, due its utmost grievous conclusions. They indicate that the warming in the climate system is unequivocal, concerning to the climate changes and their consequences, as well as the causes of the warming, which are related to the emission of greenhouse gases. They are anthropogenic and not natural. The impacts on nature and society are already tangible [3]. The current situation has aggravated. 2016 was the warmest year since the beginning of temperature measurement in 1880, when this record had been broken for the third consecutive year [4]. The projections of the climate science are already indicating the catastrophic increase of 3°C (37.4° F) in the global average temperature [5]. In this scenario, the existence of extreme climate-environmental phenomena is recurrent: droughts, hurricanes, floods, etc. Such phenomena have become gradually more intense, until the moment when a war-vocabulary word had been lent to the ecological repertoire with the figure of the "climate refugee" or "environment refugee," which are already millions of people on the planet. In 2001, the International Red Cross published the "World Disasters Report," predicting the existence of 50 million climate refugees in 2050 [6]. However, the climate changes as well as the global warming are only the more evident face of a deeper crisis. It is directly related to the current configuration of the Capitalist mean of productionwith its development model grounded on the fossil fuel paradigm and its productive-consumerist–centered vision.

Such social-environmental has multiple nuances, and the hydric problem is one among them. It has been manifested in the planetary order. According to the UN, water shortage affects more than 40% of the global population and must increase. It is estimated that 783 million people have no access to clean water and more than 1.7 billion people nowadays live in hydrographic basins where the use of water exceeds the reloading capacity [7]. Historically marked by inequality of access to water, the Northeastern region of Brazil, where the Pecém Port Complex is located, subsidized by tariff and tax instruments, is the part of the country where droughts are more usual. According to the Brazilian Panel for Climate Change, the decrease in rainfall during the Winter can reach 50% by the end of the century [8]. It is important to add to this a physical-climate factorthe fact that the lands of the State of Ceará are in the drought-polygon, right in the Northeastern semi-arid. In such region, the evaporation amount exceeds the precipitation one, which aggravates the climate situation: in the analysis made by Frischkonr, Araújo and Santiago:

A mean annual rainfall of about 900 mm competes with a potential evaporation of 2200 mm powered by 3000 h of sunshine. Real evapotranspiration is of the order of 700 mm (SUDENE 1980; corresponding to 78% of rainfall), leaving only about 120 mm (13%) for runoff and 80 mm (9%) for percolation. Specific runoff in the region is of the order of 4 L/s/km^2 **to be compared with 21 L/s/km^2 for all of Brazil (Barth et al. 1987)** [9]. In this scenario – a collapse – in the environmental, climate and hydric spheres, we intend to research, in the following, the Right to Water and the violation to it, what happens because of the development policies adopted by the last governments of the State of Ceará.

3. WATER: A COMMON GOOD AND A FUNDAMENTAL HUMAN RIGHT AND THE DENYING OF IT AS HYDRIC UNFAIRNESS

3.1. The right to water in the international law

The United Nations broach the Right to Water in many of its documents, some of them centerpiece here: The General Commentary n. 15, from November 2002, from the United Nations Committee for Economic and Social Rights, for instance, affirmed that "the human right to water presupposes that everybody should have sufficient, safe, acceptable and physically accessible water with reasonable prices for personal and domestic use."[4] [10] And the Resolution 16, from April 2011, from the Council for Human Rights, with the adoption of the access to potable and safe water and sanitation as human rights. However, the major centerpiece is the Resolution A/RES/64/292 [11], passed on July 28, 2010, by the General Assembly of the United Nations[5] [10], which declares that clean and safe water and sanitation are an essential human right for the full enjoyment of rights, as well as for all the other rights. For Wolkmer and Melo, the international recognizing of the Right to Water made the international community commit—by the National states—to the protection and tutelage of such right [12]. Nevertheless, in the field conventionally called Latin-American Neo-constitutionalism, particularly in the case of multinational States, such as Bolivia and Ecuador—countries where the Andean indigenous tradition of Well Living is spread, we can find the best deal of the hydric problem (as well as for the other environmental problems), specially from the innovating concept that Nature is itself a rights holder.

The Mother-Earth Act (*"Ley de Derechos de la Madre Tierra"*) **in Bolivia, for instance, recognizes the rights of Earth as a living system.** [13] In Ecuador, similar mechanisms can be found in the Constitution of the Republic itself. [14] For Marques, the recognizing of the rights of nature stands beyond the "long history of the universalization of the subjects of right." Indeed, the author considers unsurpassable concept that it emanates from the demand of the conservation of the planetary biota to save, ultimately, the survival of the current society [15]. From that notion, water can be considered, in this eco-centered or bio-centered background, as a rights holder subject. Ana Alice de Carli defends this concept from the fundamental necessity of "awaking the ecological conscience and the duty of taking care of the water of all people." [16]. In the same direction, there have been taken important decisions in March 2017, in India, where the Ganges and Yamuna Rivers had obtained the status of "an alive human entity," and in New Zealand, where the Whanganui River obtained the same rights of a human being [17]. Following, it will be shown that the Brazilian law takes the management of hydric resources and the right to access to water according to the main documents of International Law, which assure the Right to Water, embodying such right into the National Law.[6]

3.2. The right to water in the Brazilian law

The conception that the political formula for the Brazilian Constitution of 1988 is the State of Environmental Law (or, in a more detailed definition, a socio-environmental democratic state under the rule of law), results of a dialectical synthesis "post-positivist," which surpasses the antinomy jusnaturalism x positivism [18], according to Belchior. It acknowledges the status of self-applicable juridical rule, and not only as a promise of rights. Marlmestein refers to what he defines as the "triumph of constitutionalism, with the renovation of the thinking and the judges in charge of the Supremo Tribunal Federal (also known as STF) the Brazilian supreme court. In his analysis of court works, he observes that"[...] nowadays, it is matter of no discussion in the jurisprudence of the STF, the understanding that it is possible to extract from the constitutional principles direct commands on the lawmakers [19], by force of the maximal effectiveness of the constitution." Among those fundamental rightsof socio-environmental nature, strictly according to the already mentioned meaning by Sarlet and Fenterseifer [20]there are the Right to an Ecologically Balanced Environment, to Health and to Water. The Brazilian Constitution directly recognizes the first and the second ones in its own text. Even though expressed in different articles of the Constitution, there is no possibility to interpret them independently from the Rights to Health, presupposed in the Article 196, as well as the Right to Balanced Environment, in the Article 225.

The relation between the quality of the environment, which is supposed to be ecologically balanced, and the healthy quality of life, presupposed in the Article 225, can be found in the synthesis definition of the World Health Organization (WHO) that states health as "a complete state of physical, mental and social well-being and not merely the absence of disease and infirmity" [21]. Thus, there is no possible way to think a dignified life in a non-balanced, non-healthy and non-sustainable environment—in its natural, artificial or cultural dimensions. Machado stands by the idea of water as a fundamental human right, as a direct consequence of the Rights to a Balanced Environment and to Health, since the access to the "precious liquid," even in quantity or decent quality, is a *conditio sine qua non* **for a healthy quality of life. In his own words:**

The individual access to water deserves to be understood as a universal human right, which means that any person, in any part of the planet, can collect, use or appropriate water to the specific intend of survival, in other words, to not die because of lack of water, and at the same time, to enjoy the Right to Life and to Ecological Balance [22]. D'Isep, after adducing that the Right to Water is a precursor of all the other rights, clarifies a series of definitive conclusions in which those rights are present and states that the Right to Water is manifest as a "universal principle of the fundamental right to water-life" [22]. The Right to

Water and Right to Sanitation are also encountered in the reflections of Sarlet and Fernsterseifer, when the authors state that it is in the theoretical framework of the State of Environmental Law that one can find what he/she denominates as the fundamental socio-environmental rights. This concept is related to the idea of indivisibility and interdependence of the fundamental human rights, in which the authors gather the rights, which are, at the same time, social and environmental. In their own words:

The environmental protection [...] is directly related to the guarantee of the social rights, since the enjoyment of these ones is dependent of favorable environmental conditions. As in the case, for instance, of the access to potable water (through sanitation, which is also a fundamental social right of the minimal necessary to existence.) [...] The effectiveness of the supply service of water and sanitary sewage integrates, directly or indirectly, the normative field of diverse fundamental rights (but, especially, the social rights), as the Right to Health, the Right to Decent Dwelling, the Right to Environment and the "forthcoming" Right to Water (essential to human dignity) as well as, in extreme cases, also the Right to Life [22].

What the authors denominate "forthcoming" rightdespite the claim of its insertion in the current positive normative framework of the Constitution of the Republic, as required by Machado [22]is already present in some recent acts, such as the *Estatuto da Cidade* **(the Basic Law of the City, Act 10.257/ 2001), the** *Lei de Saneamento Básico* **(Sanitation Act, Act 11.445/2007), and specially, the Act that instituted the National Policy for Hydric Resources (Act 9.443/1997).**[7]

Whereas in the first rule*the Estatuto da Cidade*the right to the environmental sanitation integrates the first list of guarantees of the so-called right to sustainable cities (one of the guidelines of urban policy), presupposed in its Article 2, Incise 1; the Act 11.445/ 2007 in its Article 3, Incise 1, defines sanitation as a collection of services, infrastructure and logistic installations of "potable water supply, sanitary sewage, urban cleanness and management of solid resources and drainage and management of urban rain water." (Act 11.445/2007, Article 3, Incise I.) The act also established as one of its fundamental principles the universalization of access (the progressive enlargement of access of sanitation for all occupied residences), in the words of its Article 2, Incise 1, combined with Article 2, Item 3.

Finally, the Act that instituted the National Policy for Hydric Resources, in this search for grounding of the fundamental socio-environmental right to water, should not be forgotten. It is the Act 9433/1997, especially concerned with the use of raw water, since the issues of potable water are part of the already mentioned policy of sanitation.

It is important to say that the principles of the National Policy of Hydric Resources (article 1 of the law) bring fundamental (some contradictory) definitions for the treatment of the right to water, namely, the character of water as a "public property" (which is consonant with the concept of the environment as "good of common use of the people", inscribed in article 225 of our Constitution) and endowed with "economic value" - which could, in theory, contain a term contradiction.[8]

The act also deals with a vision of "multiple uses" in the management of hydric resources, which alludes a perspective of conflict of the terms in a quarrel of a limited resource, as the act itself acknowledges and tends to deepen in times of climate change. It also assures that, in the situation of scarcity (and only in such cases, which is the other contradiction with the guarantee of the Right to Water), the prior use of water will be destined for human consumption and animal watering.

Water shortage, treated as a "calamity," is one of the circumstances that can lead to the suppression, partial or total, definitively or with no determined deadline, of the grants of the right to the use of hydric resources, besides other cases, such as the prevention or reversal of severe environmental degradation or the necessity to respond to prior uses, of collective interest, for those there are no other alternative source (Article 15, PNRH). According to D'Isep, the instrument of granting is an answer to the rarity of such resource, since "it legitimates the intervention of the State into the management of the access to water, therefore, in the regimentation of its use, in order to assure the social satisfaction, which is the healthy and dignified life" [22]. The grants of the rights of hydric resources consist in the instrument created to guarantee the "quantitative and qualitative control of the uses of water and the effective activation of the rights to access to water" (Article 11, PNRH) in order to guarantee, at least instance, the prime objective of the National Policy of Hydric Resources, which is, "assuring to this generation and to the next to come, the necessary availability of water, within the adequate patterns of quality to its respective uses."

And it is precisely this instrument created to guarantee the Right to Water for present and future generations that can, on the other hand, be responsible for situations of what can be called today water injustice, a concept that stems from environmental justice conception developed by Acselrad et al. [23], for whom this is a set of principles and practices aimed at equity, access to information and, fundamentally, democratic and participatory processes of defining not only the uses of environmental resources and the destination of tailings, but mainly, of public policies, especially those of socioeconomic development. In a counterpoint, the authors define environmental injustice as the mechanism through which unequal societies, from an economic and social view, allocate the major amount of environmental damage in lower income populations, groups racially discriminated, traditional ethnic peoples, workers' neighborhoods, the marginalized and vulnerable populations [23]. Martinez Alier, on the other hand, works with this conceptenvironmental justiceas one of the chains of the ecologic movement, synonym of *ecology of the poor,* or *popular ecology.* For that author, the Ethics of this movement is decurrent of the demand for social justice. According to him, "disgracefully, economic growth implies in bigger impacts on the environment, drawing one's attention to the geographical displacement of the sources of resources and the areas for waste discard" [24]. When that fair distribution of social and environmental goods is alluded, it must include water among them, a good of public domain (Article 1, Incise 1, Ac 9.433/1997) and an essential factor to healthy quality of life, preconized by the Article 225 of the Brazilian Constitution. The unfair distribution, the denial or the obstruction of that common good, as already mentioned, as well as the favorability to economic groups instead of human populations, is considered, evidently, as hydric injustice.

Working the concept of hydric injustice, as taught by Porto-Gonçalves, means thinking of water as a territory, or in other words, "[...] as the inscription of society in nature, with all the contradictions implied in the process of appropriation of nature by man and women through their social relations of power" [25]. It is interesting in this research to observe how the economic legal instruments of taxation and tariff are related to the promotion or reduction of this water injustice from the empirical case study. Those relations of power are exactly what produce environmental injustice, through the private appropriation of hydric resources, even when legalized by the instrument of grant of the right to use. The case of the "thirsty industries," in other words, hydro-intensive, located in the Industrial and Port Complex of Pecém (CIPP, in Portuguese) in the Municipality of São Gonçalo do Amarante, in the State of Ceará is a relevant example of the exposed scenario.

4. THE TAX BENEFITS FOR THE HYDRO-INTENSIVE INDUSTRIES OF THE COMPLEX OF PECÉM: A DEBATE ON ITS (UN) CONSTITUTIONALITY

The economic policy of the Estate of Ceará is inserted in the context of neo-developmentism [26], associated with neo-extractivism [27]. Both share the idea of progress with unlimited growth, a perspective that justifies the appropriation of environmental goods and the conception that the state and the market consist of complementary fields, to provide economic growth, powered by large-scaled enterprises.

In such context, it is important to highlight the fundamental role the state plays in the contribution of these large-scaled enterprises. The case of CIPP is not different from others, for which the state works as a factor of stimulation and facilitation for their installation. The specific literature indicates the recurrence of environmental conflicts involving a productive hydro-extensive matrix subsidize by the state. In Ceará, the following cases are remarkable: the agribusiness in the Chapada do Apodi [28], the project of mining of uranium and phosphates in Santa

Quitéria [29, 30] and the shrimp production in traditional Quilombos' lands [31].

A distinctive trace of those enterprises is in the emphasis of this research: the state subsidizing of the enlargement of environmental goods supplies, violating the nature of water as a human right and a common good [32], as discussed in the previous chapters. The character of economic worth that is also attributed to water by the normative system is defined by Enrique Leff as a process of privatization of water, which would be "promoted in a narrative that intends to obtain the 'rational use and efficient management of water,' turning the users into payers for the 'real cost' of the resource supplying." And, in addition to that, it is characterized as one of the "strategies of the expansion of the natural capital to absorb environmental goods and services, in other words, the natural common goods of humankind." However, large-scaled enterprises happen to be polluting and hydro-extensive, in which we observe the perverse inversion in the logic of pricing of the environment: those with major economic capacity receive tax benefits from the state.

Here, there is the core of the proposed work, which is the analysis of the anti-law nature and the hydric injustice in the subsidizing granted by the state to the Industrial and Port Complex of Pecém. But before going into the analysis itself, it is important to briefly define the enterprise in question. Only for the Steel Company of Pecém, there are innumerous other public grants, and their operation obtained the grant of 1500 L a second for the company. Also, the infamous thermal-electric power plants of Pecém are owners of grants of voluminous water flows, available in the Portal Hidrológico do Ceará (Hidryc Website of Ceará, in free translation) Below follow the systemized grants:

1. Grant n. 41. Granted volume: 9.460.800 m^{3}flow 300 1/sRecipient: PORTO DO PECÉM GERAÇÃO DE ENERGIA S/A;
2. Grant n. 136. Granted volume: 15.768.000 m^{3}flow 500 1/sRecipient MPX Mineração e Energina LTDA;
3. Grant n. 454/2016. Granted volume: 9.460.800 m^{3}flow 300 1/sRecipient MPX PECEM II GERAÇÃO DE ENERGIA S/A;
4. Grant n. 577. Granted volume: 2.57.944flow 891 1/sRecipient TERMOCEARÁ LTDA.

To guarantee the feasibility of the hydric consume of the enterprise, the fifth part Eixão das Águas was inaugurated in 2014. It consists in a mean for transferring of water and interlinking of hydric basins. Besides that, the other source of water supply for the thermal-electric power plant of Pecém was the Reservoir of Sítios Novos. Its data in 2015 indicated it supplied a volume of 600 L a second, which caused its drain. In February 2017, its volume was 0.07% of its natural capacity, according to Portal Hidrológico [33].

Observing the investigative purposes of this research, initially the analysis is centered in the benefits that grant a reduction of 50% in the water tax for thermal-electric power plants and for the steel industry of the Complex. It is also remarkable how the tax subside is inserted in a complicated contribution of fiscal reductions and the availability of public infrastructure for the enterprise. This is State Law No. 14,920/2011 and State Law No. 14456/2009.

Having said that, the analysis goes through the comprehension on the juridical nature of the apparatus of the water bill. It is consistent with the propitious way that establishes the public prize and tax for the industrial consumers, presupposed in the National Policies (Federal Act n. 9433/1997) and in the State Policy of Hydric Resources (State Act n 14.844/2010). Both laws state the function of the apparatus, which is to guarantee a rational use of water.

The Act that instituted the National Policy of Hydric Resources has one chapter dedicated to the apparatus of billing water, discussing on its criteria, later regimented by the State Decree n. 32.032, on September 2, 2016. It confirms the prime goal of water bill, seen as an instrument of rationalization of water use.[9]

In Ceará, it is used as a model of billing water different from the billing used in other hydrographic basins. It is as follows:

... it is characterized by its binomial form, grounded in its marginal cost of management of hydric resources and in its capability of payment of each category of consumer. [...] However, in consequence of the necessity of structuration of the management authority, the universalization of grant, as well as a wider comprehension and acceptance of the consumers, the charging was implemented in a mononomial form, admitting taxes only defined by the water consumed. (Consumer tax) [34].

For the juridical doctrine, billing water is an instrument capable to promote sustainable development. Because of its character of public good of common use, it is affirmed that "the payment of the use does not imply in the creation of any kind of right on the water, as already observed, for being a public good, it is inalienable [35].

In the case of Ceará, the Decree that regiments the billing water presupposes different taxes for "enterprises considered as structuring for the State of Ceará" (Article 9, Decree n. 32.032/2016), which threatens the prime goals of the instituted bill.

The unsustainable water demand of the project caused the State of Ceará to approve, by law, the creation of the Emergency Water Charge, which burdened the water consumption of the thermals. In reaction to the measure, the two largest coal-fired thermals, Pecém I and II, contacted the National Electric Energy Agency (Aneel) stating that they would not be able to continue operating if the price adjustment of the energy tariff is not allowed, as a way of compensating the increase in water costs. The request was rejected by the Agency and later by the Judiciary.

The Contingency Tariff consists of an instrument authorized by State Law 16.103/2016, which created the Contingency Tariff for the use of water resources during a critical situation of scarcity. The norm was regulated by the Resolution of CONERH (Council of Water Resources of the State of Ceará) number 006/2016, providing that:

Article 1. Establish the value of contingency tariff for the use of the water resources of the State of Ceará, in the industrial purpose, granted to thermoelectric companies Porto do Pecém Generation of Energy, MPX Pecem II Generation of Energy S/A and MPX Mining and Energia Ltda.

In its sole paragraph, it remains clear that "The contingency fee for the use of water resources differs from the tariff for the use of water resources because it is transitory, objective to cover the additional expenses arising from the Critical Situation of Water Scarcity and stimulate rational use".

That would be sufficient to ensure that there was no confusion between the legal instruments at issue. Thus, it should also be clarified that the Resolution established that:

Article 2. The contingency tariff for the use of water resources applied to users established in the caput of Article 1 will have the value of R $ 7210.00/1000 cubic meters.

Sole Paragraph. The amount indicated in the caput of this article will be added to the value of the collection fee for the use of water resources and applied to all the volume consumed.

Article 3. The value of the contingency fee for the use of resources provided for in this Resolution shall be charged for the duration of the Declaratory Act no. 01/2015/SRH, published in Official Gazette of October 7, 2015.

The act to which Article 3 refers consists of a Statement of Critical Situation of Water Scarcity in the State of Ceará. According to Article 2, the Tariff will have the value of R $ 7210.00 /1000 cubic meters. If the Tariff, which is eminently transitory, is no longer applied, the companies benefiting from State Law 14,920/2011 would pay half of the industrial tariff.

It should be noted that, despite the mitigation measure created with the Emergency Charge, the consumption of water by the thermals is not decreasing, nor has the volume granted been altered, revealing that the measure proves insufficient to guarantee the protection of human supply and that there must be a complete revision of the tariff economic instruments on a permanent and non-temporary basis.

That said, it is considered that economic compensation measures cannot be ignored to reduce water consumption and increase efficiency in economic activity, either because these companies tend to pass the costs of the tariff to the price of electricity or because costing and profitability remain in force, even though the economic sector is strained by passing on the increase in costs.

In this research, it is remarked that the subject does not approach exclusively to a discretionary politic decision, since the fundamentality of the Right to Water and the infra-constitutional regimenting of the hydric management institutions conditionate and design the discretionary margin of the state agencies.

The second legal regime that merits analysis concerns tax exemptions, according to the distinction made in the introduction of this research. In the present case, in addition to the reduction on the water tariff price, the State of Ceará also reduces taxes on the main inputs of the project, notably the tax called ICMS, Service and Goods Circulation Tax.

It occurs that taxes, a kind of tribute, instituted by law and regulated under a specific legal regime, are disciplined under their own norms and principles. In Brazilian systematics, ICMS is a tax of an extra-fiscal nature, which is a competence of all the states of the federation, subject to the principles of selectivity and essentiality, that is, to the regime of harmonious protection of assets protected by the constitutional order.

On the tax instruments, then, we must make some observations. The principle of selectivity consists of an instrument of state extrafiscality and includes a minimum selection of taxes, among them the ICMS, which was reduced as a financial contribution to the industries of the Pecém Complex. Extrafiscality consists in the use of instruments of the Tax Law whose primary purposes are not cash collection, but non-fiscal objectives, of stimulus or control to certain behaviors and economic activities.

On the other hand, the principle of selectivity establishes that, for goods of greater essentiality, the rate will be lower, and the inverse will occur for less essential (or harmful) goods. It applies to indirect taxes, that is, those that have repercussions on the final consumer, and still, a fiscal justice technique to foster the progressiveness of the tax system. It is expressly provided for in the constitutional text:

Article 153:

Paragraph 3. The tax established in item IV:

I - will be selective, depending on the essentiality of the product;

Article 155:

§ 2. The tax provided in item II shall comply with the following:

III - may be selective, depending on the essentiality of goods and services;

Although subsection III, Paragraph 2 of Article 155, regarding the ICMS speaks of "may", the application of selectivity does not consist of a faculty. The correct and predominant interpretation is that the term "may" corresponds to a "must," as it is present in item I of Paragraph 3 of Article 153 of the Brazilian Federal Constitution of 1988, which establishes on the principle of selectivity also for the Industrialized Products Tax. Thus, there is no faculty, but mandatory in observance of the principle, this being the dominant understanding and that appears in the Proposal of Constitutional Reform Tax, in process in the National Congress. In RMS n° 28.227/GO, from the report of the Minister Herman Benjamin, the Second Panel of the Superior Court of Justice unanimously decided that "there is no doubt that the state legislature can not simply disregard the norm set forth in Article 155, § 2°, III, of CF, because of the inherent appropriateness of the expression "should be selective."

It should be noted that the National Tax Code also enshrines the norm, stating in Article 48 that "The tax is selective according to the essentiality of the products.". Essentiality, which guides the application of tax selectivity, is not only a moral or ideological conception, but a real verification of the importance of a merchandise or service for tax justice. The possible tax favorability seeks facilitate access to essential products for a life with quality and dignity. This is why the state charges cigarettes and alcoholic beverages, for example, and exempts medicines, food and items essential to human dignity.

It is also necessary to understand the relationship between essentiality, instruments of fiscal justice and the promotion of material equality. One of the elements that guides the extrafiscality has to be to ensure that those with greater capacity, expecially when they profit from economic activity whose nature involves risks and damage to the environment and health, deal with the tax burden. In the present case, large industries are benefiting from the fiscal renunciation of the State, with full tax capacity, making the rules that subsidize it even more incompatible with the legal system.

On the other hand, the data that indicate the annual liquid profit of the company EDP Energias do Brasil (Holder of Porto do Pecém Geração de Energia S/A – Pecém I) are relevant. It was 1265 billion Reais [36], making evident the economic capacity of the sector. It corroborates the thesis of the absence of reasonable and juridical justification and normatively based of the granted subsidies.

Synthesizing, the normative aim is to privilege the essential products for a good life, dignity, social justice, and not extremely polluting economic activities that have ample capacity to bear the regular tax burden. Therefore that is no reason to go against the increase of the final product, considering that the objective of the extra-fiscal standard is exactly discourage harmful behaviors to the community, such as the intensive and wasteful use of water, in addition to the environmental pollution caused by the thermoelectric company of the Pecém Complex.

Thus arises the reflection about the compatibility between, on one hand, the water tax reduction and subsides offered by the CIPP and, on another hand, the normative content of the constitutional principles that found the juridical order. Taking a look at the issue, the policy of subsidies with the effectiveness of the constitutional right to the balanced environment and the healthy quality of life, from which the democratic and regulated access of essential goods to guarantee human dignity, consonant with the theoretical contribution exposed in the previous items of the research.

The normative environmental discipline also deals with the protection of the hydric resources. *A priori*, it is important to remark water as a member constituent of the environment and include it in the words of the Article 225 of the Brazilian Constitution.

The constitutional embodiment of water and other rules characterizes the phenomenon denominated "Constitution of the Environment and Ecology of the Law" [37]. The normative analysis of the subject, presented in the initial chapters of this work, indicates an incongruence between the Right to Water and to Environment and the grant of tax subsidies for hydro-intensive enterprises.

In addition to that, it is worth to mention that the Article 225 also emanates from other related principle, which finds technical terminologies differenced in the doctrine, such as "the Principle of Obligation of Intervention of the Public Force," in Machado. [22] Such intervention is oriented under the criteria of distributive justice, social equality and the maximal environmental tutelage. Therefore, the state intervention in the case of CIPP is a threat to this paradigm.

Finally, the principles that interest the debate concerning water should not exclude the principles of precaution and preventive actuation, which are founded in Principle 15, of the Declaration of Rio on Environment and Development, which Brazil signs. Paulo de Bessa Antunes [38] indicates that the principle of prevention should be applied when the possible impacts in the future are acknowledged, whereas the principle of precaution (or caution) should be applied when the probable impacts are uncertain or unknown. In both cases, when the impacts are known and in front of scientific indications for the scenario of climate change, the incentive to the intensive, prodigal and polluting use of environmental goods violates the normative protective mark of the environment.

Looking at the Constitution of the State of Ceará [39], it can be observed that its text presents regimenting apparatus and its normative content is deeply damaged by the public subsidies grant to the hydro-intensive enterprises of CIPP. In its Article 318, the constitutional text states that "the State and the Municipalities have the duty do preserve their waters and to promote its rational use." In the Article 326, it states that the administration should guarantee "the multiple use of hydric resources and the apportionment of cost of the respective works in the rule of law" (Article 326, II, C.E.) and "the protection of water against actions that might compromise its present or future use" (Article 326, III, C.E.). The duty to preserve the waters, promote their rational use, and priority for human use and animal watering, are guidelines that can be observed in all legal systems in the country and state.

Thus, it can be also observed that the billing of use of hydric resources constitutes an indispensable instrument to the legality of the public management of water. This is not an option, or a discretionary act of the Administration, which can change depending on the individual to be disadvantaged. This is an administrative act fully linked to the law and its regimentations.

Therefore, our understanding is that a total or partial exemption from the billing of the use of hydric resources, with no justification under proportionality and impersonality criteria, violates the normative constitutional order. In addition to that, it does not consider the dictates of the National Policy and the State Policy of Hydric Resources in their priority of water supplying to human individuals, also damaging the principles of proportionality, reasonability and isonomy. It happens because the economic sector has a rather differenced treatment with no juridical justification.

Such considerations associated to the fatidic scenario and its severity should not be despised. In Ceará, the basin Gavião, which supplies water to the Metropolitan Zone of Fortaleza, with the Castanhão as the main reservoir in the state lands, is found in grievous situation. This reinforces the state of water shortage in Ceará and the necessity to take urgent decisions in hydric management, to guarantee the legal dictate that establishes the priority for water supplying for human individuals. It should also be highlighted that Castanhão had 4.94% of its water volume in February 2017. Currently, even after a rainfall period, the reservoirs in the state have 12.3% [40] of their capacity. On April 18, 2017, the State of Ceará declared Situation on Emergency in 168 of its municipalities for water shortage [41].

Thus, the tax and tariff instruments must be managed in accordance with the constitutionally defined environmental protection.

5. CONCISE SUMMARY

In conclusion, we present the following considerations as a contribution to the field of environmental critical investigation:

1. There is an intimate relationship between the increasing climate change, the actual hydric crisis in the State of Ceará and the scarcity of water for the human supply service in diverse locations of the state, which tend to turn for the worse under the direction of the financial policy adopted by the state.
2. The Brazilian and Ceará's normative legal milestone allows to understand water as a human right and a common good.
3. The high consumption of water by the Industrial and Port Complex of Pecém (CIPP in Portuguese) materializes a case of hydric injustice and violates the priority of human water supply, established by the National Policy of Hydric Resources, as well as by the State Policy for Hydric Resources.
4. The granting of tax and tributaries benefits, constituent part of the context neo-developmentism, outrages the juridical nature of the instrument of billing of the use of water and the legal text of the National Policy and the State Policy for Hydric Resources, which state the rational use of water and the priority of human supply, and still defies the principles of the tax order. Both legal institutes, although of a distinct nature, are configured in economic instruments that must be in harmony with the system of environmental protection.
5. The reduction of 50% in the water tax for thermal-electrical power plants, as well as for the steel industry in CIPP, is unconstitutional, for the direct outrage it does to the Article 225 of the Federal Constitution of Brazil, in addition to its fundamental principles, as well as the Article 226 of the State Constitution of Ceará.

AT A GLANCE

The objective of this study is to assess the compatibility of taxation and tariff instruments applied to the enterprises inside the Industrial and Port Complex of Pecém. The aim is to analyze their conformity with the Brazilian legal system and determine if they are constitutional or not. Given the global prevalence of the water issue, particularly in the semi-arid state of Ceará, effective water management is crucial. Taxes serve as a means to do this, and their misallocation can lead to significant water inequality. To progress in this research, we conducted an extensive bibliographical and documentary examination, as well as a case study, to explore the intimate connection between the state's economic policy and the current shortage of water for human consumption. Based on the Brazilian normative framework, which recognizes water as a fundamental right and a public resource, the tax and tributary benefits given to the Industrial and Port Complex of Pecém are in violation of Article 225 of the Federal Constitution and Article 326 of the State Constitution, making them unconstitutional.

REFERENCES

1. Morin E, Kern AB. Terra-Pátria. Translated into Brazilian Portuguese by Paulo Azevedo Neves da Silva. 5th ed. Porto Alegre: Sulima; 2005
2. <http://www.ibama.gov.br/noticias/422-2017/1066-ibama-multa-ceara-portos-em-r-13-8-milhoes-por-lancamento-de-carvao-mineral-na-praia-do-pecem> [Accessed: April 20, 2017]
3. IPCC. Fifth Assessment Report (AR5). Available on <http://www.ipcc.ch/report/ar5 /index.shtml > on March 28, 2017
4. Information available on <https://climate.nasa.gov/news/2537/nasa-noaa-data-show-2016-warmest-year-on-record-globally/> [Accessed: April 15, 2017]
5. Güstschow J et al. INDCs lower projected warming to: Significant progress but still above 2°C. Climate Action Tracker. Disponível em: www.climateactiontracker.org/publications/briefing/223/INDCs-lower-projected-warming-to-2.7C-significant-progress-but-still-above-2C-.html [Accessed: October 15, 2015]
6. Hood M. Climate change: The increasing in the dangers for the future refugees. Available on <www.noticias.uol.com.br/ultnot/afp/2007/01/31/ult1806u5420.jhtm.> [Accessed: March 28, 2017]
7. Available on <http://www.un.org/en/sections/issues-depth/water/index.html> [Accessed: March 3, 2017]
8. Brazilian Panel for Climate Change (PBMC, in Portuguese acronym). Impactos, vulnerabilidades e adaptação **às** mudanças climáticas. In: Assad ED, Magalhães AR, editors. Contribuição do Grupo de Trabalho 2 do Painel Brasileiro de Mudanças Climáticas ao Primeiro Relatório da Avaliação Nacional sobre Mudanças Climáticas. COPPE. Rio de Janeiro, RJ, Brasil: Universidade Federal do Rio de Janeiro. p. 414
9. Frinschkorn H, Araújo JC, Santiago MMF. Water resources of Ceará and Piauí. In: Gaiser T, Krol M, Frischkorn H, de Araújo JC, editors. Global Change an Regional Impacts: Water Availaibility and Vulnerability of Ecosystems and Society in the Semiarid Northeast of Brazil. Berlin, Heidelberg, New York, Hong Kong, London, Milan, Paris, Tokyo: Springer; 2003. p. 87

10. Riva GR, Saab. Água, um direito humano. São Paulo: Paulinas; 2016. p. 80
11. United Nations. Available on: http://www.un.org/ga/search/view_doc.asp?symbol=A/RES/64/292> [Accessed: April 04, 2017]
12. Wolkmer MFS, Melo MP. O Direito Fundamental à Água: convergências no plano internacional e constitucional. In: Moraes GO, Marques Júnior WP, Melo ÁJM, org. As águas da UNASUL na Rio+20: direito fundamental à água e ao saneamento básico, sustentabilidade, integração da América do Sul, novo constitucionalismo latino-americano e sistema brasileiro. Curitiba: CRV; 2013. p. 13
13. Bolivia. Available from: http://bolivia.unfpa.org/content/ley-no-71-de-derechos-de-la-madre-tierra [Accessed: March 10, 2017]
14. Ecuador. Available from: http://www.asambleanacional.gob.ec/sites/default/files/documents/old/constitucion_de_bolsillo.pdf [Accessed: March 10, 2017]
15. Marques L. Capitalismo e colapso ambiental. Campinas, SP: Editora da UNICAMP; 2015. p. 609
16. De Carli AA. Água é vida: eu cuido, eu poupo: para um futuro sem crise. Rio de Janeiro: Editora FGV; 2015. p. 43
17. Information available on: <https://www.publico.pt/2017/03/21/mundo/noticia/foi-a-vez-dos-rios-ganges-e-yamuna-conseguirem-os-direitos-de-um-ser-humano-1765964> [Accessed: March 10, 2017]
18. Belchior GPN. Hermenêutica Jurídica Ambiental. São Paulo: Saraiva; 2011. p. 90
19. Marlmestein GL. 25 anos da Constituição de 1988: presente, passado e futuro. In: Paulo Rogério MC, Maria Vital da Rocha, organizadores. 25 anos da Constituição de 1988: os direitos fundamentais em perspectiva. Fortaleza: Expressão Gráfica; 2013. p. 29
20. Sarlet IW, Fensterseifer T. Estado socioambiental e mínimo existencial (ecológico?): algumas aproximações. In: Sarlet IW, org. Estado socioambiental e direitos fundamentais. Porto Alegre: Livraria do Advogado Editora; 2010
21. WHO. Definition of Health. Disponível em: <http://www.who.int/about/definition/en/print.html> [Accessed: May 25, 2017]
22. Machado PAL. Direito Ambiental Brasileiro. 22.ed. ver, ampl. e atual. São Paulo: Malheiros; 2014
23. Acselrad H et al. O que é justiça ambiental. Rio de Janeiro: Garamond; 2009. p. 4

24. Martinez Alier J. O Ecologismo dos Pobres: conflitos ambientais e linguagens de valoração. Tradução de Mauricio Waldman. São Paulo: Contexto; 2007. pp. 33-34

25. Porto-Gonçalves CW. O desafio ambiental. Rio de Janeiro: Record; 2004. p. 152

26. SampaioJr.,PlíniodeArruda.Desenvolvimentismoeneodesenvolvimentismo: tragédia e farsa. Vol. 112. São Paulo: Revista Serv. Soc. Soc.; 2012. pp. 672-688

27. Milanez B, Santos RSP. Neodesenvolvimentismo e neoextrativismo: duas faces da mesma moeda?. In: 37o. Encontro Anual da ANPOCS, 2013, Águas de Lindóia. Annals of the 37th The Annual Meeting of the Association of the Post-Graduations of Social Sciences (ANPOCS, in Portuguese acronym); 2013

28. Rigotto RM et al. Agrotóxicos, trabalho e saúde—vulnerabilidade e resistência no contexto da modernização agrícola do Baixo Jaguaribe, Ceará. 1ª ed. Fortaleza: Editora UFC e Coedição Expressão Popular; 2011

29. Melo RD. Riscos Ambientais e Processos de Vulnerabilização: diálogos e controvérsias em torno do Projeto de Mineração de Urânio e Fosfato em Santa Quitéria, Ceará [thesis (Master in Environment and Development)]. Fortaleza: Universidade Federal do Ceará (UFC); 2015

30. Montezuma TFPF. Licenciar e Silenciar: análise do conflito ambiental nas audiências públicas do Projeto Santa Quitéria, CE [thesis (Master in Law)]. Universidade Federal do Ceará (UFC): Fortaleza; 2015

31. Meireles AJ, Cassola R, Tupinambá SV, Queiroz LS. Impactos ambientais decorrentes das atividades da carcinicultura ao longo do litoral cearense, Nordeste do Brasil. Mercator—Revista de Geografia da UFC, the 6th Year, n. 12; 2007

32. Leff E. Discursos Sustentáveis. São Paulo: Cortez; 2010. p. 110

33. Ceará. Portal Hidrológico. Disponível em **http://www.hidro.ce.gov.br/# [Accessed: April 20, 2017]**

34. Finkler NR, Mendes LA, Bortolin TA, Schneider VE. Cobrança pelo uso da água no Brasil: uma revisão metodológica. Revista Desenvolvimento e Meio Ambiente. 2015;33:33-49 [abr]

35. Barros WP. A água na visão do direito. Porto Alegre: Tribunal de Justiça do Rio Grande do Sul, Departamento de Artes Gráficas; 2005. p. 97

36. Information available on: <http://edp.infoinvest.com.br/static/ptb/dividendos.asp?language=ptb [Accessed: March 10, 2017]

37. Benjamin AH. Direito Constitucional Ambiental Brasileiro. In: Canotilho JJG, Morato Leite JR, orgs. Direito Constitucional Ambiental Brasileiro. 2nd ed. São Paulo: Saraiva; 2008

38. Antunes PB. Direito Ambiental. Rio de Janeiro: Lumen Juris; 2007. pp. 37-39

39. Ceará. The State Constitution. Available on: http://www.ceara.gov.br/simbolos-oficiais/constituicao-do-estado-do-ceara [Accessed: April 15, 2017]

40. Ceará Portal Hidrológico. Available on <http://www.hidro.ce.gov.br/#> [Accessed: April 4, 2017]

41. Diário do Nordestes. Emergência é decretada em 61 municípios do CE. Available on http://diariodonordeste.verdesmares.com.br/cadernos/regional/emergencia-e-decretada-em-61-municipios-do-ce-1.1740441 [Accessed: April 20, 2017]

9 Chapter

THE PRESENT CONDITION AND CHALLENGES ASSOCIATED WITH THE FOREST INHERITANCE TAX IN JAPAN

1. INTRODUCTION: AN OVERVIEW

Approximately 66% of Japan's total land area is comprised of woods, which are categorized based on ownership. As of March 31, 2012, the national forest covered 7.7 million hectares, which accounted for 30.6% of the entire forest area. Public forest, mostly held by prefectural and local governments, covered 2.9 million hectares, representing 11.6% of the total forest. Private forest covered 14.4 million hectares, making up 57.6% of the total forest area (Forestry Agency [1]). Private forest encompasses several forms of ownership, with the majority being held by individual private foresters, commonly referred to as "forest owners" or "private forest owners." A significant number of these individuals were previously small-scale farmers. There are 1,018,752 individuals who own forests, and the combined size of these forests is 5.7 million hectares.1 The majority of forest owners in Japan possess relatively tiny forested areas, with around 761,086 out of 1,018,752 proprietors owning less than 5 hectares of forest.Two Historically, the vast majority of privately owned forest land has been acquired through the process of inheriting it from family members. However, this trend has recently changed.

Japan is one of the most swiftly aging societies globally, with 26.6% of its population being over the age of 65 in 2015, surpassing any European country. Depopulation and aging have occurred concurrently, especially in mountainous locations. In 2000, approximately 44.4% of forest households had householders who were 65 years old or older [2]. Consequently, the percentage of homes with a householder who is 75 years old or older is on the rise. The criteria specified will lead to an increase in forest inheritance, which is expected to result in imminent issues pertaining to forest inheritance.

Due to the incomplete national land survey, the number of forested areas with unknown boundaries is growing, as many owners are unaware of the precise limits of their forests. In the 1950s, forest owners exhibited a greater level of consciousness regarding their limits due to the consumption of fuelwood for heating purposes. The bond between the forest and the forest owner became less strong when the usage of fuelwood declined. Furthermore, due to a decline in population and an increase in the elderly population, several small villages have ceased to exist [3]. In these districts, the newly acquired forested land was often inherited by non-residents who were prone to neglect any forest management endeavors.

An inheritance tax is levied on the transfer of any property, including forest, that is received by inheritance. Nevertheless, private forest owners found themselves burdened by the inheritance tax and annual fixed property tax once they ceased to get any more economic advantages from the forest. The economic significance of broad-leaved trees experienced a significant decline once the use of fuelwood ceased, and the prices for harvesting coniferous plantation forests, such as Cryptomeria japonica and Chamaecyparis obtusa, also saw a substantial fall. This issue arises when owners are unable to bear the expenses of planting and weeding following the act of cutting, particularly when the stumpage price is low. Additionally, they face difficulties in harvesting the coniferous trees.

The complexities of forest inheritance are intricately linked to a multitude of variables and issues that revolve around Japanese forestry. This chapter examines the issues of the transfer of forests in the present and upcoming years, specifically focusing on the implications of the inheritance tax system. Section 2 outlines the research approach. Section 3 provides a comprehensive overview of the Japanese and forest inheritance tax systems. Furthermore, this analysis addresses three existing issues: the implementation of preferential treatments to decrease the forest inheritance tax, the correlation between the forest inheritance tax and the forest planning system, and the connection between the forest inheritance tax and the amount of forest holdings. In Section 4, the text concludes and presents potential study areas.

2. METHODS

This research included a literature survey and analysis based on government statistics, predominantly from three sources.

The first data source was the National Tax Agency Annual Statistics Report,[3] in particular the national total number of ancestors and value of forest land properties from a breakdown table of inherited property by type. Although this data provided information on the ancestors, it was difficult to obtain data on inheritors. The value of timber was based on the price of standing timber at the standard cutting age, which is published almost annually in the form of a circular notice on legal interpretation from the Director General of the National Tax Agency to the heads of regional taxation bureaus. For example, in Yoshino, the calculation was based on the Yoshino forestry area of Nara prefecture under the authority of the Osaka Regional Tax Bureau.

The second source of data was the Census of Agriculture and Forestry, which included basic statistics related to forest owners, although the data were not always continuous due, for example, to national budget cuts. The minimum holding size of forest land included in the survey was 0.1 and 1 ha in the 1990 and 2000 censuses, respectively. Moreover, since 2005, the survey interval changed from 10 to 5 years, and the survey method changed completely. To account for these differences, only forest owners with ≥1 ha were considered in this study.

Finally, the third source of data was Housing and Land Statistics. The Statistics Bureau of Ministry of Internal Affairs and Communications collect this data every 5 years. Although the main objective of these statistics is to survey the housing situation, survey items related to land owned by each household were added in the 1998 survey. There are two surveys: survey A was completed by approximately 3 million householders and survey B was completed by 0.5 million householders. For the first time in the 2013 survey, survey A included a survey item on ownership of land other than current residence, including farmland and forest land.

In this chapter, examples of tax calculations for forest owners were not included, in part because the inheritance tax is estimated for all inheritance properties including forest and it is difficult to show a separate calculation for forests. Usui and Hayashi [4] noted that the contents of inheritance properties differ, and the value of the inheritance tax for forest and the burden it places on the inheritor may differ. Furthermore, it is generally difficult to determine all inheritance property based on on-site surveys.

3. STATUS OF FOREST INHERITANCE TAX

3.1. Inheritance tax

All inheritors must pay an inheritance tax, which is applied to all inherited properties, including forests. The amount charged is the exempted amount subtracted from the total value of the property. The current exemption is 30 million yen plus 6 million yen per inheritor. The tax rate is determined by the classification of the chargeable amount. A progressive taxation system is used, and the current rate is 10–55%. In 2015, the exemption was reduced from 50 to 30 million yen and the exemption per person was reduced from 10 to 6 million yen, resulting in a decrease in the minimum value for inheritance tax. In addition, the tax rate classification table was changed in 2015, and the maximum taxation rate was raised from 50 to 55%. The current tax rate table is shown in Table 1. The maximum tax rate decreased from 75 to 70% in 1988, and from 70 to 50% in 2003. In 2015, the maximum rate increased to 55%.[4]

Table 1. Tax rate.

Chargeable amount (million yen)	Taxiation Rate (%)
less than 10	10
10-30	15
30-50	20
50-100	30
100-200	40
200-300	45
300-600	50
600 and over	55
Source: National Tax Agency.	

3.2. Forest inheritance tax

The major taxes related to private forest owners include inheritance tax, which is a national tax, fixed property tax, which is paid as an annual municipal tax, and forest income tax, which is a national sales tax that must be paid by sellers of standing trees.[5]

Forests are evaluated by dividing the area into forested land and standing trees. The forested land evaluation is calculated by multiplying the evaluation of the property tax[6] by a constant number. When forest land is located near an urban area, its value is generally high due to the effect of the housing land price.[7]

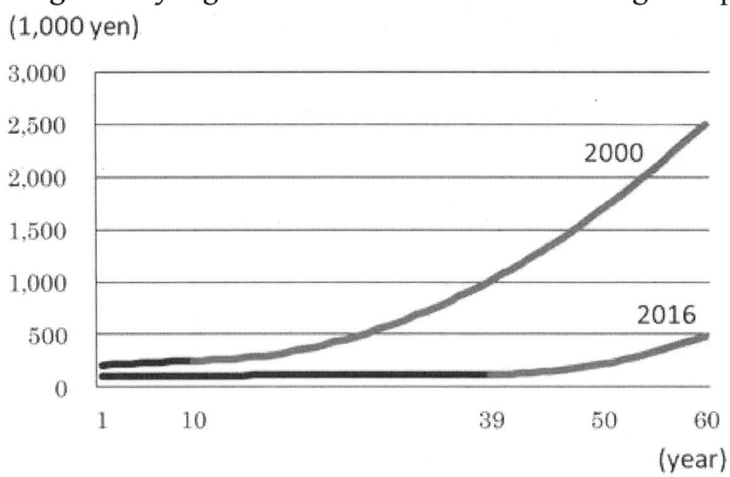

Figure 1. Example of evaluation of standing trees. Note: This is an example calculated using the final cutting age and the value of standing C. japonica trees at the final cutting age in the Yoshino forestry area.

The current method to calculate standing trees is as follows [10]. The value of 1- to 39-year-old standing trees is based on the standard reforestation cost, in which the value for a 1-year-old tree is determined by the national tax office, and the value for 2- to 39-year-old trees is calculated as 1.5% the compound interest rate. The value of trees from 40 years old to the standard final cutting age[8] is calculated using the Glaser formula. Figure 1 shows an example of this calculation based on *C. japonica*, with a standard final cutting age of 60 years.[9] In Figure 1, the black line shows the value from 1-year old to the fixed tree age and the red line shows the value from the fixed tree age to the standard final cutting age calculated using the Glaser formula.

In 2004, the compound interest rate was reduced from 2 to 1.5%, the fixed tree age at which the calculation method changed rose from 10 to 39 years, and the standard reforestation cost decreased.[10] Figure 1 shows examples of the calculations before and after the 2004 amendment. The value of standing trees per ha decreased markedly for all tree ages after these changes.[11]

To calculate the value of trees older than the standard final cutting age, the value of standing trees, from the standard final cutting age to twice the standard final cutting age, is calculated based on a 2% compound interest rate.[12] The value of standing trees over twice the standard final cutting age is estimated based on expert opinions.[13]

The standard value of the standard final cutting age changes based on the actual stumpage price. The example in Figure 1 is based on the standard value at the standard final cutting age in the Yoshino forestry area of Nara Prefecture, under the jurisdiction of the Osaka Regional Tax Bureau, a representative privately owned traditional forestry area in Japan. The standard value at the standard final cutting age in this area is shown in Figure 2. Over the past 20 years, the value has decreased, although this decreasing trend recently stopped.[14]

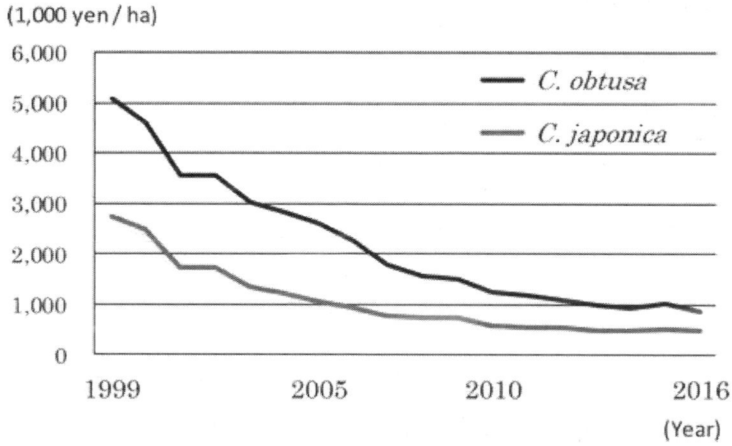

Figure 2. The standard value of standing trees at the standard final cutting age. Source: National Tax Agency. Note: Example in the Yoshino forestry area. As data are lacking for 2002, values for 2002 are the same as those for the previous year.

Table 2 shows the standard values per ha at the standard final cutting age in 1999 and 2016. The standard values decreased in all forestry areas. The value in the Yoshino forestry area, used in the example of Figure 1, decreased at a rate of 82.5%, showing the maximum decrease.

Table 2. Standard value at the standard final cutting age of *C. japonica*.

(1,000 yen %)				
Prefecture	**Forestry area**	**1999**	**2016**	**Change**
Miyagi	North part of Miyagi	1,530	560	-63.4
Tochigi	Watarasegawa	1,860	710	-61.8
Tokyo	Tama	1,750	390	-77.7
Shizuoka	Tenryu	1,710	480	-71.9
Fukui	Echizen	2,140	550	-74.3
Nara	Yoshino	2,750	480	-82.5
Shimane	Hiigawa	1,440	470	-67.4
Ehime Imabari and Matsuyama		1,400	480	-65.7
Fukuoka	Chikugogawa and Yabegawa	1,110	330	-70.3
Kumamoto	Kumagawa	1,020	440	-56.9
Source: National Tax Agency.				

As a result of a number of changes, including the standard value of standing trees at the standard final cutting age, the value of standing trees has decreased in recent years.

3.3. Measures to reduce the forest inheritance tax

After evaluating forested land and standing trees, several tax reductions are available. If the forest is specified as a protected forest under the Forest Act (Act No. 249 of 1951), the value of the forest land and standing trees is reduced by 30–80% according to the cutting method allowed (Table 3). In forests where cutting activities are completely prohibited, the reduction rate is 80%.

Table 3. Value reduction rate of protected forests.

Category	Rate (%)
Clear cutting	30
Selective cutting	50
Single tree selective cutting	70
Cutting is prohibited	80

If a forest falls under a forest management plan in the Forest Act, a 5% reduction has been applied to the evaluation values of the forest land and standing trees since 2002.[15]

A 15% reduction is applied to the evaluation value of standing trees. For example, if an inheritor takes possession of a 20-year-old plantation forest and sells the forest when the trees are 50 years old, the forest income tax on 50-year-old trees will be applied. However, because the forest was inherited, ancestor(s) owned from the planting year until they were 20 years old. Thus, the 15% reduction rule[16] was introduced for standing trees across the board to cancel out future income tax related to the first 20 years of ownership by ancestor(s).

3.4. Number of ancestors and evaluation value of forest property

Table 4 summarizes the land characteristics of all properties in 2014. In 2014, there were 56,329 ancestors, and 93% (52,327) of ancestors had land property. The inheritance tax is necessary in cases when the total evaluation of properties exceeds the value of several exemptions. However, the inheritance tax tends to be applicable when there is land included as property.

Table 4. Land property in 2014.

Category	Number of ancestors (number)	Percentage (%)	Value of properties (million yen)	Percentage (%)	Average
Rice field	11,133	21.3	263,646	5.1	23.7
Farm land	14,358	27.4	593,975	11.5	41.4
Housing land	51,513	98.4	3,781,938	73.5	73.4
Forest land	10,929	20.9	74,034	1.4	6.8
Other land	14,863	28.4	487,309	9.5	32.8
Total	52,327	100.0	5,146,902	100.0	98.4

Source: National Tax Agency Annual Statistics Report.

Note: The total of number of ancestors is the actual number of ancestors. In cases of rice fields and farmland, cultivation rights and perennial tenant rights are included. In the case of housing land, leaseholding is included.

Of the 52,327 ancestors with land property, 51,513 cases included housing land, meaning that in most cases, including forest land, the land property included housing land. This is in agreement with the results of the 2013 Housing and Land Statistics conducted by the Statistics Bureau of the Ministry of Internal Affairs and Communications, which estimated that 2,673,000 households owned forest land, of which 2,569,400 households (96.1%) had their own house. Therefore, only a small percentage of cases included inherited land property that was only forest land.

In total, 20.9% of ancestors had land properties that included forest land. However, these properties only accounted for 1.4% of the total value of properties. The average value of forest land per ancestor was 6.8 million yen, much less than the values of housing land, farmland, and rice fields.

Figure 3 shows the number of ancestors with property that included forested land and the value of forest land per ancestor from 1988 to 2014.

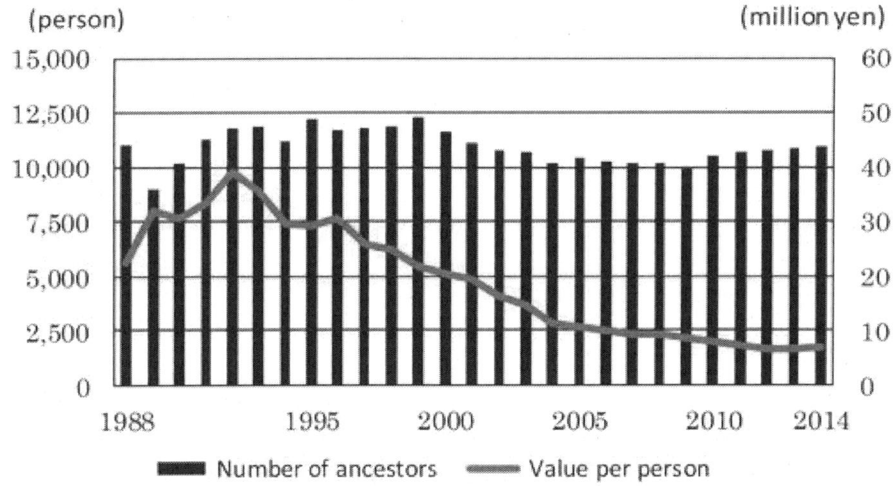

Figure 3. Number of ancestors and value of forest land. Source: National Tax Agency Annual Statistics Report.

About 10,000 inheritances that included forested land were required to pay inheritance tax. The evaluated value of forest land per inheritance has decreased since 1992. For example, when the value in 1992 is fixed to 100, the value in 2014 is 17.4. The reason for this decrease is the decrease in the value of forest land, since the values of both forest land and housing land have decreased. Figure 4 shows the number of ancestors and value of housing land. The pattern of the graph is similar to that of forest land, and when the peak value in 1992 is fixed to 100, the value in 2014 is 36.1.

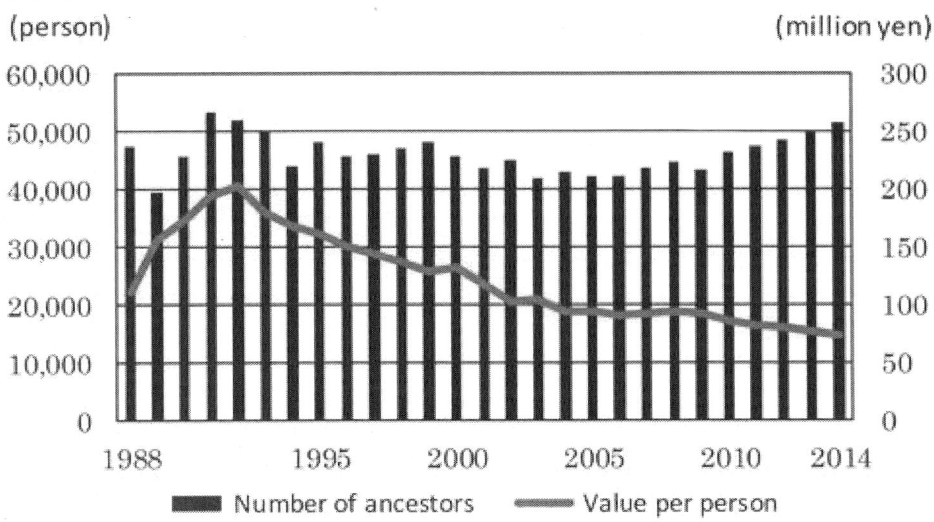

Figure 4. Number of ancestors and value of housing land. Source: National Tax Agency Annual Statistics Report.

Figure 5 shows the number of ancestors and value of the inherited property when only standing trees are considered and forest land is excluded, both of which are decreasing.

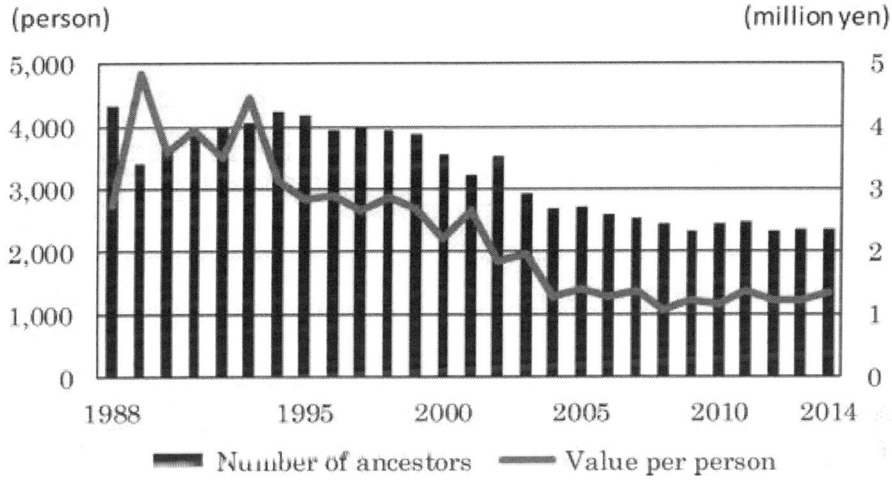

Figure 5.Number of ancestors and value of standing trees. Source: National Tax Agency Annual Statistics Report.

3.5. Decrease in the value of forest and stumpage price

The value of forest land per ancestor has decreased since 1992 (Figure 3). The value in the peak year (1992) was 39 million yen, which decreased to 6.8 million yen in 2014. The reason for this decrease is a decrease in the standard value at the standard final cutting age due to decreases in both forest land and stumpage prices (Figure 6).

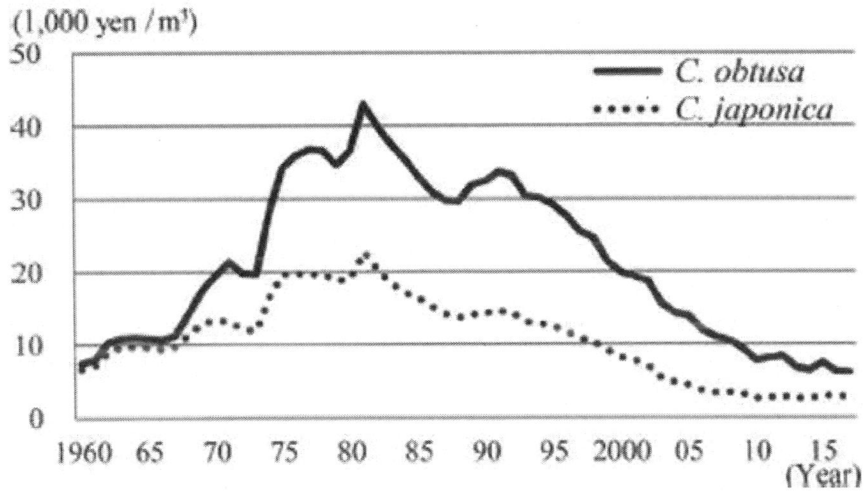

Figure 6. Stumpage price. Source: Forestry Agency, Annual Statistics of Forestry, Annual Statistics of Forest and Forestry; original source is the Japan Real Estate Institute. Note: As of March 31.

The stumpage prices of *C. japonica* and *C. obtusa* peaked in 1980, and have been decreasing since. Setting the stumpage price in 1980 to 100, the stumpage price in 2016 was 12.3 for *C. japonica* and 14.4 for *C. obtusa*. Compared to the stumpage prices in 1960, 7,148 yen and 7,966 yen for *C. japonica* and *C. obtusa*, respectively, the stumpage prices in 2016 were 39.2 and 77.2% of those in 1960, respectively. Since this represents the nominal price, a long-term increase in prices should be considered. Using the Corporate Goods Price Index of 2005 by the Bank of Japan, the index was 50.8 and 105.0 in 1960 and 2011, respectively. Using the Consumer Price Index of 2010 by the Bank of Japan, the index was 19.1 and 99.7 in 1960 and 2011, respectively. In other words, between 1960 and 2011, the Corporate Goods Price Index increased twofold and the Consumer Price Index increased fivefold. Under such long-term increases in the price index, the nominal prices of 2016 were 39.2 and 77.2% of those in 1960, showing a decrease in price.

The large decrease in stumpage price has affected the value of forests during evaluations for inheritance tax. Since the area of inherited forest is not included in the National Tax Agency Annual Statistics Report, further statistical analysis is difficult, and analyses related to on-site surveys is a topic of future research.

Given the large decreases in stumpage price, it is possible that the stumpage price will decrease beyond the break-even point. When forest owners cannot expect any income from cutting after inheritance, the inheritance tax is only a burden to the inheritor. This would create a scenario where there is a probability that some forest owners would cut standing trees to reduce the standing tree value before their death.[17] Since many plantation forests planted after World War II are now reaching the standard cutting age, and thinning has been promoted by the Forestry Agency, the value of standing trees is increasing. To reduce the burden of the inheritor further, forest owners may sell not only standing trees, but also the forest land.

It has been noted that some forest owners, for example, older owners without an inheritor, have stopped managing their forest with the intent of selling their forest land along with standing trees to logging companies;[18] however, it is difficult to determine the statistics behind this trend. It should be mentioned that the reason for such action is not limited to inheritance, as the decrease in stumpage price (Figure 6) and decrease in log price have led to decreases in income from timber sales. Table 5 shows statistical indexes of forest management. Net income (subtracting column (B) from column (A)) has recently decreased. The percentage of tax in which forest inheritance tax is not included in the statistics based on the total cost is almost 6–8%; however, the amount of tax currently yields a net income. This management situation is the foundation of the current abandonment of forest management.

Table 5. Index of forest management.

(1,000 yen) Holding size	Year	Gross income (A)	Cost (B)	(A)-(B)	Tax	Tax/(B)	Tax/(A-B)
Total	2003	2,751	2,235	516	156	7.0	30.2
	2008	1,784	1,681	103	136	8.1	132.0
	2013	2,484	2,371	113	145	6.1	128.3
20 -50 ha	2003	1,598	953	645	82	8.6	12.7
	2008	1,225	938	287	75	8.0	26.1
	2013	2,773	2,013	760	131	6.5	17.2
50 – 100 ha	2003	2,312	1,748	564	140	8.0	24.8
	2008	1,098	1,191	-93	108	9.1	
	2013	1,742	1,652	90	106	6.4	117.8
100 – 500 ha	2003	3,460	3,108	352	225	7.2	63.9
	2008	3,218	2,959	259	209	7.1	80.7
	2013	3,198	3,309	-111	224	6.8	
500 ha and over	2003	60,253	63,495	-3,242	2,303	3.6	
	2008	30,302	28,131	2,171	2,357	8.4	108.6
	2013	9,346	13,851	-4,505	415	3.0	

Source: Ministry of Agriculture, Forestry and Fisheries, Statistics of Forest Management.[19]
Note: In this case, tax refers to taxes, public dues, various burden charges, etc.

4. DISCUSSION

4.1. Preferential treatment for forest inheritance tax

4.1.1. Changes in the background of preferential treatment for the forest inheritance tax

Several forest inheritance taxes have been reduced for forest land and standing trees. As a background, forests were necessary for daily life in the past, and forestry practices and maintenance were conducted mainly by the forest owner, who invested in the forest over the long-term, but with low profitability. However, this background has changed.

4.1.1.1. End of fuelwood use

As a result of the end of fuelwood use, the importance of fuelwood in forest management has decreased. Figure 7 shows the percentage of fuelwood to the total cutting volume. At the beginning of the 1940s, the percentage was over 60%. After World War II, it decreased in a linear manner, and fell to only 3% in 1972. Because of the end of fuelwood consumption, daily use by forest owners and their family almost disappeared, except for activities such as mushroom production.

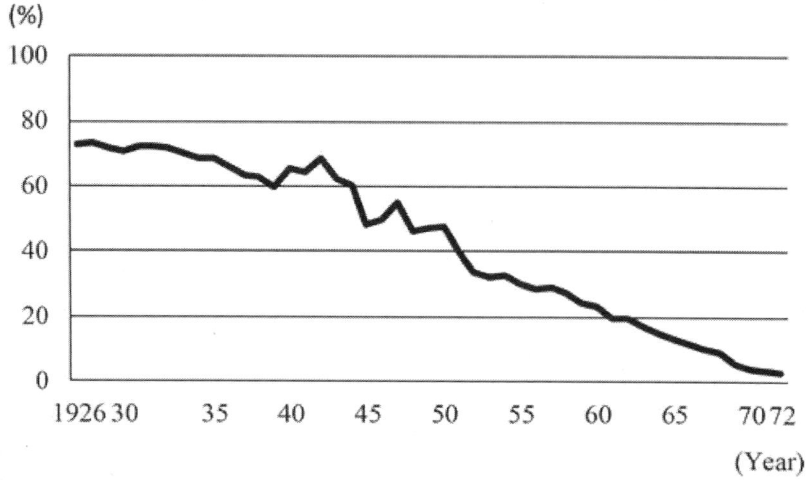

Figure 7. Percentage of fuel wood for the total cutting. Source: Forestry Agency, Division of Research [17], Forestry Agency [18–20].

During the period when fuelwood consumption decreased, the Forestry Agency strongly promoted the planting of coniferous trees such as *C. japonica* and *C. obtusa*. Figure 8 shows the area of plantation. In the 1950s and 1960s, the annual plantation area was approximately 300,000 ha, which began to decrease in the 1970s and is currently around 20,000 or 30,000 ha, less than 10% of the peak.

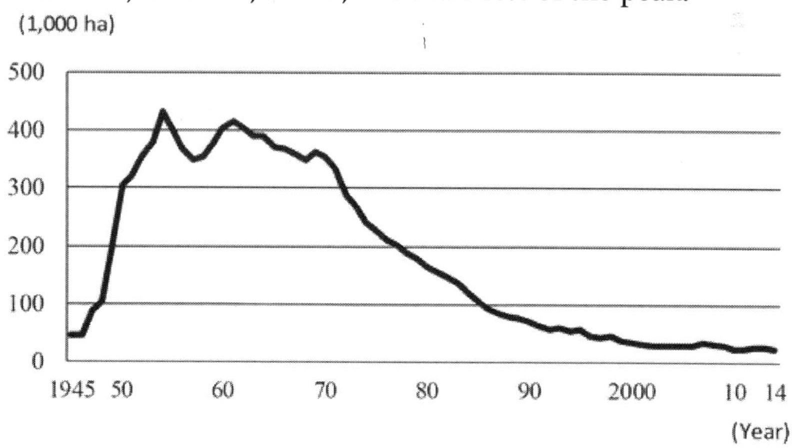

Figure 8.Area of plantation. Source: Forestry Agency, Division of Research [17], Forestry Agency [1, 18–20].

To create coniferous plantations, a large amount of labor was necessary to conduct planting and initial treatment, such as weeding. In the 1950s and 1960s, the peak period of planting, family labor within the forest owner's household and employees of forest owners' cooperatives had large roles in private forestry. The forests planted during that time are now about 50 years old, and require thinning and final cutting, but these activities are conducted by forestry companies or forest owners' cooperatives. Since most forest owners do not have the machinery necessary for such activities, it is difficult for families to conduct cutting activities.

In the past, the relationship between forest land and agriculture was considered as a role of private forest. However, of all forest owners, 58% also owned farmland based on the 2015 Census of Agriculture and Forestry.[20] Meanwhile, based on the 2013 Housing and Land Statistics, 71% of forest owners also owned farmland [21]. Just after the end of World War II, most forest owners were probably farmers, and the percentage of non-farming forest owners has increased. In addition, in the field of farm management, the relationship to forest resources has disappeared.

4.1.1.2. Increase in non-resident forest owners

The spread of depopulation and number of non-resident forest owners is increasing throughout Japan. In the 2000 Census of Agriculture and Forestry, non-resident forest owners accounted for 24.6% of total forest owners. As the number of aged owners is increasing, inheritance appears to be increasing. In some cases, the inheritor does not live in the same municipality as the ancestor. Table 6 shows the percentage of non-resident forest owners by region, which shows regional differences. In Hokkaido, the northern-most prefecture, the percentage of non-resident forest owners reached 46.1%. In the mountainous areas of north Kanto and Kinki regions, it was ≥40%. Therefore, before discussing daily use or maintenance, it must be stressed that many owners are non-residents.

Table 6. The percentage of non-resident forest owners in 2000.

(%) Region	Urban area	Agricultural area Flat land	Medium	Mountain	Total
Hokkaido	46.1	44.7	55.5	55.6	52.6
Tohuko	14.1	17.8	14.4	13.7	14.5
Hokuriku	11.1	13.5	16.3	23.7	17.7
Kanto and Tosan	23.1	19.3	22.5	28.8	24.6
Nort Kanto	24.9	18.3	22.1	45.0	27.9
South Kanto	28.3	22.5	28.0	30.2	27.9
Tokai	30.7	21.6	23.9	32.7	30.4
Kinki	23.3	20.8	21.3	42.9	32.6
Cyugoku	8.6	11.2	12.5	16.4	13.8
Shikoku	20.1	17.1	19.7	29.8	25.9
Kyusyu	12.8	12.2	15.2	21.2	16.6
Total	19.8	12.2	15.2	21.2	16.6

Source: Ministry of Agriculture, Forestry and Fisheries, the 2000 Census of Agriculture and Forestry.

Depopulation and aging have long been a problem in Japan, and there have been a number of discussions regarding the end of hamlets. The Ministry of Land, Infrastructure, Transport and Tourism ([22], p. 12) predicted an increase and decrease in population at a 500-m mesh resolution based on the 2010 Population Census. Comparing the number of meshes between 2010 and the 2050 prediction, 19% of meshes changed from populated areas to unpopulated areas, and 44% of meshes showed a decreasing rate of population of ≥50%. In these areas, the percentage of non-resident forest owners is likely to increase.

4.1.1.3. Forest as property

Since most Japanese private forest owners have small holding areas, forest has an important role as household property. Such areas are too small to conduct planting and periodic cutting to receive a sufficient annual income from forest products to cover the household economy. Thus, the main deciding factor of whether to cut trees is related to the large expenditure, which has long been a characteristic of the Japanese private forest sector. In addition, daily use has disappeared and the number of non-resident forest owners has increased; therefore, the consideration of forest as property is further increasing.

The current situation surrounding private forest is changing. Generally, forest owners do not manage and work in their forest on a daily basis. This is in part because the number of non-resident owners is increasing, and will likely continue to increase in the future with the expansion of unpopulated areas. Moreover, forests are becoming land estates. At the same time, both the stumpage price and value of forest property have decreased. Under these conditions, ongoing tax reductions have the potential to encourage non-resident ownership, although it is highly possible that the increasing number of non-resident owners will abandon forest practices.

4.1.2. Final cutting in protected forest

The forest inheritance tax has been reduced and the fixed property tax is exempt in protected forest[21] where the cutting method is determined under the Forest Act. Namely, an inheritor can inherit protected forest with a low inheritance tax rate and hold the forested area without paying any property tax. Approximately 30% of non-national forest is protected.[22]

Under the Japanese protected forest system, forests in which cutting activities are completely prohibited exist in limited areas, while most protected forests can be cut for commercial purposes under some restrictions. However, under the current inheritance and fixed property tax, even if the forest reaches the final cutting age, protected forest owners can simply hold the forest. The government revised the Basic Plan on Forest and Forestry in May 2016, with the main goal of increasing timber production. In 2014, the domestic timber supply was 24 million m^3, which the government plans to increase to 32 million m^3 and 40 million m^3 in 2020 and 2025, respectively. However, under the current tax system, it is possible that cutting activities in private forests, especially under various restriction systems, such as protected forests, will not be realized as estimated.

4.2. Forest inheritance tax and forest planning system

4.2.1. Forest management of large-scale forest owners and forest inheritance problems

Some forest owners who hold large parcels are managing their forests full-time. At times, the inheritance tax has become a considerable burden for such owners. In particular, if a large part of inherited property is forest, the forest may be clear cut to pay the inheritance tax. Since the current stumpage price is generally low, the cutting area may be large. A forest income tax is imposed on the income generated from cutting the trees to pay the inheritance tax, which may be a burden for the inheritor ([23], p. 241). The final cutting age for *C. juponica* is around 50 years, but actual cutting tends to occur at older ages.[23] To avoid clear-cutting at the scheduled cutting age, some forest owners have performed repeated thinning after the standard final cutting age. In these cases, inheritance may occur more than once between planting and final cutting.[24] Therefore, the burden of the inheritance tax can influence scheduled forest practices.

To illustrate the effects of this, the following section describes the opinions of forest owners, including opinions on the inheritance tax, based on the results of the opinion survey on forestry management[25] conducted by the Forestry Agency in the fiscal year of 2009. Figure 9 shows the responses to the question on what support or measures are necessary for forestry management to continue in the next generation. The most frequent answer was the stabilization of timber price. This response reflects the long-term decrease in stumpage price (Figure 6). Since forest owners cannot pay the costs associated with reforestation under low stumpage prices, the second-most frequent answer was to subsidize the full cost of reforestation. Following these, a reduction in the inheritance and gift tax, development of forest owners' cooperatives and forestry entities, and reduction in fixed property tax were also deemed important. Due to the low stumpage price, it is necessary to decrease management costs, for example, by intensifying forest practices through the development of forest owners' cooperatives, etc. After these three suggestions, improvements related to taxes were selected, because the current inheritance tax has decreased correspondingly, but the decrease in the stumpage price is severe, and it is not practical for forest owners to cut standing trees under such stumpage prices.

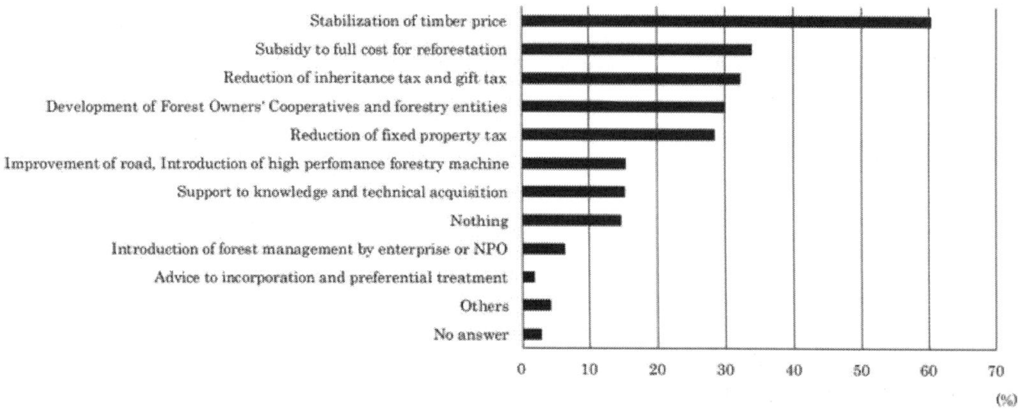

Figure 9. Forest owner opinions on strategies to support forestry management. Source: MAFF ([24], pp. 18–19). Note: Three answers were required.

Figure 10 shows the percentage of respondents who selected the two tax-related responses, a reduction in inheritance and gift tax and a reduction in fixed property tax, classified by holding area of forest. The frequency of annual fixed property tax was only larger than that of inheritance tax in the case of owners with <20 ha.[26] Among owners with ≥20 ha, the percentage of respondents who selected inheritance tax was larger, markedly so in the case of ≥500 ha, with 53.1% selecting inheritance tax. These results showed that the importance of inheritance tax increased according to holding size.

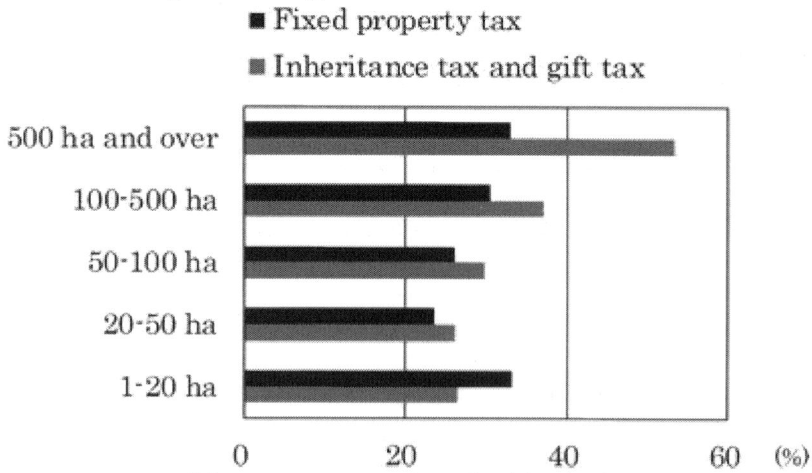

Figure 10. Percentage of forest owners classified by holding size who considered taxes to be an impediment to the continuation of forestry management. Source: MAFF ([24], pp. 18–19).

Figure 11 shows the same options related to taxes as Figure 10, but with the owners classified by management situation from the perspective of annual income. Forest owners with an annual income from timber sales more often considered the inheritance tax and gift tax to be an impediment than the property tax. Only owners holding unmanaged forested land more often selected the fixed property tax as a problem. To summarize these results, there is high demand for a reduction in the inheritance tax and gift tax among large-scale forest owners who sell timber every year.

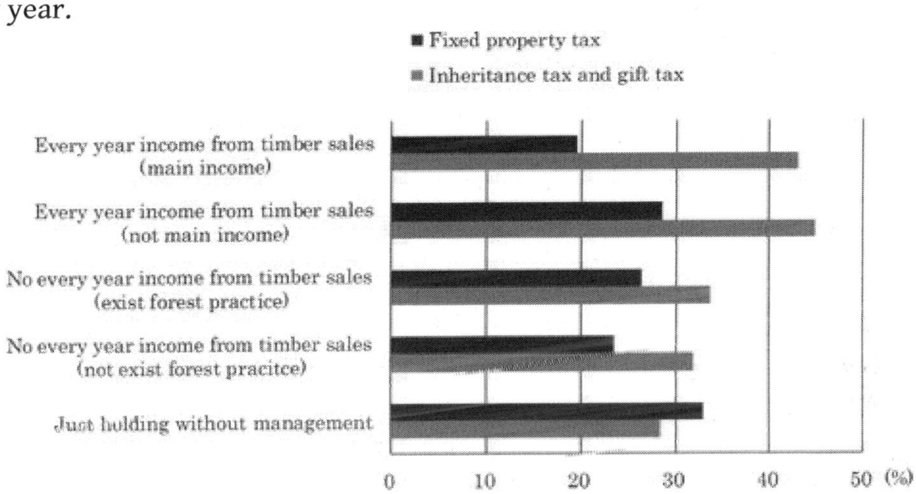

Figure 11. Percentage of forest owners classified by management situation and income who considered taxes to be an impediment to the continuation of forestry management. Source: MAFF ([24], pp. 18–19).

Figure 12 shows the results of the responses to the survey question related to future management policy. Among owners with a holding area <20 ha, approximately 80% answered that they plan to hold without management. This same response was selected by 43.9 and 33.9% of owners with holding areas of 100–500 and ≥500, respectively. Meanwhile, there was no clear relationship among owners who responded that they plan to end forestry management by holding size.[27] In addition, 4.6, 5.8, and 4.8% of owners with <20, 100–500, and ≥500 ha, respectively, responded that they plan to expand management. Finally, 35–40% of owners with ≥20 ha responded that they do not plan to make changes.

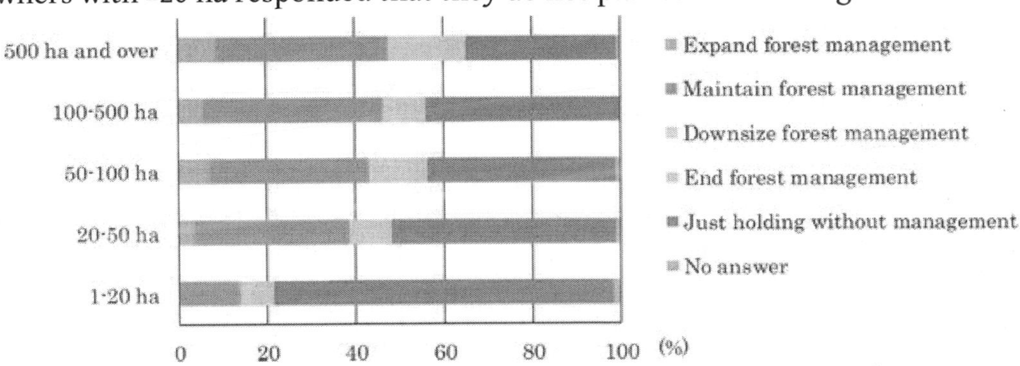

Figure 12. Forest owners intended future forestry management policy. Source: MAFF ([24], p. 11).

4.2.2. Postponement of inheritance tax payment by large-scale forest owners

4.2.2.1. New measures on the postponement of payment of inheritance tax in 2014

The government introduced a new system in April 2012 allowing the postponement[28] of the inheritance tax payment[29] under specific conditions for forest owners with ≥100 ha. The basic conditions are as follows.

For forest land, the forest management plan made by the ancestor must be certified. In addition, forest practices and the investment to forest road network must be conducted or planned for forests to be eligible for postponement, and the total forest area must be ≥100 ha.

For standing trees, the age should not have reached the standard age for final cutting, as determined in municipal forest development plans, by a specific year. The specific year is the average remaining lifetime up to 30 years. The inheritor must inherit all of the ancestor's forest management according to the forest management plan of the ancestor. The inheritor must succeed at completing the ancestor's forest management plan, continue making a forest management plan, and conduct forest practices according to the forest management plan.

The postponement of paying inheritance tax is available until the day of the death of the inheritor for up to 80% of the amount of inheritance tax imposed on forests that satisfy the above conditions. At the time of the death of the inheritor, the total amount of postponed tax is exempted. Since the new postponement has only just been introduced, data on this postponement are not available. However, Sugano and Tani ([14], p. 32) reported that applications for this tax postponement are currently very low.

4.2.2.2. Relationship between the new postponement and forest planning systems

The new postponement system introduced in 2012 has a close relationship with the forest management planning system based on the Forest Act.[30] The current forest management planning system introduced in 2012 focuses on intensive forest management and improvements to forest road networks. When the forest owner makes a forest management plan, the forest owner can receive several benefits, such as a reduction in forest inheritance tax, reduction in forest income tax, subsidy related to reforestation, or low-interest loan on forestry from the Japan Finance Corporation. Although many coniferous plantations planted after World War II now require thinning, if a forest owner wants to conduct thinning as well as construct forest or spur roads, a forest management plan is necessary to obtain a subsidy. Ultimately, forest management plans have a close relationship with government subsidies. There are three types of forest management plans, one of which can be made by sole forest owners holding ≥100 ha of forest.[31] Under the postponement system, a one-person forest management plan is necessary. The two additional conditions related to the forest management plan necessary to obtain a postponement of inheritance tax are that within 10 years after inheritance, the forest owner should expand the management area at least 30%, up to 150 ha, and should expand forest or spur roads to a level determined by the local municipal forest development plan.

In old forests with a dense forest road network, it is not necessary for forest owners to obtain a subsidy related to forest practices; therefore, there is little merit to making a forest management plan. When there are no special benefits to obtaining a subsidy, a forest management plan may constrain forest management. For example, when forest owner wants to conduct final cutting, he/she can contact a logging company without a subsidy. Furthermore, the percentage of forest owners who want to expand forest management is generally low (see Figure 12). For example, a forest owner who owns ≥500 ha would have to expand the forest management by 150 ha, which is the upper limit of the conditions related to the postponement, and only a few forest owners have conducted this expansion to postpone the inheritance tax.

Large-scale forest owners often own forest in remote areas, and some investment is necessary to satisfy the forest road network density conditions. In addition, after investing in the forest road network, the value of the land will increase.[32] Regardless, an initial cash reserve is necessary to expand the holding size or increase the forest road network. Given the long-term decrease in stumpage price, the number of large-scale forest owners who want to expand forests and invest in roads is limited.

Because the postponement measure in 2012 is connected with forest management plan, when a forest owner cannot continue the forest management plan or the certification of the forest management plan is canceled, the forest owner must pay the postponed inheritance tax. Typical examples[33] of this include the case that the forest owner cannot accomplish the objectives related to the expansion of forest management area and forest road network density, or the case that the forest owner entrusts all or a part of the forest management to others. Expanding holding forest and forest road networks are straightforward obligations. However, there is another condition as follows: in a year when the forest owner does not conduct any planting, cutting, or road construction, the forest owner must pay the postponed inheritance tax. Generally, forest management does not require forest practices annually; therefore, this condition may be too strong. When the forest owner pays the postponed inheritance tax, he/she must also pay the annual interest tax of 3.6%. Considering the payment of the interest, it may be difficult to apply the postponed tax, except cases where the inheritor decisively shows continuous forest management until death.

One final comment should be made regarding the forest planning system, which has a strong connection with the inheritance tax postponement. The forest management plan is located at the bottom of the forest planning system. First, there is the Basic Plan on Forest and Forestry at the top of the forest planning system, and the current version published on May of 2016 includes the objective of increasing domestic timber production in Japan (see Section 4.1.2). The existence of the objectives of expanding management size and forest road networks in the postponement measures seems to be related to the basic policy direction of domestic timber production. However, the method for continuing forest management differs. In cases where the holding size is large and the forest area is not dispersed, the expansion of forest management area may lead to a decrease in efficiency. In addition, once the forest road network reaches a certain density, further investment may not be necessary. The current forest road volume conditions are based on logging using vehicles. While the majority of logging systems use vehicles, there are some areas where cable logging systems are used. For example, in some steep mountainous areas, there may be an advantage to using cable logging systems. Moreover, in the Yoshino forestry area, helicopter logging is used for high quality logs. Although it may seem logical that a continuous forest management model includes the expansion of management area and forest road networks, the automatic requirement of such expansive conditions in large-scale forest management should be avoided, and should allow for practical alternative measures.

4.2.3. Problems associated with the postponement measures

Some problems are inherent in this new policy. For example, this system applies only to large-scale forest owners with ≥100 ha, and many forest owners whose families manage their forest have <100 ha. Meanwhile, many non-residential forest owners with ≥100 ha have no interest in forest management. Regarding the forest management planning system, only forest owners with ≥100 ha can make forest management plans independently. Accordingly, in both the forest planning system and the postponement system of inheritance tax, the Forestry Agency has used 100 ha as the limit of the desirable holding size.

Therefore, the relevance of using 100 ha as a criterion should be examined. After checking publications by the Forestry Agency, only a small, detailed introduction was found ([27], p. 107). In potential support of the introduction of the postponement of the inheritance tax, 53% of forest owners with ≥500 ha thought that a reduction in the inheritance tax was necessary to support the continuation of forestry management in the next generation (see Figure 10). Judging from the results of this question in Figure 10, except forest owners with <20 ha, interest in a reduction in the inheritance tax tended to increase with increased holding size. The Forestry Agency [27] explained that the objective of creating the postponement of the inheritance tax was to support a smooth business succession to the main provider and effective and stable forestry management. However, there is no basis for the use of 100 ha as the inclusion criterion. In the questionnaire survey on taxes (Figure 10) and future plans (Figure 12), the responses of forest owners differed according to holding area, but a clear reason of the use of 100 ha could not be found from these survey results.

4.3. Forest inheritance tax and forest holding size

4.3.1. Small-scale family forest management and inheritance

Before World War II in Japan, inheritance operated under a family system,[34] where the eldest son inherited essentially all family estates. In addition, the inheritance tax at the time was generally low ([28], p. 74; [12], p. 2). After World War II, the family system was abolished, and any family member could inherit forest land. In the inheritance system after the war, all children had equal rights to the inherited property, which resulted in the concern that already small farms would become further segmented ([15], p. 92). Under the new inheritance system, forest land may be divided at the time of inheritance.[35] However, actual practices regarding the division of forested land at the time of inheritance are not clear due to a lack of statistical surveys.[36]

In Japan, forest holding sizes are small. In 2015, 829,000 forest owners owned ≥1 ha. Table 7 shows the breakdown of households by forest holding size.

Table 7. Number of households classified by holding size (2015).

Holding size	Number of forest owners	Percentage (%)
1-5 ha	616,687	74.4
5-10	110,944	13.4
10-20	59,650	7.2
20-30	18,617	2.2
30-50	12,713	1.5
50-100	6,715	0.8
100-500	3,316	0.4
500 ha and over	331	0.0
Total	828,973	100.0

Source: MAFF, the 2015 Census of Agriculture and Forestry.

Note: Surveyed households had ≥1 ha.

Based on the 2013 Housing and Land Statistics by Statistics Bureau of the Ministry of Internal Affairs and Communications, 2,673,100 households were estimated to have forest land. However, as shown in Table 7, there is a large discrepancy between this estimate and the number of households determined by the Census of Agriculture and Forestry, which included forest owners with <1 ha.[37] Between 2000 and 2015, the number of households with forest land decreased by 189,779 (18.6%) (Figure 13).

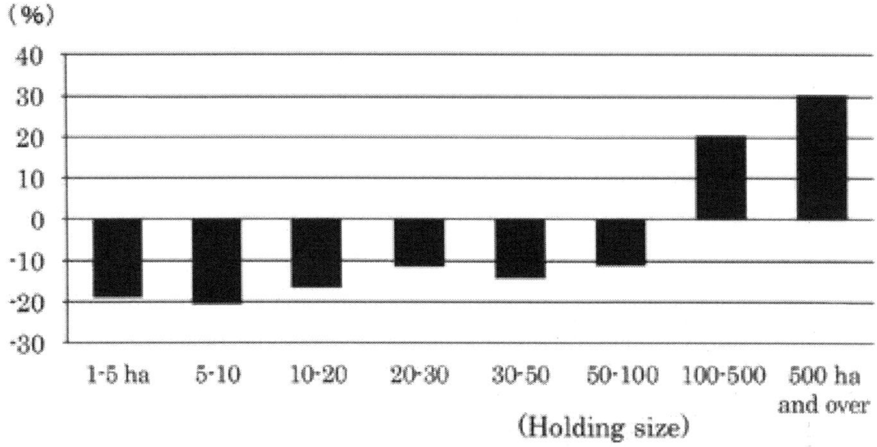

Figure 13. Change in the number of households with forest land between 2000 and 2015 classified by holding size. Source: MAFF, the 2000 and 2015 Census of Agriculture and Forestry. Note: Surveyed households had ≥1 ha.

Although there was an overall decrease of 18.6% in the number of households that owned forest land, the number of forest owners with <100 ha decreased, while the number of forest owners with ≥100 ha increased. However, because a smaller number of households had ≥100 ha, this smaller change is expressed as a large percentage. In contrast, approximately 75% of owners had <5 ha of forest land (Table 7).

Although there is no current survey on forest inheritance in Japan, the importance of demographics, such as depopulation and aging, is increasing. In the 2000 Census of Agriculture and Forestry, 65- to 69-year olds accounted for the largest proportion of householders who owned both farmland and forest land, but 41.0% of households had no successor for agriculture [2]. The number of aged forest owners with no successor is increasing, which could lead to an increase in inheritances at death. Under the inheritance rule created after World War II, there was some importance on gifting property before death.[38] Table 8 shows the number of inheritances and gifts before death in the 1960s ([18, 20], p. 18).

In the case of the household successor, 31.0% of households gifted all or a part of the forest property before death. Meanwhile, in 50.5% of cases, the land was gifted before death to someone other than the successor. This shows that, at least at that time, gifting before death had some importance for the inheritance of forest, and ancestors often gifted forest to successors or other family members before death after clear-cutting. The objective was that inheritors would not be burdened with paying the forest inheritance tax. The tax rate of the gift tax is higher than that of the inheritance tax; however, immediately after clear-cutting, the value of standing trees is negligible and only the forest land has value, which is generally low, excluding areas near cities. Even at a high gift tax rate, if the value of property is low, the ultimate amount of gift tax is low. When a forest owner conducts clear-cutting in a small area and gifts it to inheritor(s) each year, the forest inheritance tax is greatly reduced. As shown in Table 8, someone other than the successor received forest land in 109 (54.5%) of the surveyed households, indicative of segmentalization.

Table 8. Gifting of forest land before death (1960s).

Classification	Method how to get forest land	Number of household	Percentage (%)
Successor of household	Gift before death	30	15.0
	Inheritance	130	65.0
	Both	32	16.0
	Nothing	8	4.0
	Total	200	100.0
Others	Gift before death	55	50.5
	Inheritance	43	39.4
	Both	11	10.1
	Total	109	100.0

Source: Forestry Agency ([18, 20] p. 18, Table 3).
Note: Based on 200 surveyed households.

In households with both farmland and forest land, it may be possible to use both gifts before death and inheritance after death to transfer land to a successor. For example, old coniferous trees can be cut and gifted before death, while low-value broad-leaved trees are left and inherited at death to reduce the total tax. In addition to benefits to the inheritor, there is another explanation of why clear-cutting was common at that time. In the 1950s, the market share of domestic logs was high, and forest owners could sell their trees and receive income at almost any time. Therefore, both conditions, the existence of an inheritor and income from clear-cutting, were satisfied.

However, since 41% of households who owned farm and forest land in 2000 had no inheritor, many ancestors could not gift their forest before death.[39] Moreover, because of the low stumpage price, it was sometimes difficult to pay for reforestation after clear-cutting. In addition, in some areas, the deer population has increased markedly, resulting in the necessity to invest in protection against damage by deer. Without effective countermeasures for such damage, it is difficult to conduct clear-cutting and reforestation of coniferous trees such as *C. japonica* or *C. obtusa*, even in very small areas. Currently, the benefits of conducting clear-cutting to decrease the value of standing trees and gifting to successors before death seems to have decreased, especially for small-scale owners. Future research should clarify the current state of inheritance using on-site surveys.

4.3.2. Forest management intensification

One of the current main forestry policies by the Forestry Agency is cost reduction in forestry production. Concurrently, the Forestry Agency has been promoting expansion of forest management planning area, and an important objective of this policy is reducing associated costs. Article 12 of the Basic Forestry Act (Act No. 161 of 1964) determined that the expansion of forestry management was necessary for small-scale forestry. The introduction of the forest management planning system in 2012 was also related to the expansion of forest management and cost reduction; however, increases in area with forest management plans have stagnated. Although detailed figures have not been published, the Basic Forest and Forestry Plan stated in May 2016 that 28% of forests were covered by forest management plan ([32], p. 4). The reason for the lack of expansion of the area under forest management plans was not clarified due to a lack of data; however, one reason seems to be that forest management planning is closely connected to the subsidy system. This close connection is useful for forest owners who want to obtain a subsidy to conduct forest practices. For forest owners' cooperatives, such a system is beneficial, because owners in such cooperatives can work together to make and execute a plan. However, among forest owners who do not want to conduct thinning or construct forest roads, the current forest management planning system may not be attractive. Future analyses should clarify the reasons for the low percentage of planning area.

Within the scope of this study, only one relationship between aging and inheritance is discussed. Considering the relationship between householder age and the percentage of households who sold timber in the previous year based on the 2000 Census of Agriculture and Forestry, 60- to 64-year olds showed the peak percentage (5.3%). Meanwhile, 3.3 and 3.7 of 80- to 84-year olds and ≥85-year olds, respectively, sold timber in the previous year [2]. Although the current situation is unknown, because the last available data are from 2000, this trend appears to be related to the current decrease in willingness to sell timber, especially among >80-year-old forest owners. Figure 14 shows the age of the major financial supporter of households with forest from the 2013 Housing and Land Statistics.

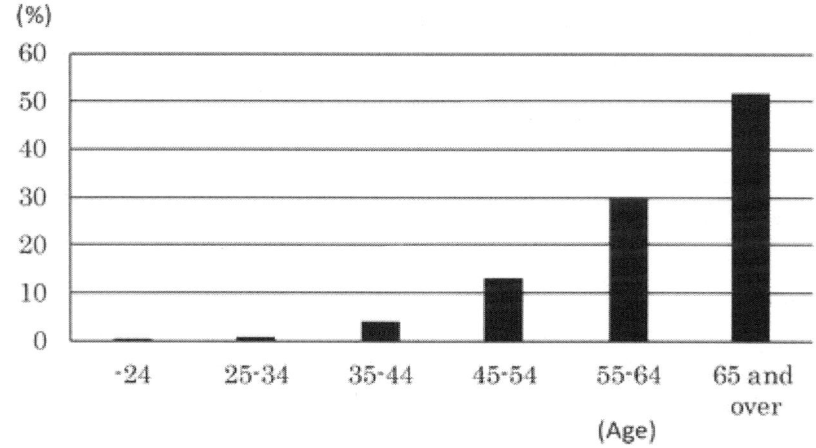

Figure 14. Age of the major financial supporter of households holding forests. Source: MIC, Statistics Bureau ([33], Table 87). Note: The major financial supporter is not the same as the householder. Generally, financial supporters are younger than householders.

In Japan, 65 is the usual age of retirement. The percentage of ≥65 years old has reached 51.8% in Figure 14. Considering that the peak age-class of timber sales was 60- to 64-year-olds in the 2000 Census of Agriculture and Forestry, the number of forest owners who want to sell standing trees may decrease. Ultimately, the low percentage of area covered by forest management plan could be related to demographic factors.

In forests owned by aging persons, especially small-scale forests without a forest management plan, there is a high likelihood that forest roads will not be constructed and the owners will simply hold the forest without managing it. In mountainous areas, where owners have small areas of farmland, forest land, and housing land, the total value of the inheritance property may be less than the minimum taxable rate, and the inheritor may continue to hold the forest without paying the inheritance tax when inheriting the forest property. This ensures that the small-sized holdings will continue in the future.

The total population of Japan reached to a peak in the 2010 Population Census, but showed a decrease in the 2015 Population Census. The National Institute of Population and Social Security Research ([34], **Table A-8**) has estimated that the total population in 100 years will decrease to almost one-third based on an analysis of the 2010 Population Census. In such a situation, if the system and conditions surrounding forest management do not change, the percentage of non-resident forest owners will increase.

Immediately after the end of World War II, most forest owners were also farmers. Since the family system was abolished after the war, children other than the successor could inherit forest, and many children moved to cities when beginning school or for a job. Therefore, the percentage of non-farmer forest owners has been increasing. In the 1990 Census of Agriculture and Forestry, 36.4% of forest owners with ≥0.1 ha were non-farmers, while 42.0% with ≥1 ha forest were non-farmers in the 2015 Census of Agriculture and Forestry.[40] The situation surrounding non-farmer non-resident forest owners is unclear, and should be examined further in future research. Regarding forest owners who live in urban areas, since the value of housing land is generally high, the total value of inheritance properties may surpass the minimum value for imposing the inheritance tax, and this set of circumstances should also be examined further in future research.

5. CONCISE SUMMARY

The existing forest inheritance tax system operates under the assumption that private woods are handled within a conventional family framework. In addition, tax reduction techniques have been used to assess forest area and standing trees, taking into account the extended production period. The Japanese forestry industry is currently encountering challenges in managing its operations, specifically due to the sustained decline in stumpage prices and the need to revise the methodologies used to assess forest area and standing trees. Consequently, the value of forests has diminished. The number is 41. Nevertheless, there has been a rise in the count of inheritors who are not residents or farmers, which calls for a reevaluation of the forest inheritance system, including the inheritance tax. This is due to the fact that the circumstances and underlying assumptions for granting preferential treatment have undergone a transformation.

There is a requirement for a fresh categorization of individuals who own private forests. Within the existing framework of forest inheritance tax system, forest owners who consistently engage in forest management, do not reside on the land, and possess no awareness or interest in their forest management practices are regarded identically, as if they were a family actively involved in forest operations. In the second scenario, this refers to the temporary possession of a property, and it is probable that the quantity of individuals who own forests of this nature will grow in the coming years. The tax reduction strategies for forest owners of this nature should be reassessed.[43] If the reduction policy were abolished for forest owners, they would have the option to engage in forest management or transfer ownership to individuals who possess the necessary skills to effectively manage it. An important challenge lies in defining the appropriate categorization of forest owners. Forest owners can be categorized as either resident or non-resident owners, with further significant elements including the presence or absence of forest management, a forest plan, investments made in the forest, and so on. Several potential technical issues may be envisioned for each of these solutions, and they should be thoroughly investigated in future research.

In 2012, a provision was implemented to allow forest owners with a minimum of 100 hectares of forest to postpone their inheritance tax. However, the low number of applications for this new system can be attributed to the presence of several restrictive requirements associated with the deferral of the tax. The management of forest owners with a forest area of 100 hectares or more is diverse. For instance, 43.9% of forest owners possess forest land ranging from 100 to 500 hectares, while 33.9% own forest land equal to or greater than 500 hectares, and they do not actively manage it. Consequently, relying solely on the size of the landholding is challenging when determining eligibility for postponing inheritance tax (Figure 12).[45].

According to the existing system for postponing inheritance tax and the forest management planning system, large-scale forest management is defined as having an area of 100 hectares or more. Nevertheless, there is a lack of theoretical or statistical foundation for employing 100 hectares as the threshold. While holding size should be taken into account as a factor, it is not necessary fair to use a 100-hectare holding size as a criterion. While it may be required to provide a suitable minimum space requirement, it is also imperative to implement additional precautions for smaller holding sizes. In addition, future studies may need to consider institutional redesign that incorporates additional criteria, such as place of residence and family workforce. The issues related to inheriting private forests are not exclusive to Japan. However, this study did not examine the forest inheritance tax from a global standpoint.[46]. The phenomenon of an increasing number of non-resident non-farmer forest owners and the aging of forest owners is observed in several industrialized nations. Exploring the international policies regarding the forest inheritance system, including inheritance tax, in light of this transition, is a subject that warrants more investigation.

AT A GLANCE

The population of elderly forest owners is growing in tandem with the aging of Japanese society and the rising number of inheritances involving forested land. The existing forest inheritance regulations, including the inheritance tax, were implemented post-World War II and necessitate immediate modification of the overall inheritance system. Despite the implementation of tax-reduction programs, private forest owners are currently grappling with a significant decline in the domestic timber market and low stumpage prices. There is a growing number of forest owners who are not residents or farmers, and this is causing a crisis for the traditional forestry system that is built on farm families. Given the declining population in Japan, particularly in rural regions, it is imperative to reassess the forest inheritance tax. This will encourage non-resident and non-farmer forest owners, who possess limited knowledge of forest management, to sell their forests to individuals or entities with a genuine interest in forest management, such as current resident forest owners and forestry companies. The 2014 legislation that defers payment of the forest inheritance tax is a crucial means of promoting sustainable forest management, particularly among owners of extensive forested areas. However, it is necessary to reassess the specific persons who benefit from this advantage.

REFERENCES

1. Forestry Agency. Shinrin Ringyo Tokei Yoran, 2016 (Annual Statistics on Forests and Forestry, 2016). Tokyo: Nihon Shinrin Ringyo Shinkokai; 2016. (in Japanese)
2. Matsushita K, Yoshida Y, Senda T. Household composition and aging of forest owners in Japan. Austrian Journal of Forest Science. 2017;134(s1):101-130
3. MLIT, Ministry of Land, Infrastructure, Transport, and Tourism. Figure II-7, 2050 nen Madeni Kyojyu Chiiki no 2 wari ga Mu-Kyojyuka. 2011. Available from: http://www.mlit.go.jp/common/000135838.pdf [Accessed: June 30, 2016]. (in Japanese)
4. Usui N, Hayashi S. Studies on problems of taxation in forest management: Especially inheritance tax. Research Bulletin of the Faculty College of Agriculture Gifu University. 1988;53:33-46. http://repository.lib.gifu-u.ac.jp/handle/123456789/5892 [Accessed: April 18, 2017] (in Japanese with English summary)
5. Butler BJ. Taxing family forest owners—Implications of federal and state policies in the United States. Journal of Forestry. 2012;110(7):371-380
6. GHQ/SCAP, General Headquarters, Supreme Commander for the Allied Powers. Forestry in Japan 1945–51. Natural Resource Section Report, No. 153. 1951
7. Forestry Agency. Forestry of Japan. 1955. pp. 199-202
8. Iwai Y. Forestry financial policy and taxation. In: Handa R, editor. Forest Policy in Japan. Tokyo: Nippon Ringyo Chosakai; 1988
9. Takagi M. Ringyo Mokuzaigyo no Tameno Zei Chisiki Nyumon (Introduction to Taxation of the Forestry and Timber Industries). Tokyo: Zenkoku Ringyo Kariyo Fukyu Kyokai; 1994. (in Japanese)
10. Yamamoto K. Sozokuzei ni okeru sanrin no hyoka no tekisei-ka tou ni tsuite (On the adjustment of the valuation of forest in the inheritance tax). Sanrin. 2004;1445:36-43. (in Japanese)

11. Sadachi K. Jizoku teki na ringyo keiei ni shisuru sozoku zeisei no jitsugen ni mukete (Toward realizing an inheritance tax that contributes to sustainable forestry management). Ringyo Gijyutsu. 1994;624:17-21. (in Japanese)
12. Tezuka H. Shinrin shisan no sozoku zeisei ni tsuite: Rongi no seijo to mondai no tenbyo (On the inheritance tax system: Brief report on examining and problems in argument). Ringyo Gijyutsu. 1986;533:2-7. (in Japanese)
13. Takagi F. Ringyo Zeisei Heno Teigen, (Suggestions Regarding Forestry Taxation). Seibunsha, Tokyo; 1988. (in Japanese)
14. Sugano T, Tani S. Sozokuzei to sanrin keiei (Inheritance tax and forest management). Sanrin. 2016;1581:27-34. (in Japanese)
15. Nagata R. Ringyo Kankei no Shin Zeisei Kaidoku (Description of New Taxation System Relating to Forestry). Tokyo: Nihon Ringyo Shiryo Kankokai; 1950. (in Japanese)
16. Tezuka H. Sairon ringyo shisan no sozoku zeisei ni tsuite (Reargument on the inheritance tax system of forestry properties). Rinkekyo Geppo. 1999;453:2-8. (in Japanese)
17. Forestry Agency, Division of Research. Ringyo Tokei Yoran 1953 (Annual Forestry Statistics 1953). Tokyo: Rinya Kyosaikai; 1953. (in Japanese)
18. Forestry Agency. Ringyo Tokei Yoran, Ruinen-Ban (Forestry Statistics, Time Series Edition). Tokyo: Rinya Kyosaikai; 1964. (in Japanese)
19. Forestry Agency. Ringyo Tokei Yoran, Jikeiretsu-Ban (Forestry Statistics, Time Series Edition). Tokyo: Rinya Kosaikai; 1982. (in Japanese)
20. Forestry Agency, Division of Research. Rinchi Sozoku ni Kansuru Chosa (Research on the Inheritance of Forest Land). Tokyo: Forestry Agency; 1964. (in Japanese)
21. Matsushita K, Yoshida Y, Senda T, Yamaguchi K. Jyutaku tochi tokei chosa ni yoru sanrin syoyu sya suu (Number of forest owners by the housing and land statistics) (in Japanese). In: 128th Annual Meeting of the Japanese Forest Society, Presentation on March 28 of 2017; Kagoshima University. 2017
22. MLIT, Ministry of Land, Infrastructure, Transport and Tourism. Mesh Betsu Syorai Jinko Suikei wo Katsuyo Shita Bunseki no Tenkai: Chiiki ni Okeru Seikatsu Kanren Service no Riyo Kanousei no Bunseki (Development of Analysis by Utilizing Prediction of Future Population as Mesh Data: Analysis on the Availability of Services Relating to Daily Life in the Region) (in Japanese). 2016. Available from: www.mlit.go.jp/common/001144843.pdf [Accessed: April 11, 2017]

23. T. Kaitei Rinseigaku (Forest Policy), Revised Version. Tokyo: Chikyusya; 1978. (in Japanese)
24. MAFF, Ministry of Agriculture, Forestry and Fisheries. Heisei 21 Nendo Ringyo Keiei ni Kansuru iko Chosa (Questionnaire Survey for Forestry Management, 2009 Fiscal Year) (in Japanese). 2011. Available from: www.maff.go.jp/j/finding/mind/pdf/ringyou_ikou.pdf [Accessed: April 18, 2017]
25. Y. A treatise on the forest succession tax in Japan. Ringyo Keizai. 1953;6(8):22-33. (in Japanese)
26. Sugano T. Sozokuzei zozei ga kongo no shinrin keiei ni ataeru eikyo: Heisei 27 nendo sozokuzei zozei ga kongo no shinrin keiei ni ataeru eikyo ni kansuru kenkyu kara (The effect of increased inheritance tax on future forest management). Sanrin. 2016;1590:11-17. (in Japanese)
27. Forestry Agency. Heisei 25 nen, Shinrin Ringyo Hakusyo (White Paper on Forests and Forestry, 2013 Fiscal Year) (in Japanese). 2014. Available from: www.rinya.maff.go.jp/j/kikaku/hakusyo/25hakusyo/zenbun.html [Accessed: April 18, 2017]
28. S. Sanrin Kazei no Genjyo to Mondai (Current State and Problems of Forest Taxation). Tokyo: Zenkoku Shinrin Kumiai Rengokai; 1957. (in Japanese)
29. Katayama S. Sanrin Zeisei Syokan: Sanrin sozokuzei wo chusin to shite (Comments on forest tax: Focus on forest inheritance tax). Ringyo Keizai. 1968;21(6):6-15. (in Japanese)
30. Forestry Agency, Division of Research and Extension. Shinrin-ku Betsu Syoyu Keitai Betsu Minyurin Menseki, Shinrin-Ku Betsu Syoyu Kibo Betsu Shinrin Shoyusya Suu (Area of Non-National Forest Classified by Forest Unit and Ownership, and Number of Forest Owners Classified by Forest Unit and Ownership). Tokyo: Forestry Agency; 1960. (in Japanese)
31. K. Tenkan-Ki Ni Tatsu Nihon Ringyo (Japanese Forestry at the Turning Point). Tokyo: Shinrin Shigen Sogo Taisaku Kyogikai; 1960. (in Japanese)
32. MAFF, Ministry of Agriculture, Forestry and Fisheries. Shinrin Ringyo Kihon Keikaku (Basic Plan of Forests and Forestry) (in Japanese). 2016. Available from: http://www.rinya.maff.go.jp/j/kikaku/plan/ [Accessed: April 19, 2017]
33. MIC, Ministry of Internal Affairs and Communications, Statistics Bureau. The 2013 Housing and Land Statistics. Vol. 1 Whole Japan. Tokyo: Japan Statistical Association; 2015. (in Japanese and English)

34. National Institute of Population and Social Security Research. Population projects for Japan: A supplement to the 2012 revision (Commentary with ancillary projections). Population Research Series. 2013;327:79-80. (in Japanese)

35. Kim EG. Sanrin sozokuzei no mondaiten to kongo no kento kadai: Shizuoka-ken Tenryu ringyo-chi no chosa jirei kara (Problems and subject of future investigation of the forest inheritance tax: From the survey results in Tenryu forestry area in Shizuoka Prefecture). Ringyo Gijyutsu. 1989;573:16-19. (in Japanese)

36. Toyama F. Shinrin Sozei no Kenkyu (Research on Forestry Taxes), Hokkaido Ringyo-kai, Hokkaido-Cho, Takushoku-Bu, Chiho-ka. Sapporo: Hokkaido Ringyo-kai; 1936. (in Japanese)

SECTION-3

TAX POLICY AND TAX SYSTEM

10 Chapter

ESSENTIAL ELEMENTS FOR DEVELOPING AN EFFECTIVE TAX POLICY TO ENSURE TAX COMPLIANCE : DOES PERCEPTION OF TAX COMPLIANCE DEVELOP IN PERSONS WHO ARE NOT TAX PAYERS YET?

1. INTRODUCTION: AN OVERVIEW

The significance of tax revenue in the overall state income can be assessed by many methods, such as examining the funding quantity in relation to the state's dominant power, the extent of its influence, and the diversity of its functions as a fiscal policy instrument. It is widely accepted by all countries that it is impossible to fully realize the potential of tax income (tax capacity). The same principle applies to the endeavors aimed at reducing the amount of tax money lost (tax effort). There is little doubt that taxpayers require apps that address both social and psychological aspects in order to prevent potential loss of tax revenue, in addition to the technical measures taken by tax legislators and offices. Tax compliance occurs within the framework of the effectiveness of tax implementation, including the adequacy of legislation, inspections, and penalties.

Turkey has done numerous rigorous research on tax compliance and its primary indicators, specifically tax ethics. Several of these were substantiated through field research. However, the research on these issues needs to be continuous because empirical studies show that changes in conditions throughout time might provide different outcomes.

This study employed a novel technique by examining the impression of tax compliance among university students with limited or no prior experience in tax implementation. The government relies largely on tax compliance for its tax income operations, and the fairness of the tax burden allocation directly impacts taxpayers' compliance. This study examines the development of tax compliance perception among highly educated individuals who are not yet taxpayers, and assesses the extent to which this impression is formed. In order to investigate the factors that influence tax compliance, a questionnaire was administered to a sample group consisting of individuals with similar characteristics, including education level, field of study, and age.

1.1. The concept of tax compliance

According to James and Alley, tax compliance refers to the extent to which taxpayers adhere to the tax legislation. Tax compliance refers to the adherence of taxpayers to tax rules and regulations. This idea posits that taxpayers willingly fulfill their tax obligations without the need for inspection, prosecution, threats, or sanctions [2]. The definition contains implicit references to the notions of tax ethics and tax consciousness. Tax consciousness refers to the essential awareness that enables individuals to understand how changes in their tax burden may impact their actions [3]. In addition, tax morale can be described as the inherent drive of taxpayers to fulfill their tax obligations, as stated in reference [4]. The more aware individuals are of their tax obligations, the greater their adherence to tax laws and ethical standards. When people become more aware of taxes and their importance, their sense of moral responsibility towards paying taxes will improve, leading to a greater overall compliance with tax regulations (see Figure 1).

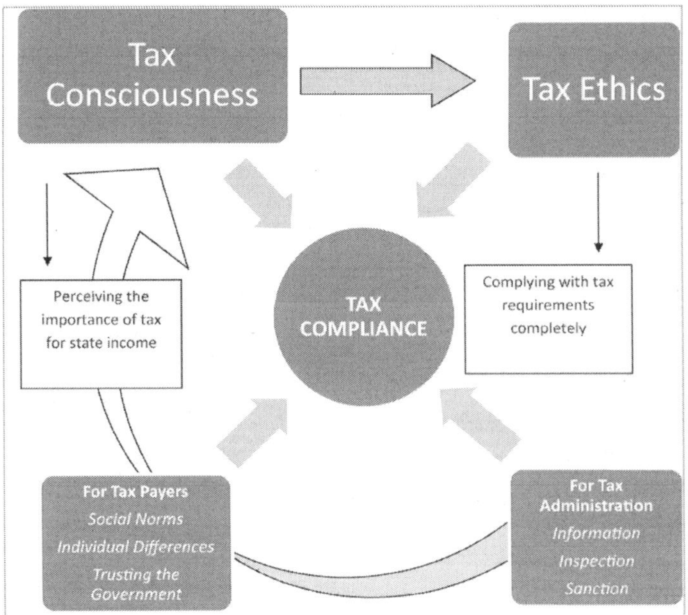

Figure 1. Forward-reverse connections of tax compliance.
Source: Author's illustration.

The tax compliance shaped by tax consciousness and tax ethics should be completed by the stages of taxing in terms of the tax payer. The content of tax compliance is described in four parts [5]:

- Complete declaration of the income to be taxed
- Accurate representation of the factors to be discounted from the tax
- Submitting the declaration on time
- Calculating the tax liability correctly.

In our study, the concept of tax compliance will be tested with empirical experiments on university students who are not tax payers yet, but have knowledge about these issues because of their level of education. For this paper, it is preferred to use lab experiment with undergraduate students. As referred in [6], most laboratory experiments which have been conducted by using students are very common. The reason is that in these experiments, it is realized that the responses of students are often heavily the same as the responses of other subject pools in similar lab experiments. Unlike Levitte and List (2007) and Kogler et al. [27], students as a subject pool are useful in many studies [7, 8, 9, 10].

Even though the study has its limitations, it will help in the development of a perception of tax compliance through information before tax-paying experience and efforts for the creation of social norms in terms of its novelty. Thus, it will show whether such efforts will have an impact on the efficiency of future tax income.

1.2. Types of tax compliance and effective factors

Tax compliance may be defined in two ways namely *formal compliance* and *financial compliance*. Formal compliance is the compliance with the formal requirements in terms of tax laws by the tax payers. Financial compliance is the compliance with the financial requirements by the tax payers based on the letter and spirit of tax laws. Formal tax compliance is a complementary factor on financial compliance. The requirement of financial compliance for the tax compliance to be complete was also indicated by Pertiwi [2].

There are fundamental factors that affect formal and/or financial compliance. The following is a list of factors that affect tax compliance [11]:

- Level of income and tax ratios
- Social and demographic factors
- Sanctions, probability of inspection, previous inspections
- Subjective and objective measures/preventions
- Effects of certified public accountants and/or tax consultants
- Moral and social dynamics
- Complexity of the tax system and tax amnesty.

Among the factors stated above, the ones emphasized here are social-demographic and moral-social dynamics that affect compliance for the tax payer and inspections-sanctions and subjective-objective measures that affect tax administration implementations. The level of knowledge and social norms gained by students in the experiment up to this study is considered to be sufficient in order to test the factors mentioned before.

In addition to the factors listed above, various financial and economic indicators that affect tax compliance may lead to a change in the tax payer's perception of compliance. These factors may be ordered as follows: tax burden, tax structure, debt burden, and underground economy (Figure 2).

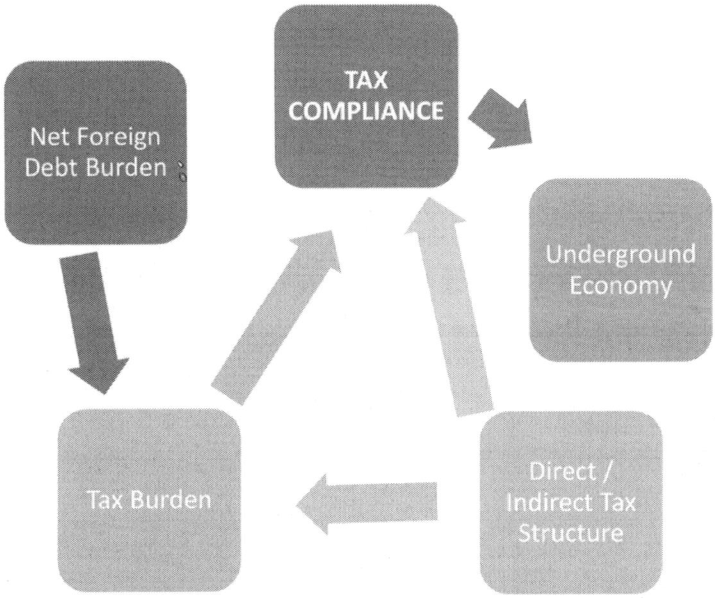

Figure 2. Influencing factors of tax compliance. Source: Author's illustration.

The most important macroeconomic parameter that affects the perception of tax compliance is the tax burden, which also affects tax consciousness. The higher the tax burden on an individual is, the more problematic the tax compliance becomes, especially because of the idea that the system is unjust. The idea that the tax burden is unjust may develop based on the ratio of direct and indirect taxes in the tax structure. As the tax payers know that indirect taxes are collected from everyone on goods and services and the burden is inversely proportionate to the income, they may develop opposite reactions. In direct taxes, such as ones collected according to a projected declaration, the tax payer may fail to comply with the declaration based on the amount of the burden. In withholding taxes, as there is no way to avoid the tax, there may be thoughts of overestimation against other tax payers. This situation in the direct and indirect tax structure may affect tax compliance by itself, as well as over the tax burden.

Debt burden normally leads to tax increases for the term following the term it is experienced. The tax burden is dependent on the magnitude of the debt burden. This is another way of which tax burden interferes with tax compliance. As Önder reports that any decrease or disappearance of the perception of tax compliance for any reason will bring an increase in underground economy [12]. In scope of this issue, the 2015 Action Plan to Eliminate Underground Economy by the Ministry of Development determined increasing the voluntary tax compliance as an important action plan component and stated that *"Economic, sociological, cultural, etc. factors that affect voluntary tax compliance will be analyzed, and solutions will be developed to increase the level of compliance by the tax payers"* [13].

Table 1 shows some indicators that affect tax compliance in Turkey with numbers from the year 2013. These data not only provide numbers important to understand the concepts used in this study but also represent factors that influence real life situations. During the experimental implementation stage of the study, the students were briefed about the data that are mentioned above. As a group which does not carry the tax burden and/or does not completely feel it yet, university students know about these issues in terms of economics and finances, and it is important to test these parameters under these conditions in order to understand the perception of tax compliance.

Table 1. Various indicators that affect the perception of tax compliance in Turkey.

2013	%
Income tax/gross domestic product (GDP)	5.02
Corporate tax/GDP	2.01
VAT + special consumption tax/GDP	10.1
Tax burden/GDP	29.3
Net foreign debt stock/GDP	27.8
The ratio of the total tax income (including social security premiums) lost because of underground economy	16

Source: [14, 15, 16].

2. GENERAL ANALYSIS CONSTRUCT AND HYPOTHESES

2.1. The construct and participatory decision structure

Experimental survey method was used for the subject of this study. The questions in the questionnaire consist of ones that were asked in a similar way in previous studies on the subject.[1] There were seven questions and they used a three-point Likert scale as in [17], which worked on *"three-point participation level determination."* Participants were asked to assign points from 1 to 3 to statements: "1" meant "I do not agree," "2" meant "I somewhat agree," and "3" meant "I agree."

The construct of the analysis is to evaluate the level of significance for the questions in the form of hypotheses and crossexamine the related hypotheses.

2.2. Participants

In total, 287 students from three different departments at the Faculty of Economics and Administrative Sciences of Ankara Gazi University took part in the study. The mean age of students was 23 (SD: 2.1).

As seen in Table 2, the departments were chosen by considering the students of these departments start taking public finance, tax law, and economics classes in their first year. Taking the courses which are public finance and tax law helps students understand the place of taxes in law implementation and public finance, whereas learning economics raises awareness on the roles taxes play in the economic system and helps students understand the relationship of taxes and macroeconomic parameters, therefore affecting tax compliance. Every student who participated has taken the mentioned courses and/or is currently taking it.

Table 2. Number of participants by department.

	Finance department	Labor economics and industrial relations department	Econometrics department
Number of participants by department	112	102	73

Source. Author's identification.

As seen in Table 3, it is important that participants are mostly third and fourth year students, as their knowledge about taxes is above a certain level and they can answer the questions with similar awareness.

Table 3. Distribution of participants by levels of grade.

	First year	Second year	Third year	Fourth year
Distribution of participants by levels	62	48	94	83

Source. Author's identification.

2.3. Hypotheses

In selection of the questions in the questionnaire according to Likert Scale Formation Technique (Summation Ordering Technique) described in detail in [18], hypotheses were developed in order to assess the fundamental content of the subjects of this study. The hypotheses are given in Table 4.

- Hypotheses H1 and H2 are for testing the tax consciousness, which fundamentally affects tax compliance. Associating paying taxes with being a good citizen and being aware of the contribution of taxes for national development will establish or improve a perception of tax compliance.

- Hypotheses H3, H4, and H5 are indicators for tax payers with established or developed perceptions of tax compliance on whether they comply with the duties of paying taxes as they must be.
- Hypotheses H6 and H7 measure the contribution of factors provided by the tax administration on the perception of tax compliance. Providing correct and fast service at the administration not only establishes/improves trust in the administration but also prevents complexities and strengthens the tax payers' perceptions of compliance.

Table 4. Hypotheses of the lab experiment.

Hypotheses	
1	H1: Being a tax payer who shows the required compliance means being a good citizen
2	H2: A compliant tax payer gained this trait as they think paying taxes helps in national development
3	H3: A compliant tax payer makes their declaration on time
4	H4: A compliant tax payer calculates their debt accurately
5	H5: A compliant tax payer is sensitive about paying their tax debts
6	H6: A compliant tax payer gained this trait because the tax administration provided correct and fast service
7	H7: A compliant tax payer gained this trait because the tax administration provided correct information about calculated tax payments

Source. Author's identification.

2.4. Limitations of the study

Fundamentally, two things may be provided as limitations of the study. The first limitation is that it is difficult to collect information on tax compliance behavior as encountered in many tax compliance studies [19].

The second limitation is that, as Kogler et al. reported, problems may arise when students are selected as a sample, as they do not have sufficient experience paying taxes. Kogler et al. indicated in 2013 that students fail to concentrate especially on tax evasion scenarios because of their lack of experience [20].

3. RESULTS OF THE ANALYSIS

3.1. General assessment

Frequencies and percentages of the responses to the hypotheses are given in Table 5. As a general assessment, considering the percentages of the responses, the perception of tax compliance decreases for the statements about the tax administration.

Table 5. Statements and the distributions of frequencies of the responses.

Statements	Responses					
	Disagree		Somewhat agree		Agree	
	Frequency	%	Frequency	%	Frequency	%
H1: Being a tax payer who shows the required compliance means being a good citizen	32	11.1	47	16.4	198	69.0
H2: A compliant tax payer gained this trait as they think paying taxes helps in national development	49	17.1	90	31.4	147	51.2
H3: A compliant tax payer makes their declaration on time	19	6.6	38	13.2	230	80.1
H4: A compliant tax payer calculates their debt accurately	33	11.5	61	21.3	192	66.9
H5: A compliant tax payer is sensitive about paying their tax debts	26	9.1	44	15.3	216	75.3
H6: A compliant tax payer gained this trait because the tax administration provided correct and fast service	90	31.4	88	30.7	109	38.0
H7: A compliant tax payer gained this trait because the tax administration provided correct information about calculated tax payments	68	23.7	92	32.1	126	43.9

Source. Author's identification.

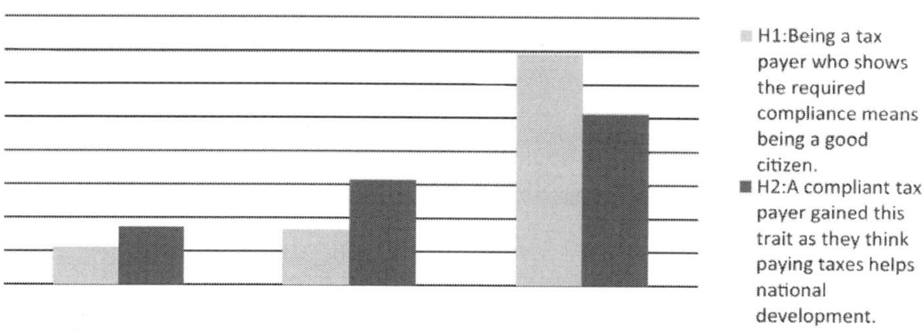

Graph 1. The percentage distribution of the H1 and H2 hypotheses.

Source. Author's calculation.

The percentage distribution of the hypotheses H1 and H2 seen in Graph 1 that the statements are related to tax consciousness and implementations toward these may increase the perception of tax compliance.

Graph 2 shows the relationship between increases in the perception of tax compliance and compliance by tax payers who show voluntary compliance, where the tendency for the participants' responses showed a relationship in the positive direction.

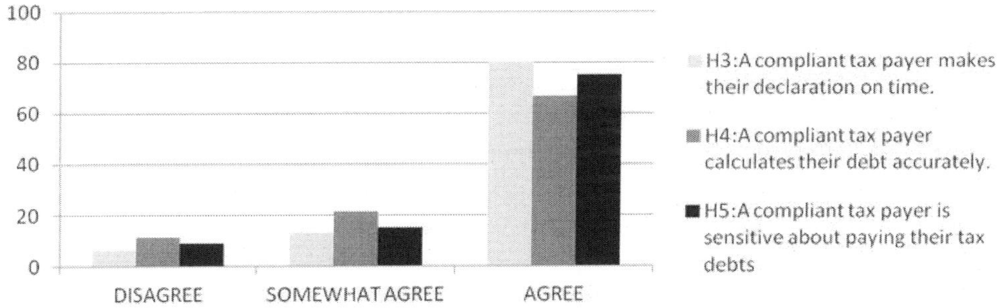

Graph 2. The percentage distribution of the H3, H4, and H5 hypotheses. Source. Author's calculation.

Graph 3 shows the distribution of responses to hypotheses testing effects of trusting the tax administration and the administration's operation on the perception of tax compliance. Participation percentages show that the administration is not considered to be providing a correct and fast service, and this is thought to decrease the perception of tax compliance. It can be seen on the distributions that supplying correct information will prevent complexities and increase the perception of tax compliance.

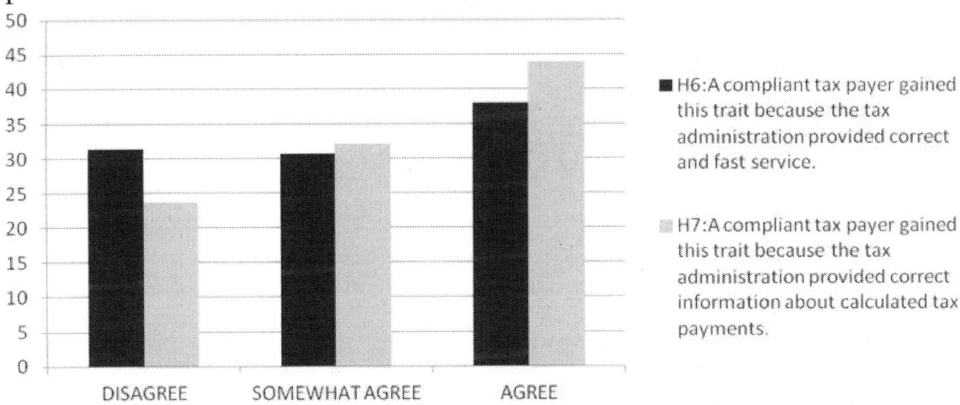

Graph 3. The percentage distribution of the H6 and H7 hypotheses. Source: Author's calculation.

3.2. Assessment by crossexamination

In this section, hypotheses found to be related to each other and with high levels of significance will be assessed by crossexamination. In crossexaminations and comments, three different stages will be followed: (1) tax consciousness and tax compliance, (2) tax payer duties and tax compliance, and (3) trusting the tax administration and tax compliance.

3.2.1. Tax compliance and tax consciousness

In this stage, the hypotheses H1 and H2 will be assessed together and the tax compliance and tax consciousness relationship will be observed.

For tax compliance, the financial, economic, and social meaning of taxes must be understood by the tax payers. Leder et al. reported that information campaigns about taxes financing public goods and services increase consciousness of tax payers about the importance of taxes, strengthen their perceptions toward financial change, and increase their compliance levels [21]. Likewise, Karakostas and Zizzo also stated that especially implementations like advertisements support the concept of norm creation toward tax compliance [22].

Significance level (P) and chi-squared (χ^2) numbers indicate that the relationship is positive with a mid-sized magnitude. As Table 6 shows, 45.3% of the participants agreed with both statements. An interesting result arose about the relationship between "being a good citizen" and "contributing to national development." In total, 6.5% of the participants agreed with being a good citizen, but disagreed with contributing to national development. Considering that participants were university students, it may be argued that even though the result covers a few people, the participants have awareness of the liability of the tax payer in terms of being a good citizen, but they do not completely grasp the economic effects of paying taxes and/or they do not think the collected taxes are used for the development.

Table 6. Tax compliance-tax consciousness relationship.

Disagree Somewhat Agree			A compliant tax payer gained this trait as they think paying taxes helps national development Agree			Total
Being a tax payer who shows the required compliance means being a good citizen	Disagree	Frequency	16	9	7	32
		%	5.8%	3.3%	2.5%	11.6%
	Somewhat Agree	Frequency	12	25	10	47
		%	4.3%	9.1%	3.6%	17.0%
	Agree	Frequency	18	54	125	197
		%	6.5%	19.6%	45.3%	71.4%
Total		Frequency	46	88	142	276
		%	16.7%	31.9%	51.4%	100.0%
χ^2 = 57.594 Level of significance (P) = 0.000						

Source: Author's identification.

3.2.2. Tax payer duties and tax compliance

In this stage, the hypotheses H3 and H5 will be assessed together, and the tax compliance and tax payer duties relationship will be observed. Complying with tax duties on time and in the way it must be done is closely related to efforts to create a social norm. Leder et al. stated that when there is a low level of tax compliance, strict policies to prevent tax evasion are not enough, but an effort to create a social norm is important [21]. Cummings et al. also stated that inspection bodies are effective on social norms about tax compliance, and these norms are dependent on the tax regime and the state's willingness to satisfy citizens' demands [23]. On the other hand, Feld and Larsen indicated that social norms and deterrence should be used simultaneously [24].

The hypothesis H3 denotes the relationship between tax compliance and making declarations on time, which is the first duty in tax responsibilities. The crossexamination here is making declarations on time and being aware of the importance of taxes in national development. Level of significance (P) and chi-squared (χ^2) numbers indicate a positive relationship with mid-sized magnitude. As it may be seen in Table 7, 47.6% of participants believe in the existence of this relationship. Similar to the interesting result of the previous test, 8% of the participants agreed with the timely submission of declarations, while they did not think taxes have a relationship with the national development.

Table 7. Tax compliance-tax payer duties relationship 1.

Disagree Somewhat Agree			A compliant tax payer is sensitive about paying their tax debts Agree			Total
A compliant tax payer makes their declaration on time	Disagree	Frequency	9	9	1	19
		%	3.1%	3.1%	.3%	6.6%
	Somewhat Agree	Frequency	17	11	10	38
		%	5.9%	3.8%	3.5%	13.3%
	Agree	Frequency	23	70	136	229
		%	8.0%	24.5%	47.6%	80.1%
Total		Frequency	49	90	147	286
%		17.1%	31.5%	51.4%	100.0%	
χ^2 = 50.782 Level of significance (P) = 0.000						

Source. Author's calculation

Lewis et al. observed that level of inspections affects tax compliance, and high inspection rates on tax evasion increased the voluntary tax compliance [25].

However, in Kastlunger et al. (2009), it was seen that inspections without increasing and/or strengthening tax compliance lead tax payers to invent new ways to evade taxes [26].

As the sensitivity to pay tax debts, as indicated in H5, is related to being a good citizen and the importance of taxes in national development, Tables 8 and 9 may be considered together. The levels of significance (P) and chi-squared (χ^2) numbers in both tests show that there is a positive relationship, while the first relationship has a small magnitude and the second has a mid-sized magnitude. Even though 60.9% participants in the first test agree with both statements in Table 5, the distinctive finding is that 5.4% of the participants agree with sensitivity to pay debts, while disagreeing with being a good citizen relationship. This may be explained by that the students are aware of tax as a compulsory and required liability, rather than being aware of taxes associated with being a good citizen. Kogler et al. stated that issuing feedback to tax payers in a timely manner about tax inspections creates positive effects on tax compliance [27]. Likewise, Castro and Scartascini found that tax payers who received feedback about deterrents to tax crimes had 5% higher amounts of positive behaviors than those who did not receive feedbacks [28].

Table 8. Tax compliance-tax payer duties relationship 2.

Disagree Somewhat Agree			A compliant tax payer is sensitive about paying their tax debts Agree			Total
Being a tax payer who shows the required compliance means being a good citizen	Disagree	Frequency	9	8	15	32
		%	3.3%	2.9%	5.4%	11.6%
	Somewhat Agree	Frequency	7	13	27	47
		%	2.5%	4.7%	9.8%	17.0%
	Agree	Frequency	9	20	168	197
		%	3.3%	7.2%	60.9%	71.4%
Total		Frequency	25	41	210	276
%		9.1%	14.9%	76.1%	100.0%	
χ^2 = 37.254 Level of significance (P) = 0.000						

Source. Author's calculation

Similarly, 44.9% of the participants in the test as shown in Table 6 above agreed with both statements. However, even though 6.7% agreed with sensitivity to pay tax debts, they disagreed with the importance of paying taxes for national development or that it will increase tax compliance. The relationship has the same direction as it is stated in the previous test.

Table 9. Tax compliance-tax payer duties relationship 3.

Disagree Somewhat Agree			A compliant tax payer gained this trait as they think paying taxes helps national development Agree			Total
A compliant tax payer is sensitive about paying their tax debts	Disagree	Frequency	14	7	5	26
		%	4.9%	2.5%	1.8%	9.1%
	Somewhat Agree	Frequency	16	15	13	44
		%	5.6%	5.3%	4.6%	15.4%
	Agree	Frequency	19	68	128	215
		%	6.7%	23.9%	44.9%	75.4%
Total		Frequency	49	90	146	285
%		17.2%	31.6%	51.2%	100.0%	
χ^2 = 50.849 Level of significance (P) = 0.000						

Source. Author's calculation.

3.2.3. Trusting the tax administration and tax compliance

Hypotheses H6 and H7 were crossexamined, and the relationship between trusting the tax administration and tax compliance was investigated.

Cummings et al. (2009) found that administration's quality of management has an observable effect on tax compliance [23]. Şafaklı and Kutlay (2014) indicated that the tax administration having strategic plans toward knowledge of tax payers of tax laws will increase tax consciousness and therefore tax compliance [29].

Table 10 shows the relationship of H6, which suggests that the tax administration provides correct and fast service and this increases tax compliance and the test of submitting declarations on time, which is the first duty in tax requirements. The level of significance (P) and chi-squared (χ^2) numbers show that there is a positive relationship, while it has a small magnitude. In total, 34.8% of the participants agreed with both statements. However, even though 22.6% agreed with the importance of submitting declarations on time, they did not agree that the tax administration works fast and correctly. It may be that students who have not experienced the tax implementation are missing trust in the tax administration or they have not developed it yet.

Table 10. Tax compliance and trusting the tax administration relationship 1.

Disagree Somewhat Agree			A compliant tax payer gained this trait because the tax administration provided correct and fast service Agree			Total
A compliant tax payer makes their declaration on time	Disagree	Frequency	10	4	5	19
		%	3.5%	1.4%	1.7%	6.6%
	Somewhat Agree	Frequency	15	19	4	38
		%	5.2%	6.6%	1.4%	13.2%
	Agree	Frequency	65	65	100	230
		%	22.6%	22.6%	34.8%	80.1%
Total		Frequency	90	88	109	287
%		31.4%	30.7%	38.0%	100.0%	
χ^2 = 19.936 Level of significance (P) = 0.001						

Source. Author's calculation.

Kogler et al. reported that the highest tax compliance and the lowest tax evasion are experienced in countries where the authority is seen trusted and effective by citizens. They argued that the state should win the citizens' trust with generally fair implementations and service-oriented behavior [20]. Verboon and Dijke stated the importance of the authorities' fair treatment of citizens in increasing tax compliance, therefore increasing the effectiveness of their sanctions [30].

When the hypotheses H6 and H7 are considered together, as shown in Table 11, significance level (P) and chi-squared (χ^2) numbers show a positive relationship with high magnitude. In total, 28.3% of the participants agreed with both statements. However, 15.7% of the participants disagreed with both statements. Both statements test the trust in the tax administration, and the number of people who chose to disagree is noteworthy. Leder et al. (2010) stated that if the tax administration shows transparency in disclosing final data about financial transition, it will be able to gain tax payers' trust, which is extremely important for tax compliance [21]. Litina and Palivos argued that individuals (tax payers) who believe that the tax administration is honest will have very high probability to respond to sanctions positively [31].

Table 11. Tax compliance and trusting the tax administration relationship 2.

Disagree Somewhat Agree			A compliant tax payer gained this trait because the tax administration provided correct information about calculated tax payments Agree			Total
A compliant tax payer gained this trait because the tax administration provided correct and fast service	Disagree	Frequency	45	29	16	90
		%	15.7%	10.1%	5.6%	31.5%
	Somewhat Agree	Frequency	14	45	29	88
		%	4.9%	15.7%	10.1%	30.8%
	Agree	Frequency	9	18	81	108
		%	3.1%	6.3%	28.3%	37.8%
Total		Frequency	68	92	126	286
%		23.8%	32.2%	44.1%	100.0%	
$\chi^2 = 97.107$ Level of significance (P) = 0.000						

Source. Author's calculation.

4. DISCUSSION

This study examines tax compliance among university students who have limited exposure to tax payment procedures. A study was conducted to assess the perspective of tax compliance among highly qualified students in specific academic fields, who are supposed to have a heightened awareness of tax-related matters.

Findings of the study were listed below:

- In terms of tax consciousness and tax compliance, it was seen that students agree that paying taxes completes the concept of being a good citizen.

On the contrary, Leder et al. in which mentioned that importance of information campaigns about taxes financing public goods and services increasing the compliance level, students do not agree with the importance of taxes in national development [21]. This means that convincing information about taxes should be made.

- In terms of tax compliance and tax payer duties, students perceive the sensitivity submitting declarations on time and showing care in paying tax debts.

Feld and Larsen (2012) indicated that social norms and deterrence should be applied simultaneously and Lewis et al. (2009) observed that high inspection rates on tax evasion increase the voluntary tax compliance, and students realizing this as a civic duty tax obligation should be inspected and audited [24, 25]. Besides that, it should be noted that on the basis of the findings of the study, students see taxes as a compulsory requirement, rather than a way for being a "good citizen."

- The situation is complicated in the relationship of the tax administration and tax compliance.

The studies by Cummings et al., Kogler et al., and Verboon and Dijke all discuss factors that influence tax compliance. Cummings et al. highlight the impact of administration quality on tax compliance, while Kogler et al. emphasize the role of a trusted and effective tax authority in promoting higher compliance levels. Verboon and Dijke stress the importance of fair treatment by authorities in increasing tax compliance. These findings are consistent across the studies [20, 23, 30]. Contrarily, in this paper, students hold unfavorable views on the transparency, accuracy, and reliability of the tax administration. The tax administration attributes the success in tax compliance to the tax payers themselves, rather than to its own efforts.

However, Litina and Palivos contended that having faith in the integrity of the tax administration enables effective enforcement of sanctions. Djawadi and Fahr also noted that transparency regarding public expenditures positively influences tax compliance. Additionally, it was found that the tax administration does not provide information on how taxes are allocated, as reported by the students [32].

AT A GLANCE

Tax compliance occurs within the context of the effectiveness of tax enforcement. The effectiveness of tax income operations relies significantly on tax compliance, while the equitable distribution of the tax burden impacts the level of compliance among taxpayers. This study examines the development of tax compliance perception among highly educated individuals who are not yet taxpayers, and the extent to which it occurs among university students. The study's findings indicate that students generally believe that paying taxes is an essential aspect of being a responsible citizen. They also recognize the importance of submitting tax declarations on time and being diligent in paying tax debts. However, students have negative perceptions regarding the transparency, accuracy, and trustworthiness of the tax administration. An effective tax policy design should prioritize the assessment of tax compliance among the taxpayers of a country as the main indicator of success.

REFERENCES

1. James S, Alley C. Tax compliance, self-assessment and tax administration. Journal of Finance and Management in Public Services. 2002;2(2):27-42

2. Pertiwi DN. The Influence of Tax Consciousness, Service Tax Authorities, and Tax Sanctions on Tax Compliance (Survey on Indıvidual Taxpayer Conducting Business Operations and Professional Service in Jakarta) [Thesis]. Jakarta: State Islamic University Syarif Hidayatullah; 2013
3. Gideon M. Do individuals perceive income tax rates correctly? Public Finance Review. 2015:1-21. DOI: 10.1177/1091142115615670
4. Lubian D, Zarri L. Happiness and tax morale: An empirical analysis. Journal of Economic Behavior & Organization. 2011;80:223-243. DOI: 10.1016/j.jebo.2011.03.009
5. Göksu GG, Saruç T. Türkiye'de Vergiye Uyum: Mülakat Çalışması. Mevzuat Dergisi; 2012. 15/176: http://www.mevzuatdergisi.com/2012/08a/01.htm Accessed: 3 February 2015
6. Levitt SD, List JA. What do Laboratory experiments measuring social preferences reveal about the Realworld? Journal of Economic Perspectives. 2007;21(2):153-174 http://www.jstor.org/stable/30033722
7. Güth W, Kirchkamp O. Will you accept without knowing what? The yes-no game in the newspaper and in the lab. Experimental Economics. 2012;15(4):656-666 ISSN 1864-7057
8. Güth W, Schmidt C, Sutter M. Bargaining outside the lab—A newspaper experiment of a three-person ultimatum game. Economic Journal. 2007;117(518):449-469
9. Alm J, Bloomquist KM, Mckee M. On the external validity of laboratory policy experiments. Economic Inquary. 2015;53(2):1170-1186. DOI: 10.1111/ecin.12196
10. Choo CYL, Fonseca MA, Myles GD. Do students behave like real taxpayers in the lab? Evidence from a real effort tax compliance experiment. Journal of Economic Behavior & Organization. 2016;124:102-114. DOI: 10.1016/j.jebo.2015.09.015
11. AndreoniJ,ErardB,FeinsteinJ.Taxcompliance.JournalofEconomicLiterature. 1998;36(2):818-860.http://www.jstor.org/table/2565123?seq=1&cid=pdf-reference#references_tab_contents. [Accessed: 02.03.2015]
12. Önder M. Türkiye'de Kayıt Dışı Ekonomi ve Uluslararası Uygulamalar Işığında Çözüm Önerileri. Mesleki Yeterlilik Tezi: T.C. Maliye Bakanlığı Strateji Geliştirme Başkanlığı; 2012
13. Republic of Turkey Ministry of Development. The tenth development plan (2014–2018). In: Unregistered Economy Reduction Program ActionPlan.2015.http://www.gib.gov.tr/sites/default/files/fileadmin/beyannamerehberi/2015kayitdisi.pdf [Accessed: 29.09.2017]

14. Revenue Administration. Budget Revenue (1923–2014). http://www.gib.gov.tr/sites/default/files/fileadmin/user_upload/ vi/gbg1.htm [Accessed: 12.04.2016]

15. Republic of Turkey. Prime Ministry Undersecretariat of Treasury. Public Debt Management Report. 2016

16. Schneider F. Tax losses due to shadow economy activities in OECD countries from 2011 to 2013: A preliminary calculation. In: Cesıfo Workıng Paper No. 5649, Category 1: Publıc Fınance. 2015 ISSN 2364-1428

17. Vagias WM. Likert-Type Scale Response Anchors. Clemson International Institute for Tourism & Research Development, Department of Parks, Recreation and Tourism Management, Clemson University; 2006. https://www.uc.edu/content/dam/uc/sas/docs/Assessment/likert-type%20response%20anchors.pdf [Accessed: 29.09.2017]

18. Bayat B. Uygulamalı Sosyal Bilim Araştırmalarında Ölçme, Ölçekler Ve "Likert" Ölçek Kurma Tekniği. Gazi Üniversitesi İktisadi Ve İdari Bilimler Fakültesi Dergisi. 2014;16/3:1-24 ISSN 1302-2024

19. Torgler B. Speaking to theorists and searching for facts: Tax morale and tax compliance in experiments. Journal of Economic Surveys. 2008;16/5:657-683. DOI: 10.1111/1467-6419.00185

20. C, Batrancea L, Nichita A, Pantya J, Belianin A, Kirchler E. Trust and power as determinants of tax compliance: Testing the assumptions of the slippery slope framework in Austria, Hungary, Romania and Russia. Journal of Economic Psychology. 2013;34:169-180. DOI: 10.1016/j.joep.2012.09.010

21. Leder S, Mannetti L, Hölzl E, Kirchler E. Regulatory fit effects on perceived fiscal exchange and tax compliance. The Journal of Socio-Economics. 2010;39:271-277. DOI: 10.1016/j.socec.2009.12.003

22. A, Zizzo DJ. Compliance and the power of authority. Journal of Economic Behavior & Organization. 2016;124:67-80. DOI: 10.1016/j.jebo.2015.09.016

23. Cummings RG, Martinez-Vazquez J, Mckee M, Torgler B. Tax morale affects tax compliance: Evidence from surveys and an artefactual field experiment. Journal of Economic Behavior & Organization. 2009;70:447-457. DOI: 10.1016/j.jebo.2008.02.010

24. Feld LP, Larsen C. Self-perceptions, government policies and tax compliance in Germany. International Tax and Public Finance. 2012;19:78-103. DOI: 10.1007/s10797-011-9196-6

25. A, Carrera S, Cullis JP. Individual cognitive and cultural differences in tax compliance: UK and Italy compared. Journal of Economic Psychology. 2009;30:431-445. DOI: 10.1016/j.joep.2008.11.002

26. B, Kirchler E, Mittone L, Pitters J. Sequences of audits, tax compliance, and taxpaying strategies. Journal of Economic Psychology. 2009;30:405-418. DOI: 10.1016/j.joep.2008.10.004

27. C, Mittone L, Kirchler E. Delayed feedback on tax audits affects compliance and fairness perceptions. Journal of Economic Behavior & Organization. 2016;124:81-87. DOI: 10.1016/j.jebo.2015.10.014

28. L, Scartascini C. Tax compliance and enforcement in the Pampas: Evidence from a field experiment. Journal of Economic Behavior & Organization. 2015;116:65-82. DOI: 10.1016/j.jebo.2015.04.002

29. Şafaklı OV, Kutlay K. A research on students' tax compliance: Case of European university of Lefke. International Journal of Academic Research in Economics and Management Sciences. 2014;3/2:1-7 ISSN: 2226-3624

30. Verboon PA, Dijke MV. When do severe sanctions enhance compliance? The role of procedural fairness. Journal of Economic Psychology. 2011;32:120-130. DOI: 10.1016/j.joep.2010.09.007

31. Litina A, Palivos T. Corruption, tax evasion and social values. Journal of Economic Behavior & Organization. 2016;124:164-177. DOI: 10.1016/j.jebo.2015.09.017

32. Djawadi BM, Fahr R. The impact of tax knowledge and budget spending influence on tax compliance. Iza; 2013 Dp No. 7255

11 Chapter

A MATHEMATICAL MODEL FOR ESTIMATING THE NUMBER OF TAXPAYERS WHO COMPLY WITH THE MEXICAN INCOME LAW

1. INTRODUCTION: AN OVERVIEW

1.1. Tributary incomes and active base of contributors

In Mexico, the total amount of tributary incomes, including taxes such as ISR (income tax), IVA (value-added tax), IEPS (special tax on goods and services), IGI (general tax on imports), and other related concepts, reached $723,130 million pesos in the first quarter of 2016. The quantity had a 6.1% growth compared to the value in the first quarter of the previous year [1]. To be more precise, the income tax (ISR) saw an increase of 8.3%, the value-added tax (IVA) increased by 5.2%, and the general sales tax (IGI) increased by 1.1% [1, 2].

The collection for the period January-March 2016 exceeded the predicted amount by $93,585 according to the Federal Income Law (LIF) [1, 3, 4, 5, 6, 7, 8]. Conversely, the tax revenue collected between 2010 and 2015 showed that over 90% was derived from Income Tax (ISR) and Value Added Tax (IVA). Specifically, the percentage of revenue from ISR was 49.71% in 2010, 55.67% in 2011, 57.74% in 2012, and 57.98% in 2013. The IVA percentages during the same period were 40.02%, 41.51%, 44.12%, and 35.65%, respectively. It is noteworthy that the proportion of IEPS in relation to the overall amount was just 0.03% in 2010 and showed a shortfall in 2011 and 2013. IEPS experienced a positive growth of 6.17% up till 2014. From the information provided, it is evident that there is a requirement to determine the makeup of donors as they play a crucial role in the process of collecting taxes. This study focuses on this issue and introduces multiple models that aim to estimate the anticipated number of contributors.

According to official information [1], the active base of contributors consists of all persons, employees, and companies who are currently engaged in the Federal Taxpayer Registry (RFC in Spanish) under a fiscal regime. By 2010, the proportion of persons in relation to the total was 36.68%, while employees accounted for 59.38% and entities made up 4.23%.

Based on the analysis of contributions from 2010 to March 2016, it was discovered that the majority, 61.64%, were employees. Individuals accounted for 34.54% while entities made up only 3.82% [1] (Figure 1).

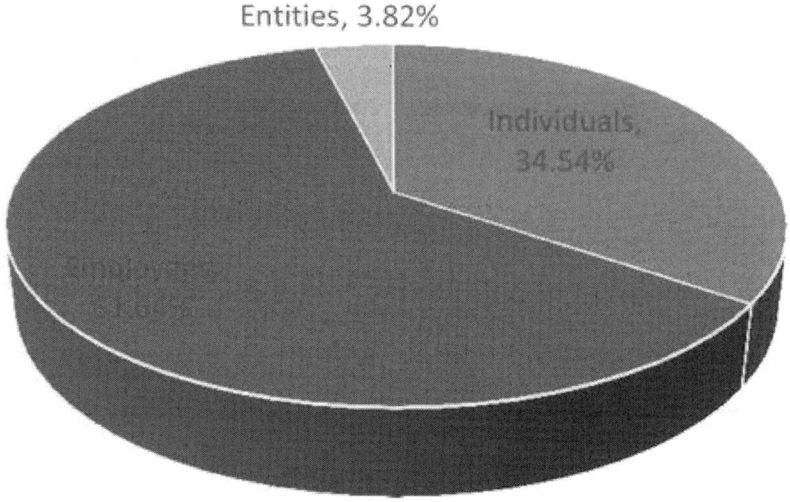

Figure 1. Composition of the active base of contributors considering general averages in 2010–2016. Source: Compiled by the authors with data from the tributary and management report up to the first quarter of 2016.

1.2. Works based on contributors

The following provides a concise overview of the research conducted on tax contributors. The description is specifically centered around a Latin-American context. In their study, Méndez, Morales, and Aguilera [9] examined the concept of contributors as integral members of a collective, highlighting that the progress of individuals is contingent upon their participation. However, only a select few assume leadership roles within the community. The authors argue that compliance with the tributary authorities is essential when analyzing contributors, as it greatly influences the adjustment of profits in their contributions. They determine that in order to increase the number of contributors and improve efficiency, it is necessary to take into account the perception and sociocultural background of individuals, as well as develop appropriate policies that promote transparency and responsibility. Contrarily, Giarrizzo and Brudersohn [10] argued that the government's role as a regulatory and executive agency may not always be beneficial for public administration. Hence, it is not possible to establish a direct relationship between exerting pressure and increasing tax collection. On the other hand, they suggest offering rewards to individuals and companies who follow the taxpaying procedure correctly, so incentivizing their efforts through clear and targeted fiscal incentives. They believe that while this incentive-based method is effective in Argentina, their suggestion may be easily applied to the current situation by identifying the number of individuals with the highest tax burden and implementing incentives accordingly. Javier Tapia [11] proposed a legal research that introduced the theories of power relations, legal-tributary relations, and the tributary function.

Rodriguez [12] highlights the importance of equality to maintain a positive perception of the base number of contributors and considers taxing financial operations. Absalón and Urzúa [13] highlight the need to analyze the base number of contributors per categories or subgroups in the same way this work does. Absalón [13] presented the effect of a fiscal reform and suggests that the negative effects are intimately related to the different regimes, categories, or group of contributors. By the use of microdata, they suggest that the impact could have been identified in specific groups, regimes, or categories.

There is a growing interest to quantify the impact of fiscal imposition on social inequality. Flores [14] analyzes the increase of value-added tax (IVA) on the poorest people and emphasizes the need for a deeper revision of a fiscal reform and claims that a tax on certain goods and services should not impact to the poorest ones.

Gómez [15] conducted a study on the fiscal impact on various demographic segments and suggested a method to streamline the taxpaying procedure in order to improve tax collection. In this study, the authors emphasize the relationship between productivity and employment using an endogenous model. They suggest implementing direct charges based on individuals' revenue levels. They assert that this will lead to societal well-being and equitable distribution of resources. To learn more about the analysis of fiscal policies, reforms, and the use of mathematical techniques to investigate factors that contribute to them, please refer to the following studies: [16, 17, 18, 19, 20, 21, 22, 23, 24, 25].

2. METHODOLOGY

2.1. Base information for developing the proposed models

The methodologies presented in this chapter are based on optimization models; the interested reader may refer to the following references for the theory [26, 27, 28, 29, 30, 31]. The variables for developing an optimization model, applied to the active base of contributors, originated from the expected collection in the income law for the fiscal years 2015 and 2016 and the number of contributors up to the fourth quarter of 2015 and first quarter of 2016. Table 1 shows the number of contributors according to the individuals, employees, and entities categories considered in the tributary and management report [1, 2] and fiscal regimes [32, 33, 34]. Tables 2 and 3 include the collection of ISR, IVA, and IEPS.

Table 1. Contributors according to the class reported in the tributary and management report.

Types of contributors	Third quarter of 2015 (millions of contributors)	Fourth quarter of 2015 (millions of contributors)	First quarter of 2016 (millions of contributors)
Individuals	19.4	19.9	19.9
Employees	29.5	29.9	30.2
Entities	1.8	1.8	1.8
Total	50.7	51.6	51.9

Source: Compiled by authors with data from the tributary and management report up to the first quarter of 2016.

Table 2. Collection of ISR, IVA, and IEPS according to the LIF of 2015.

Tax	Millions of pesos	Relation with respect to total (%)
ISR	1059206.20	55
IVA	703848.50	37
IEPS	159970.60	8
Total tax collection	1923025.30	100

Source: Compiled by authors with data from federal income law for the fiscal year of 2015 [4].

Table 3. Variation in the estimated collection for ISR, IVA, and IEPS (2015–2016).

Concept	Federal income law of 2015 (millions of pesos)	Federal income law of 2016 (millions of pesos)	Percentage (%) of increase
ISR	1′059206.20	1′249299.5	17.95
IVA	703848.50	741988.7	5.42
IEPS	159970.60	348945.2	18.13

Source: Compiled by authors with data from the federal income law in the 2015 and 2016 fiscal years.

It was important to establish within each category the ratio of participation in monetary units with respect to three classes of taxes as shown in the following tables (Tables 4 and 5):

Table 4. Ratio of participation in taxes (LIF 2015) per number contributors up to the fourth quarter of 2015.

Types of contributors	ISR (%)	IVA (%)	IEPS (%)	Total (%)
Individuals	21	14.12	3.21	39
Employees	32	21.21	4.82	58
Entities	2	1.28	0.29	3
Total	55	37	8	100

Source: Compiled by authors.

Table 5. Participation of each category with respect to the number of contributors per tax class up to the fourth quarter of 2015 (millions of pesos).

Types of contributors	ISR	IVA	IEPS	Total
Individuals	408492.31	271445.45	61694.09	741631.85
Employees	613764.83	407850.20	92696.14	1114311.17
Entities	36949.05	24552.85	5580.37	67082.28
Total	1059206.20	703848.50	159970.60	1923025.30

Source: Compiled by the authors.

The fiscal regimes, on the other hand, have 15 categories for each tax class, and the details are considered in Section 4 along with their corresponding proposals.

3.MODELSFOROPTIMIZINGTHEACTIVEBASEOFCONTRIBUTORS PER CATEGORIES

3.1. Initial model

3.1.1. Structure and assessment

The first approach was to develop a model applicable to the fiscal year of 2016 and the previous ones. The OF will consider the constant returns per million contributors up to the fourth quarter of 2015, and this will multiply the optimized number of contributors with the three tax categories considered in the tributary and management reports. The final results are the incomes by ISR, IVA, and IEPS included in the fiscal year of 2015 (Table 2)

$$Maximize = R_{4T2015PF}\tau + R_{4T2015AS}\varphi + R_{4T2015PM}\omega \qquad (1)$$

The initial model should be permitted to display the time evolution of the active base of contributors with respect to the three tax categories. The returns considered the total revenues of 2015 with respect to the census or active base of contributors up to the fourth quarter of 2015, and the restrictions were with respect to the previous quarter. The restrictions are the following[1]:

- Active base of contributors: millions of contributors up to the fourth quarter of 2015
- Individuals: millions of active contributors according to the third quarter tributary and management report of 2015
- Employees: millions of contributors according to the third quarter tributary and management report of 2015
- Entities: millions of active contributors according to the third quarter tributary and management report of 2015

$$\tau + \varphi + \omega \leq \theta \quad (2)$$

$$\tau \geq \theta_1 \quad (3)$$

$$\varphi \geq \theta_2 \quad (4)$$

$$\omega \geq \theta_3 \quad (5)$$

where τ=individuals, φ=employees, ω=entities, θ=active contributors roll, in millions; θ_τ=active roll of individuals, in millions; θ_φ=active roll of employees, in millions; and θ_ω=active roll of entities, in millions.

Based on the above, the initial model is the following:

Model 1						
Returns per million contributors **$R_{4T2015PF}$=Fourth quarter return,individuals** **$R_{4T2015AS}$=Fourth quarter return,employees** **$R_{4T2015PM}$=Fourth quarter return,entities**		**Maximize** **$R_{4T2015PF}\tau+R_{4T2015AS}\varphi+R_{4T2015PM\omega}$**				
Restriction variables	**Subjected to**					
1	θ Active base of contributors up to the fourth quarter of 2015 (millions of contributors)	τ	φ	ω	≤	θ
2	θ_1 Individuals (active contributors up to the third quarter of 2015, in millions)	τ			≥	θ1
3	θ_2 Employees (active contributors up to the third quarter of 2015, in millions)		φ		≥	θ2
4	θ_3 Entities (active contributors up to the third quarter of 2015, in millions)			ω	≥	θ3

Source: Compiled by authors

The estimated returns, R_{4T2015}, (for 2015) per million contributors, is determined by the total returns considered in the LIF of 2015 multiplied for each class of contributors with respect to the total, and the result of this is divided by the number of contributors for each class according to the tributary and management report of the fourth quarter of 2015[2]:

$$R_{2015}\tau = \left[\frac{1923025.3*0.39}{19.9}\right] = 37726.93$$

$$R_{2015}\varphi = \left[\frac{1923025.3*0.58}{29.9}\right] = 37726.93$$

$$R_{2015}\varphi = \left[\frac{1923025.3*0.03}{1.8}\right] = 37726.93$$

Based on the above, the OF is given by

$$Maximize = 37267.93\tau + 37267.93\varphi + 37267.93\omega \quad (6)$$

Subjected to restrictions

$$\begin{cases} 1\tau + 1\varphi + 1\omega \leq 51.60 \\ 1\tau + 0\varphi + 0\omega \geq 19.40 \\ 0\tau + 1\varphi + 0\omega \geq 29.50 \\ 0\tau + 0\varphi + 1\omega \geq 1.80 \end{cases}$$

$$\tau, \varphi, \omega \geq 0$$

The results obtained by using the PHP Simplex tool [35] and replicated with Solver in Excel were the following: τ=20.30 *(individualsin million contributors)* φ=29.50 *(employees,in millioncontributors)*, and ω=1.80 *(entitiesin million contributors).*

Based on the optimized number of contributors, the product of these variables with the returns, i.e., the maximized results of (6), is tested for equality with total revenue by ISR, IVA, and IEPS within the LIF for 2015.

$$Maximize = 37267.93(20.30) + 37267.93(29.5) + 37267.93(1.8)$$

$$Maximize = 1923025.20$$

As can be noted, the optimized results for the total revenue by ISR, IVA, and IEPS are the same with respect to the approved LIF for the fiscal year 2015[3] (Table 2). The proposed model indicates, however, in this scenario of constant returns per million contributors, that a better choice would be to increase the number of individuals to 20.3 million instead of the one reported in the tributary form of the fourth quarter of 2015 in which this number reaches 19.9 million. The difference, however, was in the number of employees that went from 29.5 to 29.9 million contributors [2].

3.2. A model with differentiated returns

Using the proposed model of the above section, the next model considers several types of returns per million contributors with respect to three categories, a condition that can be well estimated and updated by SAT. For this, $34,000 is considered for individuals, \$35,963.57 for employees, and \$75,000 for entities which results in an OF of the following form:

$$Maximize = 34000\tau + 35963.57\varphi + 75000\omega \tag{7}$$

The restrictions were 51.60 million contributors as the maximum allowed and that corresponds to the total number of contributors of the tributary and management report of the fourth quarter of 2015 and also the restriction which corresponds to the official number of contributors up to the third quarter of 2015 and that will allow to know the optimal change in each category.

Model 2						
Returns per million contributors $R_{dif2015PF}$=*Differenced returns,individuals* $R_{dif2015AS}$=*Differenced returns,employees* $R_{dif2015PM}$=*Differenced returns ,entities*		**Maximize** $R_{dif2015PF}\tau+R_{dif2015AS}\varphi+R_{dif2015PM}\omega$				
Restriction variables	**Subjected to**					
1	θ Active base of contributors up to the fourth quarter of 2015 (millions of contributors)	τ	φ	ω	≤	θ
2	θ_1 Individuals (active contributors up to the third quarter of 2015, in millions)	τ			≥	θ1
3	θ_2 Employees (active contributors up to the third quarter of 2015, in millions)		φ		≥	θ2
4	θ_3 Entities (active contributors up to the third quarter of 2015, in millions)			ω	≥	θ3

Source: Compiled by the authors

$$\begin{cases} 1\tau + 1\varphi + 1\omega \le 51.60 \\ 1\tau + 0\varphi + 0\omega \ge 19.40 \\ 0\tau + 1\varphi + 0\omega \ge 29.50 \\ 0\tau + 0\varphi + 1\omega \ge 1.80 \end{cases}$$

$$\tau, \varphi, \omega \ge 0$$

The results obtained by using the PHP Simplex tool [35] and replicated with Solver in Excel were the following: τ=19.40Individualsin million contributors,

φ=29.50 Employeesin million contributors, and ω=2.70 Entitiesin million contributors. Based on the optimized number of contributors, the product of these variables by the returns, i.e., the maximized result of (7), is compared with the total revenues by ISR, IVA, an IEPS within the LIF of 2015 (Table 2), i.e., $1923025.30.

Using the maximized OF of Eq. (7), the following is obtained:

$$Maximize = 34,000(19.4) + 35963.57(29.5) + 75,000(2.70)$$

$$Maximize = 1923025.31$$

Unlike the model with constant returns, in this model that considers distinct returns, the increase should have been registered in entities, and if this is not the case, the original way of considering contributors is preferred instead, even though this situation is uneven with respect to tax participation.

3.3. Prototype model with constant returns

In the following, an approach called prototype model (PM), whose objective is to give tax authorities a better idea of the capacity to adequate tax policies to obtain optimized results, is presented. The first approach is a model with constant returns[4] and whose objective function to maximize is

$$Maximize = 37929.49\tau + 37929.49\varphi + 37929.49\omega \tag{8}$$

In this new proposal[5], the restriction for entities to be at least 2.5 million contributors will be modified. Also, an additional restriction concerning the total number of active contributors and distributed in two classes (employees and entities) is that this should be at least 34.43 million.

$$\begin{cases} 1\tau + 1\varphi + 1\omega \leq 61.70 \\ 1\tau + 0\varphi + 0\omega \geq 19.40 \\ 0\tau + 1\varphi + 0\omega \geq 29.50 \\ 0\tau + 0\varphi + 1\omega \geq 2.05 \\ 0\tau + 1\varphi + 1\omega \geq 34.43 \end{cases}$$

$$-\tau, \varphi, \omega \geq 0$$

Model 3						
Return per million contributors $R_{3T2015PF}$**=Return for the third quarter of 2015, Individuals** $R_{3T2015AS}$**=Return for the third quarter of 2015, Employees** $R_{3T2015PM}$**=Return for the third quarter of 2015, Entities**		**Maximize** $R_{3T2015PF}\tau+R_{3T2015AS}\varphi+R_{3T2015PM}\omega$				
Restriction Variables	**Subjected to**					
1	θ Active base of contributors, estimated for 2016 (in million contributors)	τ	φ	ω	$\leq$	θ
2	θ_1 Individuals (millions of active contributors, third quarter of 2015)	τ			$\geq$	$\theta 1$
3	θ_2 Employees (millions of active contributors, third quarter of 2015)		φ		$\geq$	$\theta 2$
4	δ_1 [6] Minimum number of contributors for entities (in million contributors)			ω	$\geq$	$\delta 1$
5	δ_2 Minimum required number of contributors for employees and entities (in million contributors)		φ	ω	$\geq$	$\delta 2$

Source: Compiled by the authors

The results obtained with the PHP Simplex tool [35] and replicated with Solver of MS Excel were the following: τ=27.27million contributors,individuals; φ=32.38million contributors,employees; and ω=2.05million contributors,entities.

Based on the optimized number of contributors, the product of these variables by the returns, i.e., the maximized result of (19), is compared with the total revenue by ISR, IVA, and IEPS, in this case, considering the LIF of 2016. Maximizing, again, the OF of (19) results in

$$Maximize = 37929.49(27.27) + 37929.49(32.38) + 37929.49(2.05)$$

$$Maximize = 2340249.53$$ [7]

The above result represents the total expected tax collection for 2016 considering ISR, IVA, and IEPS. The results present differences in decimals due to the fact that only two decimal points were considered in the returns; however, by using the complete decimals, the result would be exact.

3.4. Prototype model with differentiated returns

In the following a model which considers increments per million contributors, where each contributor may lie within three categories, is presented (the categories may be adjusted by fiscal authorities when needed). Moreover, a restriction which considers a minimum number of contributors in the employees and entities categories is added (as before these categories may be adjusted by the goals and objectives of the fiscal authorities). The model proposes to maximize the following objective function:

$$Maximize = 40239.19\tau + 35963.57\varphi + 37000\omega \qquad (9)$$

An additional restriction is the condition that the total number of contributors (in million contributors) will reach at least 22.50

Model 4						
Returns per million contributors $R_{dif2016PF}$=2016 differenced returns, Individuals $R_{dif2016AS}$=2016 differenced returns, Employees $R_{dif2016PM}$=2016 differenced returns, Entities		**Maximize** $R_{dif2016PF}\tau+R_{dif2016AS}\varphi+R_{dif2016PM}\omega$				
Restriction variables	Subjected to					
1	θ Estimated active base of contributors for 2016 (in millions of contributors)	τ	φ	ω	≤	θ
2	θ_1 Individuals (millions of active contributors up to the fourth quarter of 2015)	τ			≥	θ1
3	θ_2 Employees (millions of active contributors up to the fourth quarter of 2015)		φ		≥	θ2
4	δ_1[8] Minimum number of contributors (entities) (in million contributors)			ω	≥	δ1
5	δ_2 Minimum number of contributors (employees and entities) (in million contributors)		φ	ω	≥	δ2
6	δ3 Minimum number of contributors (individuals and entities) (in million contributors)		φ	ω	≥	δ3

Source: Compiled by authors

$$\begin{cases} 1\tau + 1\varphi + 1\omega \leq 61.70 \\ 1\tau + 0\varphi + 0\omega \geq 19.90 \\ 0\tau + 1\varphi + 0\omega \geq 29.90 \\ 0\tau + 0\varphi + 1\omega \geq 2.05 \\ 0\tau + 1\varphi + 1\omega \geq 34.43 \\ 1\tau + 0\varphi + 1\omega \geq 22.50 \end{cases}$$

$$-\tau, \varphi, \omega \geq 0$$

The results obtained by using the PHP Simplex tool [35] and replicated with MS Excel Solver are the following: τ=27.27million contributors,individuals; φ=29.90million contributors,employees; and ω=4.53million contributors,entities.

Based on the optimized number of contributors, the next steps are to multiply these variables by the returns, i.e., the maximized result of (9), and to compare it with the total revenues by ISR, IVA, and IEPS for equality.

Using the maximized OF, (9) results in

$$Maximize = 40239.19(27.27) + 35963.57(29.90) + 37000(4.53)$$

$$Maximize = 2340243.40^{9}$$

The above result represents the total tax collection expected for 2016 for taxes ISR, IVA, and IEPS. Using exact quantities with all decimals will result in an exact value.

4. MODELS TO OPTIMIZE THE BASE NUMBER OF CONTRIBUTORS PER FISCAL REGIME

4.1. Generic model for ISR

In the following a generic model for ISR is presented. The model is structured in accordance to the official information up to September 31 of 2015 and obtained via a request of public information [33]. The authorities detail that the total number of contributors up to September 31[10], registered up to the 2009 exercise, is 11,107,553; however, in order to give an example for the following model, we will take the total number of contributors as 16,752,516. To test the model, constant returns are considered for each contributor, and these can be obtained by dividing the total collection of ISR in the fiscal year 2015 which is $1059206.20 (in million pesos) by the total number of contributors which is 16,752,516 and which results in an approximated return per contributor of 0.0632 million pesos[11]. The objective function will be represented by the returns of each fiscal regime reported by the authority. Restrictions are composed of the total number of contributors (for this case it is greater than the one reported on September 2015 which is 17,000,000[12]), and consequently a better tax collection is expected than the one that was considered for the base of the returns. The following restrictions (14 in total) will correspond each to the total number of contributors per regime[13]; the number of residents abroad without a permanent establishment in Mexico is at least 200. Also, the restriction, wages, salaries, and similar regime together with the fiscal incorporation regime are at least 10,600,000 contributors[14]. In the following, the notation is presented[15]:

$R\theta n$ = Return per restriction variable

θ=Total number of contributors for ISR in accordance to official goals and objectives

θ_1=Wages and salaries regime and wages like in comes official data

θ_2=Fiscal incorporation regime official data

θ_3=Individuals with enterprise and professional activities regimeofficial data

θ_4=General regime for the law of entities official data

θ_5=Régimen de Arrendamiento (dato official)

θ_6=Incomes by dividends regime partners and shareholders,official data

θ_7=Agriculture,forestry,livestockandPFandPMfishing regime official data

θ_8=Regime for the rest of incomes official data

θ_9=Incomes by interests regime official data

θ_{10}=Entities with non-profit purposes official data

θ_{11}=Producers cooperatives that defer their incomes official data

θ_{12}=Regime of coordinatedofficial data

θ_{13}=Corporate groups regime official data

θ_{14}=Regime of consolidated official data

δ_1=Individuals residing abroad without a physical estabishment in Mexico restricted to200

δ_2=Wages and salaries regime and fiscal incorporation regime Rrestricted to10,600,000.

Generic model for ISR

Objective function for ISR:

$$R_{\theta_1} + R_{\theta_2} + R_{\theta_3} + R_{\theta_4} + R_{\theta_5} + R_{\theta_6} + R_{\theta_7} + R_{\theta_8} + R_{\theta_9} + R_{\theta_{10}} + R_{\theta_{11}} + R_{\theta_{12}} + R_{\theta_{13}} + R_{\theta_{14}}$$

with the following restrictions:

$$1\theta_2 + 1\theta_3 + 1\theta_4 + 1\theta_5 + 1\theta_6 + 1\theta_7 + 1\theta_8 + 1\theta_9 + 1\theta_{10} + 1\theta_{11} + 1\theta_{12} + 1\theta_{13}$$

$$\theta_2 + 0\theta_3 + 0\theta_4 + 0\theta_5 + 0\theta_6 + 0\theta_7 + 0\theta_8 + 0\theta_9 + 0\theta_{10} + 0\theta_{11} + 0\theta_{12} + 0\theta_{13} +$$

$$\theta_2 + 0\theta_3 + 0\theta_4 + 0\theta_5 + 0\theta_6 + 0\theta_7 + 0\theta_8 + 0\theta_9 + 0\theta_{10} + 0\theta_{11} + 0\theta_{12} + 0\theta_{13} +$$

$$\theta_2 + 1\theta_3 + 0\theta_4 + 0\theta_5 + 0\theta_6 + 0\theta_7 + 0\theta_8 + 0\theta_9 + 0\theta_{10} + 0\theta_{11} + 0\theta_{12} + 0\theta_{13} +$$

$$\theta_2 + 0\theta_3 + 1\theta_4 + 0\theta_5 + 0\theta_6 + 0\theta_7 + 0\theta_8 + 0\theta_9 + 0\theta_{10} + 0\theta_{11} + 0\theta_{12} + 0\theta_{13} +$$

$$\theta_2 + 0\theta_3 + 0\theta_4 + 1\theta_5 + 0\theta_6 + 0\theta_7 + 0\theta_8 + 0\theta_9 + 0\theta_{10} + 0\theta_{11} + 0\theta_{12} + 0\theta_{13} +$$

$$\theta_2 + 0\theta_3 + 0\theta_4 + 0\theta_5 + 1\theta_6 + 0\theta_7 + 0\theta_8 + 0\theta_9 + 0\theta_{10} + 0\theta_{11} + 0\theta_{12} + 0\theta_{13} +$$

$$\theta_2 + 0\theta_3 + 0\theta_4 + 0\theta_5 + 0\theta_6 + 1\theta_7 + 0\theta_8 + 0\theta_9 + 0\theta_{10} + 0\theta_{11} + 0\theta_{12} + 0\theta_{13} +$$

$$\theta_2 + 0\theta_3 + 0\theta_4 + 0\theta_5 + 0\theta_6 + 0\theta_7 + 1\theta_8 + 0\theta_9 + 0\theta_{10} + 0\theta_{11} + 0\theta_{12} + 0\theta_{13} +$$

$$\theta_2 + 0\theta_3 + 0\theta_4 + 0\theta_5 + 0\theta_6 + 0\theta_7 + 0\theta_8 + 1\theta_9 + 0\theta_{10} + 0\theta_{11} + 0\theta_{12} + 0\theta_{13} +$$

$$\theta_2 + 0\theta_3 + 0\theta_4 + 0\theta_5 + 0\theta_6 + 0\theta_7 + 0\theta_8 + 0\theta_9 + 1\theta_{10} + 0\theta_{11} + 0\theta_{12} + 0\theta_{13} +$$

$$\theta_2 + 0\theta_3 + 0\theta_4 + 0\theta_5 + 0\theta_6 + 0\theta_7 + 0\theta_8 + 0\theta_9 + 0\theta_{10} + 1\theta_{11} + 0\theta_{12} + 0\theta_{13} +$$

$$\theta_2 + 0\theta_3 + 0\theta_4 + 0\theta_5 + 0\theta_6 + 0\theta_7 + 0\theta_8 + 0\theta_9 + 0\theta_{10} + 0\theta_{11} + 1\theta_{12} + 0\theta_{13} +$$

$$\theta_2 + 0\theta_3 + 0\theta_4 + 0\theta_5 + 0\theta_6 + 0\theta_7 + 0\theta_8 + 0\theta_9 + 0\theta_{10} + 0\theta_{11} + 0\theta_{12} + 1\theta_{13} +$$

$$\theta_2 + 0\theta_3 + 0\theta_4 + 0\theta_5 + 0\theta_6 + 0\theta_7 + 0\theta_8 + 0\theta_9 + 0\theta_{10} + 0\theta_{11} + 0\theta_{12} + 0\theta_{13} +$$

$$\theta_2 + 0\theta_3 + 0\theta_4 + 0\theta_5 + 0\theta_6 + 0\theta_7 + 0\theta_8 + 0\theta_9 + 0\theta_{10} + 0\theta_{11} + 0\theta_{12} + 0\theta_{13} +$$

$$1\theta_2 + 0\theta_3 + 0\theta_4 + 0\theta_5 + 0\theta_6 + 0\theta_7 + 0\theta_8 + 0\theta_9 + 0\theta_{10} + 0\theta_{11} + 0\theta_{12} + 0\theta_{13} +$$

Generic model for ISR

Objective function for ISR:

$$R_{\theta_1} + R_{\theta_2} + R_{\theta_3} + R_{\theta_4} + R_{\theta_5} + R_{\theta_6} + R_{\theta_7} + R_{\theta_8} + R_{\theta_9} + R_{\theta_{10}} + R_{\theta_{11}} + R_{\theta_{12}} + R_{\theta_{13}} + R_{\theta_{14}}$$

with the following restrictions:

$$\begin{cases}
1\theta_1+1\theta_2+1\theta_3+1\theta_4+1\theta_5+1\theta_6+1\theta_7+1\theta_8+1\theta_9+1\theta_{10}+1\theta_{11}+1\theta_{12}+1\theta_{13}+1\theta_{14}\leq 17000000\\
1\theta_1+0\theta_2+0\theta_3+0\theta_4+0\theta_5+0\theta_6+0\theta_7+0\theta_8+0\theta_9+0\theta_{10}+0\theta_{11}+0\theta_{12}+0\theta_{13}+0\theta_{14}\geq 6155456\\
0\theta_1+1\theta_2+0\theta_3+0\theta_4+0\theta_5+0\theta_6+0\theta_7+0\theta_8+0\theta_9+0\theta_{10}+0\theta_{11}+0\theta_{12}+0\theta_{13}+0\theta_{14}\geq 4444544\\
0\theta_1+0\theta_2+1\theta_3+0\theta_4+0\theta_5+0\theta_6+0\theta_7+0\theta_8+0\theta_9+0\theta_{10}+0\theta_{11}+0\theta_{12}+0\theta_{13}+0\theta_{14}\geq 3764639\\
0\theta_1+0\theta_2+0\theta_3+1\theta_4+0\theta_5+0\theta_6+0\theta_7+0\theta_8+0\theta_9+0\theta_{10}+0\theta_{11}+0\theta_{12}+0\theta_{13}+0\theta_{14}\geq 1496588\\
0\theta_1+0\theta_2+0\theta_3+0\theta_4+1\theta_5+0\theta_6+0\theta_7+0\theta_8+0\theta_9+0\theta_{10}+0\theta_{11}+0\theta_{12}+0\theta_{13}+0\theta_{14}\geq 547070\\
0\theta_1+0\theta_2+0\theta_3+0\theta_4+0\theta_5+1\theta_6+0\theta_7+0\theta_8+0\theta_9+0\theta_{10}+0\theta_{11}+0\theta_{12}+0\theta_{13}+0\theta_{14}\geq 324011\\
0\theta_1+0\theta_2+0\theta_3+0\theta_4+0\theta_5+0\theta_6+1\theta_7+0\theta_8+0\theta_9+0\theta_{10}+0\theta_{11}+0\theta_{12}+0\theta_{13}+0\theta_{14}\geq 187716\\
0\theta_1+0\theta_2+0\theta_3+0\theta_4+0\theta_5+0\theta_6+0\theta_7+1\theta_8+0\theta_9+0\theta_{10}+0\theta_{11}+0\theta_{12}+0\theta_{13}+0\theta_{14}\geq 45000\\
0\theta_1+0\theta_2+0\theta_3+0\theta_4+0\theta_5+0\theta_6+0\theta_7+0\theta_8+1\theta_9+0\theta_{10}+0\theta_{11}+0\theta_{12}+0\theta_{13}+0\theta_{14}\geq 18337\\
0\theta_1+0\theta_2+0\theta_3+0\theta_4+0\theta_5+0\theta_6+0\theta_7+0\theta_8+0\theta_9+1\theta_{10}+0\theta_{11}+0\theta_{12}+0\theta_{13}+0\theta_{14}\geq 5577\\
0\theta_1+0\theta_2+0\theta_3+0\theta_4+0\theta_5+0\theta_6+0\theta_7+0\theta_8+0\theta_9+0\theta_{10}+1\theta_{11}+0\theta_{12}+0\theta_{13}+0\theta_{14}\geq 5043\\
0\theta_1+0\theta_2+0\theta_3+0\theta_4+0\theta_5+0\theta_6+0\theta_7+0\theta_8+0\theta_9+0\theta_{10}+0\theta_{11}+1\theta_{12}+0\theta_{13}+0\theta_{14}\geq 3918\\
0\theta_1+0\theta_2+0\theta_3+0\theta_4+0\theta_5+0\theta_6+0\theta_7+0\theta_8+0\theta_9+0\theta_{10}+0\theta_{11}+0\theta_{12}+1\theta_{13}+0\theta_{14}\geq 1275\\
0\theta_1+0\theta_2+0\theta_3+0\theta_4+0\theta_5+0\theta_6+0\theta_7+0\theta_8+0\theta_9+0\theta_{10}+0\theta_{11}+0\theta_{12}+0\theta_{13}+1\theta_{14}\geq 626\\
0\theta_1+0\theta_2+0\theta_3+0\theta_4+0\theta_5+0\theta_6+0\theta_7+0\theta_8+0\vartheta_9+0\theta_{10}+0\theta_{11}+0\theta_{12}+0\theta_{13}+1\theta_{14}\geq 200\\
1\theta_1+1\theta_2+0\theta_3+0\theta_4+0\theta_5+0\theta_6+0\theta_7+0\theta_8+0\theta_9+0\theta_{10}+0\theta_{11}+0\theta_{12}+0\theta_{13}+0\theta_{14}\geq 10600000
\end{cases}$$

The generic model of ISR presented above along with their objective function permitted to obtain a tax collection for $1,074,400. Due to the fact that two restrictions conditioned the increase of certain fiscal regimes below the one expected in the LIF. The optimized number of contributors with the above restrictions are **θ_1=6,155,456; θ_2=4,444,544; θ_3=3,764,639; θ_4=1,349,998; θ_5=547,070; θ_6=324,011; θ_7=187,716; θ_8=45,000; θ_9=18,337; θ_{10}=5,577; θ_{11}=5,043; θ_{12}=3,918; θ_{13}=1,275; θ14=626; and θ_{15}=200.**

As can be noted, the differences are presented in three of the fiscal regimes. In wages, salaries, and similar regime, the official value went from 6,056,971 to 6,155,456; in the leasing regime went from 547,070 to 693,660; and finally in the other incomes, regime went from 42618.00 to 45000. In the individuals residing abroad without a physical establishment, regime went from 173 to 200 contributors.

5. CONCISE SUMMARY

The initial model, which was supported by official information up to the fiscal year 2015, provided evidence of the functionality of the system. It allowed for establishing a correlation between the number of active contributors and the projected collection in the LIF. This implies that the approach can be applied in several different contexts.

The performance of the initial model for the first scenario, which adheres to the LIF of 2016, imposes limitations on the official count of individuals and employees, as well as two additional constraints. Furthermore, it establishes a minimum target of achieving at least 2.05 million entities. The second requirement, which mandates that the total number of employees and entities must be at least 34.43 million, led to the following breakdown: 27.27 million individuals, 32.38 million employees, and 2.70 million contributing entities.

The aforementioned ideas not only enable the adaptation of the model to the tax authorities' returns, but also facilitate the imposition of constraints based on data from previous exercises, such as the prototype models mentioned above. It is crucial to acknowledge that certain scenarios depicted in this study rely on the returns derived from official data. Consequently, if these returns cannot be obtained, conducting an active census for each category will impose an extra financial burden on the same number of contributors. Furthermore, this will perpetuate a risky trend observed over the past decade, wherein the number of individuals and employees has been increasing, but not the number of entities.

AT A GLANCE

This chapter presents proposed approaches for calculating the overall number of taxpayers in Mexico's tax system. The techniques are founded on the principles of optimization theory and comprise of an initial model that yields distinct outcomes, a prototype model that generates consistent and distinct returns, and a generic model specifically designed for Mexican income tax (ISR). According to the theoretical findings, the models allow for efficient estimation of the anticipated number of contributors in various scenarios. Furthermore, when the estimated data is compared to the official data, they yield satisfactory findings. The presented models have the potential to be customized to suit the specific circumstances of the Mexican tributary authority. They could serve as a valuable tool for the Mexican government in managing their fiscal process.

REFERENCES

1. Servicio de Administración Tributaria. Informe Tributario y de Gestión Primer Trimestre 2016, México [Online]. 2016. http://www.sat.gob.mx/transparencia/transparencia_focalizada/Documents/itg2016_t1/ITG_T1_2016.pdf
2. Servicio de Administración Tributaria. Informe Tributario y de Gestión Cuarto Trimestre 2015, México [Online]. 2016. http://www.sat.gob.mx/transparencia/transparencia_focalizada/Paginas/informe_tributario_gestion.aspx
3. Congreso de la Unión. Ley de Ingresos de la Federación para el Ejercicio Fiscal 2016. Diario Oficial de la Federación [Online]. Nov. 2015. http://www.diputados.gob.mx/LeyesBiblio/pdf/LIF_2016.pdf

4. Congreso de la Unión. Ley de Ingresos de la Federación para el Ejercicio Fiscal de 2015, Diario Oficial de la Federación [Online]. Nov. 2014. http://www.dof.gob.mx/nota_detalle.php?codigo=5368103&fecha=13/11/2014
5. Congreso de la Unión. Ley de Presupuesto y Responsabilidad Hacendaria, México; 2016
6. SHCP. Documento relativo al cumplimiento de las disposiciones contenidas en el Artículo 42, Fracción I, de la Ley Federal de Presupuesto y Responsabilidad Hacendaria, México [Online]. 2015. http://finanzaspublicas.hacienda.gob.mx/work/models/Finanzas_Publicas/docs/paquete_economico/precgpe/precgpe_2016.pdf
7. SHCP. Paquete Económico y Presupuesto, México [Online]. 2016. http://finanzaspublicas.hacienda.gob.mx/es/Finanzas_Publicas/Paquete_Economico_y_Presupuesto
8. SHCP. Presupuesto de Egresos de la Federación, Proyecto 2016 versión ciudadana,México[Online].2015.http://www.transparenciapresupuestaria.gob.mx/work/models/PTP/Presupuesto/Presupuestacion/ppef2016.pdf
9. M, Aguilera O, Morales N. Cultura Tributaria y Contribuyentes: Datos y apectos metodológicos, Fermentum. Revista Venezolana de Sociología y Antropología, septiembre-diciembre [Online]. 2005. pp. 332-352. http://www.redalyc.org/articulo.oa?id=70504404
10. V, Brudersohn S. Premiar al buen contribuyente. Un recorrido por los Incentivos Positivos aplicados en Argentina para mejorar el Cumplimiento Fiscal, Documentos y Aportes en Administración Pública y Gestión Estatal [Online]. 2013. pp. 7-48. http://www.redalyc.org/articulo.oa?id=337530224001
11. Tapia J. Bases para un debido proceso tributario: tres teorías acerca de la relación entre el estado y los contribuyentes. Revista Chilena de Derecho, Mayo-Agosto [Online]. 2005. pp. 329-362. http://www.redalyc.org/articulo.oa?id=177021336006
12. Rodríguez J. El impuesto a las operaciones financieras y la equidad tributaria. Cuedernos de Economía [Online]. 2002;21(37):1-21 http://www.scielo.org.co/pdf/ceco/v21n37/v21n37a08.pdf
13. Absalón C, Urzúa C. Modelos de micro-simulación para el análisis de políticas públicas, Gestión y Política Pública [Online]. 2012. pp. 87-106. http://www.redalyc.org/articulo.oa?id=13323078003
14. Flores D. Un incremento en la tasa del IVA sobre alimentos ¿eficiencia, equidad o recaudación?, Ensayos [Online]. 2003. pp. 1-14. file:///C:/Users/Sergio%20Lagunas/Downloads/Un_incremento_en_la_tasa_del_IVA.pdf

15. Gómez M. Reforma fiscal y bienestar en la economía de México. Economía Mexicana, Economía Mexicana Nueva Época, XIII segundo semestre [Online]. 2004. pp. 161-189. http://www.redalyc.org/articulo.oa?id=32313202

16. Pádurean E, Leonida L. Impact of the Fiscal Policies on the standard of living of the employees, Financial Studies [Online]. 2013;17(1):58-67. http://fs.icfm.ro/7_IMPACTOFTHEFISCALPO-LICIESONTHESTANDARDOFLIVINGOFTHEEMPLOYEES.pdf

17. Ailinca A, Iordache F. The current reforms of the labour markets and of the related social policies at European Union level – are they the best solution to solve the problems which appeared during the crisis?. Financial Studies [Online]. 2012;16(2):147-163. ftp://www.ipe.ro/RePEc/vls/vls_pdf/vol16i2p147-163.pdf

18. Ramírez E. Por una política fiscal contracíclica, Problemas del Desarrollo [Online]. 2006. http://www.ejournal.unam.mx/pde/pde147/PDE14704.pdf

19. P. The Return of Fiscal Policy: Can the New Developments in the New Economic Consensus Be Reconciled with the Post-Keynesian View? New York [Online]. 2008. http://www.levyinstitute.org/pubs/wp_539.pdf

20. Ban C. Austerity Versus Stimulus? Understanding Fiscal Policy Change at the International Monetary Fund since the Great Recession, Boston [Online]. 2014. http://www.relooney.com/NS3040/000_New_947.pdf

21. The World Bank. Fiscal Policy and Economic Growth Lessons for Eastern Europe and Central Asia, Washington [Online]. 2008. http://siteresources.worldbank.org/INTECA/Resources/257896-1182288383968/FiscalPolicy&EconomicGrowthinECA_FullReport.pdf

22. Robles A, Huesca L. Incidencia fiscal en México: ¿Es posible aumentar la recaudación sin afectar a la población? Finanzas y Política Económica [Online]. 2013;5(1):59-78. file:///C:/Users/Sergio%20Lagunas/Documents/CARPETA%20DE%20TRABAJO/PUBLICACIONES/IMEF%202016/OPTIMIZACION%20CONTRIBUYENTES/INCIDENCIA%20FISCAL%20EN%20MEXICO.pdf

23. JY, Jalbert V, Araar A. Classical Horizontal Inequity and Reranking: an Integrating Approach, Canadá [Online]. 2003. http://www.cirpee.org/fileadmin/documents/Cahiers_2003/CIRPEE03-06.pdf

24. C. Un modelo microeconómico de la economía peruana (una aplicación de programación lineal), Economía [Online]. 1982. pp. 47-84. revistas.pucp.edu.pe/index.php/economia/article/download/161/157

25. F. A contribution to the theory of taxation. Economic Journal. 1927;37:47-61
26. Render B, Stair R, Hanna M. Métodos cuantitativos para los negocios. Pearson: México; 2012
27. D, Sweeney D, Williams T, Camm J, Martin K. Métodos cuantitativos para los negocios. CENGAGE Learning: México; 2011
28. A, Almazán O, Cabello A, Blanco G, Herryman M. Aplicación de la modelación matemática en el análisis de diferentes esquemas de producción integrada de alcohol, azúcar y electricidad, ICIDCA. Sobre los Derivados [Online]. 2007. pp. 26-30. http://www.redalyc.org/comocitar.oa?id=223114970005
29. B. Principles of Linear Programming. Problems of Economic Transition [Online]. 1932;5(2):16-27 http://mesharpe.metapress.com/link.asp?target=contribution&id=1541170H83X62004
30. S. An Introduction to Linear Programming, Rhode Island [Online]. 2007. https://web.williams.edu/Mathematics/sjmiller/public_html/BrownClasses/54/handouts/LinearProgramming.pdf
31. A, Sánchez P, Ferrer JM, Barquín J, Linares P. Modelos Matemáticos de Optimización, Madrid [Online]. 2010. https://www.gams.com/docs/contributed/modelado_en_gams.pdf
32. de Administración Tributaria. Respuesta a Requerimiento de Información Folio 0610100140715 Administración Central de Identificación del Contribuyente, México, 2015
33. de Administración Tributaria. Respuesta a requerimiento de información Folio 0610100140515 Administración Central de Identificación del Contribuyente, México, 2015
34. de Administración Tributaria. Respuesta a Requerimiento de información Folio 0610100140915 Administración Central de Identificación del Contribuyente, México, 2015
35. Izquierdo D, Ruíz J. PHP Simplex [Online]. http://www.phpsimplex.com/index.htm. 2016, May

12

Chapter

TAX PRACTITIONER COMPLIANCE

1. INTRODUCTION: AN OVERVIEW

The purpose of this chapter is to examine previous research on tax practitioners and offer insights into their conduct that impacts taxpayer compliance. Tax compliance has been a topic of significant interest to scholars from various academic disciplines, such as accounting, economics, history, law, psychology, political science, and sociology, for the past forty years [1]. Numerous research have made significant contributions to the tax literature by uncovering the elements that influence taxpayer compliance behavior. However, the majority of these studies concentrate on the taxpayer's behavioral reactions to the tax system and fiscal policies.

Taxation is a meticulously organized procedure involving several entities such as taxpayers, tax practitioners, tax administration, and government officials responsible for making tax laws [2]. In addition, tax compliance is an intricate phenomenon involving several participants in the sector, and their interactions significantly influence the behavior of individual taxpayers [3]. Therefore, a deficiency in studies regarding significant entities can weaken our comprehension of tax compliance behavior, which is closely interconnected [4].

Professional tax methods are crucial in determining taxpayer compliance in the real world. Tax practitioners have the ability to significantly impact taxpayers during the tax compliance process by either assisting them in adhering to or taking advantage of the tax legislation [5]. Due to the enormous quantities and confusing jargon in tax regulations, many people seek guidance from tax specialists who are knowledgeable about the complex tax rules. In addition, due to their limited resources, taxpayers frequently rely on tax practitioners to make crucial decisions regarding their tax affairs. Hence, it is crucial to comprehend the factors that contribute to practitioners' adherence and the methods they employ to ensure compliance in the taxpayer compliance process. Nevertheless, there is a dearth of scientific studies examining the relationship between tax procedure and taxpayer compliance. Moreover, there is a lack of consensus on the definition of tax practitioner compliance.

The primary aim of this chapter is to enhance the comprehension of tax scholars, tax practitioners, and tax authorities about tax practitioner compliance in relation to taxpayers' selection of their tax position. In pursuit of this objective, I extract valuable insights from research discoveries and combine them to elucidate the significance of tax compliance in the context of taxpayers and tax practitioners, as well as their interactions. In this context, tax practitioners are defined as private sector tax specialists who assist taxpayers in the preparation of their tax returns and offer guidance on tax-related issues. This category includes accountants, paid preparers, lawyers, and other relevant professionals.

The conduct of tax practitioners is a matter of significant concern for both taxpayers and tax authorities. According to Shafer and Simmons [6], tax consultants have prioritized commercialism over the public interests. The difficulty primarily stems from their dual responsibility as both a client advocate and a gatekeeper ensuring the fairness of the tax system. Put simply, tax practitioner compliance involves dealing with the tension between advocating for clients and fulfilling professional obligations [7]. According to Mason and Garrett Levy (8), client advocacy is defined as a mental condition in which one's primary loyalty is towards the taxpayer. The individual demonstrates a strong commitment to advocating for the taxpayer within legal limits and a willingness to vigorously defend their interests.

For instance, a noncompliant practitioner may be inclined to engage in excessively aggressive or even fraudulent tax reporting if they believe that the chances of being caught and punished are relatively low. Nevertheless, a crucial inquiry remains unsettled. Should tax practitioners' assertiveness in advising tax treatment be considered noncompliant without any consideration? Does tax practitioner compliance occur when the practitioner adopts an excessively cautious tax stance that favors the government, potentially in the interest of the public?

This chapter aims to elucidate the function of tax practitioners in the self-assessment system (SAS) with respect to income tax return reporting positions, in order to unravel the enigmatic idea of tax practitioner compliance. Previous studies mostly focus on examining tax compliance within the context of individual taxpayers' decision to evade taxes, taking into account the danger of being detected. As a result, the terms tax compliance and taxpayer compliance are frequently used interchangeably. However, it is important to make a clear distinction between tax compliance and taxpayer compliance for the purpose of this essay. I understand tax compliance to pertain to the proactive process of adhering to tax obligations, rather than the reactive consequences that arise after declaring tax liabilities. This process involves the participation of all individuals working in the area to ensure compliance. Similarly, Boll [9] contends that tax compliance is a socio-material configuration, and the act of complying is a collective effort involving various actors within the tax system.

2. THE CONCEPTUALIZATION OF TAX COMPLIANCES

Taxpayer noncompliance encompasses any failing to fulfill tax duties, regardless of whether there is a desire to pay less tax than legally required. It can arise from intentional underreporting, unintentional misreporting, or failure to file a tax return. The tax gap is a widely used indicator of noncompliance at a collective level. It refers to the discrepancy between the amount of tax actually collected and the amount that could be collected if everyone fully complied with tax regulations [10]. The term "tax noncompliance" encompasses three types of actions: nonfiling, underreporting, and underpayment of taxes. Nonfiling refers to the failure to submit tax returns, underreporting refers to the inaccurate reporting of income or deductions, and underpayment refers to the failure to pay the full amount of taxes owed.

Tax evasion and tax avoidance include intentional acts of noncompliance. Tax evasion is the deliberate act of not paying the full amount of taxes by purposefully hiding taxable resources. On the other hand, tax avoidance is generally seen as a lawful method of decreasing the amount of taxes owed. Tax avoidance, although frequently in violation of the intent of the rules, is subject to potential scrutiny by tax officials and ultimately classified as noncompliance. Most scientific research on tax compliance focus on individuals' decision to evade taxes by either underreporting their taxable income or making unjustified deductions. Specifically, the most of them are focused on the issue of SAS, where taxpayers have the chance to inaccurately disclose their income and their initial tax obligations are based on self-declaration. The actual income remains hidden from tax authorities unless a tax audit is carried out. Tax noncompliance, in its most limited interpretation, pertains to the lack of honesty exhibited by taxpayers in their tax reporting.

It is important to acknowledge that, from the perspective of taxpayers, the problem of noncompliance is not limited to undercompliance alone. Noncompliance can occur not only due to underreporting or underpayment, but also as a result of overreporting or overpayment. Unintentional failure to comply may occur due to errors and oversights made by taxpayers or tax professionals. However, the issue of overcompliance has received minimal attention from researchers and policymakers. Perhaps it is expected that taxpayers possess enough rationality to handle tax affairs, and so, the detection of underreporting should be considered the result of their deliberate wrongdoing. Based on the assumption of rationality, any errors can be attributed not to ineptitude but to a lack of dedication in accurately reporting a tax return [13].

The tax rules are becoming more extensive, and the provisions of the law can be exceedingly complex and difficult to comprehend in their entirety. Meeting tax requirements requires a significant amount of time and effort. Even with careful attention to detail, unintentional errors can still occur. Additionally, the interpretation of confusing tax situations can lead to uncertainty regarding tax liabilities. To enhance comprehension, the subsequent section delves into the matters of tax law intricacy and vagueness.

3. TAX LAW COMPLEXITY AND AMBIGUITY

In practice, many taxpayers are faced with the complexity of tax laws and the uncertainty of enforcement. In most developed countries, tax law is complex, and it requires a very high reading age to be correctly understood [14]. Taxation cost (taxes and compliance cost) is perceived to be much more painful loss for small business taxpayers because they lack sufficient resources to manage their business [15].

If tax laws are vague and complicated, it may be difficult to fully comply with the law even with no intention to evade. Owing to the complex nature, ordinary taxpayers cannot cope well with tax requirements. Sakurai and Braithwaite [16] showed that the most important reason that their survey respondents gave for using tax service was that the desire to avoid the risk of potential tax penalties resulting from inaccurate tax returns. The professional tax knowledge that prevents the taxpayer from unintentional overpayment as well as underpayment can be purchased from the tax practitioners. Thus, an aspect of tax practitioner compliance can be better construed in connection with professional competence that ensures correct tax reporting.

McKerchar [17] maintains that tax complexity is a double edge sword for practitioners: on one side, it induces taxpayers into the arms of practitioners facilitating the market for tax service; but sometimes, it is too much a burden even for them to juggle. Although compliance duties can be addressed more correctly by the tax practitioner, the assistance of the tax practitioner cannot eliminate the risk of inadvertent noncompliance due to the complexity inherent in the law.

Carnes and Cuccia [18] argue that complexity is a source of unintentional noncompliance, and it may represent opportunities for intentional noncompliance as well. More often, tax practitioners can only reduce the uncertainty by assessing the likelihood a tax treatment will be sustained on its merits [19]. That said, inadvertent noncompliance is in part attributable to tax law ambiguity. A tax situation is ambiguous if its proper tax treatment is not *ex-ante* deterministic.

Aggressive tax treatment involves a reasonable probability that the reporting position will not be upheld in a tax audit [20]. Aggressive tax practitioners are more likely to interpret the ambiguous tax situation to the benefit of their clients.

Studies on tax practitioner behavior attempt to discover the conditions in which tax advisors would recommend more aggressive reporting position [21]. A number of studies have been conducted investigating factors that impact tax practitioners' willingness to accept aggressive reporting positions; among them are attitude toward risk [22], the threat of penalties [23], and client's risk preference [24]. In particular, Prospect theory [25] may also serve as a theoretical basis to explain tax practitioner's behavior. According to the Prospect theory, people exhibit risk seeking tendency in a loss situation, while being risk averse in a gain situation. Newberry et al. [26] found that CAPs were more likely to sign a tax return containing a large and ambiguous deduction to retain an existing client than to gain new one.

However, tax practitioner studies tend to avoid compliance or noncompliance, directly focusing instead on aggressiveness [27]. Phillips and Sansing [28] underline that conservative and aggressive are *ex-ante* labels that characterize a reporting position when the law is ambiguous. They go on emphasizing that taxpayer compliance is an *ex-post* and hypothetical concept, because in the real world, many of the reporting positions will not be evaluated by tax inspectors. Put differently, contrary to taxpayers' common beliefs, in many cases, tax compliance is not deterministic in spite of tax practitioners being involved, but it is stochastic depending on the enforcement activities of the tax administration.

4. THE WORK OF TAX PRACTITIONERS

There are a variety of motives in hiring tax practitioners. As it is, the role of tax practitioners in tax compliance process can be best understood considering the multifaceted aspects of tax service. Frecknall-Hughes and Moizer [29] argue that the work of tax practitioners in its broadest way can be divided into two kinds: tax compliance and tax planning/avoidance advice; the formal relates to resolve uncertainty in which tax position can be correctly settled, and the latter is associated with ambiguous tax situations in which legitimate tax position is not deterministic. Stephenson [30] discovered four separate constructs underlying the demands for tax practice: legal compliance, time savings, money savings, and protection from the tax authority.

Many taxpayers tend to claim accuracy as their main objective in tax preparation [31]. In that case, the quality of tax service is to ensure the tax returns do not contain inadvertent errors or omissions. It is somewhat evident that taxpayers hire tax practitioners to save time and effort required to achieve compliance. They will delegate tax return preparation to the practitioner, if the opportunity cost of self-reporting exceeds the service fee. Tax practitioners are also expected by their clients to reduce the chances of audit and penalty, thereby lowering monetary and psychic costs associated with audits that would otherwise have occurred [32]. Tax practitioners may provide professional assurance of compliance by verifying and assessing acceptable tax positions in the SAS [33].

Every tax legislation, however, contains "gray" areas that produce ambiguous tax situations. Tax practitioners cannot get rid of entire uncertainty, but they can only gauge the likelihood the position not being upheld by the tax court. The tax position is subject to some uncertainty and hence may step into a process of negotiation with the tax authorities [29]. Indeed, Frecknall-Hughes and Kirchler [34] came up with negotiation theory as a conceptual framework for understanding the nature of tax practice. They argue that the tax advisor/preparer and the tax inspector (who are the employee of revenue authority) are negotiators who act respectively on behalf of a client and the tax authority. While laypersons may see the task of trials and tax audits as revealing the truth about the matter, many practitioners approach their job as being able to negotiate the best settlement for their clients [35].

Some tax practitioners promote unacceptable tax minimization arrangements, assisting their clients in devising strategies to exploit legal ambiguities [36]. They are inclined to view testing the outer limits of the tax law as a natural and acceptable feature [37]. In recent decades, their role has become more complicated and sophisticated with the special tax knowledge required to facilitate tax avoidance [38]. For example, Sikka and Hampton [39] criticize that accountancy firms have sold tax avoidance schemes to corporations and wealthy individuals, which they refer to as tax solutions or tax strategies.

Nevertheless, it is important to distinguish legally permissible tax planning from potentially unacceptable tax scheme. Adapting motivational postures theory [40], Kang [41] coined two terms indicating differentiated features of tax avoidance: deferential avoidance and defiant avoidance, while deferential avoiders stand firm within the boundaries of the law, defiant avoiders try to push the boundaries of the law's intent by self-serving in terms of law interpretation.

The role of tax practitioners has been viewed as representative of both taxpayers and the government [42]. One might argue that they have to act as advocates for their clients and to serve as intermediaries in the tax system. Tax practitioners should be concerned not only with their client's interest but also with general publics in conducting their practices. Indeed, OECD [43] published a report highlighting the importance of trilateral relationships among tax authorities, taxpayers, and tax intermediaries in promoting taxpayer compliance. In a nutshell, tax practitioners have a legitimate and efficient function as intermediaries or "knowledge brokers" between taxpayers and revenue authorities [44]. They can provide a useful line of communication between tax inspectors and taxpayers. Furthermore, tax professionals can provide a check-and-balance function that prevents tax authorities' possible extortion or tax inspectors' harassment on the part of taxpayers, thereby safeguarding the equity of a tax system [7].

There are a variety of expectations for tax practitioner work, and sometimes an "expectation gap" arises from the misperception of each other's expectation. Expectations gap refers to the difference between client expectations and the professional's perceptions of those expectations and vice versa [20]. Christensen [45] argues that tax preparers' perceptions of what clients expect from tax service differ significantly from clients' expectations. Tax preparers may rationalize it is their clients who demand aggressive tax reporting. Schisler [24] maintains that many taxpayers insist on aggressive tax advice. In contrast, according to Tan [46], taxpayers favor conservative tax advice if the taxpayers' main objective is filing an accurate tax return. This issue is worthwhile to be explored in more depth in the following section.

5. INTERACTIONS OF THE TAXPAYER AND THE TAX PRACTITIONER

Research on the interaction between taxpayers and tax practitioners exists much less than is required, providing the immense amount of time and money spent on tax compliance [20]. Kaplan et al. [5] emphasize the role of tax practitioners in tax compliance by demonstrating that if a tax practitioner provides aggressive tax advice, the taxpayer is likely to take the aggressive tax position that might not be upheld in a tax audit. On the contrary, Hite and McGill [47] argue that taxpayers tended to disagree with aggressive advice and to agree instead with conservative advice. Or, there is also evidence that conservative taxpayers defer to the opinion of aggressive tax practitioners [48]. Not surprisingly, there are taxpayers who will still accept whatever types of advice their practitioners recommend.

For the tax practitioner, clients' risk preferences could influence the willingness of practitioners to recommend aggressive positions [49]. Cloyd [50], Cuccia et al. [51], and Schisler [24] indicate tax practitioners' tendency to recommend more aggressive positions when taxpayers are more aggressive (risk seeking). Notably, Duncan et al. [52] found the opposite evidence showing the more risk-averse the taxpayer, the more aggressive the tax practitioner, and the more aggressive the taxpayer, the more conservative tax position recommended by the practitioner. Furthermore, Bobek et al. [53] examined how the role of client advocacy influenced tax professionals' decision processes and outcomes and provided empirical results revealing that client characteristics influence tax professionals' advocacy attitudes. These findings suggest that taxpayers and tax practitioners' decisions are interdependent, and studies on their interaction dynamics could be a promising approach to find new insights into tax compliance.

Wurth and Braithwaite [54] underline that practitioners are responsive to influences from many sources—clients, tax authorities, professional associations, governments, international bodies, and the organizations and cultures. For example, Doyle et al. [55] investigated the moral reasoning of tax practitioners in social contexts and in tax contexts, and they found tax practitioners' significantly lower level moral reasoning than nonpractitioners in tax contexts. The study implies that client advocacy may deter tax practitioners' moral reasoning. Reckers et al. [23] pointed out that less important taxpayers are more likely to receive more conservative advice from the tax practitioners. On the contrary, Bandy et al. [56] asserted that economic importance of the taxpayer had little effect on tax practitioners' willingness to be aggressive in terms of providing advice or signing aggressive tax return. Spilker et al. [57] provide evidence that tax practitioners interpret ambiguity in the tax law differently in planning than in compliance stage because they are more vulnerable to problematic tax advice that might result in litigations and reputational loss.

In connection with taxpayer compliance, Practitioner-Client role model developed by Tan [58] recognizes two parties' expectations, and behavioral dynamics can emphasize that how taxpayers and tax practitioners interact with each others are likely to affect each other's tax decisions. Similarly, The Wheel of Social Alignments put forth by Braithwaite and Wenzel [59] synthesizes the drivers of tax compliance regarding tax practitioners as alternative authorities to tax officials.

Some taxpayers exhibit their preference of conservative advice over aggressive one. However, Sakurai and Braithwaite [60] show that some taxpayers prefer "no risk no fuss" type. As with their diverse motivational postures [40], it is natural of taxpayers to exhibit diversity in their preference over tax advice as well as tax position. It is therefore in communicating with their clients, tax practitioners should educate, persuade, and encourage taxpayers to acknowledge the responsibility for their decisions in order to reduce expectation gap [61]. In many cases, ineffective communication is attributable to the failure to achieve compliance procedures accompanied by unintended consequences. The absence of clear communication and the failure to make reasonable enquiries when information or documentation provided by a client appears to be inaccurate or incomplete [62] tend to engender the disappointment in their tax service experienced.

Tax practitioner self-seeking behavior together with compliance cost can afford unique opportunities to explore taxpayer decision. Tax law complexity increases the cost of compliance, and compliance costs are widely regarded as high. For the part of taxpayers, it may seem unfair to hire a tax professional in order to understand the laws. Taxpayers may expect their compliance cost to be offset by the tax service. If they deem the service fee as a mere expense accompanied by no additional benefit, they will be likely to be more aggressive in order to restore equitable condition. For instance, Jackson et al. [63] well demonstrated how taxpayers and tax practitioners decisions are interrelated. Drawing on mental accounting theory, they postulate mental aggregation of preparation cost with taxes, and tax professionals may place their clients in positive prepayment positions. The concept of mental accounting derived from research on prospect theory describes the set of cognitive operations used by individuals to organize, evaluate, and keep track of financial activities [64]. Then, they provide evidence that tax return preparation fees are larger for taxpayers who receive tax refunds than for taxpayers who owe additional taxes. It is argued that compliance costs paid to the tax preparer and the expected tax refund occur in the same mental account. Thus, taxpayers who have a favorable mental representation of tax return preparation fees may be willing to pay for higher costs incurred by tax practitioners.

6. CONCISE SUMMARY

In this chapter, I aim to differentiate between tax practitioner compliance and taxpayer compliance in order to enhance our comprehension of the tax compliance process. Furthermore, I argue that the conduct of tax practitioners can be evaluated in relation to tax compliance, which offers a fresh outlook on the existing body of tax compliance literature. Given the importance of tax practice in relation to tax compliance, it is valuable to examine the definition of tax compliance in relation to the behavior of tax practitioners.

Similar to taxpayer compliance, tax practitioner compliance can occur either unintentionally or deliberately. The loss of professional competence and objectivity is the outcome of tax practitioner noncompliance. However, it is somewhat unavoidable for them to make errors due to the inherent uncertainty and complexity of the tax legislation. To maintain compliance, tax practitioners must continuously enhance their professional abilities and be well-informed about current tax concerns that might have either favorable or bad effects on their clients. Additionally, the tax practitioner should demonstrate adaptability to both customer preferences and legal regulations. Nevertheless, the ethical assessment made by professionals should remain unaffected by any influence exerted by clients.

Professions have certain responsibilities towards their clients, coworkers, and society as a result of their esteemed status [65]. The concept of tax compliance encompasses adherence to both the literal requirements of the law and a respectful approach towards the intentions of the law and fiscal policy. In the case of tax practitioners, compliance can also be understood in terms of their decisions and underlying attitudes towards clients, colleagues, and the tax system. As a service provider, the tax practitioner should aim to minimize discrepancies between client expectations and actual experiences. As a professional in the field of taxation, the tax practitioner avoids engaging in fraudulent tax methods that may encourage institutional corruption. It is the responsibility of the tax practitioner to protect the integrity of the tax system in their professional capacity. Essentially, tax practitioners should position themselves as vigilant intermediaries between tax authorities and their clients, ensuring the integrity of the tax system.

Noncompliance among tax practitioners can manifest in two extremes. On one end, it involves disregarding clients' lawful entitlement to minimize their tax obligations. On the other end, it arises from tax practitioners willingly accepting or colluding in tax evasion. Therefore, tax authorities must recognize that tax practitioners have a crucial role in implementing effective measures to enhance taxpayer compliance. Primarily, it is the responsibility of the practitioners to dissuade taxpayers from adopting excessively aggressive or illegal tax positions. Moreover, company taxpayers and their tax practitioners have a strong interdependence, as tax practitioners often serve as trusted advisors to businesses [67].

Numerous domains of research have received insufficient attention. Within this context, a conflict of interest arises between taxpayers and tax practitioners. While the taxpayer hires the tax practitioner, the practitioner may prioritize their own interests instead of working for the advantage of their clients. This difficulty primarily occurs due to the asymmetry of information between the taxpayer and the tax practitioner. Certain individuals may use confidential information for their personal gain. It is worth exploring the conflict of interest between taxpayers and tax practitioners in order to build a comprehensive body of literature on tax compliance.

AT A GLANCE

This chapter seeks to examine previous research on tax practitioners and offer insights into the conduct of tax practitioners that impact taxpayer compliance. In conclusion, I strive to differentiate between tax practitioner compliance and taxpayer compliance in order to enhance our comprehension of the tax compliance process. In my view, the evaluation of tax practitioner compliance can be analyzed in relation to tax compliance, which can provide a fresh outlook on the existing tax compliance literature. The tax practitioners strive to enhance their professional skills to guarantee compliance. Additionally, the tax practitioner should demonstrate adaptability to both client preferences and legal constraints imposed by tax legislation. Nevertheless, the ethical assessments made by professionals should remain unaffected by any pressure exerted by clients. Tax practitioner compliance, as a component of tax compliance dynamics, encompasses their decisions and underlying attitudes towards clients, coworkers, and the tax system. As a service provider, the tax practitioner should aim to minimize discrepancies between client expectations and actual experiences. As a professional in the field of taxation, the tax practitioner avoids engaging in fraudulent tax schemes that may encourage unethical practices within institutions. It is the responsibility of the tax practitioner to ensure the integrity of the tax system.

REFERENCES

1. Torgler B. Can tax compliance research profit from biology? Review of Behavioral Economics. 2016;3(1):113-144
2. Pickhardt M, Prinz A. Behavioral dynamics of tax evasion – A survey. Journal of Economic Psychology (Special Issue on Behavioral Dynamics of Tax Evasion). 2014;40:1-19
3. Alm J, Kirchler E, Muehlbacher S. Combining psychology and economics in the analysis of compliance: From enforcement to cooperation. Economic analysis and Policy. 2012;42(2):133-151
4. Long SB, Swingen JA. Taxpayer compliance: Setting new agendas for research. Law & Society Review. 1991;25(3):637-683
5. Kaplan SE, Reckers PM, West SG, Boyd JC. An examination of tax reporting recommendations of professional tax preparers. Journal of Economic Psychology. 1988;9(4):427-443
6. Shafer WE, Simmons RS. Social responsibility, Machiavellianism and tax avoidance: A study of Hong Kong tax professionals. Accounting, Auditing & Accountability Journal. 2008;21(5):695-720
7. Brock G, Russell H. Abusive Tax Avoidance and Institutional Corruption: The Responsibilities of Tax Professionals. Edmond J. Safra Working Paper No. 56. 2015
8. Mason JD, Garrett Levy L. The use of the latent constructs method in behavioral accounting research: The measurement of client advocacy. In: Advances in Taxation. Yorkshire: Emerald Group Publishing Limited; 2001. pp. 123-139
9. Boll K. Mapping tax compliance: Assemblages, distributed action and practices: A new way of doing tax research. Critical Perspectives on Accounting. 2014;25(4):293-303
10. Gemmell N, Hasseldine J. Taxpayers' behavioural responses and measures of tax compliance 'gaps': A critique and a new measure. Fiscal Studies. 2014;35(3):275-296

11. IRS. Tax Gap for Tax Year 2006: Overview. 2012. Available form: https://www.irs.gov/pub/newsroom/overview_tax_gap_2006.pdf
12. Elffers H, Weigel RH, Hessing DJ. The consequences of different strategies for measuring tax evasion behavior. Journal of Economic Psychology. 1987;8(3):311-337
13. Niemirowski P, Wearing AJ. Taxation agents and taxpayer compliance. Journal of Australian Taxation. 2003;6:166
14. Lewis A. The Psychology of Taxation. Oxford: Martin Robertson; 1982
15. Kamleitner B, Korunka C, Kirchler E. Tax compliance of small business owners: A review. International Journal of Entrepreneurial Behavior & Research. 2012;18(3):330-351
16. Sakurai Y, Braithwaite V. Taxpayers' Perceptions of the Ideal Tax Adviser: Playing Safe or Saving Dollars?. Working Paper No 5. 2001
17. McKerchar M. Impact of income tax complexity on practitioners in Australia. Australian Tax Forum. 2005;20(4):529-554
18. Carnes GA, Cuccia AD. An analysis of the effect of tax complexity and its perceived justification on equity judgments. Journal of the American Taxation Association. 1996;18(2):40-56
19. Cloyd CB, Spilker BC. The influence of client preferences on tax professionals' search for judicial precedents, subsequent judgments and recommendations. The Accounting Review. 1999;74(3):299-322
20. Stephenson T. The gap between what taxpayers want and what tax professionals think they want: A reexamination of client expectations and tax professional aggressiveness [doctoral dissertations]. University of Kentucky. 2006
21. Outslay E. The State of Behavioral Tax Research: An editor's Perspective. Behavioral Tax Research: Prospects and Judgment Calls. Sarasota. Florida: American Accounting Association; 1995
22. Carnes GA, Harwood G, Sawyers R. The determinants of tax professionals' aggressiveness in ambiguous situations. Advances in Taxation. 1996;8:1-26
23. Reckers PM, Sanders DL, Wyndelts RW. An empirical investigation of factors influencing tax practitioner compliance. The Journal of the American Taxation Association. 1991;13(2):30-46
24. Schisler DL. An experimental examination of factors affecting tax preparers' aggressiveness – A prospect theory approach. The. Journal of the American Taxation Association. 1994;16(2):124

25. Kahneman D, Tversky A. Prospect theory: An analysis of decision under risk. Econometrica: Journal of the Econometric Society. 1979;47(2):263-291

26. Newberry KJ, Reckers PM, Wyndelts RW. An examination of tax practitioner decisions: The role of preparer sanctions and framing effects associated with client condition. Journal of Economic Psychology. 1993;14(2):439-452

27. Cloyd CB. Prior knowledge, information search behaviors, and performance in tax research tasks. The Journal of the American Taxation Association. 1995;17:82

28. J, Sansing RC. Contingent fees and tax compliance. Accounting Review. 1998;73(1):1-18

29. Frecknall-Hughes J, Moizer P. Assessing the quality of services provided by UK tax practitioners. eJournal of Tax Research. 2015;13(1):51-75

30. Stephenson T. Measuring taxpayers' motivation to hire tax preparers: The development of a four-construct scale. Advances in Taxation. 2010;19:95-121

31. Collins JH, Milliron VC, Toy DR. Factors associated with household demand for tax preparers. The Journal of the American Taxation Association. 1990;12(2):9-25

32. Andreoni J, Erard B, Feinstein J. Tax compliance. Journal of Economic Literature. 1998;36(2):818-860

33. Wurth E. A will and a way: An analysis of tax practitioner preparation compliance [PhD thesis]. Austrian National University; 2013

34. Frecknall-Hughes J, Kirchler E. Towards a general theory of tax practice. Social & Legal Studies. 2015;24(2):289-312

35. Stalans L, Lind EA. The meaning of procedural fairness: A comparison of taxpayers' and representatives' views of their tax audits. Social Justice Research. 1997;10(3):311-331

36. Erard B. Taxation with representation: An analysis of the role of tax practitioners in tax compliance. Journal of Public Economics. 1993;52(2):163-197

37. Salter MS. Lawful But Corrupt: Gaming and the Problem of Institutional Corruption in the Private Sector. Harvard Business School Research Paper (11-060). 2010

38. Lipatov V. Corporate tax evasion: The case for specialists. Journal of Economic Behavior & Organization. 2012;81(1):185-206

39. Sikka P, Hampton MP. The role of accountancy firms in tax avoidance: Some evidence and issues. Accounting Forum. 2005;29(3):325-343
40. Braithwaite V. Dancing with tax authorities: Motivational postures and non-compliant actions. In: Braithwaite V, editor. Taxing Democracy. Understanding Tax Avoidance and Evasion. Aldershot: Ashgate Publishing Limited; 2003. pp. 15-39
41. Kang M. A psychological perspective on tax avoidance: Deferential avoidance vs. defiant avoidance. eJournal of Tax Research. 2016;14:235-246
42. Brody R, Masselli J. Tax preparers: Whose team are they on. The National Public Accountant. 1996;41(3):18-20
43. OECD. Study into the Role of Tax Intermediaries. Paris: OECD; 2008
44. Hasseldine J, Holland K, van der Rijt P. The market for corporate tax knowledge. Critical Perspectives on Accounting. 2011;22(1):39-52
45. Christensen AL. Evaluation of tax services: A client and preparer perspective. The Journal of the American Taxation Association. 1992;14(2):60
46. Tan LM. Taxpayers' preference for type of advice from tax practitioner: A preliminary examination. Journal of Economic Psychology. 1999;20(4):431-447
47. Hite PA, McGill GA. An examination of taxpayer preference for aggressive tax advice. National Tax Journal. 1992;45(4):389-403
48. Murphy K. 'Trust me, I'm the Taxman': The Role of Trust in Nurturing Compliance. Centre for Tax System Integrity Working Paper No. 43. Canberra: The Australian National University; (ACT, Australia) 2002
49. D, Reckers PJ. An empirical examination of the influence of selected factors on professional tax preparers' decision process. Advances in Accounting. 1989;7(1):37-50
50. Cloyd CB. The effects of financial accounting conformity on recommendations of tax preparers. The Journal of the American Taxation Association. 1995;17(2):50
51. Cuccia AD, Hackenbrack K, Nelson MW. The ability of professional standards to mitigate aggressive reporting. Accounting Review. 1995;70(2):227-248
52. WA, LaRue D, Reckers PM. An empirical examination of the influence of selected economic and noneconomic variables in decision making by tax professionals. Advances in Taxation. 1989;2(1):91-106
53. Bobek DD, Hageman AM, Hatfield RC. The role of client advocacy in the development of tax professionals' advice. Journal of the American Taxation Association. 2010;32(1):25-51

54. Wurth E, Braithwaite V. Tax practitioners and tax avoidance: Gaming through authorities, cultures and markets. RegNet Research Paper No. 119. School of Regulation and Global Governance (RegNet). 2016
55. Doyle E, Hughes JF, Summers B. An empirical analysis of the ethical reasoning of tax practitioners. Journal of Business Ethics. 2013;114(2):325-339
56. Bandy D, Betancourt L, Kelliher C. An empirical study of the objectivity of CPAs' tax work. Advances in Taxation. 1994;6:1-23
57. Spilker BC, Worsham Jr RG, Prawitt DF. Tax professionals' interpretations of ambiguity in compliance and planning decision contexts. Journal of the American Taxation Association. 1999;21(2):75-89
58. Tan LM. Understanding the tax practitioner-client relationship: Using a role theory framework. Procedia-Social and Behavioral Sciences. 2014;164:242-247
59. Braithwaite V, Wenzel M. Integrating explanations of tax evasion and avoidance. In: Lewis A, editor. The Cambridge Handbook of Psychology and Economic Behaviour. Cambridge: Cambridge University Press; 2008
60. Sakurai Y, Braithwaite V. Taxpayers' perceptions of practitioners: Finding one who is effective and does the right thing? Journal of Business Ethics. 2003;46(4):375-387
61. Tan LM, Braithwaite V, Reinhart M. Why do small business taxpayers stay with their practitioners? Trust, competence and aggressive advice. International Small Business Journal. 2014;34(3):329-344
62. Marshall RL, Armstrong RW, Smith M. The ethical environment of tax practitioners: Western Australian evidence. Journal of Business Ethics. 1998;17(12):1265-1279
63. Jackson SB, Shoemaker PA, Barrick J, Burton F. Taxpayers 'prepayment positions and tax return preparation fees. Contemporary Accounting Research. 2005;2:409-447
64. Thaler R. Mental accounting matters. Journal of Behavioral Decision Making. 1999;12(3):183-206
65. Loeb SE. A survey of ethical behavior in the accounting profession. Journal of Accounting Research. 1971;9(2):287-306
66. James SR. A Dictionary of Taxation. 2nd ed. Cheltenham: Edward Elgar Publishing; 2012
67. Blackburn R, Carey P, Tanewski GA. Business Advice to SMEs: Professional Competence, Trust and Ethics. ACCA research report no. 119. London: Certified accountants educational trust; 2010

13 Chapter

AN ANALYSIS OF THE TAX BURDEN OF LOCAL GOVERNMENTS IN BRAZIL, FOCUSING ON ITS EVOLUTION AND CHARACTERISTICS

1. INTRODUCTION: AN OVERVIEW

In the 1980s and 1990s, numerous countries underwent state reforms characterized by the privatization of the state's production sector and the decentralization of social policy. The World Bank implemented decentralization as a method to enhance the efficiency of public service provision and increase social accountability to the populace [1]. Therefore, these policies were implemented in countries with unitary and federalist political systems. However, it was only in the Brazilian federation that the local government was recognized as a federative institution.

The establishment of federalism at three levels of government (Union, 26 states and the federal district, and 5570 municipalities) grants individuals a wide range of political, administrative, legislative, and financial independence. The symmetrical federalism in question fails to acknowledge the economic differences and unequal distribution of the population within the national area. Only 17.1% of the Brazilian population resides in 70% of the municipalities, indicating a high concentration of people in large cities. Specifically, 29.3% of the population lives in 38 municipalities with over 500,000 residents. However, about 50% of the local tax collection is likewise centralized in these specific towns [2].

This discrepancy would result in varying levels of financial autonomy among municipalities: larger municipalities have a greater ability to generate their own revenue, while a significant majority of small municipalities rely on income from intergovernmental transfers. The acknowledgement of territorial imbalances in this context presents significant obstacles for the federative collaboration in Brazil. It involves beyond the limitations set forth in this chapter.

Typically, in the majority of federalist nations, local governments possess the most modest budget compared to other tiers of government. Due to the fragmented nature of this level of government and its focus on specific segments of the population through simpler public policies, local governments naturally have fewer resources compared to state/regional governments and the central government.

In Brazil, the situation is similar, but it is vital to emphasize the consistent and growing involvement of municipalities in the overall income of the public sector. In 2014, municipalities collected around 7% of the total tax burden in the country. After intergovernmental transfers, they retained little under 20% of this sum. In 1987, one year prior to the implementation of the Federal Constitution, the respective percentages for these shares were 2.5% and 12.6% [4]. The growth trend is sufficiently stable that municipalities now possess a budget that is nearly as significant as that of state governments. This observation has prompted certain authors, such as Afonso and Araujo [5], Castro and Afonso [6], and Fernandes and Wilson [7], to categorize fiscal federalism in Brazil as "fiscal municipalism" or "municipal federalism."

If a significant portion of this expansion can be attributed to the rise in intergovernmental transfers, the enhanced ability of local governments to impose taxes was equally significant. Serra and Afonso [8] argue that the subnational governments' capacity to impose their own taxes increased and solidified after the implementation of the Constitution of 1988. This occurred at the same time that the overall tax burden of the country expanded [9]. Specifically, the involvement of local government in this responsibility increased precisely at a period when the Brazilian welfare state developed with the advancement of social rights in the current constitution.

As the influx of money has risen, the distribution of public policies has also been expanding rapidly. In the 1990s, the Union started adopting unconventional methods for intergovernmental relations due to reduced participation in revenue caused by decentralization, as well as the need for fiscal adjustment and macroeconomic stabilization. It became customary for tax collection efforts to focus on revenue sources that were not shared, such as social contributions [11], and for responsibilities to be transferred to other levels of government [12]. This was supported by the 1988 Constitution, which established obligations that apply to multiple levels of government.

Although municipalities have gained autonomy within the Brazilian federation, there are still evident challenges with the execution of public policy and the management of tax collection and administration at the local level. When it comes to spending, it is worth noting the challenges that arise from inter-municipal collaboration in providing public services through consortia. These challenges are further exacerbated by the horizontal inequalities within the federation, leading to inefficiencies in public expenditure. In terms of revenue, tax management continues to suffer from inefficiency, particularly in areas with smaller populations and less economic influence that heavily depend on federal and state subsidies. Municipal tax authorities in these localities face significant administrative expenses.

This study specifically focuses on addressing the aforementioned question. Given that the financial capacity of the public sector mostly depends on its tax collection, it is imperative to examine municipal taxation. Ingram and Hong [15] assert that examining municipal finances is crucial due to the role of cities and their environs as catalysts for economic growth. They argue that the efficient provision of public services can generate the right incentives for businesses and people. The insufficient provision of infrastructure and urban services, such as public transportation, by local governments often results in decreased productivity, which in turn undermines the local economy [16].

The significance of this analysis extends beyond that. Only a limited number of studies have opted to conduct an evaluation specifically centered on this topic in Brazil. In general, the majority of the research conducted in Brazil about taxation focuses on the federal level or the overall public sector. At the local level, it is typical to come across articles that focus on taxation and provide detailed information about a particular tax or present case studies.

Hence, the objective of this study is to examine the tax burden imposed on local governments in Brazil, with a specific focus on its historical progression, involvement in the federation, magnitude, tax foundation, and allocation of revenue among locals based on their size and region. It is crucial to emphasize that the tax burden in this context will be evaluated comprehensively, encompassing not only direct income taxes but also the tax revenue generated by other levels of government and allocated to municipalities, which is known as available revenue. In order to accomplish this goal, a comprehensive examination of data, exclusively sourced from official channels, will be conducted. This analysis will be supplemented by relevant bibliographic sources pertaining to the subject matter.

Furthermore, apart from this introductory piece, five further sections are provided: Section 2 outlines the development of local taxes, connecting it to the overall tax burden. Section 3 analyzes the economic impact of local taxation, specifically in comparison to the broader public sector's tax base. Section 4 provides data categorized by population and region, aiming to comprehend how taxation varies based on the size and location of municipalities. Section 5 provides a concise international comparison of the scale of local governments in fiscal federalism. Lastly, Section 6 offers concluding remarks on the subject.

2. HISTORICAL DEVELOPMENT OF LOCAL TAXATION

The tax burden refers to the direct correlation between the amount of resources obtained via taxation and the gross domestic product (GDP) of a specific area during a specific timeframe. Typically, the tax burden is determined on a national scale by taking into account the overall amount of tax revenue collected in a country during a specific year. This study will focus exclusively on taxes imposed by local governments, rather than adopting a more general and comprehensive approach to the tax burden. Put simply, the research will concentrate solely on taxes that pertain to municipalities and the intergovernmental transfers they receive. This analysis will not include any comparisons of this nature with other levels of government.

The primary resource for referencing municipal revenue is the publication Brazil's Finance (Finbra) provided by the Brazilian National Treasury (STN). The GDP is calculated using the System of National Accounts (SCN) in collaboration with the Brazilian Institute of Geography and Statistics (IBGE). Other government areas were consulted using additional official sources, including the Union Balance Sheet (BGU) and Budget Execution of the States (EOE) from the STN; the System S Transfer Report from the Brazilian Internal Revenue Service (RFB); and the Workers' Severance Guarantee Fund (FGTS) Report, provided by the Federal Social Bank (CEF). In addition, data was collected from the STN, National Petroleum Regulatory Agency (ANP), and National Electrical Energy Regulatory Agency (Aneel) to create the database on intergovernmental transfers.[1]

In 2016, municipalities in Brazil directly collected taxes that amounted to around 2.37% of the country's GDP. This accounts for around 7.2% of the total tax burden for that year. Since the Constitution of 1988, the municipal tax burden has been consistently increasing. In 2016, it reached its highest level ever recorded in the country's history, surpassing the GDP of 1987 by 1.77 percentage points. 1987 was the first year of the National Constitutional Assembly, which led to the creation of Brazil's current constitution. Table 1 displays the changes in the tax burden of each sector of the Brazilian Government, in terms of direct collection and income, starting from 1960.

Table 1. Evolution of the Tax Burden's Federal Share by level of government, 1960/2016.

Year	Tax Burden (% of GDP)				Composition (% of Total)			
	Union	States	Municipalities	Total	Union	States	Municipalities	Total
DIRECT COLLECTION								
1960	11,14	5,45	0,82	17,41	64,0	31,3	4,7	100,0
1970	17,33	7,95	0,70	25,98	66,7	30,6	2,7	100,0

Year	Tax Burden (% of GDP)				Composition (% of Total)			
1980	18,31	5,31	0,90	24,52	74,7	21,6	3,7	100,0
1990	19,29	8,52	0,97	28,78	67,0	29,6	3,4	100,0
2000	20,38	8,45	1,73	30,56	66,7	27,6	5,7	100,0
2010	22,36	8,81	2,07	33,23	67,3	26,5	6,2	100,0
2015	21,65	8,80	2,36	32,80	66,0	26,8	7,2	100,0
2016	21,37	8,95	2,37	32,69	65,4	27,4	7,2	100,0
AVAILABLE REVENUE								
1960	10,37	5,94	1,11	17,41	59,5	34,1	6,4	100,0
1970	15,79	7,59	2,60	25,98	60,8	29,2	10,0	100,0
1980	16,71	5,70	2,10	24,52	68,2	23,3	8,6	100,0
1990	16,95	7,94	3,89	28,78	58,9	27,6	13,5	100,0
2000	17,07	8,16	5,33	30,56	55,9	26,7	17,5	100,0
2010	18,76	8,34	6,13	33,23	56,5	25,1	18,4	100,0
2015	18,10	8,22	6,48	32,80	55,2	25,1	19,8	100,0
2016	17,61	8,41	6,67	32,69	53,9	25,7	20,4	100,0

Elaborated by the authors. Primary sources: Varsano et al (1998), Afonso and Castro (2016), STN, RFB, CEF, ANP, Aneel and IBGE.

Broad methodology: includes taxes, fees and contributions, including FGTS, royalties, revenue from fines and active debt. Available revenue = tax collection plus/minus constitutional sharing of tax revenue and other compulsory transfers.

At the same time as their own collected revenue increased, the municipalities experienced a substantial rise in intergovernmental transfers: an increase in transfers from the Municipal Participation Fund (FPM), the creation of the Fund for Maintenance and Development of Basic Education and Valorisation of Education Professionals (Fundeb), as well as the expansion of municipal participation from 20 to 25% of the state Tax on the Circulation of Goods and Services (ICMS) collected, were the main events to have contributed to such scenario.

The increase in transfers from the Union and the states made the municipalities' available revenue (direct collection plus transfers) increase from 2.98% of GDP in 1987 to 6.67% of GDP in 2016—a growth not as intense (in relative terms) as in the case of direct collection, but still very expressive and unparalleled in the Brazilian federation. To have a basis for comparison, in the same period, state governments increased their available revenue by 2.86 pp. of GDP, below the 3.68 pp. of local governments. Municipal participation in federal and state revenue is fundamental for understanding the strong growth of local governments' role in the Brazilian federation—not only through increased revenue, but also due to the fact that local governments have become responsible for implementing much of the country's social policies. The significant participation of the municipalities in the public sector's available revenue (around 20%) was achieved due to two decentralising movements provided by the Constitution of 1988: granting tax autonomy (their own revenue) and intensification of intergovernmental transfers. This aspect is important in the Brazilian Federal debate because, as indicated by Afonso and Araujo [5], the idea that the municipalities' revenue has grown since the 1980s exclusively due to federal and state transfers is not unusual.

The municipalities' own resources were and have been such important factors to the "fiscal municipalism" in Brazil that in recent years, it is possible to identify an interesting aspect about the direct collection of local governments: the continuing tendency of an expanding tax burden even with the economic crisis that took hold of the country from 2014 [17]. The country's total tax burden has been showing a pattern of contraction since 2011, leading Ribeiro [18] to point out the existence of a structural break in Brazilian tax elasticity with respect to economic performance from the subprime crisis of 2008. Apparently, this break applies to the public sector as a whole, but not specifically for local governments.

Breaking down the municipal tax burden, one can see that it is determined primarily by two taxes: the Tax on Services of any Nature (ISS) and the Property Tax (IPTU). While the first is an indirect tax, levied on the service sector's production, the second is a direct tax on urban real estate. Between 1980 and 2016, these two taxes accounted for, on average, more than 60% of the municipal tax burden. In 2016, this participation was 57.7%. Figure 1 shows the trajectory of the municipal tax burden and its main components since 1980.

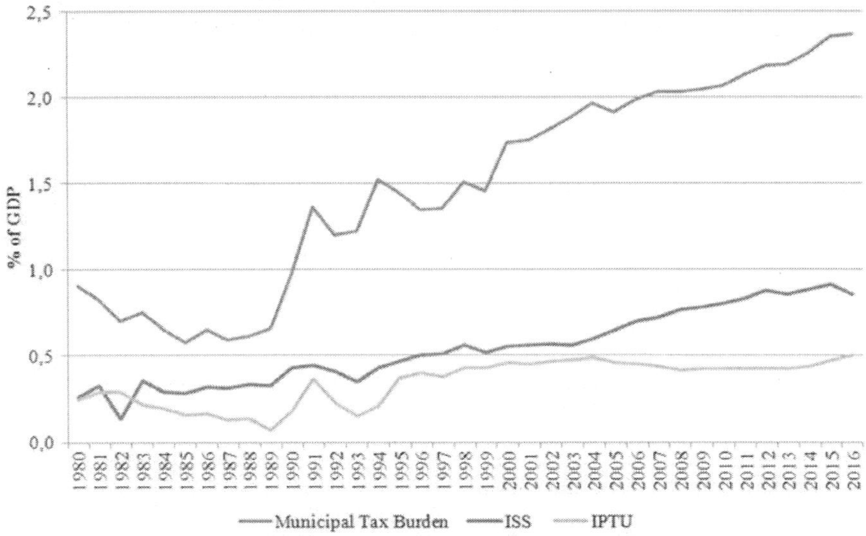

Elaborated by the authors. Primary sources: Varsano et al (1998), Afonso and Castro (2016), STN, RFB, CEF and IBGE.

Figure 1. Evolution of the municipal tax burden and its main components, 1980/2016.

Although both taxes present an expansionary trend from a historical perspective, this is most evident in the case of the ISS, especially from 2003 onwards. Some explanations may be suggested in this case: First, the modern economy is leaning increasingly towards the service sector, especially those services of higher added value, related to innovation and technology [19], and, in Brazil's case, especially in metropolitan areas [20]; second, the enactment of Amendment No. 116 in 2003, which increased the activities subject to the ISS; third, the advent of the electronic invoice in local governments, which modernised tax management and supervision [21] and consequently, the revenue collected [22, 23] and fourth, the relatively low IPTU collection in light of its potential [24, 25, 26, 27].

3. TAX BURDEN BY TAX BASE

Assessing the tax burden by tax base intends to identify which economic categories underpin the tax wedge, thus being able to make some inferences about the characteristics of the tax system studied such as fairness and distributive efficiency.

According to Afonso and Castro [3], the Brazilian tax burden (total) is markedly characterised by a high incidence of taxes on the sale of goods and services. In fact, the data from the 2016 tax burden point in this direction, as evidenced in Figure 2. However, the picture is significantly different when the municipal taxation is examined separately.

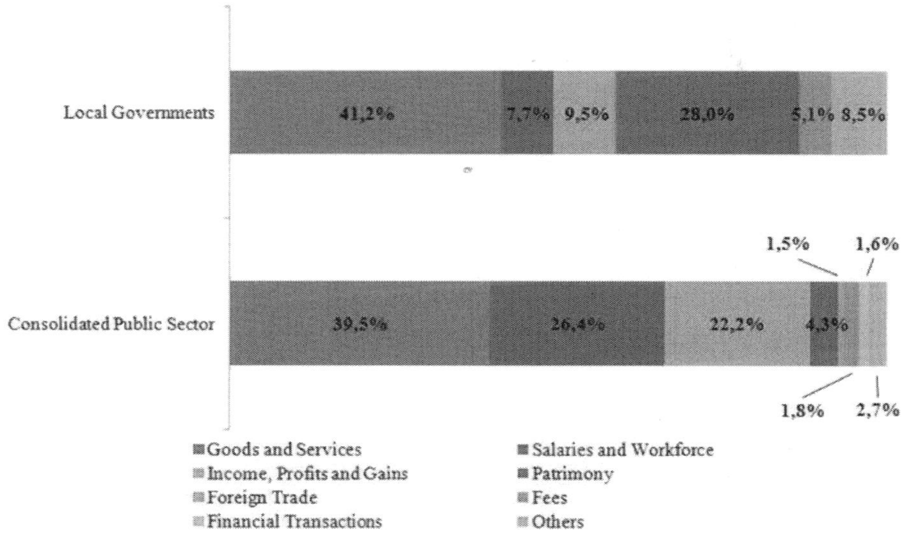

Elaborated by the authors. Primary Sources: STN, RFB, CEF and IBGE.

Figure 2. Composition of the tax burden by tax base, 2016.

Despite the taxation on goods and services being pretty close in both cases, the way in which the taxes are levied (direct and indirect) acts slightly differently in the two cases. Adding the base of goods and services to taxation on foreign trade, financial fees and transactions (plus "others"), makes up the framework of indirect taxation in the country—which is usually regressive [28, 29], helping to accentuate social inequalities.

The burden of indirect taxation [...] is high in Brazil. The so-called indirect taxes, included in the prices of goods and services are collected by third parties, responsible for charging, but effectively borne by final consumers. Such taxes, by their nature, affect consumers indiscriminately, regardless of their level of income. Therefore, mainly the poorest, who spend their entire income on consumption, are encumbered. The ultimate effect of this taxation is highly regressive and concentrating [30], p. 85.[2]

As Figure 3 shows, this indirect base has greater importance in the municipal taxation (50.6%) than in the consolidated public sector taxation (45.7%), which could indicate a worse tax structure in the municipal scope.

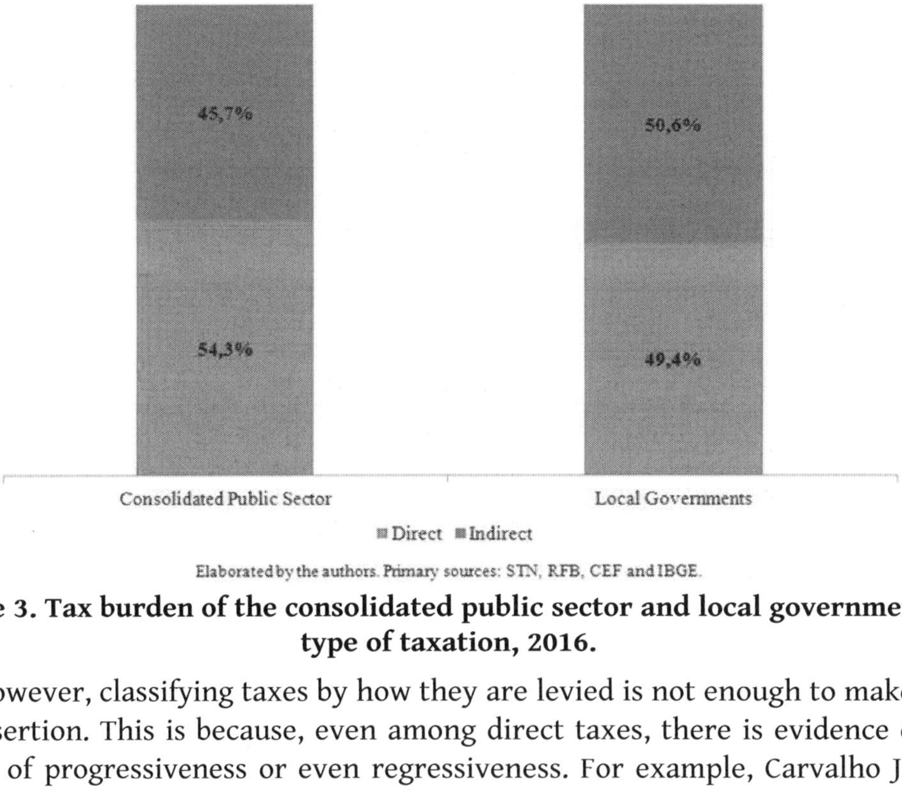

Figure 3. Tax burden of the consolidated public sector and local governments by type of taxation, 2016.

However, classifying taxes by how they are levied is not enough to make such an assertion. This is because, even among direct taxes, there is evidence of low levels of progressiveness or even regressiveness. For example, Carvalho Jr. [31] is categorical in stating that IPTU—despite being a direct asset tax—is regressive, within the realm of real contributors (taxpayers). Another case is that of the social security contribution (tax base "salary and labour") which, "[...] by virtue of the upper limit of contribution, acts regressively" [32], p. 13.[3] In the same sense, Mélo and Campos [33] point to a historical process of deterioration in progressiveness of taxation on income and patrimony.

In this way, considering indirect taxation's greater weight in the tax authorities of local governments, along with the fact that IPTU (the second largest municipal tax) also presents regressive characteristics, it is reasonable to assume that the municipal taxation contributes to accentuating social inequality in Brazil, following a characteristic which is inherent in the Brazilian tax system as a whole [9].

4. TAXATION BY SIZE OF MUNICIPALITY AND REGION

Following the evaluation of the municipal tax burden, this section aims to breakdown municipalities into groups by population and region of the country. An analysis focused on this is important to see how the tax burden of local governments behaves as the socioeconomic profile of the localities is changed, allowing questions such as: "do bigger cities have a higher tax burden?" or "what is the profile of a municipality that receives relatively more transfers?" to be asked.

Due to the information that is presented in this section being in greater detail, it has not been possible to present data as recent (2016) as that of the two previous sections. Since the last GDP for municipalities released by the IBGE refers to 2014, this section is related to 2014. Therefore, the main base of information (Finbra) was also from that year. This on the other hand was reedited to remove major errors such as zero or negative values, but providing a final sample of 4866 municipalities -87.4% of the total number of municipalities in Brazil (5570) in 2014. To calculate the burden, the municipalities were divided into six bands of populations[4] and five regions.[5]

Given these brief methodological considerations, Figure 4 presents the municipal tax burden (% of GDP) in terms of direct taxation and available revenue in each of the six population bands and the general average.

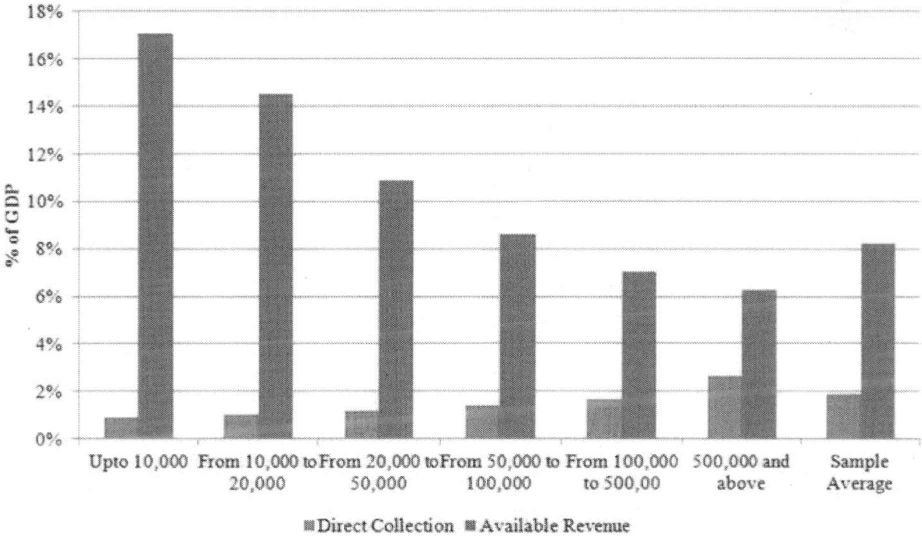

Elaborated by the authors. Primary Sources: Finbra/STN and GDP of Local Governments/IBGE.

Figure 4. Direct collection and available municipal revenue by band of population, 2014.

Figure 4 presents two clear movements when the data are observed from the smaller to the higher population range: first, the local governments' own direct collection grows in relation to the size of the municipality in terms of population and second, the available revenue (including transfers) presents an opposite trend, having an inverse relationship with the size of the municipality in terms of population.

A few observations can be made from these results. Firstly, regarding the relatively higher tax burden in the larger cities, the evidence is consistent with the literature that points to a tendency of service agglomeration in major urban centres [34, 35], especially the more sophisticated services which are connected to industrial activity [36]. Therefore, considering it is the municipality's responsibility to levy tax on the services sector, it is expected that the municipal tax burden would tend to be larger in larger cities. Furthermore, the concentration of these services and population in a limited area of the region raises the value of the urban properties, providing greater potential for revenue gained from tax levied on real estate assets [37] such as IPTU.

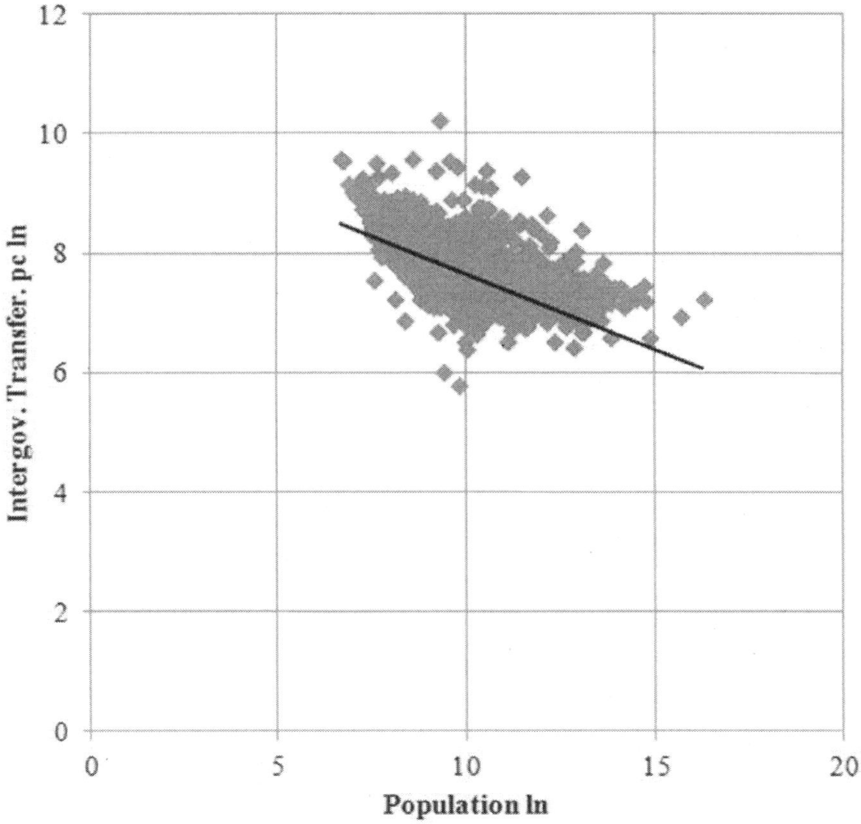

Elaborated by the authors. Primary Sources: Finbra/STN.

Figure 5. Intergovernmental transfers per capita × population, 2014.

Secondly, a big distortion can be seen when analysing the resources actually available to local governments after transfers from other spheres of government. As there is a clear difference in cities' abilities to levy taxes, intergovernmental transfers—notably those with unconditional redistributive characteristics such as the FPM—come into play to reduce horizontal inequalities between localities. However, as shown by the data, in fact, this does not happen. This had already been demonstrated by other authors such as Prado [38] in stating "[...] the Brazilian federation has a tax system which lacks an efficient and dynamic method for reducing disparities" [38], p. 41.[6]

In fact, intergovernmental transfers—especially the FPM and the State Participation Fund (FPE)—tend to accentuate the horizontal inequalities by prioritising the allocation of resources to locations with less population. Figure 5 shows the relationship between transfers distributed to municipalities per capita and the size of the municipalities' population, in which a negative relationship between the volume of resources received and the size of the population can be seen.

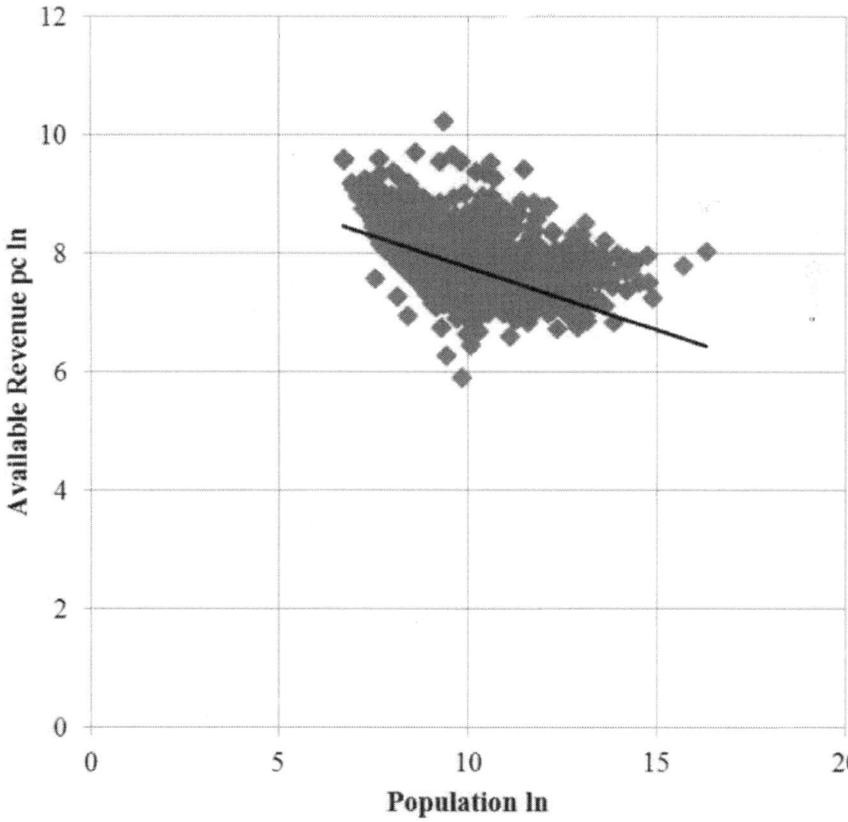

Elaborated by the authors. Primary Sources: Finbra/STN.

Figure 6. Available revenue per capita × population, 2014.

Once the Union and state transfers represent a relatively larger portion of the municipalities' disposable income than the local taxes levied, it is established that an unbalanced distribution of resources via intergovernmental transfers distributed horizontally (between municipalities), as shown in Figure 5, goes hand in hand with a lack of equality in available revenue. Figure 6 shows that even adding their own revenue to transfers, available revenue per capita tends to be higher in the municipalities with smaller populations.

In an ideal scenario, the trend line in Figure 6 should be completely horizontal: that is, the available revenue per capita should be exactly the same for all municipalities. This ideal scenario would use as a criteria only the population (number of residents) as a proxy for the level of demand for public goods in municipalities.

However, the scenario is a little more complex: the most populated cities require a greater volume of resources to meet the population's needs, due to the population density, the higher rates of urban problems (violence, traffic, etc.) and the greater complexity of services demanded (better informed voters with higher levels of education). At the same time, the less populated locations have fewer resources to co-finance a growing number of policies formulated by the federal government and assigned to local governments. A significant part of municipal spending on social policies is protected by the Constitution, which makes the allocation of fixed percentages in state and municipal budgets for the health and education sectors mandatory [39]. In 2016, the governmental level which showed the bulk of spending on health and education, approximately 50% of the spending that year, was the municipal governments, according to STN [40].

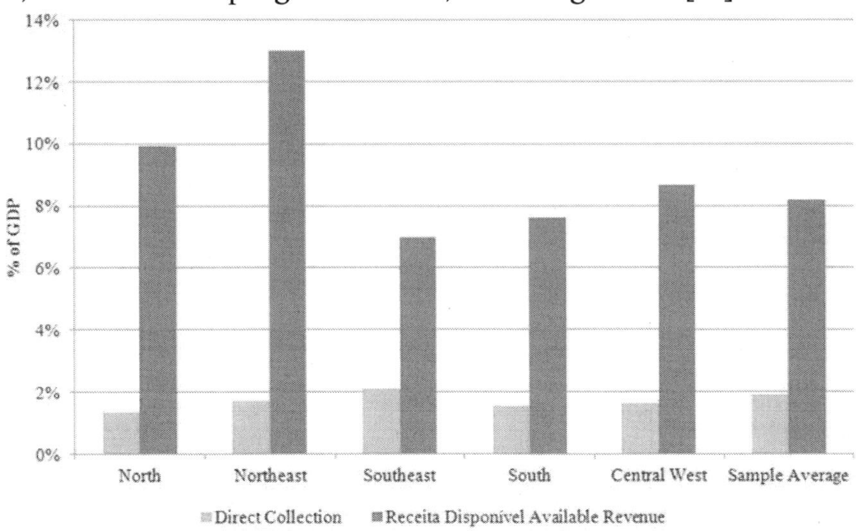

Elaborated by the authors. Primary sources: Finbra/STN and GDP of Local Governments/IBGE.

Figure 7. Direct collection and available municipal revenue by region, 2014.

Another way to observe the inequality between the different locations, from both of the aforementioned points of view of the municipal tax burden, is separating by region, as shown in Figure 7.

Here, there is a pattern quite similar to that obtained in Figure 4, in which regions with lower socioeconomic development (with less populous cities) collect less tax themselves (direct collection) and have more available revenue. This is exactly the case of the North and Northeast. On the other hand, the Southeastern, which is known to be more advanced economically and in terms of population, has a higher municipal tax burden from the perspective of direct collection and a lower available revenue from the standpoint of local governments. This pattern of a smaller tax burden in poorer and less populated regions is directly related to a more restricted taxable base, in addition to the costs and administrative difficulties of the collection procedure in small municipalities [5]. Nevertheless, it is possible to affirm that with the arrival of the Public Digital Bookkeeping System (SPED)[7] and dissemination of the use of Electronic Invoices, these barriers should be reduced.

Besides the economic and administrative aspects, it is possible to point out yet another contributing factor to the lower municipal tax burden in less affluent locations: the incentive (reverse) given by intergovernmental transfers. Empirical evidence shows that, if a city receives resources from a third-party above what is required and without having to incur the administrative and political cost itself, there is a tendency for the beneficiary government to decrease in fiscal responsibility in the following ways: over-proportionately increased spending by the local government, which is known as the flypaper effect [41]; a drop in the quality of local public spending, such as a decrease in investments and an increase in running expenditure [42] and, finally, the disincentive to raise their own revenue [43].

5. INTERNATIONAL COMPARISON

Section 2 of this chapter shows, through official statistics and other authors, that municipalities have had an expressively increased participation in the fiscal federalism in Brazil, especially after the 1988 Constitution, which raised local governments to the level of a federated entity and made them responsible for implementing much of the social policies.

Despite the intense development of municipalities with regard to the decentralisation of resources, the current position of local governments in the national tax burden can expand even more. At least, this is the evidence that emerges from a quick comparison of Brazilian data with the position of countries in the Organisation for Economic Cooperation and Development (OECD), as can be seen in Figure 8.

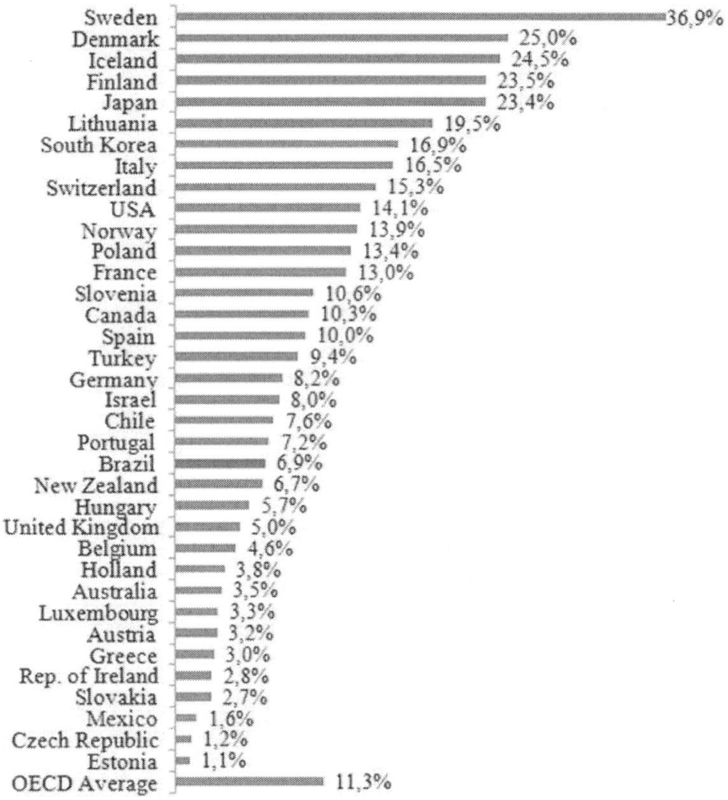

Elaborated by the authors. Primary Sources: Afonso and Castro (2016) and OECD Statistics.

Figure 8. Local governments' participation in the National Tax Burden (% of the total), 2014.

Brazil's position in the list of local governments' share in the national tax burden is neither the highest nor the lowest, but rather falls in the middle. In 2014, the country's participation rate was roughly 6.9%, which was far below the average of the OECD. The country also lagged behind other nations that have a federal system, such as Germany, Canada, the USA, and Switzerland. The justification for comparing Brazil with OECD countries lies in two factors: firstly, Brazil's overall tax burden aligns with the average of this group [3], and secondly, the Brazilian government has just submitted an application for membership to the OECD.

6. CONCISE SUMMARY

This study aimed to provide a succinct and diverse analysis of the tax burden faced by municipal governments in Brazil. Through the examination of official statistics and previous literature, it has been determined that the fiscal decentralisation that has taken place since the Constitution of 1988 has greatly benefited the municipalities. This is evident in the simultaneous rise in direct taxation and increased transfers from higher levels of government. As a result, the municipalities have gained fiscal autonomy and a significant role in the federation, which is unprecedented in the country's history.

Although there has been progress, there is a discussion that emphasizes how reallocating resources to municipalities may not align with their increased obligations of implementing the expanding social programs set by the federal government.

At present, the municipalities' revenue amounts to approximately 20% of the total taxes collected in the country. This revenue is primarily generated through taxes that have significant potential for growth, as they are based on the development of urban features, the provision of improved services (ISS), and the appreciation of land value (IPTU). Additionally, there is an increase in transfers of funds to the municipalities.

The disaggregated data on the local tax burden reveal certain unfavorable attributes. Initially, the examination of the tax base revealed that the local taxes exhibit a comparable pattern to the overall Brazilian tax system, displaying a strong inclination towards regressive taxation. This exacerbates the existing social disparities within the country. Furthermore, when examining the burden based on population, it becomes evident that there is an unequal distribution of available revenue, with less populous areas receiving a disproportionate amount. This puts a strain on the budgets of big centers, which are responsible for meeting the high demand for public goods and services. An analogous characteristic is observed when the weight is examined by partitioning the country into different areas. Simultaneously, smaller and economically disadvantaged municipalities face more challenges in meeting the increasing demands of vertically dictated social policies.

Without recognizing the significant diversity among municipalities (with 70% of the 5570 municipalities having a population of less than 20,000 inhabitants), the Brazilian fiscal federalism requires adjustments to achieve a proper balance between funding sources and the responsibilities assumed by local governments.

Based on an international comparison using OECD data, it has been demonstrated that although local governments in Brazil have made significant progress in the past 30 years, there is still room for improvement in increasing the participation of municipalities in the overall tax burden. This is due to their intermediate position in the ranking of this index.

AT A GLANCE

Since the implementation of the 1988 Constitution, Brazil has experienced a shift towards fiscal and administrative decentralization, granting more power and duties to local governments. In recent times, as municipalities have gained a significant position in the federation comparable to that of states, it has become increasingly crucial to do a comprehensive analysis of their tax burden. From the year preceding the Constitution to 2016, the amount of taxes collected by municipalities increased by about two-fold, while the amount of revenue available to them more than doubled. The growth persisted even after 2011, despite a decline in the national tax burden. An analysis utilizing the tax base indicates a regressive form of local taxation, mirroring the overall structure of the Brazilian tax system. An examination based on population and geographical location reveals that direct municipal taxation is more pronounced in affluent and densely populated districts, whereas the significance of available revenue is greater in economically disadvantaged and sparsely populated places. Although municipalities have made significant progress inside the Federation, a comparison with other countries reveals that there is still potential for local governments to further enhance their fiscal expansion.

REFERENCES

1. World Bank. Summary of the 1997 World Development Report (WDR): The State in a Changing World. Washington, DC: World Bank; 1997. 28 p
2. Santos AMSP. Política urbana no contexto federativo brasileiro: aspectos institucionais e financeiros. Rio de Janeiro: EDUERJ; 2017. 288 p
3. Afonso JRR, Castro KP. Carga Tributária en Brasil: Redimensionada y Repensada. Revista de Administración Tributaria CIAT. 2016;40:1-16
4. Varsano R et al. Uma Análise da Carga Tributária no Brasil. Texto para Discussão IPEA. 1998;583:55
5. Afonso JRR, Araujo EA. A Capacidade de Gasto dos Municípios Brasileiros: Arrecadação Própria e Receita Disponível. Cadernos de Finanças Públicas. 2000;1(1):19-30
6. Castro KP, Afonso JRR. Gasto social no Brasil pós-1988: uma análise sob a ótica da descentralização fiscal. Política. Planejamento e Gestão em Saúde. 2010;1:33-56
7. ASA, Wilson RH. Mudança institucional e gestão metropolitana no Brasil: o municipalismo autárquico e as finanças municipais metropolitanas. Revista de Administração Pública. 2013;47(3):777-800. DOI: 10.1590/s0034-76122013000300011
8. Serra J, Afonso JRR. El federalismo fiscal en Brasil: una visión panorámica. Revista de la CEPAL. 2007;91:29-52
9. Afonso JRR, Soares JM, Castro KP. Evaluation of the Structure and Performance of the Brazilian Tax System: White Paper on Taxation in Brazil. Discussion Paper IDB-DP. 2013;265:116 p

10. Ter-Minassian T. Brazil. In: Ter-Minassian T, editor. Fiscal Federalism in Theory and Practice. Washington: International Monetary Fund; 1997. pp. 438-456

11. Affonso RBA. Descentralização e reforma do Estado: a Federação brasileira na encruzilhada. Economia e Sociedade. 2000;9(1):127-152

12. Abrucio FL. Descentralização e Coordenação Federativa no Brasil: Lições dos Anos FHC. In: Abrucio FL, Loureiro MR, orgs. O Estado Numa Era de Reformas: Os Anos FHC—Parte 2. Brasília: Ministério do Planejamento, Orçamento e Gestão; 2002. pp. 143-245

13. Cunha RE. Federalismo e relações intergovernamentais: os consórcios públicos como instrumento de cooperação federativa. Revista do Serviço Público. 2004;55(3):5-95

14. Arretche M. Federalismo e políticas sociais no Brasil: Problemas de coordenação e autonomia. São Paulo em Perspectiva. 2004;18(2):17-26. DOI: 10.1590/s0102-88392004000200003

15. Ingram GK, Hong Y. Municipal revenue options in a time of financial crisis. In: Ingram GK, Hong Y, editors. Municipal Revenues and Land Policies. Cambridge: Lincoln Institute of Land Policy; 2010. pp. 3-25

16. Inman RP. Financing cities. In: Ingram GK, Hong Y, editors. Municipal Revenues and Land Policies. Cambridge: Lincoln Institute of Land Policy; 2010. pp. 26-44

17. Paula LF, Pires M. Crise e perspectivas para a economia brasileira. Estudos Avançados. 2017;31(89):125-144. DOI: 10.1590/s0103-40142017.31890013

18. Ribeiro L. Sobre Arrecadação e Atividade Econômica. Nota Técnica FGV IBRE. 2016;[s.v]:10 p

19. Miles I. Services in the new industrial economy. Futures. 1993;25(6):653-672. DOI: 10.1016/0016-3287(93)90106-4

20. Lemos MB et al. Empresas estrangeiras em espaços periféricos: o caso brasileiro. In: Negri JA, Salerno MS, orgs. Inovações, padrões tecnológicos e desempenho das firmas industriais brasileiras. Empresas estrangeiras em espaços periféricos: o caso brasileiro. Brasília: IPEA; 2005. p. 425-475

21. Mello NO et al. The implementation of the electronic tax documents in Brazil as a tool to fight tax evasion. In: Proceedings of the 13th WSEAS International Conference on Systems (WSEAS 13); 22-24 July 2009; Rodos. Wisconsin: WSEAS; 2009. pp. 449-456

22. Mattos E, Rocha F, Toporcov P. Programas de incentivos fiscais são eficazes?: Evidência a partir da avaliação do impacto do programa nota fiscal paulista sobre a arrecadação de ICMS. Revista Brasileira de Economia. 2013;67(1):97-120. DOI: 10.1590/s0034-71402013000100005

23. Angeli Neto H, Martinez AL. Nota Fiscal de Serviços Eletrônica: Uma Análise dos Impactos na Arrecadação em Municípios Brasileiros. Revista de Contabilidade e Organizações. 2016;10(26):49-62. DOI: 10.11606/rco.v10i26.107117

24. De Cesare CM, Marín JFL. Impuestos a los patrimonios en América Latina. Macroeconomía del Desarrollo CEPAL. 2008;66:111

25. Afonso JRR, Araujo EA, Nóbrega MAR. IPTU no Brasil: Um Diagnóstico Abrangente. Rio de Janeiro: FGV Projetos/IDP; 2013. 79 p

26. Santos AMSP. O IPTU em Foco: uma análise da perspectiva dos municípios fluminenses. Revista Paranaense de Desenvolvimento. 2016;37(131):199-214

27. Castro KP, Afonso JRR. IPTU: Avaliação de Potencial e Utilização Sob a Ótica da Teoria dos Conjuntos Fuzzy. Revista de Administração Pública. 2017;51(5):828-853. DOI: 10.1590/0034-7612160295

28. Tanzi V. Foreword: Tax systems and tax reform in Latin America. In: Bernardi L et al., editors. Tax System and Tax Reform in Latin America. Roma: Societá Italiana di Economia Pubblica; 2007. pp. 1-21

29. Silveira FG. Tributação, previdência e assistência sociais: impactos distributivos [thesis]. Campinas: Universidade Estadual de Campinas; 2008

30. Cardoso FH. Mãos à obra, Brasil: proposta de governo. Rio de Janeiro: Centro Edelstein de Pesquisa Social; 2008. 131 p

31. Carvalho Junior PHB. Aspectos Distributivos do IPTU e do Patrimônio Imobiliário das Famílias Brasileiras. Texto para Discussão IPEA. 2009;1417:50

32. Rodrigues JJ. Carga Tributária Sobre os Salários. Texto para Discussão da Secretaria da Receita Federal. 1998;1:23

33. Mélo LGG, Campos GCN. A Tributação Sobre o Patrimônio e a Renda: Mais um Caso de Injustiça Fiscal. Revista do Programa de Pós-graduação em Direito da Universidade Federal da Bahia. 2016;26(28):329-347

34. Friedmann J, Wolff G. World city formation: An agenda for research and action. International Journal of Urban and Regional Research. 1982;6(3):309-344. DOI: 10.1111/j.1468-2427.1982.tb00384.x

35. Sassen S. The Global City: New York, London, Tokyo. Princeton: Princeton University Press; 1991. 396 p

36. Kon A. Economia de Serviços: Teoria e Evolução no Brasil. Rio de Janeiro: Elsevier; 2004. 288 p

37. Bahl R, Martinez-Vazquez J. The Property Tax in Developing Countries: Current Practice and Prospects. Lincoln Institute of Land Policy Working Paper. 2007;[s.v.]:26 p

38. Prado S, org. Transferências Intergovernamentais na Federação Brasileira: Avaliação e Alternativas de Reforma. Caderno Fórum Fiscal dos Estados Brasileiros. 2009;6:323 p

39. Santos AMSP. Descentralização e Autonomia Municipal: uma análise das transformações institucionais no federalismo brasileiro. Revisa GEO UERJ. 2012;2(23):825-852

40. Secretaria do Tesouro Nacional. Balanço do Setor Público Nacional. Exercício de 2016. Brasília: STN; 2017. 73 p

41. Wyckoff PG. A bureaucratic theory of flypaper effects. Journal of Urban Economics. 1988;23(1):115-129. DOI: 10.1016/0094-1190(88)90009-5

42. Gomes GM, Mac Dowell MC. Descentralização Política, Federalismo Fiscal e Criação de Municípios: O que É Mau para o Econômico nem sempre é Bom para o Social. Texto para Discussão IPEA. 2000;706:27

43. Mendes M, Miranda RB, Cosio FB. Transferências Intergovernamentais No Brasil: Diagnóstico e Proposta de Reforma. Texto para Discussão da Consultoria Legislativa do Senado Federal. 2008;40:111

FOOTNOTE

Chapter 1

[1]Vide Law of 15 February 1992 o podatku dochodowym od osób prawnych [on Corporate Income Tax] (OJ 2000 r. No. 54, pos. 654 with later modifications, Art. 7, par. 2; Art. 10, Art. 11.

[2]Vide draft directive Article 9 general principles:When calculating the tax base, only effective gains and losses are taken into account.Transactions and taxable events are measured individually.The calculation of the tax base is carried out in a uniform manner, unless exceptional circumstances justify a change in the method of calculation.Unless otherwise provided, tax base is determined for each tax year. Unless otherwise provided, tax year is any period of twelve months. Also, WP/066/2008, p. 2 item 5.

[3]Expenses that are not deductible for tax purposes are defined by the legislator in Art. 16, par. 1

[4]The basic condition for the recognition of the expense as a deductible cost is the absence of this expense in the catalogue of expenditures that are not recognized by the legislature as deductible costs. A list of these expenditures is set out in the law on corporate income tax.

[5]The exception is made when the lawmakers reer directly to the provisions of other acts.

[6]Article 12 of the draft directive Deductible expenses

[7]A common consolidated EU corporate tax base, Commission Non-Paper to Informal Ecofin Council, 10 and 11 September 2004 (http://ec.europe.eu/taxation_customs)

[8]Proposal for a council directive on a common consolidated corporate tax base of 16 March 2011{SEC(2011) 315}{SEC(2011) 316}

[9]The strategy is aimed at smart, sustainable and inclusive growth. The Europe 2020 strategy has defined the following three interrelated priorities:Smart growth: development of the economy based on knowledge and innovationSustainable growth: supporting the economy based on a more efficient use of resources, more environmentally friendly and more competitiveInclusive growth: supporting the economy characterized by a high employment rate, providing social and territorial cohesionCf. Communication from the Commission

of Europe 2020: A strategy for smart, sustainable and inclusive growth (COM(2010) 2020 Brussels 3.3.2010)

[10]Communication from the Commission Towards a Single Market Act: For a highly competitive social market economy—50 proposals for improving our work, business and exchanges with one another (COM(2010) 608 Brussels 27.10.2010)

[11]Communication from the Commission Annual Growth Survey: advancing the EU's comprehensive response to the crisis (COM(2011) 11 Brussels 12.01.2010).

[12]Calculations made with reference to multinational enterprises operating in the EU indicate that about 50% of multinational financial groups and 17% of multinational nonfinancial groups may receive direct compensation for cross-border losses.

[13]Cf. Council directive on a common consolidated corporate tax base (CCCTB); Brussels, COM (2011) 121/4, 2011/0058 (CNS){SEC(2011) 315}{SEC(2011) 316}. According to the estimates made by the European Commission, a new regulation would enable to save about 700 million Euro annually in the European Union on the costs associated with adjusting to other fiscal systems, circa 1.3 billion Euro as a result of the consolidation of calculation rules, and nearly 1 billion Euro on cross-border activity. Experts are inclined to believe that such a solution would increase the attractiveness of the EU as a location of large-scale investments.

Chapter 2

[1]Statutory, or nominal, tax rates are rates stated in a tax law (statute, code) expressed usually in percentage terms to be applied to a tax base, for example, taxable income.

[2]Like taxation of previously untaxed items such as short-term capital gains.

[3]Thin or hidden capitalization of a subsidiary arises when a foreign investor substitutes foreign debt capital for equity capital, particularly in cases where debt financing exhibits some of the characteristics of equity and the debt is owed to a related lender. (Shome, 1995)

[4]Withholding rates on cross-border interest and royalty payments are (which vary by class of payer and payee and by the financial instrument—in itself a source tax arbitrage) very low. (Cnossen, 2003)

Chapter 6

[1]This paper is adapted from the author's doctoral dissertation (in Korean).

[2]The Bohn test, which draws implications from the manner in which fiscal policy has responded to increases in public debt, is also considered the context-

embedded public finance, and it has two limitations [56]. That does not address the nonlinear relationships between primary balance and public debt and does not consider endogenous relationship between interest rates and public debt.

[3]This is based on the fact that the expenditures for that year are carried out in accordance with the previous year's budget plan. The analysis is also conducted by adding value from 5 years prior to reflect the medium-term fiscal plan in high-income countries as a 5-year plan. In the determinants of fiscal sustainability of the welfare state, the correlation between welfare expenditures and fiscal capacity may not be reflected within a short time frame. In particular, the impact of fiscal capacity on welfare expenditures is likely to be seen in the medium term, because in high-income countries, the level of public expenditures is usually determined through the medium- and long-term financial management of the country.

[4]The dependent variable is the primary balance, and the independent variables are the financial factors (national debt, public welfare expenditures, output gap, inflation rate), the economic structural factors (unemployment rate, service industry ratio, portion of involuntary part-time work, economic openness, aging rate, future old age portion), and political and financial institutional factors (election, change of ideology, mandatory political system, concentration index, fiscal rule index). In this study, it is based on the works of Ostry et al. [56] and Ghosh et al. [57], but some variables are excluded in consideration of multicollinearity.

[5]Ostry et al. [56] determined long-term interest rates in two ways. The first assumes that the observed interest rate itself reflects the perceived probability of bankruptcy of a country, so the current market rate is used as the long-term interest rate. In this case, it is possible to overestimate the maximum value of sustainable debt by overlooking the fact that the interest rate rises as the debt level approaches its limit, and the risk of bankruptcy increases. An alternative method of overcoming this limitation is to use the interest rate, which is calculated by taking into account the endogenous relationship between debt levels and interest rates. Specifically, they used the calculated interest rate, assuming a recovery rate of 90% when bankruptcy occurred. Alternative methods which they used help to accurately estimate fiscal space by reflecting endogenous relationships between interest rates and macroeconomic variables. However, the abovementioned study does not provide a clear basis for assumptions used in interest rate estimation. Therefore, it is not free of the problems caused by an arbitrary definition of the recovery rate [80]. In order to overcome these limitations, this study uses the estimates through VAR.

[6]The reason for using this method is as follows. First, it uses only one dataset, OECD national accounts, so it resolves the problem of differences in reflection times in the figures according to the differences in accounting methods by using two datasets, OECD national accounts and revenue statistics, similar to the existing studies of Mendoza et al. [81] and Carey and Rabesona [82, 83]. Second, this method overcomes the overestimation of consumption tax, one of the limitations of existing methods caused when consumption and investment taxes are not separated. In this method, the consumption tax remains separate from taxation on investments so that it can be more accurately measured.

[7]In the process of estimating the fiscal space of the welfare state not only are the demand factors reflected, which are likely to drive welfare expenditures. In this situation, if these variables included to estimate fiscal sustainability are used, there is the possibility that the endogeneity problem will occur. Therefore, it is necessary to include variables with high relevance to welfare expenditures while minimizing the problem of endogeneity.

Chapter 8

[1]In May 2012, the Government of the State of Ceará declared situation of emergency in 168 of its Municipalities, affected by drought, through the Decree n. 30,922/ 2012, because of the confirmation of the abnormal situation in function of the relevant irregularity in the amount and distribution in time and space of rainfall in the state lands. This subject will be detailed through this analysis.

[2]The Industrial and Port Complex of Pecém (CIPP, in Portuguese acronym) was founded in 1995 and is situated in an area of 32.956,445 acres, 50 km (31 miles) from the state capital city, Fortaleza. The structures of the complex include a port terminal, a retroporto and in it there is an industrial district. Among the operating factories, there is a steel industry and a thermos-electric power plant UTE Pecém (for Usina Termelétrica Energia Pecé, working since 2012. It is coal-fired and its operation supplies electric power for 5 million inhabitants. The power-plant needs an amount of 30,000 m3 of water to generate 1 Megawatt, the quantity of power required to supply energy to 1000 residences.

[3]For instance, the Brazilian Institute for the Environment and Natural Renewable Resources (IBAMA, in Portuguese) condemned Ceará Portos, the company in charge of the CIPP, to pay 13.8 million Reais for environmental damage. The discard of mineral coal on the Pecém beach was the cause. Several seizures and penalties have already been imposed to CIPP, which is operating without some of the required licenses.

[4]Gabriela Riva considers the General Commentary 15 as "the most complete document on the Right to Water, clarifying the duties decurrent of such right and defining precisely its bounders."

[5]In Riva's view, this resolution was "the greatest victory for the access to water movement [...] passed by 144 votes in favor, 41 abstentions and no vote in con. [...]"

[6]The expressed rights ant guarantees in the Constitution do not exclude other ones, decurrent of the its regime and principles, or in the international deals that the Federative Republic of Brazil participates. (The Article 5, Paragraph 2 of the Brazilian Federal Constitution.)

[7]Nowadays, the Proposes of Amendment to the Constitution n. 39/ 2007 and 213/ 2012 are submitted to the Congress examination. They propose to transform the Right to Water in a Constitutional Right.

[8]The criticism against the vision of water as a worth is well grounded by Gabriela Riva, for who "the exclusive use of the economic approach did not consider the ecological bounders imposed by the water cycle and also the economic limits imposed by poverty and inequality, having done no contribution to the conservation of water and the democratization of the access to it. (Refer to the text, p. 39.)

[9]The Decree defines the following criteria for the Industrial Water Bill: Article 3: The billing for the use of raw water in the domain of Ceará will vary according to the following categories of users, for surficial and underground collection: II – Industry: (a) The supply of water with complete collection and adduction by COGERH: T = 2.067 Reais and 59 Cents per 1000 m3; (b) The supply of water with complete or partial collection and adduction by the user from water sources, such as reservoirs, rivers, lagoons, underground lakes and rivers or channels: T = 601 Reais and 03 Cents per 1000 m3.

Chapter 9

[1]Ministry of Agriculture, Forestry, and Fisheries, the 2000 World Census of Agriculture and Forestry (in Japanese)

[2]In the 1990 World Census of Agriculture and Forestry, the minimum holding size of the surveyed forest owners was 0.1 ha, and 1,452,225 forest owners owned forest land from 0.1 ha to 1 ha.

[3]Tax statistics are available at https://www.nta.go.jp/foreign_language/tax_statics/index.htm. This statistic is published in both Japanese and English.

[4]In the United States, the maximum rate was 35% in 2011 (Butler [5], p. 374).

[5]There is limited literature related to inheritance tax in Japan in English. Examples include GHQ/SCAP ([6], pp. 64–66), the Forestry Agency [7], and Iwai [8].

[6]The registered area is used to evaluate the annual property tax ([9], p. 145). Generally, in areas where the national land survey has not been completed, the registered area is less than the actual area.

[7]Except for areas restricted to forest practices, forest owners can transfer the land use from forest to other uses, such as housing land.

[8]The standard final cutting age is determined by the circular notice from the Director General of the National Tax Agency for forestry areas. In the case of C. japonica, the standard final cutting age may be 50, 55, or 60 years, while that of C. obtusa, may be 60 or 65. In the amendment in 1993, the standard final cutting age was postponed by 5 or 10 years based on actual practices of tree cutting ([11], pp. 18–19). This postponement resulted in a decrease in the standing tree value. In the amendment, the standard distance between the location of trees to the nearest timber yard along forest road was changed. The distance changed from 1.5–2 to 0.3–0.5 km ([11], p. 19), resulting in a decrease in the evaluation of standing trees. Tezuka [12] noted that a distance of about 2 km was the average ca. 1955.

[9]This graph is based on Figure 2 of Yamamoto [10].

[10]For example, the standard reforestation cost decreased from 210,000 to 103,000 yen for C. japonica and from 245,000 to 141,000 yen for C. obtusa ([10], p. 38).

[11]The 2004 amendment resulted in an average decrease in value to 50%, and maximum decrease to almost 30% ([10], p. 40). In the example in Figure 1, the decreasing rate is greater than the average decrease in the amendment in 2004, because the standard value at the standard final cutting age decreased, as shown in Figure 2.

[12]In the example in Figure 1, the standard values per ha at the standard final cutting age, 60 years, in 2001 and 2005 were 2,500,000 and 480,000 yen, respectively. Calculated from the 2% compound interest rate until two times the standard final cutting age, the value of a 120-year-old tree would be 8,203,000 and 1,575,000 yen, respectively.

[13]This rule is based on the circular notice from the Director General of the National Tax Agency.

[14]Some individuals who elected to postpone payment of the forest inheritance tax expressed their opinion on the reduction of the payment related to the decrease in the standing value because both the stumpage price and standard value at the standard final cutting age decreased ([13], p. 128).

[15]The forest management plan in the Forest Act changed in the fiscal year of 2012. In the former system, the total area under the forest management plan was generally high, for example, around 75% in 1997. However, the percentage of forest under the new forest management plan decreased. Correspondingly, the area of forest eligible for the 5% reduction rule decreased.

[16]The rule was introduced to the Inheritance Tax Act (Act No. 73 of 1950) in the amendment of 1954 ([12], p. 3).

[17]Sugano and Tani ([14], p. 32) introduced the following management example: a forest owner conducted clear-cutting of 40- to 50-year-old C. japonica and C. obtusa, and then planted low-value broad-leaved trees. In addition to the value of standing trees, the total value of the inherited properties decreased. As a result, the tax rate (see Table 1) decreased. Nagata [15] mentioned a similar problem at the time of the post-war tax reform, in that there was a large imbalance between cases in which the forest owners conducted clear-cutting and cases in which the forest owners maintained the forest without clear-cutting.

[18]Such situations have been mentioned before 2000 (e.g., [16], p. 2).

[19]Statistics Bureau, Ministry of Internal Affairs and Communications, e-Stat, http://www.e-stat.go.jp/SG1/estat/List.do?bid=000001047783&cycode=0 [Accessed: April 18, 2017] (in Japanese)

[20]From the Department of Statistics, Ministry of Agriculture, Forestry and Fisheries. The survey was conducted for forest owners with holding areas ≥1 ha.

[21]Here, protected forest refers to Hoanrin designated as Article 25 of the Forest Act (Act No. 249 of 1951), which exists in both national and non-national forests. In practice, protected forests provide another system applied only to national forests, where commercial purposes cannot be pursued.

[22]There were 5,224,000 ha of non-national protected forest at the end of the fiscal year of 2014. The total area of non-national forest was 17,407,000 ha at the end of the fiscal year of 2011.

[23]Takagi [13] noted that the average number of years of constituting a generation change is approximately 30 years. Therefore, a cutting rotation of 60 years is equal to two generations. At least 100 years or 150 years is needed produce large high-quality logs for use in temples, etc., meaning that forest owners must pay the inheritance tax three to five times.

[24]The basic idea of the Japanese inheritance system is that all inheritance property should be valued and paid at the time of inheritance, thus inheritance may occur more than once before final cutting. In the case of the United Kingdom,

the inheritance tax is imposed only once at the time of cutting ([13], pp. 135–136).

[25]The opinion survey was conducted on March and April 2010. The survey was conducted for 1,607 forest owners selected from forest owners surveyed at the 2005 Agriculture and Forestry Census, of which 1,013 completed the survey [24].

[26]In the case of small-scale owners, owners can obtain income from timber sold at long intervals, and must pay fixed property tax every year ([25], p. 32).

[27]Sugano ([26], p. 24) conducted a questionnaire survey on forest inheritance and noted that a number of forest owners, both small- and large-scale, answered that they would dispose of their forest property if inheritance occurred.

[28]A postponement system for the delayed payment of the inheritance tax applied to all forests existed before 2012 when the new postponement for only large-scale forest owners was introduced. The main contents are as follows. The content of the postponement is equal to the payment during less than 15 years with 5.4% interest tax. For standing trees located in a forest under a forest management plan, it is an unequal payment with a reduced rate of 3.6% interest ([9], pp. 102–104). The interest tax was initially 4.8%, but decreased to 4.2% in the fiscal year of 1987, and decreased to 3.6% in the fiscal year of 1990 ([11], pp. 17–18). For forests under a special forest management plan promoting long rotation operation, the limit of the number of years for postponement was extended to 40 years in the fiscal year of 1991 ([11], p. 18).

[29]In this new measure, only inheritance tax payment can be postponed. Gift tax is not included in this new measure, which has already been introduced to farmland ([14], p. 31).

[30]In the case of exceptional measure in France, a forest plan is necessary ([16], p. 4). Based on the act enacted in 1963, forest owners who own ≥25 ha have an obligation to make a simplified forest management plan. When the forest owner follows the contents of the plan over 30 years, three-quarters of the inheritance tax is exempted.

[31]Under the amendment of the Forest Act in 1939, forest owners with ≥50 ha must make a forest plan, and forest owners with <50 ha must join a regional forest owners' cooperative, and the cooperative must have a forest plan. The current system has a common characteristic with the 1939 planning system in that it includes a forest management plan that targets large-scale forest owners with a specific minimum holding size.

[32]After the construction of forest or spur roads, the value of the standing trees along the road increases. When inheritance occurs just after a road investment, the road investment results in an increase in the inheritance tax ([23], p. 241). This is the reverse case of clear-cutting before inheritance.

[33]Based on the webpage of the National Tax Agency. https://www.nta.go.jp/taxanswer/sozoku/4149.htm [Accessed: April 20, 2017].

[34]The family system was abolished after World War II, which appears to have had an effect on long-term forest management, although this remains a topic for future research. Regarding the argument related to the inheritance tax, Tezuka [16] proposed the creation of exceptions for the inheritance of forest. It is worth noting that the following rule was included in his proposal. In the case that it was agreed upon among all related persons in an argument of the distribution of forest property that one inheritor inherit all forest property and succession was conducted by this agreement, the forest inheritance tax would be exempted. Although this inheritor is not limited to the first-born person or son in his proposal, in practice, his proposal resembled the family system before World War II. Takagi [13] pointed out that the German inheritance system includes an exemption whereby the tax differs based on the relation between the ancestor and inheritor, and the maximum exemption is given to the partner and children. This exemption system is not a family system, but supports inheritance by family members. In the Japanese system, there is no difference in the potential exemption among inheritors, except for partners.

[35]Regarding forest plots, GHQ/SCAP ([6], p.65) noted that "some will be subdivided into small and inefficient units" unless there are changes to the taxation system. Based on the Forestry Agency [18, 20], which surveyed the state of forest inheritance in 10 regions during 1963 and 1964, farm households who owned a lot of forested land tended to divide the forest land. Farm households who owned less forest land tended to divide the farmland. Moreover, forest land was easier to divide because, in the case of forested land, there was no limit to holding as in the case of farmland. As a result, forest land was easier to segment than farmland during inheritance. Katayama [29] concluded that the only way to avoid segmentation of forest at the time of inheritance was incorporation of a company to hold the forest.

[36]Sadachi [11] noted that the Forestry Agency conducted a survey on inheritance in 1980 and 1988, which found that the number of forest owners almost doubled at inheritance.

[37]The number of forest owners with 0.1–1 ha was 1,572,000 in the 1960 Census of Agriculture and Forestry. In 1960, there was another publication on the

number of forest owners conducted by Forestry Agency [30]. Here, the number of forest owners with <1 ha is 3,033,000. It is possible that the number of forest owners with <0.1 ha was approximately 1.5 million at the time of 1960.

[38]Usui and Hayashi [4], pp. 41–42) surveyed the situation surrounding forest inheritance and classified households based on the corresponding inheritance tax as follows: (1) cutting the old, natural forest, (2) compulsory destructive cutting, (3) selling real estate, (4) borrowing money, (5) planned gift before death, and (6) a combinations of the above five patterns. The best strategy was concluded to be a combination of (1) and (5), emphasizing the role of gift before death. Yamazaki [31] pointed out that there were many cases of tax avoidance by tentative division or gifting of forest before death, concluding that this situation was the forest owners' legitimate resistance to the forest inheritance tax.

[39]Attention must be paid to the difference between inheritor and successor of agriculture and forestry. Forestry Agency [18, 20] showed this point already by the on-site survey in Nagano Prefecture in the 1960s. Here, the case that children was only one son, was introduced, and whether he will succeed agriculture and forestry or not was serious interest for parents. Recently, the number of children is decreasing in Japan, this is also related to the problems of successors of agriculture and forestry.

[40]Department of Statistics of the Ministry of Agriculture, Forestry and Fisheries.

[41]Tezuka [16] pointed out the low inheritance tax in Germany. The value of 80–100-year-old spruce was almost equal to one fifteenth of 90-year-old C. obtusa. Since the value of the standing trees at the standard cutting age has decreased, as shown in Figure 2, the difference appears to be decreasing.

[42]As shown in Table 5, the total amount of various taxes or public dues is now sometimes greater than the net income from timber sales; thus, problems may exist in the taxation system beyond the forest inheritance tax; however, this was beyond the scope of this paper. Supporting this, Kim [35] noted increases in the burden of several taxes other than the inheritance tax in Japan.

[43]When non-resident forest owners want to continue just holding, the amount of inheritance tax and annual municipal fixed proper tax must be low. To maintain the low-value of standing trees, forest roads should not be developed because, after road construction, the value of the standing trees along the forest increases, resulting in higher taxes.

[44]Taxation of non-resident forest owners was discussed before World War II in Hokkaido, which had a high percentage of non-resident forest owners ([36], pp. 47–51, pp. 83–85).

[45]The current postponement of the forest inheritance tax is closely connected with the forest management plan. The period of the current plan is 5 years, and the plan focuses on forest practices and forest road construction, which are related to the subsidy system. The current management planning system appears to have problems from the perspective of the inheritance system, and should be examined further in future research.

[46]Tezuka [16] noted that the United Kingdom, Germany, and France introduced clear exemptions into the inheritance tax on forestry properties, with a common forest policy to increase the area of forest. Japan differs in this basic policy.

Chapter 10

[1]The questions included here are mostly the ones used by Diah Nur Pertiwi in 2013 for the dissertation work titled "the Influence of Tax Consciousness, Service Tax Authorities, and Tax Sanctions On Tax Compliance [Survey on Individual Taxpayer Conducting Business Operations and Professional Service in Jakarta]."

Chapter 13

[1]The entire procedure of calculating the tax burden adopted in this chapter follows the "broad" methodology of calculation, which considers all public revenue extracted compulsorily from society by part of the government (federal, state and municipal). In this way, the method used here differs from most of the tax burden estimates by including items such as royalties, economic contributions, tax fines, revenue from active tax debt and others. For more details, see [1].

[2]Translation made by the authors.

[3]Translation made by the authors.

[4]The population bands are as follows: up to 10,000 inhabitants; from 10,000 to 20,000 inhabitants; from 20,000 to 50,000 inhabitants; from 50,000 to 100,000 inhabitants; from 100,000 to 500,000 inhabitants and 500,000 inhabitants and above.

[5]The regions are according to the national geographic division: North, Northeast, Southeast, South and Central West.

[6]Translation made by the authors.

[7]Established by Decree No. 6022, of 22 January 2007, the SPED is to modernise the current performance of ancillary obligations, provided by taxpayers to the tax administrations and oversight agencies, using the digital certificate for signing electronic documents, ensuring the legal validity of those only in digital form.

INDEX